KU-654-239

Chicago

© M. L. Dembinsky/DPA

"Here, of all her cities, throbbed the true life, the true power and spirit of America; gigantic, crude with the crudity of youth, disdaining rivalry; sane and healthy and vigorous; brutal in its ambition; arrogant in the new-found knowledge of its giant strength, prodigal of its wealth, infinite of its desires."

Frank Norris, *The Pit*, 1904

Travel Publications

Michelin North America
One Parkway South, Greenville SC 29615, U.S.A.
☎ 1-800-423-0485
www.ViaMichelin.com
TheGreenGuide-us@us.michelin.com

Manufacture française des pneumatiques Michelin
Société en commandite par actions au capital de 304 000 000 EUR
Place des Carmes-Déchaux – 63 Clermont-Ferrand (France)
R.C.S. Clermont-Fd B 855 200 507

Dépôt légal: Janvier 2001 – ISBN 2-06-000061-0 – ISSN 0763-1383
Printed in France 12-01/3.2

Typesetting: NORD-COMPO, Villeneuve d'Ascq
Printing: I.M.E. Baume-les-Dames
Binding: I.M.E. Baume-les-Dames

Cover design: Carré Noir, Paris 17ᵉ arr.

THE GREEN GUIDE:
The Spirit of Discovery

*The exhilaration of new horizons,
the fun of seeing the world,
the excitement of discovery: this is
what we seek to share with you.
To help you make the most of your
travel experience, we offer first-hand
knowledge and turn a discerning eye
on places to visit.
This wealth of information gives
you the expertise to plan your own
enriching adventure. With THE
GREEN GUIDE showing you the way,
you can explore new destinations
with confidence or rediscover old
ones.
Leisure time spent with THE GREEN
GUIDE is also a time for refreshing
your spirit, enjoying yourself, and
taking advantage of our selection
of fine restaurants, hotels and other
places for relaxing.
So turn the page and open a window
on the world. Join THE GREEN
GUIDE in the spirit of discovery.*

Contents

Clock Tower, Wrigley Building

© Robert Frerck/Odyssey

Fado Irish Pub, River North

Buddy Guy's Legends Blues Club

Clock on Marshall Field & Co. Building

Maps and Plans

COMPANION PUBLICATIONS

Map 491 Northeastern USA, Eastern Canada

Large-format map providing detaile road systems and including driving dis tances, interstate rest stops, border cros ings and interchanges.

– Comprehensive city and town index

– Scale 1:2,400,000 (1 inch = approx. 38 miles)

Map 930 USA Road Map

Covers the principal US road netwo and presents shaded relief detail of th overall physiography of the land.

– Features state flags with statistical da and state tourism office telephone num bers

– Scale 1:3,450,000

City of Chicago (1892)

MUSEUM PLANS

Historic Urban Plans

Using this guide

● The Sights section of this guide is divided into five areas: Chicago's Downtown, North Side, West Side, South Side and Excursions from the city. Within these sections, each Entry Heading is followed by public transportation information (if applicable) and a map reference.

● In the text, useful information such as sight location or street address, opening hours, admission charge, telephone number and Web address appears in *italics*. In addition, symbols indicate the nearest rapid-transit or bus stop ; wheelchair access &; on-site eating facilities ✗; camping facilities ⚠; on-site parking ☐; sights of interest to children ; and long lines ㎜. The presence of a hotel swimming pool is indicated in by the symbol ⌁.

● Many entries feature **digressions** —entertaining breaks from sightseeing that are marked by a purple bar and indicated on maps by a purple dot ❶ with the corresponding map reference number.

● The **Address Book** section, edged with a marbleized band, at the front of the guide features detailed information about hotels, restaurants, entertainment, shopping, sightseeing, sports and recreational opportunities.

● At the back of the guide, the section of blue pages offers **Practical Information** on planning your trip, getting there and getting around and tips for international visitors.

Addresses, phone numbers, opening hours and prices published in this guide are accurate at press time. We welcome corrections and suggestions that may assist us in preparing the next edition. Please send your comments to:

MICHELIN Travel Publications
Editorial Department
P. O. Box 19001
Greenville, SC 29602-9001
Email: TheGreenGuide-us@us.michelin.com
Web site: www.michelin-travel.com.

© Robert Frerck/Odyssey

Legend

★★★ **Highly recommended**
★★ **Recommended**
★ **Interesting**

Sight Symbols

Walking tour with departure point and direction

✝ ⚲	Church, chapel		Building described
✡	Synagogue		Other building
B	Letter locating a sight	▪	Small building
▪ ▲	Other points of interest	⚑	Lighthouse
▪	Statue, monument		Park described – Other
	Fountain		Wooded park described – Other
※ ⚶	Panorama – View		Cemetery described – Other

All maps are oriented north, unless otherwise indicated by a directional arrow.

Other Symbols

	Interstate Highway	44 US Highway	55 Other Route
	Highway, interchange	🛈	Visitor information
	Toll road, bridge	✚	Hospital
	Tunnel with ramp		Gift shop
	One way street	🚻 ✗	Restrooms – Restaurant
	Pedestrian street – Steps	⇕	Elevator
	Airport – Subway station	P ✉	Parking – Post Office
	Train station – Bus station		Railroad passenger station
	Ferry: cars and passengers		Gate
	Ferry: passengers only	►	Golf course – Stadium
	Harbor cruise	❶	Digressions

9

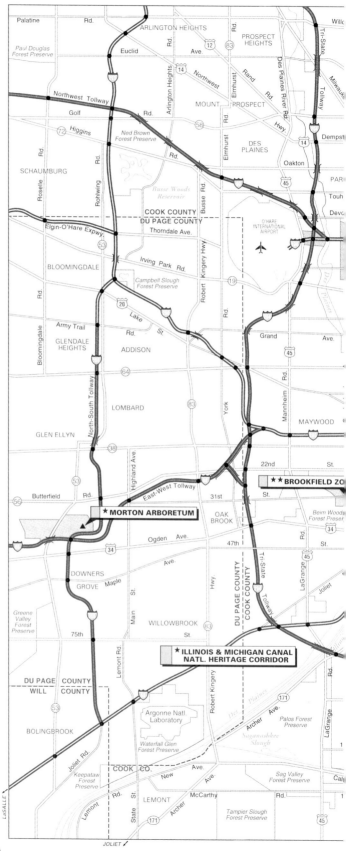

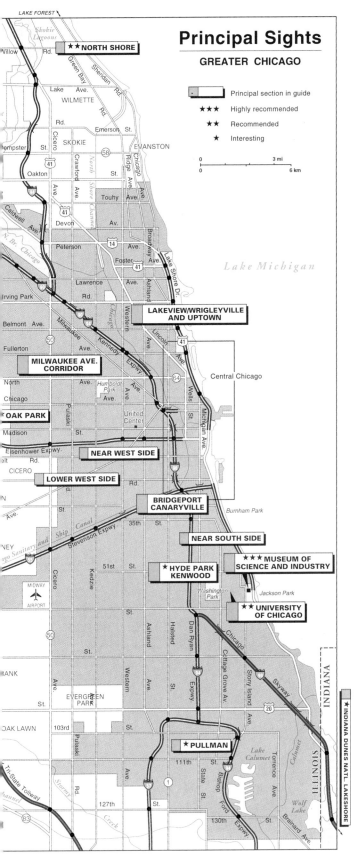

Principal Sights

GREATER CHICAGO

	Principal section in guide
★★★	Highly recommended
★★	Recommended
★	Interesting

0   3 mi
0   6 km

Lake Michigan

★★ **NORTH SHORE**

LAKE FOREST

Skokie Lagoons

Willow Rd.

Green Bay Rd.

Sheridan Rd.

Lake Ave. WILMETTE

Cicero Rd. Emerson St.

Dempster St. SKOKIE EVANSTON (58)

Oakton (41) Crawford Ave. Ridge Ave. Chicago Ave.

Caldwell Ave. Touhy Ave.

Devon (41) Av.

Peterson (14) Broadway Ave.

Foster (41) Ashland Ave.

Lawrence Ave.

Irving Park Rd.

Belmont Ave. Milwaukee Ave. Western **LAKEVIEW/WRIGLEYVILLE AND UPTOWN**

Fullerton (50) Ave. Kennedy Expwy. Lincoln Ave. (41)

MILWAUKEE AVE. CORRIDOR

North Ave. Humboldt Park (64) Central Chicago

Chicago Ave. Wells St.

OAK PARK Pulaski United Center Michigan Ave.

Madison St.

Eisenhower Expwy. **NEAR WEST SIDE**

CICERO Belt Rd.

LOWER WEST SIDE Rd.

Ave. St. **BRIDGEPORT CANARYVILLE** Burnham Park

Ship Canal 35th St.

Chicago Sanitary and Stevenson Expwy. **NEAR SOUTH SIDE**

Cicero Kedzie 51st St. **★ HYDE PARK KENWOOD** **★★★ MUSEUM OF SCIENCE AND INDUSTRY**

MIDWAY AIRPORT Washington Park Jackson Park **★★ UNIVERSITY OF CHICAGO**

St. Ashland Ave. Halsted St. Dan Ryan Expwy. Chicago Cottage Grove Ave. Stony Island Ave. Skyway

(50)

BANK St. Western Ave. INDIANA

EVERGREEN PARK

OAK LAWN 103rd Pulaski St. (20)

111th St. State St. **★ PULLMAN** Lake Calumet Torrence Ave. Calumet ILLINOIS INDIANA

Tri-State Tollway (1) Bishop Ford Expwy. Wolf Lake

(83) 127th Rd. St. 130th St. Brainard Ave.

Stony Creek

★ INDIANA DUNES NATL. LAKESHORE

11

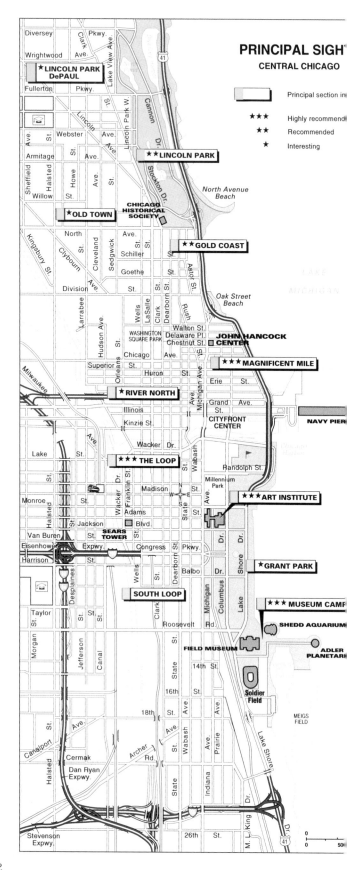

PRINCIPAL SIGH

CENTRAL CHICAGO

Principal section in

★★★ Highly recommend

★★ Recommended

★ Interesting

★ LINCOLN PARK DePAUL

★★ LINCOLN PARK

★ OLD TOWN

★★ GOLD COAST

★★★ MAGNIFICENT MILE

★ RIVER NORTH

★★★ THE LOOP

★★★ ART INSTITUTE

★ GRANT PARK

★★★ MUSEUM CAMP

SHEDD AQUARIUM

ADLER PLANETARI

SOUTH LOOP

CHICAGO HISTORICAL SOCIETY

JOHN HANCOCK CENTER

CITYFRONT CENTER

NAVY PIER

SEARS TOWER

FIELD MUSEUM

Soldier Field

MEIGS FIELD

North Avenue Beach

Oak Street Beach

WASHINGTON SQUARE PARK

Millennium Park

LAKE MICHIGAN

12

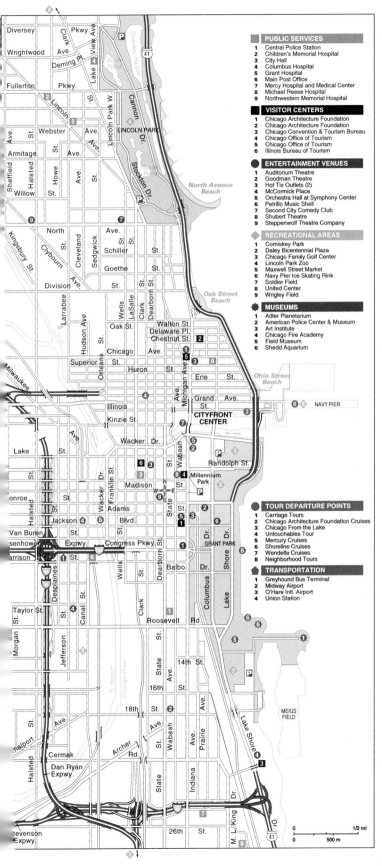

PUBLIC SERVICES
1 Central Police Station
2 Children's Memorial Hospital
3 City Hall
4 Columbus Hospital
5 Grant Hospital
6 Main Post Office
7 Mercy Hospital and Medical Center
8 Michael Reese Hospital
9 Northwestern Memorial Hospital

VISITOR CENTERS
1 Chicago Architecture Foundation
2 Chicago Architecture Foundation
3 Chicago Convention & Tourism Bureau
4 Chicago Office of Tourism
5 Chicago Office of Tourism
6 Illinois Bureau of Tourism

ENTERTAINMENT VENUES
1 Auditorium Theatre
2 Goodman Theatre
3 Hot Tix Outlets (2)
4 McCormick Place
5 Orchestra Hall at Symphony Center
6 Petrillo Music Shell
7 Second City Comedy Club
8 Shubert Theatre
9 Steppenwolf Theatre Company

RECREATIONAL AREAS
1 Comiskey Park
2 Daley Bicentennial Plaza
3 Chicago Family Golf Center
4 Lincoln Park Zoo
5 Maxwell Street Market
6 Navy Pier Ice Skating Rink
7 Soldier Field
8 United Center
9 Wrigley Field

MUSEUMS
1 Adler Planetarium
2 American Police Center & Museum
3 Art Institute
4 Chicago Fire Academy
5 Field Museum
6 Shedd Aquarium

TOUR DEPARTURE POINTS
1 Carriage Tours
2 Chicago Architecture Foundation Cruises
3 Chicago From the Lake
4 Untouchables Tour
5 Mercury Cruises
6 Shoreline Cruises
7 Wendella Cruises
8 Neighborhood Tours

TRANSPORTATION
1 Greyhound Bus Terminal
2 Midway Airport
3 O'Hare Intl. Airport
4 Union Station

NAVY PIER

CITYFRONT CENTER

LINCOLN PARK

North Avenue Beach

Oak Street Beach

Ohio Street Beach

GRANT PARK

Millennium Park

MEIGS FIELD

| 0 | 1/2 mi |
| 0 | 500 m |

13

Buckingham Fountain in Grant Park

Introduction
to Chicago

Geographical Notes

Located in Illinois, less than an hour's drive from Indiana to the southeast and Wisconsin to the north, Chicago occupies a strategic position on the southern end of Lake Michigan, at the point where America's heartland abuts the Great Lakes. Residences, commerce and industry crowd the shoreline, all vying for visual and physical access to the vast body of water, the only Great Lake whose borders lie entirely within the US. The lake has played a significant role in Chicago's phenomenal transformation into the commercial center of the country's agricultural midsection and hub of a national transportation network, funneling the Midwest's goods across the country and out to the world.

■ Quick Facts

Location:	Latitude 41° 50' N
	Longitude 87° 37' W
Area of city:	228sq mi/591sq km
Metro area:	4,653sq mi/12,051sq km
Elevation:	578ft/176m above sea level
Recreation:	551 parks, 31 beaches and 8 harbors totaling 6,756 acres
Lake Michigan:	Fifth largest freshwater body in the world
Area of lake:	22,300sq mi/57,757sq km
Deepest point:	923ft/282m
Chicago shoreline:	29mi/47km
Water intake:	4,200mi/6,758km of water mains pump a billion gallons of water from the lake into the city daily

An Inauspicious Site – Today's sprawling city lies on a plain flattened by glaciers and their meltwaters some 13,500 years ago. At that time, the site was located 60ft below the surface of glacial Lake Chicago (the ancestor of Lake Michigan). The weight of the ice and of the lake compacted a heavy layer of clay over the dolomite-limestone bedrock (Niagaran formation), which stretches across the Great Lakes area. The poor drainage of the soil above the clay created a very swampy, inhospitable site. Gradually, the glaciers retreated and, in places, the land rose, creating a subcontinental divide between the Great Lakes and the Mississippi River. The divide was defined by the Valparaiso Moraine—a glacial ridge that circles the southern end of Lake Michigan about 8mi from the present shoreline—which contained the waters of Lake Chicago. The moraine was breached at the **Chicago Portage**, located at the southwestern edge of the modern city, and the lake's outflow carved the Des Plaines and Illinois River valleys as the water drained toward the Mississippi River Valley. Originating in wetlands north and southwest of present-day Chicago, the Chicago River came into existence about 6,000 years ago; through the years, it remained a small, muddy channel that followed a meandering sandbar and emptied into Lake Michigan.
Around 4,000 years ago, the waters receded farther and the earth rebounded, allowing the ridge to rise again and separate the Des Plaines and Illinois rivers, which continued to flow toward the Mississippi from the Chicago River.

Overcoming the Quagmire – The Potawatomi Indians populating the region in the 17C named the area around the present-day city *Checaugou*, referring to the garlic growing wild throughout the swamp. Not considered suitable for defense or settlement by Native Americans, the area was nevertheless chosen by trader **Jean Baptiste Point du Sable**, who erected a homestead here in 1779. The Chicago Portage—one of the shortest and lowest points in the divide—provided a crucial link between the Great Lakes and the Mississippi River and would soon become the key to a major travel route through the middle of the continent. Native Americans, traders and settlers portaged their canoes between the Des Plaines River and a low, wide, swampy fork of the Chicago River called "Mud Lake"; when the water was high, the portage even became navigable. Already in 1673 French explorer Louis Jolliet had proposed the construction of a canal to bridge the divide and effectively link the Atlantic Ocean to the Gulf of Mexico. The canal would be realized almost two centuries later, spurring Chicago's growth.
The city's early history was characterized by the muddy soil on which the city rests. The quagmire not only thwarted road and building construction, but also contributed to the spread of disease in the population. In the 1850s the city began installing sewers throughout the settlement. Since laying the lines underground proved nearly impossible, they were placed at street level and the streets and existing structures were raised or jacked up around them, sometimes by up to 12ft. Unfortunately, the sewers

mped both storm overflow and sewage into the Chicago River, which emptied into
ke Michigan, the source of the city's water supply. To keep the drinking water safe,
gineers had to devise a way to reverse the flow of the river. A canal would not only
ovide a link from the Chicago River to the Des Plaines River, but—if deep enough—
uld also allow the river's waters to be diverted into it. Rather than continuing its
tural course toward the lake, the river would empty into the canal. At the same
ne, locks would be needed to regulate the amount of lakewater now draining into
e unused section of the original riverbed and into the canal.

■ A Feat of Engineering

The earliest designs for the **Illinois & Michigan Canal** called for a channel 8ft deep
and 60ft wide. Owing to financial constraints, the original canal bed was dug
only 6ft in depth; the proper water level was to be maintained by a pumping
station and feeder canals. Although it was deepened to the planned 8ft in 1871,
the canal remained too shallow to allow for the river's permanent reversal.
Devastating epidemics—blamed on polluted drinking water—decimated the city
in the 1880s, and the weary populace clamored for action. A Sanitary District
was quickly created with a mission to dig a new, larger and more effective
channel. The resulting Sanitary & Ship Canal was 25ft deep, 100ft wide and
over 30mi long. Its construction entailed the removal of more earth than that
of the Panama Canal, and when completed in 1900, it easily reversed the flow
of the sluggish Chicago River. The Sanitary District also built the Calumet Sag
Channel and North Shore Channel in the early 20C to maintain water flow in
the correct (wrong) direction. However, the combined storm and sewer system
continued to back up after heavy rains, and the river would occasionally flow
back into the lake. By the 1970s, the Sanitary District (now known as the
Metropolitan Water Reclamation District of Greater Chicago) began construction of the Tunnel and Reservoir Project (TARP) consisting of tunnels 30ft in
diameter and 300ft deep, plus three surface reservoirs that store storm runoff
until it can be treated. The tunnels will run 109mi through the metropolitan
area when finally completed.

Illinois & Michigan Canal (1859)

Chicago Historical Society (ICHi-05843)

The swampy juncture of the sluggish Chicago River and Lake Michigan was valued
Native Americans and 17C French traders as a link between the Great Lakes a
Mississippi River Valley settlements. After the US gained control of the area in the l.
18C, the potential for a canal between Lake Michigan and the Illinois River led to 1
establishment of Fort Dearborn. It was around this fort that the fledgling settleme
of Chicago arose.

c.AD 1000	Native Americans in Illinois begin to form larger, more permanent sett ments and elaborate burial mounds under the influence of the Caho civilization near St. Louis.
c.1500	The prevalence of bison causes Illini tribes to adopt a more mot lifestyle and traverse the Chicago Portage between Lake Michigan a the Illinois River Valley.
c.1660	Iroquois tribes begin to raid Illini settlements in northeastern Illinois. 1800, Potawatomi replace the Illini in the region.
1673	French explorer **Louis Jolliet** and missionary **Jacques Marquette** encounter t Grand Village of the Illinois near Starved Rock and are directed throu the Chicago Portage to Lake Michigan. A year later Marquette wint at Chicago, dying the following spring in Michigan.
1779	Trader **Jean Baptiste Point du Sable** becomes the first permanent settler Chicago, building a cabin and trading post on the north side of t Chicago River.
1803	US soldiers build **Fort Dearborn** on the south side of the Chicago Riv
1812	Frontier tensions spurred by war with England lead to a massacre Potawatomi natives of 52 settlers fleeing Fort Dearborn.
1816	The Indian Boundary, securing a canal corridor from Chicago to t Illinois River, is established by treaty. Fort Dearborn is rebuilt after t War of 1812.
1830	The Illinois & Michigan Canal Commission hires surveyor Jam Thompson to plat two towns along the canal route, Chicago and Ottaw
1832	Native tribes are expelled from Illinois following the suppression of uprising led by **Chief Black Hawk**.
1833	About 400 residents incorporate the village of Chicago. The first balloo frame structure, St. Mary's Church, is built from pre-sawn boards a nails.

Canal construction turns Chicago from a frontier outpost into a boomtown, bringi
waves of Yankee migrants, Irish canal workers and skilled Germans fleeing persec
tion after the failed 1848 revolutions in Europe. The city grows too fast for its ow
good, tardily adding sewers, parks and other basic amenities while culture languish
in the pursuit of fast money in real estate, lumber, agriculture, steel and livestoc
Innovations like the grain elevator and refrigerated railroad car make Chicago t
conduit for the nation's cereal and meat products. The city mushrooms from less th
4,000 persons to over 300,000 in less than 35 years.

1836	Chicago is in the fever grip of land speculation as construction begi July 4 on the **Illinois & Michigan Canal**.
1837	4,000 citizens incorporate the City of Chicago on March 4. The natio wide Panic of 1837 deflates local real-estate speculation and eventua slows canal construction.
1847	The agricultural boom in the Illinois countryside, where the rich prair soil is producing some of the nation's highest yields, leads **Cyrus H McCormick** to move his reaper factory from Cincinnati to Chicago. With two years, he is expanding to fill 1,500 orders per year.
1848	A boatload of sugar and other goods traverses the newly opened Illino & Michigan Canal en route from New Orleans to New York. Agricultu goods begin to flow east from Chicago, and the Chicago Board of Trad is created to regulate the grain trade. Chicago's first railroad, the Chicag and Galena Union, inaugurates service on A 10mi route.
1852	The city allows the Illinois Central Railroad to run tracks along the lak front in exchange for building a breakwater to prevent erosion.
1855	**Lager Beer Riots**: immigrant Germans protest Mayor Levi Boone's tempe ance edicts, which prohibit the drinking of beer on Sunday, labeling th action "un-American."

1856 | **Chicago Historical Society** is created. US Senator Stephen A. Douglas founds the first University of Chicago in alliance with the Baptist church.

1860 | **Abraham Lincoln** is nominated for president by the new Republican Party in Chicago's Wigwam Hall, built for the occasion at Lake and Market (now Wacker Dr.) Streets. Chicago is the center of the world's largest railroad network, totaling almost 3,000mi of track.

1865 | The **Union Stock Yards** are organized on Chicago's South Side to consolidate the city's slaughterhouses around a central railroad yard. Marshall Field and Levi Leiter form a dry-goods store that will become Marshall Field & Co.

1867 | Chicago labor leaders begin the struggle for the 8-hour workday, choosing May 1 as the day to celebrate the contributions of labor to the American economy.

1869 | Chicago's Parks and Boulevards System is created—over 1,600 acres of green space ringing the city in A 28mi loop. The three-part system is designed by Frederick Law Olmsted and Calvert Vaux (South Park, now Washington and Jackson parks), William Le Baron Jenney (West Parks, including today's Humboldt Park), and Swain Nelson (Lincoln Park). The **Chicago Water Tower** is constructed to regulate the pressure of water pumped into the city from Lake Michigan.

Chicago in Flames (1871)
View from Randolph Street Bridge

Chicago Historical Society (ICHi-02953)

HE FIRE

ne devastation of the Chicago Fire appears catastrophic in the destruction of homes nd businesses throughout the central area, but the city's enviable water and rail connections—and the majority of its industries—remain unscorched, and rebuilding mmences immediately. Chicago's phenomenal growth continues as the population ples in the decade after the fire. The fire also draws architects from across the untry, who eventually develop the Chicago school. By the 1880s up to 10,000 immiants arrive in the city each week, leading to health problems and overcrowding.

1871 | A "deep cut" of the Illinois & Michigan Canal attempts to reverse the Chicago River to limit pollution of drinking water taken from the lake. On October 8, the **Great Chicago Fire** starts in the barn behind Mrs. O'Leary's house on DeKoven Street. For three days, the fire burns north and east, destroying the whole of downtown Chicago and much of the North Side. Some 300 die and a third of the city's population of 335,000 is left without shelter.

1877 | The Great Railroad Strike affects Chicago as 30 workers are killed in the "Battle of the Viaduct" on Halsted Street.

19

1879   The Chicago Academy of Design (founded in 1866) is reorganized to include a school and a museum, the **Art Institute of Chicago**. In 1885 the institute constructs its first edifice (since demolished), designed by Burnham & Root, at Michigan Avenue and Van Buren Street.

1880   George Pullman hires architect Solon S. Beman to design the town and railroad-car factories of **Pullman** near Lake Calumet.

1884   The first steel-frame building, the 10-story Home Insurance Building, is erected in the Loop, designed by **William Le Baron Jenney**.

1886   Striking workers meet to hear the mayor and other speakers at a May 4 meeting in Haymarket Square. As the meeting disperses, 170 policemen arrive. Someone throws a bomb, killing seven policemen. Eight anarchist labor leaders are brought to trial in an event that garners worldwide attention, but Chicago civic leaders and newspapers condemn the anarchists. Four are eventually hanged and one commits suicide while three remain in jail. The incident becomes known as the **Haymarket Riot**.

1889   Social reformers Jane Addams and Ellen Gates Starr found **Hull-House** on the Near West Side to aid the immigrant population, which outnumbers Chicago's US-born population. The **Auditorium Building** by Adler & Sullivan is completed.

WORLD'S FAIR, WORLD CITY

The city determines to prove that it is not an uncultured hog town by inviting the world to the largest party of the 19C, the World's Columbian Exposition of 1893. The fair's gleaming Neoclassical buildings celebrate the progress of the American Republic in sciences and arts, creating a seemingly perfect "White City." The success of the fair engenders the "City Beautiful" movement nationwide. Chicago continues to feed the East and reap the West as an increasing populace migrates across the continent.

1891-92   Theodore Thomas founds the **Chicago Symphony Orchestra**. The **University of Chicago** opens in Hyde Park thanks to the beneficence of oil magnate John D. Rockefeller. Local artists form the **Little Room** salon.

1893   The **World's Columbian Exposition** opens in Jackson Park, drawing 27 million visitors to the 650-acre "White City" over the summer. The adjacent midway features the first Ferris wheel and the racy "hootchie-kootchie" dancing of Little Egypt. The city's first elevated train brings visitors to the fair from the Loop. Illinois governor **John Peter Altgeld** pardons the three surviving Haymarket defendants, earning the enmity of business and anti-immigrant forces. The Field Columbian Museum, later the **Field Museum of Natural History**, is founded.

1894   In the midst of an economic depression, the **Pullman Strike** disrupts railroad traffic nationwide as workers suffer layoffs and wage cuts in George Pullman's company town. President Grover Cleveland sends federal troops to break the strike. **Clarence Darrow** defends the strikers in a trial that leads to the end of the company town.

1897   The **Union Loop Elevated Railroad** is completed, girdling the city's core with steel.

1900   The **Chicago Sanitary and Ship Canal** opens, permanently reversing the flow of the Chicago River. By 1914 it will replace the Illinois & Michigan Canal as the city's primary shipping route. The Union Stock Yards' hundred companies employ 30,000 persons.

1903   A fire at Chicago's Iroquois Theatre kills 596 persons.

1905   **Robert S. Abbott** founds the *Chicago Defender* to serve the city's growing African-American community.

1906   Upton Sinclair's novel **The Jungle** is published. His descriptions of the meatpacking industry lead to the reforms of the Pure Food and Drug Act.

1909   Daniel Burnham and Edward Bennett's **Plan of Chicago** is released, providing a Classical template for the city's future development. Frank Lloyd Wright's quintessential Prairie-style **Robie House** is completed in Hyde Park.

1912-19   The **Chicago Literary Renaissance**, a school of social realism in literature, flourishes in Chicago. Margaret Anderson founds the *Little Review*; Edgar Lee Masters' *Spoon River Anthology* and Carl Sandburg's *Chicago Poems* are published. Theodore Dreiser and Sherwood Anderson release their early novels.

1919   A **race riot** leaves 40 dead and hundreds injured on the city's South Side. The Chicago White Sox lose the World Series, and a year later eight players are banned for conspiring with gamblers to "throw" the series

Al Capone at Comiskey Park (1931)

PROGRESS AND PROHIBITION

Civic leaders work to transform downtown Chicago into a modern civic center with the creation of Wacker Drive, North Michigan Avenue and the museums of Grant Park. But the Roaring Twenties leave Chicago with a permanent scar, as bootlegging gangs commit hundreds of murders in their attempts to control the illegal liquor business. **Al Capone** (1899-1947) becomes Chicago's most notorious figure, heading a large criminal syndicate that survives his imprisonment.

1922	The *Chicago Tribune* announces a worldwide competition to design its new skyscraper as Wacker Drive and North Michigan Avenue usher in modern development.
1924	There are approximately 20,000 illegal retail liquor outlets in Chicago. Bootlegger Dion O'Banion is killed in his North Side flower shop as Al Capone seeks to expand his empire.
1929	Seven members of the rival Bugs Moran gang are gunned down on North Clark Street by Al Capone's men in the **St. Valentine's Day Massacre**. Capone, now a media celebrity, earns roughly $50 million a year bootlegging.
1931	Al Capone is sent to prison for tax evasion. He is released eight years later, his body and brain wracked by syphilis.
1933	Chicago Mayor **Anton Cermak** is killed in Miami by an assassin's bullet intended for President-elect Franklin Delano Roosevelt. The mayor's office falls to **Ed Kelly**, who with Pat Nash founds the city's Democratic political machine, which dominates for the next 50 years.
1933-34	Chicago's **Century of Progress International Exposition** draws millions to a new lakefront site inspired by the Burnham Plan. The fair focuses on the innovations of the modern era with exhibits such as an all-glass house, a windowless Electrical Building and Buckminster Fuller's Dymaxion car. The **Museum of Science and Industry** opens in Jackson Park. Public Enemy Number One John Dillinger is shot to death by federal agents outside the Biograph Theater.
1937	Ten striking steelworkers and sympathizers are killed by police on Memorial Day as they march on the Republic Steel plant in South Chicago.

MID-TO-LATE 20C

Chicago's population peaks in 1950, and the ensuing decades witness large-scale expressway and urban-renewal projects that mark the triumph of the personal automobile. Chicago becomes the center of the nation's airline system at Midway and O'Hare airports. The social turbulence of the 1960s reaches one of its peaks at the Democratic National Convention in 1968. By the 1970s Chicago is in decline as its industrial base bleeds away and an increasing number of white middle-class residents move to the suburbs. The city's new ethnic mix elects the first African-American mayor in 1983 while Chicago's continuing role as a financial and commercial center spurs new urban redevelopment efforts.

1942   Enrico Fermi and a team of University of Chicago scientists create the first controlled, self-sustaining **nuclear reaction** underneath the school's abandoned football stands.

1949   Construction begins on 860-880 N. Lake Shore Drive by **Ludwig Mies van der Rohe**. Mies continues to design the Illinois Institute of Technology campus, where he has presided over the architectural program since 1937.

1955   **Richard J. Daley** is elected mayor of Chicago for the first of six times. He will die in office in 1976. O'Hare Airport opens on the northwestern fringe of the city.

1968   The assassination of **Dr. Martin Luther King, Jr**. leads to widespread rioting on the South and West Sides. In August demonstrators converge on the **Democratic National Convention**, provoking a violent response from police and US National Guard forces. Confrontations in Grant and Lincoln parks resound with the chant "The whole world is watching." The **Chicago Seven** trial the following year holds radicals and student leaders responsible for the melees.

1971   The Union Stock Yards close. McCormick Place Convention Center, the largest in the world, opens on the south lakefront.

1974   **Sears Tower** is topped off as the tallest building in the world.

1979   A January blizzard dumps a record amount of snow and freezes the city for over a month. City Hall's unpreparedness and lack of response to the snow lead to the ouster of Mayor Michael Bilandic by **Jane Byrne**, Chicago's first female mayor.

1983   **Harold Washington** becomes Chicago's first African-American mayor. A city council majority of 29 white aldermen struggles for power during three years of bitter "council wars."

1987   Mayor Washington dies seven months after his resounding re-election, leading to a traumatic 10-hour city council session that elects **Eugene Sawyer** as mayor.

1988   Lights for night baseball are installed at **Wrigley Field**.

CONTEMPORARY CHICAGO

A century after it first sought the world's approval, Chicago again seeks recognition as a world-class city. Still the fulcrum of American commerce, the city is redeveloping from within, transforming industrial land into middle-class neighborhoods, solidifying its role as a financial center and convention venue, and building its reputation as a tourist destination and cultural metropolis.

1989   **Richard M. Daley**, son of Richard J. Daley, is elected mayor.

1991   **Michael Jordan** and the **Chicago Bulls** win the National Basketball Association championship for the first time, and proceed to triumph again in 1992, 1993, 1996, 1997 and 1998.

1992   A company driving pilings into the Chicago River pierces a portion of the city's old freight-tunnel system, causing flooding in basements throughout the Loop and the evacuation of the entire Downtown in the middle of a business day.

1994   The first **World Cup** soccer tournament in the US opens in Chicago with a 1-0 victory by Germany over Bolivia.

1995   A summer heat wave kills more than 700 Chicagoans as the temperature reaches 106°F.

1996   The Democratic National Convention returns to Chicago. The Petronas Towers in Kuala Lumpur, Malaysia, surpass the Sears Tower as tallest buildings in the world.

1997   Field Museum of Natural History purchases a *Tyrannosaurus rex* skeleton for $8.3 million. With completion of its 60,000sq ft addition, the Chicago Board of Trade becomes the largest futures- and options-trading facility in the world. *Chicago Tribune* columnist **Mike Royko** (1932-97) dies.

1998   Long-time Chicago Cubs broadcaster **Harry Caray**, known for leading home crowds in singing "Take Me Out to the Ball Game," dies at age 77. The Chicago Bulls win their sixth NBA championship in eight years.

1999   City promotes "The Milly" dance for the new millennium with references to local landmarks and sports heroes.

      Michael Jordan retires from basketball in January.

2000   Residents move into historic and modern homes at Fort Sheridan, the decommissioned North Shore military base.

Economy

Chicago's economy has been shaped by its location at the nexus of the great inland waterways and at the heart of the nation's rich agricultural midsection. Throughout the 19C, as the central marketplace and entrepôt for the bounty of Midwestern farms and fields, Chicago achieved its legendary status as "wheat stacker, hog butcher, and freight handler to the world," in the words of Carl Sandburg. Still the most important railroad-freight hub in North America, the international center of futures trading and a major producer of food products, the Chicago metropolitan area cultivates roots in its economic past, while a booming service economy propels the city into the 21C.

From Grain to Brain – The features that made Chicago a funnel for the foodstuffs of the Midwest—location and accessibility—also led to its growth as an industrial center of the Western world. The earliest industries were closely related to agriculture and husbandry: milling, tanning, woodworking and food processing. After the Civil War, the city began to expand its industrial base, as big steel, heavy manufacturing and meatpacking came to dominate its economy. European immigrants flocked in by the thousands hoping for employment with giant United States Steel, International Harvester or the Union Stock Yards, or any of the hundreds of factories that lined the river and encircled the central business district. By 1960 manufacturing accounted for more than one-third of local jobs, but the stockyards closed forever in 1971, and the steel industry fell victim to recession. In recent years, as companies downsize and the manufacturing base dwindles further, the city has come to rely more and more on a service economy-from the largest accounting firms to the smallest shoeshine parlors-for its livelihood. Today the service sector, including government, retail, transportation, hospitality, educational, legal and medical workers, claims nearly three-fourths of the local work force.

■ Made in Chicago:

At the 1893 World's Columbian Exposition, Mayor Carter Harrison observed that Chicago "knows nothing that it fears to attempt, and thus far has found nothing that it cannot accomplish." Indeed the city's unofficial slogan—I Will-conveys the sense of purpose that built the following list of innovations.

Ferris wheel: George W.G. Ferris created A 264ft "bridge on an axle" for the Columbian Exposition. A modern rendition now dominates Navy Pier.

Skyscraper: William Le Baron Jenney designed the Home Insurance Building on LaSalle and Adams Streets around an iron-and-steel frame in 1884, thereby instituting the lineage of Chicago's 20C pride and joy, the Sears Tower.

Juvenile Court system: Established in 1899, this division of the Circuit Court of Cook County was the brainchild of Julia Lathrop, an associate of pioneering social worker Jane Addams.

Lie detector: Leonarde Keeler, an employee of the Scientific Crime Detection Laboratory (the nation's first) at Northwestern University, devised the Keeler Polygraph. His invention earned him a part in the 1948 film *Call Northside 777*.

Successful heart surgery: Dr. Daniel Hale Williams, the first African-American member of the American College of Surgeons, saved James Cornish's life by tying off a severed artery and suturing the heart sac after a near deadly barroom brawl in 1893.

Blood bank and trauma center: Cook County Hospital opened the nation's first blood bank in 1937 and the first trauma center in 1966.

Drugstore lunch counter: Faced with a cold winter and falling ice-cream sales, Myrtle Walgreen, wife of the drugstore's founder, began serving hot meals at their soda fountain counter around 1909.

Ice-cream sundae: Around 1900, ice-cream-parlor owner Deacon Garwood circumvented temperance laws that forbade ice-cream sodas on Sundays by dishing up a concoction of ice cream and syrup he called a sundae.

Ovaltine, Twinkies, Cracker Jacks, Dove Bars: These popular sweets all originated in Chicago between 1893 and 1952.

Zipper: Called the "hookless fastener" when exhibited at the 1893 Columbian Exposition, the device would be dubbed "zipper" by the B.F. Goodrich Company, who used it on overshoes.

Roller skates: Levant M. Richardson made possible the modern roller skate when he invented the ball-bearing wheel in 1884.

Pinball: The automatic-game rage began in Chicago in 1930 with the ten-balls-for-a-nickel Whoopee Game.

City vs. Suburb – Another factor complicates regional economics: the relationship between the city proper, suburban Cook County and the collar counties, a symbiosis that is impossible to ignore. Many local employers have fled downtown for less expensive, more hospitable locations outside the city limits, creating thriving economic corridors in surrounding communities like Schaumburg and those of Du Page County. As a result, of the 4.5 million people at work in the metropolitan area, less than half are employed in the city. Some analysts predict a slowing of the trend as the cost of downtown office space comes into line with suburban prices, and most agree that a balance between city and outskirts must be maintained for the economic good of the region.

Commercial Crossroads – As the freight hub of North America, Chicago supports a complex network of railroad, trucking, waterborne shipping and air-freight services. The nation's major inland port, Chicago is connected to the Atlantic Ocean via the St. Lawrence Seaway, which opened in 1959, and to the Gulf of Mexico via the Sanitary & Ship Canal and the Mississippi River. Even with the decline of the steel industry, iron ore remains the largest volume commodity to enter the port aboard deep-draft carriers, and grain is still exported by water around the world. Two commercial airports serve the city: **Midway**, the city's original air terminal on the southwest side; and **O'Hare International**, the country's second-busiest airport (recently surpassed by Atlanta's Hartsfield International Airport), which served more than 70 million passengers in 1997.

As the national hub of passenger rail travel, downtown's **Union Station** served some 2.2 million Amtrak riders in 1999. On a local scale, the buses, subways and elevated trains of the largely urban Chicago Transit Authority travel more than 375,000mi daily. A consortium of suburban rail lines known as Metra operates over 425mi of track in Illinois, with an additional 75mi that terminate in Kenosha, Wisconsin, and South Bend, Indiana. Altogether, this integrated system of rail, elevated, subway and bus lines ferries nearly two million commuters to work and back each day along with thousands of occasional riders.

Future Games – The **Chicago Board of Trade (CBOT)**, founded in 1848 and today the world's oldest and largest futures exchange, is a testament to Chicago's agrarian origins. Established to trade grain futures-bulk commodities bought and sold at a pre-determined future time-in the days when 60 million bushels passed through the city each year, the CBOT now handles an array of commodities and financial futures. The **Chicago Mercantile Exchange (CME)**, historically the world's busiest market for perishable commodities such as pork bellies, now trades futures and options on agricultural commodities, interest rates, stock market indexes, gold and foreign currency futures through an international trading link established with Singapore in 1984. In 1992 the exchange launched an electronic after-hours trading system to open up a truly global market. Generally, some 900,000 contracts trade daily at the CME; on one record-breaking day in 1994, 2.4 million contracts changed hands. Together the CBOT and the CME make Chicago a world leader in futures trading. The **Chicago Stock Exchange**, which opened in 1882, is second only to its New York counterpart in terms of the dollar value of shares traded. In 1999 the Chicago Stock Exchange traded more than 14 billion shares worth over $580 billion.

Chicago Mercantile Exchange Trading Floor

Corporate Superlatives – A survey of the highest income-earning public corporations in the Chicago metropolitan area reveals the wide range of concerns that make up the area's diversified economic base. Included among the 37 Fortune 500 companies located in Chicago are retailer Sears Roebuck and Co., Sara Lee Corp., Motorola, Inc., Ameritech Corp., State Farm insurance and UAL Corp. (parent of United Airlines). The national drugstore chain Walgreen Co., and McDonald's Corp., the nation's largest seller of hamburgers, maintain headquarters outside Chicago. In addition, Chicago has ranked second to New York as a publishing center since the turn of the century, specializing largely in encyclopedias and educational materials.

Conventions and Tourism – Chicago ranks as the undisputed convention capital of the US. In 1999 the city hosted 35,000 conventions, trade shows and corporate meetings, from the mammoth National Restaurant Show to such smaller, specialized events as the conference for the Royal Order of Jesters. This $5.3-billion-a-year industry brings more than four million visitors to the city annually. Estimates indicate that one convention alone can generate revenues as high as $95 million in six days, as delegates purchase goods and services during their stay. The centerpiece of Chicago's convention business is **McCormick Place**, the country's largest exhibition facility. Its $987-million expansion completed in 1997, the three-building complex now offers 2.2 million square feet of exhibit space. The city is becoming an increasingly popular destination for tourists as well, 26 million of whom visited in 1998. And according to the US Travel and Tourism Administration, Chicago ranks as the ninth most-visited US city for overseas visitors.

Ivory Towers – Among Chicago's 96 colleges and universities can be counted the top graduate fine-arts program in the nation at the School of the Art Institute of Chicago; the University of Chicago's law, medical, MBA, music and graduate programs, none of which ranks below eighth in the nation; and the well-respected Medill School of Journalism at Northwestern. The University of Illinois at Chicago has the largest enrollment with some 25,000 students, followed by Northwestern (its main campus is located in suburban Evanston) with 17,000.

Chicagoans who travel abroad are used to the reaction that the mention of their home city usually elicits. The city's historic reputation for vice and corruption, epitomized by the machine-gun-toting gangsters of the 1920s, casts a long shadow over those other ingredients that today make it a world-class metropolis.

This dual nature defines Chicago in all of its aspects, particularly politics. The city struts its gruff frontier reputation while successfully cultivating the trappings of class and sophistication. In city politics, the simultaneous tension and symbiosis between vice and virtue have created the inextricable tangle of good government and power politics that ultimately gave rise to the country's most enduring political machine: a mighty Democratic Party exerting influence and dispensing favors to keep the city running smoothly. Indeed, the successful among Chicago's 45 mayors have understood that the electorate's primary concern is the efficient delivery of city services—from garbage pickup to safety on the streets. In 1837 Chicago's first mayor, **William Butler Ogden**, used his own wealth to finance city improvements and even bailed out the city on his personal credit when financial panic struck.

Political Prelude – As the city's population soared in two decades to over 93,000, the adolescent boomtown seethed with prostitution, gambling and crime. Subsequent mayors—largely symbolic leaders with little real authority—turned a blind eye to the flourishing netherworld, but 6ft 6in **"Long John" Wentworth** burst into office in 1857 determined to purge the vice districts, perhaps the first effort at reform in Chicago. In a dramatic move, he and a posse literally pulled down the ramshackle brothels, saloons and gambling dens situated in a seedy patch by the river known as the Sands. Though demonstrative, his other attempts to eradicate such areas had little effect. Chicago's underworld had already taken sturdy root, and it would be for later mayors to discover the value of compromise.

The Smoke Clears – As Chicago reinvented itself in the aftermath of the Great Fire of 1871, the breach between wealth and poverty widened, enhancing the city's split personality. Growth continued unabated, dictating a personal kind of politics conducted in the neighborhoods. Vast inner-city immigrant populations represented powerful voting blocs, and ward bosses were quick to exchange jobs and other favors for their support. Nurtured by this ward-by-ward spoils system, the "Machine" began to incubate.

After the fire, the Democratic Party gained momentum, propelled by the votes of the huge foreign-born population. With the election in 1879 of **Carter Harrison I**, a flamboyant Kentuckian with empathy for the working man and a live-and-let-live philosophy, Chicago had a modern mayor who understood his constituents' practical needs. His appeal crossed class and ethnic lines and his belief in personal liberties endeared him to the city's considerable underworld. He served four consecutive terms between 1879 and 1887, only to be assassinated in 1893 by a disgruntled office seeker on the heels of his proudest accomplishment: serving a fifth term as Chicago's "World's Fair Mayor" during the Columbian Exposition.

In spite of his tolerance of powerful gambling kingpin **Michael McDonald**, Harrison earned the devotion of the electorate as well as a reputation for honesty, even among his detractors. Meanwhile, "King Mike" presided over a wide-ranging empire—which included much of the county board, the police department, the Democratic Party and the Cook County sheriff, along with bunco artists and con men—from offices in the largest of his gambling emporiums, a lavish downtown establishment known as The Store. In years to come, Mike McDonald's most famous heir would be Al Capone.

From Saloon to City Hall – Harrison's tolerant administration—and the five intermittent terms served by his son, Carter Harrison II, between 1897 and 1915—achieved a precarious balance between vice and virtue that later mayors would envy. Still, power resided in the wards and the saloons where the likes of Aldermen **"Bathhouse" John Coughlin** and **Michael "Hinky Dink" Kenna** held sway. Their rollicking First Ward included the infamous Levee, the city's sprawling underbelly and home of the **Everleigh Club**, the most elite of 200 brothels in the district. Not satisfied with the take from protection money they earned in the Levee, the two staged annual First Ward balls to line the coffers of the ward organization. To these drunken brawls came prostitutes and politicians, policemen and aldermen, all players in an absurd parody of city government.

By the 1890s aldermen were learning that more profit and long-term reward might be garnered in collusion with businessmen than on the streets of the Levee. Utilities wishing to lay cable and traction magnates seeking rights of way along city streets paid the aldermen thousands of dollars in "boodle" annually for favorable votes in council. In return, Chicago gained a modern transit system with electrified trains, and the burgeoning Machine rose from the saloons to City Hall.

In the meantime, the face of organized crime in Chicago was changing, developing into a vicious and insidious network supervised by the likes of Johnny Torrio, "Big Jim" Colosimo, Al Capone and their rivals. Whereas gambling had been the mainstay of the Victorian warlords, the gangsters of the Prohibition era made bootlegging their stock in trade, and by 1920 the "Outfit" had a lock on the city that would last for decades. **Alphonse Capone** initiated the most infamous six years in Chicago's history when he succeeded Johnny Torrio as head of Chicago's syndicate in 1925. Capone eliminated his rivals in a bloody gang war that culminated in the 1929 St. Valentine's Day Massacre, when hit men rubbed out several of gangster Bugs Moran's associates in a North Side garage. Between 1925 and 1931, 439 gangland slayings rocked Chicago, most of which were never solved. Indeed, bombastic mayor **William Hale "Big Bill" Thompson**, indebted to Capone for political and financial support, coddled the mob, and some Chicagoans even considered the ruthless Capone a folk hero. Although brought down by tenacious federal agent Eliot Ness for income tax evasion in 1931, Capone had established a dynasty that would last well beyond his death from syphilis in 1947.

The Modern Machine – Throughout the 1920s, "new-breed" Democrats had been working to create an organization with widespread influence over all of city government. Their quest to institutionalize the Machine coalesced under the leadership of **Anton J. Cermak**, who succeeded Thompson in 1931. Cermak built a revolutionary multi-ethnic coalition unified by a powerful party organization. He advocated reform, efficiency and economy and backed up his promises with the strength of that organization. Even though an assassin's bullet meant for President-elect Franklin Delano Roosevelt cut short his term in 1933, Anton J. Cermak had paved the way for the legendary Richard J. Daley.

In most cities the Great Depression marked the end of urban self-sufficiency. Local organizations could no longer control money, policy and jobs because of the increasing presence of the federal government and unions. But the Chicago Machine gained momentum, expanding its base of support as far as Washington, DC, where leaders recognized the importance of a friendly Chicago mayor. At the same time, organized crime generated considerable income for the Machine through gambling and protection monies. The party courted and won the support of the city's increasing African-American population, only to stumble later over issues of open housing and desegregation.

The Machine hit its stride under **Richard J. Daley**, "Hizzoner da Mare," between 1955 and his death in 1976. A consummate administrator and career politician, Daley, like Cermak, believed in good government through party politics. He brought the rambunctious city council under control, consolidated the power of the mayor's office and extended his reach to state and nation. He engaged professionals to streamline the system. His "City that Works" did so because Daley understood how to exchange influence and favors to get things done. The stronger and more centralized his office, the greater his clout.

By the late 1960s, however, chinks had begun to show in the armor. Daley grew more conservative, his organization less able to please and appease the city's increasingly disparate communities split by racial and political strife. Open housing marches, riots following the assassination of Dr. Martin Luther King, Jr., violence surrounding the

President Prado of Peru *(left)* and Richard J. Daley (1961)

1968 Democratic National Convention, and the mayhem of the Days of Rage the following summer pushed the Machine to the limit. Still, Daley prevailed through a tumultuous time when other big-city mayors failed. He cultivated a reassuring civic stability that played well among a largely conservative electorate confused and somewhat threatened by rapidly changing times, and he delivered city services, thereby guaranteeing loyalty.

The period following Daley's sudden death in 1976 could not have provided more of a contrast. Disputes over his successor set the tone as African-American politicians and their constituents—led by the **Rev. Jesse Jackson**—clamored for recognition, and Poles, feeling too long estranged from City Hall themselves, put forth their own candidates. Ultimately, mild-mannered **Michael Bilandic**, a Bridgeport alderman, came to office first as acting mayor and then by election in 1977. Although a competent mayor, he lacked Daley's ability to consolidate power, and the factions that had begun to form in the party gained strength.

It was a January blizzard in 1979 that sounded the death knell for the old Machine. Unable to liberate the city from its snowy grip, Mayor Bilandic succumbed to a challenge from the irrepressible, reform-minded **Jane Byrne**, Chicago's first woman mayor. With power leaking from the mayor's office, the next few years passed in a tumultuous free-for-all fueled by strikes and a difficult economy. When **Harold Washington**, the city's first African-American mayor, took office in 1983, the rhetoric turned shrill and racist, leading to a standoff between mayor and council that immobilized the city. Promising peacemaking efforts that marked Washington's second term were cut short by his untimely death in 1987.

The furor quieted in the 1990s. **Richard M. Daley**, at first indebted to his father's legacy, has emerged as a no-nonsense mayor of moderation. He presides over a multicultural city council—one alderman for each of 50 wards—whose attentions have shifted from parochial infighting to the staggering concerns of all American cities: revenue generation, a growing underclass and gang violence, a deteriorating infrastructure and an economic challenge from the suburbs.

Addresses, telephone numbers, opening hours and prices published in this guide are accurate at press time. We apologize for any inconvenience resulting from outdated information. Please send us your comments:

*Michelin Travel Publications
Editorial Department
P. O. Box 19001
Greenville, SC 29602-9001
Email: TheGreenGuide-us@us.michelin.com*

ranked in population size only by New York and Los Angeles, Chicago remains the
d and brash metropolis that Norman Mailer called "perhaps the last of the great
erican cities." In this polyglot city of nearly 3 million, the neighborhood is the
mon measure of all, a source of identity and pride and a lingering reflection of
ago's incredible immigrant heritage. A patchwork of neighborhoods, some 175 in
unfurls westward from the lakefront, from tiny Old Town Triangle on the North
e to the anchor communities of Rogers Park and Englewood. Some are the stuff
developers' dreams; others trace their outlines around historic ethnic enclaves.

creators of this patchwork have been an eclectic lot since **Jean Baptiste Point du Sable**,
ur trader of French, Caribbean and African descent, built the earliest permanent
elling on the banks of the river in 1779. At first a blended society of French, English
Indian settlers, the town developed a growing reputation for opportunities and
essibility, luring refugees from Europe by the 1830s. Fleeing famine, persecution
revolution, great waves of immigrants poured in between 1840 and 1924. By
0 the foreign-born (largely German, Irish and Scandinavian) and their children
ounted for 79 percent of a population of about 1.2 million. They transplanted their
etls, villages and parishes to the shores of Lake Michigan, establishing neighbor-
ds that offered the familiarity of home. In a pattern that would repeat again and
in, newcomers settled near downtown and then dispersed outward—ultimately to
suburbs—as the next groups arrived.

Population from 1837 to 1996

7	4,066	Chicago incorporates as a city.
8	20,243	**Chicago and Galena Union Railroad**, the city's first, begins operation.
0	112,172	Chicago has become the center of the world's largest railroad network. The building of the railroads attracts workers from the US and abroad.
1	335,000	The **Chicago Fire** in October flattens much of the city, but the immediate push to rebuild sustains it through the financial panic of 1873.
9	1,098,576	Chicago annexes 120 surrounding square miles by popular referendum, thereby boosting the population over the one million mark. The federal census of 1890 marks Chicago's official status as "**Second City**," its population having surpassed that of Philadelphia.
3	1,315,000	**World's Columbian Exposition** is held in Chicago.
0	1,698,575	Chicago's population now includes more Poles, Swedes, Czechs, Dutch, Danes, Norwegians, Croatians, Slovaks, Lithuanians and Greeks than any other American city.
4	2,437,526	Immigration from Europe slows with **World War I**. The migration of southern blacks, drawn in part by war-industry jobs, begins.
0	2,701,705	African-American population reaches 109,000 and will continue to grow to a quarter million by 1929.
4	2,939,605	The **Johnson-Reed Act** essentially ends foreign immigration through quotas.
2	3,236,913	Chicago is hard hit by the **Great Depression**; more than 750,000 are unemployed. Chicago grows by only 20,000 between 1930 and 1940.
0	3,620,962	A strong postwar economy along with the baby boom and the annexation of 41 additional square miles boosts Chicago's population to its peak.
6	3,552,300	**O'Hare Airport** opens and soon becomes the world's busiest, maintaining Chicago's position as transportation hub. The urban population has started to fall, however, and the flight to the suburbs begins.
0	2,783,903	The population of the city proper falls below 3 million for the first time in 70 years. Los Angeles replaces Chicago as the official "Second City."
2	2,768,483	According to the 1992 census estimate, the city's population continues to decline.
8	2,802,079	Chicago remains the nation's third-largest city.

s migratory ebb and flow has yielded a city that today is 40 percent African
erican, nearly 20 percent Hispanic and close to 4 percent Asian. Some 80 ethnic
ains enrich the mix, from American Indians to Czechs, and Pacific Islanders to
yrians.

Ukrainian Independence Day Celebration

Irish – First to arrive in large numbers, the Irish came to build the Illinois & Michi[gan] Canal in 1836 and to flee the potato famine of the 1840s. Many settled along [the] South Branch of the Chicago River in an area now called **Bridgeport**, which in the [?] would produce four Chicago mayors of Irish descent, including **Richard J. Daley**. Fr[om] humble beginnings as laborers, teamsters and domestic servants, Chicago's Irish r[ose] to prominence in politics, the police department and the Catholic church.

Germans – The failed revolution of 1848 drove Germans from their homeland by [the] thousands, and by 1860 they outnumbered other groups in Chicago. They moved no[rth] from Chicago Avenue, through **Old Town** and Lakeview and up along Lincoln Aven[ue] where **Lincoln Square** remains a center of Teutonic society. Germans were as active [in] the labor movement as in the development of Chicago's culture, organizing trade uni[ons] and fraternal groups, singing and sporting clubs. In the shadow of anti-German se[nti]ment during two world wars, German solidarity faded in favor of greater assimilat[ion].

Scandinavians – Swedes, Norwegians and Danes streamed steadily into Chicago o[ver] the years, some to stay, others to seek out the rich farmland of the northern Midw[est]. Settling in shantytowns near the central city, they prospered in the constructi[on] trades, small businesses and later in the professions, eventually migrating north [and] northwest. **Humboldt Park** was once a center of Norwegian and Danish life, and [in] Andersonville on the Far North Side of the city, the Swedish influence lingers in sh[ops] and restaurants.

Jews – Jewish immigrants arrived in two great migrations. First came the gener[ally] affluent and secular German speakers from Central Europe, and beginning in [the] 1880s, mostly Orthodox refugees fleeing pogroms in Eastern Europe flocked to [the] city's crowded **Near West Side**. The urbane Germans assimilated easily, building re[tail] and dry-goods businesses and adopting something of a paternalistic attitude tow[ard] their impoverished Russian and Polish counterparts abiding in the ghetto arou[nd] Maxwell Street. Out of that ghetto, however, came a profusion of actors and writ[ers,] jurists and businessmen. Many Jews now live on the city's Far North Side and in [the] northern suburbs.

Poles – Chicago is home to more than a million residents of Polish ancestry. T[hey] arrived in droves between 1870 and 1930, bringing a devotion to Catholicism t[hat] manifested itself in the building of elegant churches at the centers of their commu[ni]ties. Over the years, the Poles moved northwest along **Milwaukee Avenue**, which rem[ains] in places a Polish commercial corridor. Today many Poles live in the Avondale neighb[or]hood. Another wave of immigration followed the Solidarity movement in Poland [in] 1980.

Italians – Beginning in the 1880s Italians flocked to Chicago. Hailing mostly fr[om] southern Italy, they sometimes transplanted entire villages to the New Wo[rld.] Newcomers were often at the mercy of unscrupulous padrones—labor agents— [for] railroad and construction work. As they settled in, however, many Italians ope[ned] small businesses, took up public service and went into stonecutting and masonry. **L[ittle] Italy** on Chicago's Near West Side celebrated its heyday in the 1920s, and, though [dis]rupted by urban renewal, remains a center of Italian culture today.

eeks – Latecomers to Chicago, Greeks arrived after the turn of the century to settle the Delta on the **Near West Side**. Almost half of them were single men who came me to earn a living and return to Greece. Still, by the late 1970s, Chicago had the gest Hellenic population outside Greece. As restaurateurs the Greeks have been remely successful; by 1919 they already owned one out of three Chicago eating ablishments.

ican Americans – Blacks had lived in Chicago since its first settler, and their nbers grew with the city's reputation for abolitionism. Not until the 1910s, vever, did they arrive en masse during the Great Migration, seeking jobs in an dus from the increasing hardships of the rural South. The most populous "black ::" developed along the **Near South Side**. At its heart, Bronzeville, "the Harlem of :cago," pulsed with daily and nightly life, its lively restaurants, cabarets and the-rs the incubators of the hot, new Chicago-style blues. Gradually, competition with ites for work and housing created conflict; at the same time, prejudice and racism nted the progress of blacks attempting to escape the ghetto. The advent of public using in the 1940s relieved the worst of the slums, but institutionalized over-wding in African-American neighborhoods, a situation that is being addressed with transfer of public-housing authority to the federal government. On the other hand, rowing middle class, inheritors of the considerable legacy of Chicago's early African-erican professionals and entrepreneurs, is dispersing throughout the metropolitan a, somewhat relieving the city's reputation for segregation.

spanics – Under the broad rubric "Hispanic" exists a tremendous divergence of erience. Mexican immigration began in earnest around 1916, as the railroads and el mills recruited workers to make up for slackening European immigration in the e of World War I. Combined, the **Pilsen** and Little Village neighborhoods are today ne to the largest Mexican-American population in the region. Young Puerto Ricans, king a chance at prosperity on the mainland, are among the poorest Chicagoans, ile Cubans, who first came in 1959 as political rather than economic refugees, have t with greater success. Central and South Americans are now increasing the nbers—and diversity—of Chicago's Hispanic community.

ans – Located south of the Loop, **Chinatown** is the city's oldest extant Asian ghborhood, established in 1912 by Chinese businessmen when the existing down-n enclave became overcrowded. By the 1920s Filipinos and Japanese had also tled in the city. The greatest influx of Asian immigrants began in the 1960s and s, largely Southeast Asian refugees who established New Chinatown along **Argyle et** on the city's North Side. Farther north, along **Devon Avenue**, Chicago's Asian ians and Pakistanis have developed a bustling commercial corridor, and many of city's Koreans have settled in Albany Park.

e welcome corrections and suggestions that may assist us
preparing the next edition. Please send us your comments:
        Michelin Travel Publications
        Editorial Department
        P. O. Box 19001
        Greenville, SC 29602-9001
        Email: TheGreenGuide-us@us.michelin.com

Performing Arts

It is the "lively arts" that give true expression to Chicago's character. Swagger
Chicago-style theater, the wail of the blues, the sardonic world of improvisational com
and even television programs and movies all feed on the city's rough-cut persona.

Theater District Marker

Theater – Some 120 pro
sional theaters through
Chicago present everyth
from sweeping Broadway m
sicals like *Show Boat* a
Phantom of the Opera to
classics of Shakespeare a
Tennessee Williams. E
Chicago's native theatrical
dition has little to do with s
crowd pleasing. The gr
edge of "off-Loop" theat
perhaps best exemplified
the work of local playwri
David Mamet *(American Buff
Glengarry Glen Ross)* and
acting of John Malkovich
William L. Petersen, is in p
the legacy of the Hull-Ho
Players. Conceived by pione
ing social worker Jane Adda
as part of her community w
at the turn of the century,
Players were reactivated in
revolutionary 1960s, introd
ing avant-garde theater
Chicago with plays by Edw
Albee, Samuel Beckett, At
Fugard and their contem
raries. Featuring difficult s
jects staged and acted with
intensity, Hull-House prod
tions prepared audiences to
preciate what would evo
into the visceral Chicago style. Small, innovative theaters with elemental names—B
Politic, Organic, and Remains—flourished in the ensuing years, fueled by enthusia
audiences, generous donors and an energetic crop of young performers, writers
directors. As the Chicago style matures at theaters like Steppenwolf in an atmosph
of more restrained funding, scores of upstart, itinerant companies work to remain
ventive and solvent, continuing to experiment with new and often outrageous
proaches to stagecraft.

Dance – Although most of the performing arts have long found expression he
Chicago has been a slow starter when it comes to dance. In spite of the efforts of s
dance greats as Ruth Page and Maria Tallchief Paschen,
traditional ballet companies failed initially to gain a solid
toehold in the city. In 1987 Ballet Chicago was established, and more recently, in 1995, artistic
director Gerald Arpino moved his Joffrey
Ballet from New York City to Chicago.
However, it is **Hubbard Street Dance Chicago**
that has truly put the city on the terpsi-
chorean map. Founded in 1977 by
Lou Conte, the company pioneered
a hybrid, thoroughly American style
that incorporates the excitement
and energy of jazz with the precision
of ballet. In 1990 choreographer
Twyla Tharp chose Hubbard
Street as a repository for her
small-scale works. Other notable Chicago dance ensembles
include the Joseph Holmes
Chicago Dance Theater, Gus Gior-
dano Jazz Dance Chicago and Shirley
Mordine and Company Dance Theater.
A number of ethnic troupes interpret folk
dances from Africa to Ireland.

Hubbard Street Dance Chicago

medy – The twin muse of Chicago's dark dramatic style is the satirical, incredulous "improv" comedy that has shaped the national sense of humor since the television show *Saturday Night Live (SNL)* took to the air in 1975. Also vestiges of Hull-House, improvisational exercises were employed by recreational counselors there to help immigrants adjust to their new life. Modern progenitor of the style, **The Second City** was founded in Hyde Park in 1955 as the Compass Players and today thrives in Old Town. Scores of comedians started there, including Alan Alda, Elaine May, Ed Asner, Ann Meara, Joan Rivers and a galaxy of *SNL* stars led by John Belushi, Dan Aykroyd and Gilda Radner. Traditional comedy nightclubs throughout the city and suburbs feature stand-up comics both known and new.

Cinema

Between 1897 and 1918, Chicago prospered as the capital of American filmmaking. William Selig built the world's first movie studio on the Near South Side in 1897, followed a decade later by George Spoor and Gilbert "Bronco Billy" Anderson's Essanay Motion Picture Co. Among them they produced thousands of pictures and employed hundreds of local vaudeville and entertainment professionals. Essanay signed a young Charlie Chaplin for $1,250 a week in 1915, and Selig Polyscope made more than 200 cowboy films featuring Tom Mix.

Eventually, California's better weather and new laws regarding motion picture rights ended the city's movie-making dominion. The lull lasted until 1976 when Chicago began an aggressive campaign to sell itself to location scouts. Since then, over 200 feature films have been made in the metropolitan area, their producers attracted by the city's fresh profile and cooperative atmosphere. Television dramas such as *Chicago Hope* and *ER* have discovered that Chicago's working-class, no-nonsense ethos makes a good setting, apart from the well-worn stereotypes of New York and Los Angeles.

■ Starring Chicago

Underworld (1927)
The Front Page (1931)
Little Caesar (1931)
Scarface (1932)
In Old Chicago (1937)
His Girl Friday (1940)
Call Northside 777 (1948)
Wabash Avenue (1950)
Native Son (1950, 1986)
The Man with the Golden Arm (1956)
Al Capone (1959)
Compulsion (1959)
A Raisin in the Sun (1961)
Robin and the Seven Hoods (1964)
Gaily, Gaily (1969)
Medium Cool (1969)
The Sting (1973)
Carrie (1976)
The Fury (1978)

The Blues Brothers (1980)
My Bodyguard (1980)
Ordinary People (1980)
Risky Business (1983)
Sixteen Candles (1984)
Ferris Bueller's Day Off (1986)
About Last Night (1986)
The Color of Money (1986)
The Untouchables (1987)
Eight Men Out (1988)
Music Box (1989)
Backdraft (1991)
The Fugitive (1993)
Blink (1994)
While You Were Sleeping (1995)
Home Alone III (1996)
Blues Brothers 2000 (1997)
Stir of Echoes (1998)
Message in a Bottle (1998)

Music

Chicago's development as an immigrant city has imbued it over the years with a r[...] musical heritage. But the most interesting phenomenon has been the power of t[...] city to transform certain styles. The **blues**, for one, would never be the same once th[...] came to Chicago. From the hollows, fields and churches of the rural South, migra[...] brought their music to the city in the 1910s. As artists such as Big Bill Broonzy a[...] Papa Charlie Jackson began to play together, a hybrid guitar-driven style based [...] urban themes emerged. In the 1940s musicians experimented with amplification a[...] by 1950, Chicago surfaced as the capital of the hard-driving electric blues, with **Mu[...] Waters** (McKinley Morganfield) as its king. Other greats like Willie Dixon, Howlin' W[...] and Sunnyland Slim spent their careers in Chicago, and today, veterans Buddy C[...] and Koko Taylor (the preeminent female blues artist) each own a local club. Eve[...] summer the public flocks by the thousands to the Chicago Blues Festival to hear t[...] world's best sing the blues.

Jazz came up from the South as well after the fall of New Orleans' Storyville vice d[...] trict and in Chicago became an integrated art. During the 1920s, when jazzmen K[...] Oliver and Louis Armstrong came to play the clubs in the Black Belt, young and re[...] less white musicians like Gene Krupa, Bud Freeman and Jimmy McPartland embrac[...] their style. The resulting hybrid Chicago-style jazz pulsed with a hot tempo, explos[...]

rhythm sections and elabor[...] instrumental interplay. Mu[...] fine jazz, from traditional [...] contemporary, can be heard [...] clubs and cabarets around t[...] city to this day, as well as [...] the **Chicago Jazz Festival** h[...] each summer in Grant Pa[...] Chicago remains a center of [...] novation when it comes to co[...] temporary music, particula[...] **rock**. In the early 1980s cuttin[...] edge Chicago disc jockeys p[...] duced a frenetic, fast-pac[...] dance music called "hous[...] that went on to have consid[...] able influence in current r[...] and "industrial" rock tren[...] After the meteoric ascent [...] the Smashing Pumpkins, [...] Phair, Veruca Salt and Ur[...] Overkill in the early 1990[...] some industry prognosticato[...] predicted that Chicago wou[...] rise to the top of the rock p[...] With hundreds of venue[...] scores of recording studios, t[...] ented managers and enthusi[...] tic audiences, the ascent see[...] likely. However, it remains [...] be seen whether a recognizab[...] "Chicago-style" rock will co[...] lesce from this diverse scene[...]

Andy's Jazz Club

Classical Music – Chicago[...] considerable classical music heritage harkens back to the early city elite who wish[...] to convey a sophisticated image of Chicago by encouraging the development of "hi[...] culture." The first orchestra performed in 1850, and an opera house opened in 18[...] Visiting artists and ensembles reinforced a taste for the classical, and by 1891 c[...] boosters realized that a permanent orchestra would enhance Chicago's reputation. T[...] **Chicago Symphony Orchestra (CSO)** was thus founded under the direction of Theodo[...] Thomas of New York. Over the years the CSO has grown in stature under the bato[...] of such luminaries as Frederick Stock, Fritz Reiner, Sir Georg Solti and most recent[...] Daniel Barenboim and Pierre Boulez.

Opera has always found a willing audience in Chicago, but the grand Italian style [...] expensive to produce, and at least six major companies have come and gone over t[...] years. Finally in 1954, under the visionary leadership of Carol Fox, the **Lyric Op**[...] opened its first season with a performance of *Norma* featuring Maria Callas in h[...] American debut. Currently under the general direction of William Mason, the Ly[...] continues to be one of the world's most exciting opera companies. Small ensembl[...] choruses and ethnic companies abound in Chicago, and early music is particula[...] popular, especially when performed by Music of the Baroque, now the largest pr[...] fessional chorus and orchestra of its kind in the country.

isual Arts

cago is today a city of great museums, ubiquitous public sculpture, active arts orga-
tions, insightful critics, enthusiastic collectors and innovative artists, but a tension
ween its origins in industry and commerce and its early aspirations to gentility has
/ed a major role in its uneasy artistic growth.

Matter of Taste – The World's Columbian Exposition of 1893 did much to estab-
an artistic aesthetic that prevailed in the city for 40 years. The Art Institute of
cago had been organized in 1879, and its president Charles L. Hutchinson believed
ongly in the power of great art to uplift the human spirit and counter civic and
merical corruption. He also felt that a respected art museum would elevate
cago's image. In the same vein, the hardworking industrial city hoped that the glit-
ng Beaux-Arts World's Fair would appear sophisticated and genteel to the rest of
world, proving conclusively that though their money had been made in railroads
meatpacking, Chicago's elite had also developed considerable taste. More than
000 art objects crowded the huge Palace of Fine Arts, most of them European
rks of conservative appeal. Volume and predictability, it seems, equaled culture.
haps the most representative local artist of the day was sculptor **Lorado Taft**, whose
rks can be seen today in parks and cemeteries throughout the city. Employing a
hly allegorical style, Taft believed in the ennobling power of art. His monumental
intain of the Great Lakes (1914), outside the South Wing of the Art Institute, was
first public sculpture to be underwritten by the Ferguson Fund, established in 1905
wealthy lumberman Benjamin Franklin Ferguson to decorate Chicago with European-
e monuments. Even the School of the Art Institute, the Midwest's preeminent
demy of the fine arts, trained students under the French academic plan, empha-
ng the naturalistic rendering of the human form and the copying of classical art.
ong collectors, the impetus to acquire art was inspired largely by investment value
I fashion, and focused on the works of European artists. The lavish collecting style
the Potter Palmers, eventually responsible for much of the Art Institute's famous
nch Impressionist collection, contrasted sharply with the more curatorial approach
later collectors like Arthur Jerome Eddy and Frederic Clay Bartlett, who champi-
ed the Modernist movements of the teens and twenties.

rning Point – In 1913 the controversial **Armory Show** in New York City contested
olic taste by introducing Modernism into this milieu. The works of, among others,
uguin, Picasso and Duchamp met with widespread chagrin, moving students at the
ool of the Art Institute to hang Matisse in effigy. Chicago's art world faced off:
juried exhibitions challenged the conservative standards of the Art Institute and a
v echelon of collectors promoted the avant-garde. A community of Modernists
gan to grow, among them painter Rudolph Weisenborn (*Chicago*, 1928), who may
best remembered for organizing several anti-establishment artists' groups. Highly
erse in style, Chicago's young artists shared instead a rejection of formal art training
I, like abstract master Wassily Kandinsky (1866-1944), sought the inspiration of
er experience, a common thread in subsequent Chicago art. Finally, by 1933, the
ntury of Progress Exposition proudly proclaimed Chicago's embrace of the modern.
e Art Institute exhibited 27 galleries of Modern art, signaling a mainstream accep-
ice of the movement.

om the American Scene to the Imagists – Some Chicago artists of the 1920s and
30s combined elements of Modernism and Realism to depict the urban landscape
ound them, making the city a center of American scene painting. Inspired by the
ef teaching stint of social realist George Bellows at the School of the Art Institute,

nters like Emil Armin (*Towers*, 1931)
d Ramon Shiva (*Chicago MCMXXIV*,
24) rendered the city with an expres-
nistic edge and an honesty reminiscent
New York's Ashcan school. African-
nerican painter **Archibald Motley, Jr.**
891-1981) created lively scenes of life
Chicago's black neighborhoods (*Black
lt*, 1934). Linked to the larger Region-
st movement made popular by Art In-
tute students **Grant Wood**, John Steuart
rry and Thomas Hart Benton, the
icago scene painters shared a sense of
ice, recognizing Chicago's gritty urban
idscape to be as legitimate a subject as
e French countryside.

embers of the most recognizable
icago school came to be known in the
060s as **Imagists**. Precursors of the move-
ent included **Ivan Albright** (*That Which
Should Have Done I Did Not Do*,

American Gothic (1930) by Grant Wood

Museum of Contemporary Art

Adria (1976) by Ed Paschke

1931-41), whose disturb
canvases express a personal
sion rather than an external
ality, and artists June Le
H.C. Westermann and Le
Golub. Their work, dubb
"monster art" for its toten
elemental style, drew inspi
tion from the Art Brut mo
ment of the 1950s populari
by Jean Dubuffet (1901-8
The Imagists, too, relied he
ily on inner experience and p
sonal imagery; their dispar
work catalogs a fantasti
world of organic abstract
with stronger ties to Surreal
than to the Abstract Expr
sionism of Jackson Pollo
Among the best known of
Imagists were the **Hairy Who**
band of artists—includi
Gladys Nilsson, Art Green, K
Wirsum, James Falconer a
Suellen Rocca—whose gro
shows in the 1960s set of
flurry of outrageous exhib
that were part theater and p
art. From the vibrant and a
biguous portraits of **Ed Pasc**
(*Elcina*, 1973) to the darkly comic, misshapen figures of Jim Nutt (*Is This the Ri*
Way, 1979), the fantasies of Imagism have influenced a generation of Chicago artis

The Contemporary Scene – In recent years Chicago has seen a burgeoning of inter
in art and a commensurate increase in related activities. Since 1967 the Museum
Contemporary Art has made the artists of the avant-garde accessible to a broad a
eager audience. That same year came the unveiling of the 50ft Picasso sculpture
Daley Plaza, one of Chicago's first non-commemorative public artworks. Public scu
ture has since proliferated, thanks in part to the **Percent for Art Program** enacted by
city in 1978, which mandates that one percent of the cost of every city project w
public access be applied toward the purchase of art for the site. The million-dollar c
lection of art at the Harold Washington Library Center represents the largest proj
the program has undertaken.

A new generation of artists seeking inspiration beyond Imagism emerged in the l
1980s, fueling a phenomenal boom in the number and popularity of art galleries.
the same time, the Wicker Park neighborhood grew into one of the country's m
popular habitats for young artists. **Art Chicago**, the latest of several prestigious int
national art expositions held each spring at Navy Pier, ranks among the world's leadi
art marketplaces.

The Other Arts – Chicago occupies an undisputed place in the history of design a
photography. European Modernist **Laszlo Moholy-Nagy** brought the principles of
German Bauhaus to the city in 1937, establishing a school that would evolve into t
Institute of Design, a part of the Illinois Institute of Technology since 1949. The holis
curriculum reflected a well-integrated variety of disciplines from industrial and grap
design to architecture. As a center for the teaching of photography as art, the scho
boasts a fine roster of instructors over the years—Harry Callahan, Arthur Siegel a
Aaron Siskind among them—as well as a long list of prominent graduates. Major c
lections of photography are located at the Art Institute and the Museum
Contemporary Photography.

"Chicago is the archetypal American city ....
For visitors who are interested in a city that's really America,
this would be the one to visit."
Studs Terkel

◼ Outdoor Sculpture

Chicago is a veritable treasure trove of public art. Below is a selection of works of sculpture found in and around the Loop.

Sculptor/*Work*	Location
Ivan Mestrovic *The Bowman and The Spearman*	Grant Park, Grand Entrance
Alexander Calder *Flamingo*	Federal Center plaza
Augustus Saint-Gaudens *The Seated Lincoln*	Grant Park, Court of Presidents
Lorado Taft *Fountain of the Great Lakes*	Art Institute of Chicago, South Wing
Edward Kemeys *Lions*	Art Institute, main entrance
Dankmar Adler and Louis Sullivan *Chicago Stock Exchange Arch*	Art Institute, Columbus Dr. entrance
Marc Chagall *Four Seasons*	First National Bank Plaza
Louise Nevelson *Dawn Shadows*	Madison Plaza
Joan Miró *Miró's Chicago*	Washington St., next to Chicago Temple
Pablo Picasso *Untitled*	Daley Center Plaza
Virginio Ferrari *Being Born*	Corner of State & Washington Sts.
Jean Dubuffet *Monument with Standing Beast*	James R. Thompson Center Plaza
Jerry Peart *Splash*	Corner of S. Michigan Ave. & Lake St.

Monument with Standing Beast by Jean Dubuffet

Literature

The explosive growth that propelled Chicago from frontier outpost to major industrial center far surpassed any development in the arts—including literature—or in other refinements associated with civilization. The city throbbed with power, and when literary culture did bloom in the late 19C, it was indelibly marked by the earthy money-grubbing nature of the immigrant metropolis. Its tradition of social realism and street-level literature continues to present-day with poet Gwendolyn Brooks and, until recently, columnist Mike Royko (1932-97).

Literature in the Capital of Capital – The writings emerging in Chicago during the mid-19C were indistinguishable from the mass of other moralistic or romantic works churned out by artists from London to New York to Los Angeles. Only after the 1893 Columbian Exposition focused world attention on this vibrant city did local writers emerge with a style to match the pace of Chicago life. During that frenetic decade, the city began to reduce its cultural shortcomings by erecting a new art institute (1893) and the first permanent library (1897), and by developing its musical and literary tastes. Still, the business of Chicago was business, and writers focused on the race to riches in novels like *The Cliff Dwellers* (1893) and *With the Procession* (1895) by Henry Blake Fuller, and *The Pit: A Story of Chicago* (1904) by Frank Norris. These early social realists, part of the **Little Room** salon, began exploring the contradictions of a society that, though modeled on democracy, favored the industrial elite over the working classes. This was the first literary school to look at both the front and the back, at the public and the private, and in so doing, discovered subject matter so rich that it remains fertile to this day.

Best known of these early novels is **Upton Sinclair's** *The Jungle* (1906), a stark, heart-wrenching story meant to waken awareness of the plight of immigrant workers; instead, it fomented a reform of food laws following Sinclair's harrowing descriptions of life in the stockyards. Lamented the author: "I aimed at the public's heart, but by accident I hit it in the stomach." Probably the most important novel of the period was **Theodore Dreiser**'s *Sister Carrie*, written in 1900 but suppressed until 1912 due to the risqué nature of the story, which celebrates a heroine who parlays her lost innocence into a successful career. It inspired the next generation of Chicago writers, who peered behind every street lamp and back alley in their search for the raw, rude stories of a fast-paced American city.

Many Chicago writers worked for the newspapers, and added a journalistic and often humorous strain to the Chicago tradition, as seen in Finley Peter Dunne's "Mr. Dooley" series and Ring Lardner's fictionalized sports stories. Some preferred fantasy to the starkness of urban life: L. Frank Baum and artist William Denslow completed the American classic *The Wizard of Oz* in 1900; and Edgar Rice Burroughs' 1912 *Tarzan* series was inspired by his visits to the Lincoln Park Zoo.

Milestones in Chicago Literary History

1872	1903	1912	1916	1935

1872
E.P. Roe, *Barriers Burned Away*

1880
The Dial founded

1893
Harriet Monroe, *Columbian Ode*

Henry Blake Fuller, *The Cliff Dwellers*

1895
Henry Blake Fuller, *With the Procession*

1900
Theodore Dreiser writes *Sister Carrie*. Frank L. Baum and William Denslow complete *The Wizard of Oz*

1903
Will Payne, *Mr. Salt*

1904
Robert Herrick, *The Common Lot*

Frank Norris, *The Pit: A Story of Chicago*

1906
Upton Sinclair, *The Jungle*

1909
Jane Addams, *Twenty Years at Hull-House*

1911
Harriet Monroe founds *Poetry* magazine

1912
Sister Carrie released

1914
Margaret Anderson founds *The Little Review*. Theodore Dreiser, *The Titan*

1915
Edgar Lee Masters, *Spoon River Anthology*. Willa Cather, *The Song of the Lark*. Sherwood Anderson, *Windy McPherson's Son*

1916
Carl Sandburg, *Chicago Poems*. Ring Lardner, *You Know Me Al*

1919
Sherwood Anderson, *Winesburg, Ohio*

1920
Floyd Dell, *Moon-Calf*

1928
Ben Hecht and Charles MacArthur, *The Front Page*

1929-34
James T. Farrell writes *Studs Lonigan* trilogy

1935
Willa Cather, *Lucy Gayheart*

■ Chicago *(Carl Sandburg, 1916)*

Hog Butcher for the World,
Tool Maker, Stacker of Wheat,
Player with Railroads and the Nation's Freight Handler;
Stormy, husky, brawling,
City of the Big Shoulders:
They tell me you are wicked and I believe them, for I have seen your
    painted women under the gas lamps luring the farm boys.
And they tell me you are crooked and I answer: Yes, it is true I have
    seen the gunman kill and go free to kill again.
And they tell me you are brutal and my reply is: On the faces of women
    and children I have seen the marks of wanton hunger.
And having answered so I turn once more to those who sneer at this
    my city, and I give them back the sneer and say to them:
Come and show me another city with lifted head singing so proud to
    be alive and coarse and strong and cunning.
Flinging magnetic curses amid the toil of piling job on job, here is a tall
    bold slugger set vivid against the little soft cities;
Fierce as a dog with tongue lapping for action, cunning as a savage
    pitted against the wilderness,
        Bareheaded,
        Shoveling,
        Wrecking,
        Planning,
Building, breaking, rebuilding,
Under the smoke, dust all over his mouth, laughing with white teeth,
Under the terrible burden of destiny laughing as a young man laughs,
Laughing even as an ignorant fighter laughs who has never lost a battle,
Bragging and laughing that under his wrist is the pulse, and under his
    ribs the heart of the people,
        Laughing!
Laughing the stormy, husky, brawling laughter of Youth, half-naked,
    sweating, proud to be Hog Butcher, Tool Maker, Stacker of
Wheat, Player with Railroads and Freight Handler to the Nation.

hicago Literary Renaissance – In 1911 Harriet Monroe, whose "Columbian Ode"
elebrated the 1893 World's Fair, founded *Poetry* magazine. The publication included
he pioneering work of poets Marianne Moore and William Carlos Williams, and cre-
ted a stir by publishing the modern, free-verse works of T.S. Eliot and Carl Sandburg.
Margaret Anderson's *Little Review* was born at the Fine Arts Building in 1914. In it

1940 — **1950** — **1960** — **1965** — **1975** — **1982**

1940
Richard Wright,
Native Son

1942
Nelson Algren,
*Never Come
Morning*

1944
Saul Bellow,
Dangling Man

1945
Gwendolyn
Brooks, *A Street
in Bronzeville*

1949
Nelson Algren,
*The Man with the
Golden Arm*

Gwendolyn Brooks,
Annie Allen

1951
Nelson Algren, *Chicago:
City on the Make*

1953
Hugh Hefner creates
Playboy magazine

1954
Saul Bellow,
*The Adventures
of Augie March*.
Nobel Prize
to Ernest
Hemingway

1959
Lorraine Hansberry,
A Raisin in the Sun

1960
Gwendolyn Brooks,
The Bean Eaters

1965
Saul Bellow, *Herzog*

1967
Studs Terkel,
*Division Street
America*

1971
Mike Royko, *Boss:
Richard J. Daley
of Chicago*

1974
Studs Terkel,
Working

1975
Saul Bellow,
Humboldt's Gift

1976
Nobel Prize
to Saul
Bellow

1982
Saul Bellow,
*The Dean's
December*

Carl Sandburg (c.1925)

she serialized James Joyce's *Ulysses*, a novel that so scandalized conservative Midwesterners that the US Postal Service refused to handle the magazine; by 1917, Anderson and her path-breaking review had left town for New York. The year 1915 saw the publication of Edgar Lee Masters' *Spoon River Anthology*, a stark portrayal of the underside of small-town life. Sherwood Anderson continued the tradition of exposing rural America's hidden foibles in *Windy MacPherson's Son* (1916) and *Winesburg, Ohio* (1919), while Dreiser created more novels of the failings of the American Dream with *The Financier* (1912) and *The Titan* (1914). While a reporter for the *Chicago Daily News*, **Carl Sandburg** published his *Chicago Poems* (1916) and later won a Pulitzer Prize for his biography of Abraham Lincoln. Sandburg's poem "Chicago" remains the most frequently quoted description of the "City of the Big Shoulders."

The Daily News and the Depression – The Chicago literary renaissance ebbed in the 1920s, but the gutsy, lusty style of Chicago writing continued at the *Chicago Daily News*, where reporters Ben Hecht and Charles MacArthur penned *The Front Page* (1928), a hilarious send-up of journalistic moxie. Like many Chicago writers, the pair tasted success and soon moved to New York. The *Daily News* was also home to Eugene Field, the "children's poet" who rhymed the classics "Wynken, Blynken and Nod" and "Little Boy Blue."

The Depression set the tone for a return to social realism, and the Federal Writers' Project brought together the next generation of authors, including James T. Farrell, **Richard Wright, Nelson Algren, Gwendolyn Brooks**, Studs Terkel and Saul Bellow. Farrell recollected his rowdy Washington Park youth in the *Studs Lonigan* trilogy (1935), while Wright's epochal *Native Son* (1940), set on the South Side, launched a career that took him not only out of Chicago but out of the country whose racism he so eloquently exposed. The publication of Algren's first novel *Never Come Morning* (1942) was marred by the political reaction of Chicago's Polish community, who cringed at having their seamy underside exposed. Algren achieved greater success describing a war veteran hooked on morphine and poker in *The Man With the Golden Arm* (1949). Brooks—first black female Pulitzer Prize winner (1949)—published her first collection of poems, *A Street in Bronzeville*, in 1945, and remained in Chicago despite her fame. Today she is Poet Laureate of the State of Illinois.

The Last Few Decades – Oak Park native **Ernest Hemingway** was awarded the Nobel Prize for Literature in 1954. A year earlier, Hemingway won a Pulitzer Prize for his magnificent novel, *The Old Man and the Sea*. Lorraine Hansberry completed *A Raisin in the Sun* in 1959 before leaving for New York. Two writers emerged in the 1960 and 70s from the old Federal Writers' Project circle: **Saul Bellow** and **Studs Terkel**. Bellow released a series of novels that culminated in *Humboldt's Gift*, for which he received the 1976 Nobel Prize, while Terkel honed his skills as the nation's best interviewer with his television and radio programs and award-winning oral histories, including *Division Street America* (1967), *Working* (1972) and *The Good War* (1984). Newspaper columnist Mike Royko captured Mayor Richard J. Daley in *Boss* (1971) and carried on the tradition of Algren, Sandburg and Dreiser. Current literary figures include mystery writer Sara Paretsky, Larry Heineman *(Paco's Song)*, James McManus *(Going to the Sun)* and Scott Turow *(Presumed Innocent, Burden of Proof)*.

Architecture

For over a century, Chicago has been the capital of modern architecture. In the years following the Great Fire of 1871, architects came from all over the country to help rebuild the world's fastest-growing city and in the process created the skyscraper, America's great contribution to architecture. Chicago also nurtured the Prairie school architects who followed Frank Lloyd Wright in developing the clean horizontal lines of the modern American residence. The city remains a mecca for an international coterie of architects wishing to leave their mark on the famous skyline.

From Sticks to Steel – The earliest buildings date to the city's founding in the 1830s and exhibit the design features of the Greek Revival style popular throughout Jacksonian America. In 1833 Chicago wrought its first architectural innovation with the development of the **balloon frame**, so dubbed because it supposedly made house construction as easy as blowing up a balloon. Balloon framing involved the substitution of thin plates and studs, held together only by nails, for the ancient and expensive system of mortise-and-tenon joints. This method permitted the rapid construction of economical, lightweight buildings and was particularly suited to the Chicago area's relative lack of forests. Unfortunately, the preponderance of structures made of small timbers meant that the city was built of kindling, as it learned following the dry summer of 1871, when the Great Fire leveled the budding metropolis. Wood-frame construction was banned after the Fire, but intact rail connections and industry ensured that the city would be rebuilt, and soon architects and engineers migrated en masse to Chicago. At first the city reassembled its pre-1871 self, as local architects John Mills Van Osdel and William Boyington rebuilt a downtown of four- and five-story italianate buildings—often from pre-fire plans. However, the Great Fire had proven that even castiron facades were vulnerable, and Chicago architects were called upon to develop better fire prevention techniques.

Frederick Wacker House, 1874

Civil War engineer **William Le Baron Jenney**, trained at the École Polytechnique and École Centrale in Paris, came to Chicago in 1870 to design the West Parks and Boulevards. Jenney advocated an iconoclastic "Western" style of architecture in contrast to the European models employed on the nation's East Coast, and helped train Chicago School architects **Louis Sullivan**, **William Holabird** and **Martin Roche**. It was Jenney who developed the skeletal steel frame that allowed skyscrapers to be built. The steel members were sheathed in brick for fire prevention, and his 1884 Home Insurance Building (demolished 1929) was the first true skyscraper.

In traditional masonry construction, the walls support the weight of the building. Jenney reversed this previously unquestioned principle of architecture. For the first time, the building supported the walls, which could be draped on the frame like a curtain. Since less space was needed for support, larger windows and hence more light and air could be admitted to upper-floor office spaces. This principle, called curtain-wall construction, made possible the development of modern high rises.

Other technical problems needed to be overcome to allow for buildings of more than nine or 10 stories. First, the refinement of the elevator in the 1870s provided efficient vertical transportation. Secondly, Jenney and other Chicago architects developed a series of bracing techniques to reduce the effects of wind on tall buildings. A more difficult problem was posed by foundations sinking in Chicago's swampy, shifting soil. John Wellborn Root developed a floating foundation for the Montauk Block in 1882 that allowed building loads to spread out and grab hold in the infirm soil. Adler & Sullivan improved on the design with the development of the caisson foundation, still used today.

The Chicago School – These innovations, conceived and executed within the decade of the 1880s, gave birth to the Chicago school of architecture, recognized as the first significant new architecture since the Italian High Renaissance and characterized by the work of four prominent firms. William Le Baron Jenney's engineering innovations exceeded his talent for facade design in buildings such as the 1891 Manhattan Building, but he also helped usher in the department store with his Second Leiter Building of the same year. The partnership of **Daniel Burnham & John Wellborn Root** constructed the Montauk Block (demolished) in 1882, and followed with the Rookery in 1888, which used a partial steel frame, floating foundations, and featured an elegant terra-cotta

Reliance Building, 1895

facade and stunning light court. In 1891 the fir[st] also designed the tallest office building utilizing tr[a]ditional masonry construction, the 16-story Mona[d]nock Building. After Root's untimely death in 189[2] Burnham's firm turned to more traditional style[s]. One notable exception was the Reliance Building [of] 1895 (now the Hotel Burnham), designed b[y] **Charles B. Atwood**. With its protruding bays, huge wi[n]dows and narrow bands of white terra-cotta orn[a]ment, the building anticipated the glass skyscraper[s] of the 1980s. **Dankmar Adler & Louis Sullivan** combine[d] the former's engineering and acoustical genius wit[h] the latter's unparalleled gift for ornament in th[e] stunning Auditorium Building of 1889. This edifi[ce] owed some debt to the work of Bostonia[n] H.H. Richardson, who had begun to reinterpret R[o]manesque architecture in a distinctly American vei[n]. The firm's finest office structures were the Chicag[o] Stock Exchange (1894-1972) and the Prudenti[al] Building (1894) in Buffalo, New York. Sullivan we[nt] on to design the Carson, Pirie, Scott & Co. depar[t]ment store in 1899, where his ornamental desig[n] explode onto the street. The firm of **William Holabi[rd] & Martin Roche** combined the Chicago school innov[a]tions into a formula that was repeated in ov[er] 80 Loop buildings. Their Pontiac Building (1891[)], Marquette Building (1895) and Chicago Building (1905) stand as excellent exampl[es] of Chicago school skyscrapers.

"Form Follows Function" — While many of the new skyscrapers were cloaked wit[h] traditional ornament, a significant number abandoned historical precedent, notably th[e] 1891 Monadnock Building, where the only modulation was provided by protrudi[ng] bay windows and a gentle flaring at the roof and base. Sullivan, more than any oth[er] architect, enunciated the new design philosophy with the phrase "form follows fun[c]tion" and encouraged an approach to high-rise construction that expressed the ste[el] frame beneath. The base should be distinct as the entrance of the building, accordin[g] to Sullivan, who favored a semicircular arched entrance. The top of the building shou[ld]

Chicago Historical Society (ICHi-13745)

Louis Sullivan (1919) by Frank A. Werner

be an overhanging cornice th[at] terminates the compositio[n]. Between the base and the to[p] the office floors should be ide[n]tical and create a vertical effe[ct] so that the building would b[e] "every inch a proud and soa[r]ing thing." Holabird & Roch[e] effectively utilized the styl[e] which saw the grid of ste[el] girders expressed on the ext[e]rior in brick or terra-cott[a] while the bulk of the wall plan[e] was filled with Chicago win[dows], composed of a larg[e] fixed pane flanked by smalle[r] sliding sashes.

The World's Columbian Expos[i]tion, under the direction [of] Daniel Burnham, adopted [a] Neoclassical style to celebra[te] the new American empir[e]. Louis Sullivan's acclaime[d] Transportation Building, wit[h] its telescoping arched en[t]rance, was the only building a[t] the fair to follow Chicag[o] school precedents. He late[r] lamented that the expositio[n] set American architecture bac[k] 50 years.

The Prairie Style — As Sullivan was working on the pivotal Auditorium Building, h[e] hired a young draftsman from Wisconsin, **Frank Lloyd Wright**, who left to form his ow[n] practice in 1893. In contrast to the soaring skyscrapers, Wright developed home[s] inspired by the flat Midwestern prairie, with overhanging eaves, horizontal lines an[d] banded windows of stained glass. Wright also "broke the box" of traditional domest[ic] architecture by allowing rooms to flow into one another, rather than organizing squar[e]

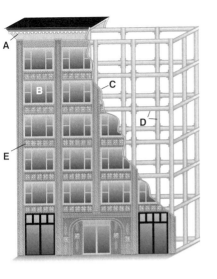

A Cornice
B Chicago-style window
C Curtain wall
D Steel frame
E Spandrel

rooms along long corridors. He eschewed attics and basements as unnecessary, and projected porches and rooflines in an attempt to meld building with landscape. His designs for Unity Temple and Robie House caused a worldwide stir when published in Germany in 1910. Wright's contemporary George Washington Maher developed a more formal and symmetrical take on the horizontal Prairie style in a wealth of residential commissions at the turn of the century, while many other Prairie school architects-among them Walter Burley Griffin, Marion Mahony Griffin, Francis Barry Byrne and John Van Bergen-learned their trade in Wright's Oak Park office. Wright's practice became more eclectic in the 1920s after he left the Chicago area. Wright designed a "mile-high" skyscraper in his later years, but the horizontal lines of his early Chicago and Oak Park homes still define his role as America's most prominent architectural figure.

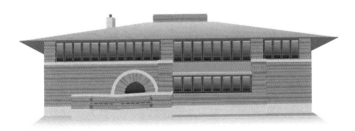

Arthur Heurtley House, 1902

Reaction and Revolution – By the 1910s architectural styles in Chicago and America entered a conservative period, as new skyscrapers were clad in traditional styles, like the Renaissance-inspired People's Gas Building of 1910 and the Wrigley Building of 1921. In 1922 the *Chicago Tribune* held an international competition to design a new high rise for the newspaper, which drew 280 entries from around the world. While the winning design by Hood & Howells of New York had a Norman Gothic exterior, it was the second-place entry by Eliel Saarinen of Finland that garnered the approval of architectural critics for its modern verticality devoid of historical ornament. Saarinen's design also fit in with new zoning ordinances that called for stepped setbacks in high-rise construction. By 1928 Chicago boasted several Vertical style, or Art Deco skyscrapers, including 333 North Michigan Avenue and the Palmolive Building by Holabird & Root (the successor firm to Holabird & Roche) and the Daily News Building by Graham, Anderson, Probst & White (the successor firm to D.H. Burnham & Co.).

International Style Comes to Chicago – The International style, which saw buildings as almost purely sculptural objects, originated in many ways with the Bauhaus of Germany in the 1920s and 30s. When the rise of Nazism precluded the modernistic innovations of the Bauhaus, one of its leading lights, **Ludwig Mies van der Rohe**, emigrated to Chicago. As chairman of architecture at the Illinois Institute of Technology, Mies ushered in what came to be called the Second Chicago school. Following World War II, Mies designed new steel-and-concrete high rises in a completely stripped-down style where attached I-beams provided the only ornament. Deceptively simple, the new

Ludwig Mies
van der Rohe (c.1961)

architecture depended on a rigid calculation of proportion that allowed little room for error in design. Mies inspired a new generation of architects with designs like 860-880 North Lake Shore Drive and Federal Center. Jacques Brownson of C.F. Murphy Assocs. contributed the 1965 Richard J. Daley Center, perhaps the best Miesian building not designed by Mies.

Emerging as the premier firm in postwar Chicago, **Skidmore, Owings & Merrill** established an international practice in the design of modern high rises. The Inland Steel Building of 1958 first expressed the possibilities of improved construction techniques with its column-free floors and double-glazed walls. Engineer Fazlu Khan helped Skidmore create Chicago's modern land marks, first with his innovative X-shaped cross bracing on the 1969 John Hancock Center, and finally with the bundled-tube construction of the Sears Tower.

Post-Modern Era – The formula of the Skidmore firm held sway throughout the 1970s, as dark steel-and-glass office blocks filled Chicago's Loop. By 1980 the post-Modern movement had arrived, and in Chicago its standard-bearer was German-born **Helmut Jahn**, whose sculptural facades of mirrored glass seemed to echo the streamlined machine aesthetic of the Art Deco period. His Xerox Centre (now 55 West Monroe Building) of 1980 led the way, followed by the daringly different James R. Thompson Center of 1985 and United Airlines Terminal of 1990. Jahn is noted for his soaring interior atrium spaces.

As the 1990s ushered in an era of real estate consolidation, Chicago also witnessed new buildings by architects from Japan, Spain, Italy and New York. Skidmore, Owing & Merrill joined the post-Modern fray with the 1989 NBC Tower by Adrian Smith. In the 90s post-Modern construction followed either a classical model with modulated concrete surfaces and punched window openings-exemplified by the R.R. Donnelley Building and Park Tower-or an expressionistic one that employs angular contrasts between glass and masonry forms and often suggests the virtuality of the digital world with curving, screen-like facades enlivened by optics and mirrors, such as that of Disney Quest.

Although A 1990 recession put a hold on plans for new skyscrapers in the Loop, at the dawn of the 21C, Chicago is experiencing a building boom the likes of which the city has not seen since World War II. And the much-touted Millennium Park, which will blanket a former rail yard along South Michigan Street, will feature an exuberant bandshell design by Frank Gehry.

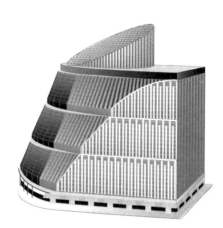

James R. Thompson Center, 1985

rchitectural Glossary

eek Revival (1820-1860) – Popular throughout America, the style adopts the pediented, symmetrical order of Greek temples in a simplified vernacular form suitable modest homes, grand mansions and larger public buildings. Classical columns in Doric, Ionic and Corinthian orders ornament the pedimented facade; roofs are en shallow, supported by a heavy cornice, and may include a cupola. The 1836 rke House is a rare Chicago example.

thic Revival (1830-1870) – The picturesque, assymetrical forms of Gothic Revival ades often include towers, battlements and pointed-arch windows with leaded ined glass. Smaller homes have intricately decorated bargeboards at the eaves and eply pitched roofs. The Chicago Water Tower is the city's most notable example.

lianate (1840-1880) – This style defined much of 19C America through flat-ofed homes and storefronts with overhanging eaves and brackets. Long, narrow idows with rounded arches often include incised decoration at the lintels and sills. re elaborate homes in the style include rusticated corner quoins and a Classical oola or tower modeled on Italian villas. The cast-iron front was usually Italianate, seen in Chicago's Page Brothers Building and Berghoff Restaurant *(see The Loop)*. good residential example is the Nickerson House.

cond Empire (1860-1880) – Inspired by Baron Hausmann's redesign of Paris in e 1850s, this grandiose style is characterized by the short, steeply pitched mansard of pierced by dormer windows. Generally symmetrical facades include quoined rners, projecting bays, windows flanked by pilasters, balustrades and an abundance Classical decoration. Often mansard roofs were added to Italianate buildings in a se approximation of the style. Examples can be found in the Jackson Boulevard d Wicker Park historic districts of Chicago.

manesque Revival (1860-1900) – The round arches, deeply inset windows and or openings and rough stone finishes of the Romanesque style suggest Medieval tles and inspired architects attempting to create permanence amid the rapidly anging landscape of late-19C America. The style was refined by Boston architect H. Richardson, who designed the John Jacob Glessner House in 1886. Burnham & ot's St. Gabriel's Church is a fine example, as are the former Chicago Historical ciety and the Newberry Library by Henry Ives Cobb.

een Anne (1870-1900) – This style is the one most commonly identified as ictorian" with its assymetrical composition, exuberant ornamentation and picresque design marked by conical towers, projecting bays, elaborately decorated rmers and gables. Adapted to both large residences and city row houses, the style found throughout Chicago's historic districts, especially Old Town, Pullman and cker Park.

nicago School (1880-010) – The design of the orld's first skyscrapers celeated their engineering and rpose, summed up by Louis Illivan's phrase "form follows nction." The steel-framed iildings express their con-ruction in a gridlike facade of ick or terra-cotta, pierced by ge areas of glass. A defined se, or entry level, is sur-ounted by a series of identi-l office floors with large

> "Make no little plans; they have no magic to stir men's blood and probably themselves will not be realized. Make big plans; aim high in hope and work, remembering that a noble and logical diagram once recorded will never die, but long after we are gone will be a living thing, asserting itself with growing intensity. Remember that our sons and grandsons are going to do things that would stagger us. Let your watchword be 'order' and your beacon 'beauty.'"
>
> The oft-repeated exhortation of Daniel Burnham

hicago windows" characterized by a fixed single-pane window in the center flanked smaller double-hung sliding sash windows. The roofline is capped by a cornice. The st 1880s skyscrapers borrowed elements of Romanesque, Italianate and Queen Anne chitecture, but by 1894 most were adopting the new aesthetic of functionalism, eschewing historical ornament to create vertical sculptures made of piers, spandrels and ndows. Four firms, **Adler & Sullivan, Burnham & Root, Holabird & Roche**, and **William Le Baron nney**, are the standard-bearers of the Chicago school and are credited with estabhing the Modern movement in the US. Chicago's Rookery and Monadnock Building itomize the early Chicago school, while the Marquette and Chicago buildings demonrate its maturity. The Reliance Building of 1895 (now the Hotel Burnham) is agreed be a worldwide landmark, prefiguring the present-day glass-and-steel skyscrapers.

eoclassical or Beaux-Arts (1893-1920) – The success of the 1893 World's olumbian Exposition brought a revival of Roman Imperial architecture, symbolizing e rise of the American Republic as a world power. Unlike the simpler Greek Revival, eoclassical architecture revels in ornamentation: Arched and arcaded windows, lustrades at every level, grand staircases, applied columns, decorative swags,

garlands and even statuary embellish the edifices. A good residential example
1500 North Astor Street in the Gold Coast. Sometimes called Beaux-Arts for its as
ciation with Paris' École des Beaux-Arts, the style was well-suited to public and cultu
buildings, such as the 1893 Art Institute and 1897 Chicago Cultural Center.

Prairie Style (1895-1915) – Largely identified with **Frank Lloyd Wright**, the Prairie s
revolutionized traditional residential architecture by creating low, horizontal comp
tions inspired by the flat Midwestern prairie. Roofs are very shallow in pitch and h
long, overhanging eaves. Windows are casements, often arranged in broad bands
stained and leaded glass. Roman brick with raked horizontal joints further emphasi
the horizontal, and entrances, instead of being the organizing principle of the hom
facade, are often hidden. Interior rooms flow into each other rather than being or
nized around corridors. Attics, basements and ancillary spaces are rare. Many of
style's premier examples are in Chicago and Oak Park, including Wright's Robie Hou
Unity Temple, Heurtley House and Laura Gale House.

Arts and Crafts (1895-1920) – In response to the proliferation of machines in
industrial age, Englishmen William Morris and John Ruskin called for a return to ha
crafted articles of everyday life and reveled in simplicity. Frank Lloyd Wright and oth
responded to the movement, which in architecture is characterized by overhang
wooden beams, delicately mortised together to form the gable ends and porches
homes.

Art Deco or Moderne (1925-1940) – Rejecting the revivalist tradition, the Art D
style first appeared during the 1925 "Exposition Internationale des Arts Décoratifs
Industriels Modernes" in Paris. US zoning laws, which called for skyscrapers to "s
back" to provide light and air to the street, helped define the architectural aspects
Art Deco that favored setbacks and piers to emphasize verticality. Often designe
smooth stone or terra-cotta shiny surfaces, edifices featured highly stylized car
ornament in low relief with a pronounced muscularity and abstraction, reces
windows and spandrels. Chicago examples include the Chicago Board of Tra
333 North Michigan Avenue and the Field Museum building.

International Style (1930-1970) – Applied ornament is abandoned for sleek, scu
tural lines in buildings, furniture and other designed objects, summarized by M
dictum "Less is more." Concrete, glass and steel are celebrated in buildings w
boxlike massing and raised lobbies surrounded by arcaded overhangs. Exterior w
of glass and steel minimize both ornament and modulation, deriving their design fr
proportion and materials alone, allowing the structures to express their function. T
Federal Center by Mies and 860-880 North Lake Shore Drive, along with
Richard J. Daley Center by C.F. Murphy Assocs., are some of the best examples
Chicago.

Post-Modern Style (1975-present) – This style is characterized by cavalier appli
tion of historical elements and references to buildings that express modern mater
of mirrored glass, concrete and surfaces generally more colorful and modulated th
the severe lines of the International style. Helmut Jahn brought the style to Chica
with his 1980 Xerox Centre, now 55 West Monroe Building, and exposed both
ambition and failings in his 1985 James R. Thompson Center and Citicorp Center.
the 1990s, post-Modern architecture followed two tracks. A new classicism offe
rectilinear concrete wall surfaces and neatly punched window openings, enlivened
dramatic curving entrances and awnings. This style, seen in the R.R. Donne
Building (1992, Ricardo Bofill) and 730 North Michigan Avenue (2000, Elk
Manfredi), occasionally veers into an homage to Art Deco, notably in the NBC Tov
(1989, Adrian Smith) and the Park Tower (2000, Lucien LaGrange), both off t
Magnificent Mile.
Expressionistic post-Modernism continued the deconstructivist style first seen in t
1980s and epitomized by the curving sculptural forms of Frank Gehry's bandsh
which will grace the new Millennium Park when it is completed in 2001.

Sports

Chicago's muscle-bound image is nowhere more apparent than in the fanaticism of its sports enthusiasts. The Saturday Night Live "Superfans" skit parodied supporters of "Da Bears" for years after their lone Super Bowl victory in 1986, and the team remains a paragon of old-style ground-game football that eschews the ballet of long passes. In baseball both White Sox and Cubs fans are devotedly loyal, despite the fact that neither team has won a World Series since World War I. Although the nation's professional baseball and football leagues trace their origins to Chicago, it was basketball superstar **Michael Jordan** and six nearly consecutive NBA titles (1991-93, 1996-98) that gave the city its most dominant sports team and a personality to outshine mobster Al Capone in worldwide notoriety.

Baseball – The **Chicago Cubs** are the oldest original franchise in professional sports, dating back to the founding of the National League by team president Walter A. Hulbert in 1876. Nicknamed the "lovable losers" of the North Side, the Cubs last won a World Series in 1908. In 1916 the team moved to their present home of Wrigley Field, which hosted several World Series in the 1920s and 30s. The 1969 season saw the first-place Cubs fade in the face of the New York "Miracle Mets," denying star slugger **Ernie Banks** a shot at the World Series. The team was purchased from the Wrigley family by the Tribune Company in 1981, and has had some moderate success with division titles in 1984 and 1989. In the historic 1998 season, Cubs MVP **Sammy Sosa** slugged 66 home runs.

Members of the American League, the **Chicago White Sox** (founded in 1901) draw support from South Siders. In 1991 the State of Illinois built a new Comiskey Park replacing A 1910 stadium that hosted the first All-Star game and the first Negro League All-Star game. White Sox fans are undying in their support of a team that last went to a World Series in 1959 and last won one in 1917. In 1920 the "Black Sox" scandal revealed that eight players in the 1919 World Series had conspired to "throw" the games for gamblers. The infamous episode is best remembered by a child's legendary confrontation with **"Shoeless Joe" Jackson**, when he sobbingly asked the star slugger to "Say it ain't so, Joe!" When the team advanced to the World Series in 1959, Mayor Richard Daley set off air-raid sirens, frightening a portion of the populace. Recently the team has reemerged as a contender, winning division titles in 1983 and 1993.

■ Legend of the Lovable Losers

The Chicago Cubs have not won a World Series since 1908 and have not appeared in the fall classic since 1945. Cub fans have wallowed in failure for so long that in 1989, newspaper columnist Mike Royko (1932-97) popularized a new baseball statistic invented by local writer Ron Berler: the ex-Cub factor. Essentially, the claim is that any baseball team with three or more former Cubs players cannot win the World Series, having been "infected" by association with the lovable losers. Each year, Royko pointed out which teams would be unable to triumph because they had too many ex-Cubs on their roster. To date, the ex-Cub factor has proved to be an accurate prognosticator. Another local legend began when Sam Sianis, owner of the Billy Goat Tavern (*see* Magnificent Mile), was denied entry into Wrigley Field with his famous pet goat and placed a curse on the team to prevent its success. Years later, Sianis' son was invited by Cub management to attend a game with his goat to remove the curse, but even this bit of ungulate hoodoo has not brought success to the North Siders.

Football – The University of Chicago produced a Big Ten conference powerhouse in the early 1900s, the "Monsters of the Midway," under coach Amos Alonzo Stagg. Football was abolished there in 1939, leaving Northwestern University to carry on the Big Ten tradition at Dyche Stadium in Evanston. George S. Halas founded the **Chicago Bears** and the National Football League in 1920, pioneering the "T" formation and launching a team defined by defense and running plays. Known for ferocious tacklers like **Dick Butkus** and elusive runners like **Gale Sayers** and **Walter Payton**, the Bears won their only Super Bowl in 1986, a dominating victory that prompted tens of thousands of fans to celebrate in the streets despite the icy cold. In 1971 the Bears moved from Wrigley Field to Soldier Field for their home games.

Basketball – Professional basketball was a latecomer to this sports-minded city: the **Chicago Bulls** were formed in 1966, 70 years after the University of Chicago beat the University of Iowa in the first modern college basketball game in 1896. The Bulls' first championship came in stellar fashion in 1991 as **Michael "Air" Jordan** led the team to the first of three consecutive titles. Jordan retired in 1993 and dabbled in baseball before returning to Chicago in 1995 for three more championship seasons (1996, 1997 and 1998). When Jordan retired from basketball for good in 1999, his lifetime scoring average led the league. The Bulls play at United Center on the Near West Side.

Hockey – Like many North American cities, Chicago has a small but devoted cadre of hard-core hockey fans who regularly fill the seats at United Center to watch the **Blackhawks**. The team last won the coveted Stanley Cup in 1961 and earned A 1967 division title, thanks to stars **Bobby Hull** and **Stan Mikita**.

Soccer – In 1994 Chicago hosted the first **World Cup** soccer match in the US as Germany defeated Bolivia 1-0. Three years later, Chicago entered Major League Soccer with the **Chicago Fire** playing at Soldier Field. The team ended the reign of Washington, DC's United in October 1998, claiming A 2-0 victory in the MLS Cup match held at the Rose Bowl. On October 30, the Chicago Fire became the second team in three years to capture the American "double."

Boxing – Chicago earned brief renown as a national boxing center in the early 20C, when Soldier Field was selected as the site for the "Long Count" championship, allowing heavyweight Gene Tunney to beat Jack Dempsey in 1927. Ten years later, **Joe Louis** began his string of victories with a triumph over Jim Braddock at Comiskey Park, while the Chicago Stadium hosted middleweight **Sugar Ray Robinson**'s epic 1951 defeat of Jake LaMotta and **Rocky Marciano**'s win over Jersey Joe Walcott in 1953. The city's boxing heyday ended in the 1950s when the Supreme Court ruled that its International Boxing Club held an unfair monopoly.

Other – In 1895 the *Chicago Times-Herald* sponsored the first automobile race in America, A 54mi affair completed by only two vehicles. The Chicago Golf Club in suburban Wheaton built the first 18-hole course in the US, and the Chicago area hosts the second-oldest US golf tournament, the Western Open. Every summer, colorful yachts ply the deep waters of Lake Michigan in the 333mi-long **Chicago to Mackinac Island Race**.

■ Bear Weather

Chicagoans are proud of their harsh winters. Bears' fans often speak of the advantages of "Bear Weather" to their home team, which has always played outdoors and has cultivated a tough, "smash-mouth" image. Recently, local journalists have exposed the "Bear Weather" myth, revealing that the team is just as likely to lose as win when the weather is inclement. Harder to dispute is the fact that the Bears are cursed on TV's Monday night football, losing almost twice as often as winning. The Bears' only loss in 1985 came on a Monday. The team's recent reliance on a passing game—in conflict with the Bears' earthy image—and the threat of a domed stadium in the future has many locals predicting the apocalypse.

■ His Airness

The mention of Chicago today in any language conjures up one man: Number 23, basketball superstar **Michael Jordan.** Throughout his career, Jordan succeeded in winning six NBA championships with the Chicago Bulls, two Olympic gold medals and the hearts of fans everywhere. His face is known everywhere—Jordan has lent his persona to everything from sneakers to the silver screen, where he co-starred with Bugs Bunny in the 1996 animated film *Space Jam.* Indeed, *Fortune* magazine estimated that Jordan's image and product line has been worth $5.2 billion to Nike Inc. alone.

Born in Brooklyn in 1963, Jordan grew up in Wilmington, North Carolina. In 1981 he entered the University of North Carolina at Chapel Hill and began his meteoric rise as a member of the UNC Tar Heels. That season, the squad won its first national championship with the help of its new 6'6" guard. Bound for his professional career, the NCAA College Player of the Year (1983 and 1984) left college a year early and signed with the Chicago Bulls. There he spent the next several years honing his incredible acrobatic abilities and dazzling eager audiences by scoring an average of 37.1 points per game—and often shooting over 50. In 1992 Jordan played on the Dream Team that won the gold medal at the Olympic Games in Barcelona.

The following year, after three national championships, events in Jordan's personal life took a sad turn with the senseless murder of his beloved father, James, at a North Carolina rest stop. Jordan left basketball briefly to pursue a career in baseball, but returned to the Bulls in 1995 for three more championship seasons. At his retirement from basketball in 1999, his lifetime scoring average led the league. Jordan's recent endeavors have included opening restaurants, golf centers and returning to basketball as part-owner and president of the Washington Wizards NBA team. Renowned for his athleticism, integrity, determination and personal style, "His Airness" has cast a powerful spell over Chicago, the city he now calls home.

Michael Jordan and the Chicago Bulls

Lobby, Hotel Allegro

Address Book

Where to Eat

Choosing a restaurant in Chicago can be an overwhelming task, given the quantity, variety and quality of local eateries. While famous for its pizzas and hot dogs, the city's culinary aptitude reaches well beyond those simple pleasures. As noted elsewhere in the text, ethnic eateries abound—from Ethiopian to Israeli—and little is left to be desired in the upscale restaurant department either. Top-notch chefs vie for honors here, to the benefit and great delight of Chicago's enthusiastic diners. As a result, restaurants come and go at a breakneck pace. One thing is constant, however: Chicago's dining scene offers something to satisfy every appetite and please every pocketbook.

The venues listed below were selected for their ambience, location and/or value for money. Rates indicate the average cost of an appetizer, an entrée and dessert for one person (not including tax, gratuity or beverages). Most restaurants are open daily—except where noted—and accept major credit cards. Call for information regarding reservations and opening hours.

Additional restaurants are listed throughout this guide in the form of Digressions. See Index for a complete listing of eateries described in the text.

$$$$ over $50   **$$** $15-$30
$$$ $30-$50   **$** less than $15

Luxury

Arun's – *4156 N. Kedzie Ave., Wrigleyville. Closed Mon.* ♿ ☎ *773-539-1909.* **$$$$ Thai**. Reputedly among the best Thai restaurants in the country, this elegantly appointed spot offers only a prix-fixe menu. Multiple, family-style courses invite diners to sample a delightful array of delicacies and flavors selected and blended with exquisite attention to detail. Choices can range from snapper in red tamarind sauce to "golden baskets," a house specialty of shrimp- and chicken-filled pastries. *Dinner only.*

Charlie Trotter's – *816 W. Armitage St., Lincoln Park. Closed Sun & Mon.* ♿ ☎ *773-248-6228. www.charlietrotters.com.* **$$$$ New American**. Tables at the restaurant run by culinary wunderkind Charlie Trotter—winner of the James Beard Foundation's Chef of the Year award for 1999—get booked 4 to 12 weeks in advance. The draw? One-of-a-kind dishes prepared with naturally raised meats, organic produce and vegetable-based sauces. Housed in a late-19C brownstone, the dining room's understated Biedermeier-style décor complements the food. Choose from two daily multicourse *prix-fixe* menus, the vegetable menu (*$90 per person*) or the grand dégustation menu (*$110 per person*). *Jackets required. Dinner only.*

Spiaggia – *980 N. Michigan Ave., 2nd floor of One Magnificent Mile Building. Magnificent Mile.* ♿ ☎ *312-280-2750. www.levyrestaurants.com.* **$$$$ Italian**. Overlooking the north end of Michigan Avenue, Oak Street Beach and Lake Michigan beyond, Chicago's toniest Italian restaurant offers a soaring array of dishes that are well grounded in regional Italian cookery. Try the ricotta ravioli with sweet Tuscan pecorino cheese and marsala wine glaze, or the wood-roasted diver scallops with porcini and shavings of parmigiano-reggiano. *Jackets required.* Next door, dressed-down **Café Spiaggia** serves pizzas and pastas at more palatable prices.

Mid-Range

Blackbird – *619 W. Randolph St., Near West Side.* ♿ ☎ *312-715-0708. www.blackbirdrestaurant.com.* **$$$ New American**. In contrast to its minimalist décor, the food at this fashionably tiny Market District hot spot is a feast for the eyes prepared in a style that chef Paul Kahan describes as "seasonal American with French countryside influences." Hearty ingredients anchor dishes such as osso bucco with artichokes, seared venison medallions with smoked bacon and brandied applesauce, and wood-grilled sturgeon in braised oxtail jus. The name "Blackbird" comes from French slang for a plump Merlot grape.

Harry Caray's – *33 W. Kinzie Ave., River North.* ♿ ☎ *312-828-0966. www.tribads.com/harrycarays.* **$$$ American**. Cub fans will revel in the atmosphere here, which is chock-full of baseball memorabilia and items relating to the Hall of Fame career of late baseball announcer Harry Caray. House specialty Chicken Vesuvio (chicken sautéed with garlic, then baked with crispy potatoes and served with peas and a white-wine reduction) and prime 23oz. porterhouse steaks top the menu; the 60ft bar makes a great gathering place. Prices range widely so there's something for everyone.

North Pond Café – *2610 N. Cannon Dr., Lincoln Park. Closed Mon.* ♿ ☎ *773-477-5845. www.tribads.com/northpond.* **$$$ New American**. Tucked into Lincoln Park at the edge of the North Pond, this little warming hut has been beautifully

nverted into a cozy ts and Crafts-style wel. The menu capitalzes on seasonal organic gredients, many from cal farms, such as heirom Wisconsin tomato d mozzarella tart; or an-roasted Amish icken with saffron ismati rice and Tipi rms rainbow chard. In e summertime, the ew of the city to the uth across the pond akes it easy to linger.

ne sixtyblue – *160 N. oomis St., Near West de. Closed Sun.* ♿ *312-850-0303.* **$$$** **w American**. Michael rdan is a silent partner this trendy restaunt, but celebs and lols alike come for chef atrick Robertson's iginal creations. Sleek d sexy, the loft-like ning room sets the ood for inventive otato-crusted Peekytoe ab cakes. Grilled lmon comes with crushed cucumber, walnut and date salad dressed with safon, olive oil and lemon juice. *Dinner only.*

Porterhouse Steak Italian Style at Harry Caray's

Courtesy Harry Caray's

hapsody – *65 E. Adams St., Loop.* ♿ ☎ *312-786-9911. www.cso.org/ apsody_restaurant.taf.* **$$$ New American**. Much of the charm of this elegant ban dining spot derives from its location in Symphony Center at the heart of icago's Loop, which is framed beautifully in the restaurant's glass windowalls. Eclectic dishes, such as lemon sole on a bed of basil-scented angel hair asta, and Thai chicken with straw mushrooms in a coconut and lemongrass oth, draw on flavors from around the world. Save room for the scrumptious esserts. Reserve early on performance nights. *No gym shoes, blue jeans or orts.*

ignature Room at the 95th – *875 N. Michigan Ave., Magnificent Mile.* ♿ *312-787-9596. www.signatureroom.com.* **$$$ American**. Atop the John ancock Center, this dining room and its companion lounge one flight up offer orious panoramic views of city and lake. The progressive menu includes a nice nge of contemporary dishes—vanilla-scented duck breast with chanterelle ushroom and potato pancake; applewood-smoked pork chop with crimson ntils and bourbon-and-molasses barbecue sauce—and dinner music entertains Friday and Saturday evenings and at Sunday brunch. *No gym shoes.*

opolobampo – *445 N. Clark St., River North. Closed Sun & Mon.* ♿ ☎ *312-61-1434.* **$$$ Regional Mexican**. Chef Rick Bayless has given his sophisticated isine a nationwide reputation by the skillful blending of traditional Mexican avors from Yucatán to Oaxaca. Bayless's way with chilies is particularly otable, and fish dishes, such as tequila-cured salmon or roasted stuffed trout, cel. Recipes may include such marvelous concoctions as pumpkin seed mole, arinated cactus, or roasted tomatillo sauce. The same quality—at less cost—an be found at **Frontera Grill**, which shares space with Topolobampo. Both enus change every two weeks.

infandel – *59 W. Grand Ave., River North. Closed Sun.* ♿ ☎ *312-527-1818. ww.zinfandelrestaurant.com.* **$$$ Regional American**. Diners enjoy a carefully afted selection of ethnic and regional specialties against a backdrop of colful folk art. Each month the menu highlights a different American cuisine, om Eastern Shoreline to Hawaiian. A true American among wines (with no uropean counterpart), zinfandel makes up more than half of the all-domestic ine list.

istro 110 – *110 E. Pearson St., Magnificent Mile.* ♿ ☎ *312-266-3110. ww.bistro110restaurant.com.* **$$ French**. The roasted garlic bulb that accomanies your baguette at this bright, bustling French bistro sets the tone for ood-oven-roasted meats and fish served here—all redolent with garlic. Save oom for the silky vanilla-bean crème brûlée.

Brasserie Jo – *59 W. Hubbard St., River North.* �& ☎ *312-595-080* *www.brasseriejo.com.* **$$ Alsatian French**. Chef Jean Joho (also of the dress Everest) works magic with the country fare of Alsace, offering among oth hearty dishes a marvelous sausage choucroute, a flaky onion tart, a lobs bouillabaisse, and the restaurant's Famous Shrimp Bag (shrimp and vegetab bathed in a light cream sauce and steamed in a phyllo bag). The largely Alsat wine list, good beer and authentic Parisian brasserie atmosphere complete t delightful dining experience.

Café Ba-Ba-Reeba! – *2024 N. Halsted St., Lincoln Park.* �& ☎ *773-935-500* *www.leye.com/restaurants.* **$$ Spanish**. Though other tapas bars have cropp up, this was Chicago's original. Seven seating areas decked in brig Mediterranean colors accommodate 360 diners. Ambience and food still sizz and the crowds come to enjoy hot and cold tapas ("little dishes" ordered quantity and shared), paella and a selection of Spanish wines.

Club Lucky – *1824 W. Wabansia Ave., Bucktown.* ☎ *773-227-230* *www.club-lucky.com.* **$$ Italian**. In a neighborhood where eateries come and g Club Lucky has endured. Generous portions of homestyle Italian cooking—rig toni with veal meatballs, eggplant parmigiana, scampi, chicken oreganato great martinis and funky 1940s supper-club décor team up to make th lounge/restaurant a long-lived hit.

Erwin – *2925 N. Halsted St., Lakeview. Closed Mon.* �& ☎ *773-528-7200.* **New American**. Seasonal specialties with Midwestern flavor grace this simple b robust menu. Creative vegetable and fruit preparations and savory sauces emb lish basics like roast chicken and pork tenderloin. The smallish room is cas yet chic and comfortable, with the feel of a friend's dining room. *Dinner or*

Jackson Harbor Grill – *6401 S. Coast Guard Dr., Hyde Park. Closed Mon Tues; call to check seasonal hours.* �& ☎ *773-288-4442.* **$$ Southern**. Becau much of Chicago's lakefront has been preserved as parkland, few watersi dining opportunities exist in the city. This converted century-old Coast Gua facility houses one of them. Dishing up Cajun-Creole creations, the grill off indoor and outdoor seating overlooking peaceful Jackson Harbor.

Pasteur – *5525 N. Broadway, Uptown.* �& ☎ *773-878-1061.* **$$ Vietname** Located just blocks north of Chicago's enclave of Vietnamese restaurants Argyle Street, this gem distinguishes itself in presentation, décor and cuisir Set about by palm trees, diners enjoy a range of carefully prepared region specialties from Saigon to Hanoi in the cool and inviting dining room. The cl pot chicken gets raves, and the whole red snapper is a house specialty.

Budget

Ann Sather – *929 W. Belmont Ave., Lakeview.* �& ☎ *773-348-237* *www.annsather.com.* **$ Swedish/American**. A welcoming atmosphere and hor cooking with a Swedish flair has made this a favorite among Chicagoans sin 1945. Breakfast is a specialty, and the cinnamon buns should not be misse Breakfast, lunch and dinner are served daily at t Belmont Ave. location; four other North Si branches have more limited hours.

Chicago Pizza and Oven Grinder *2121 N. Clark St., Lincoln Park.* ☎ *773-248-2570.* **$ Pizza**. Locat across the street from the site the St. Valentine's Day Massacr this nook serves unusual topsi turvy pizzas that resemble potpie Abundant salads can be share and the grinders are generou Good food and the laid-back a mosphere make this place pop lar and the waits sometim long. *Dinner only.*

© Kevin O. Mooney/Odyssey

Chicago Deep-Dish Pizza

Green Door Tavern – *678 N. Orleans St., River North. Closed Sun.* �& ☎ *31 664-5496.* **$ American**. Constructed only one year after the Chicago Fire of 187 this is among the oldest downtown buildings and shows its age in a 10-degr lean to the right and sloping floors. It's been a tavern since 1921 and tod serves good burgers, pasta and 35 different kinds of beers.

Half Shell – *676 W. Diversey Pkwy., Lincoln Park.* ☎ *773-549-1773.* **$ Seafoc** This quintessential neighborhood dive is located below street level, its dow scale atmosphere at odds with its surroundings. Though small and dark, it lur loyal locals craving wonderful fresh crab legs, shrimp, oysters and fried seafoc The curving bar takes up half the room, and eager diners are welcome to e there rather than wait for a table.

Lou Mitchell's – *565 W. Jackson Blvd., Loop.* 🔥 ☎ *312-939-3111.* **$ American.** The place for breakfast in downtown Chicago since 1923, Lou Mitchell's still serves up generous portions of oatmeal, omelets and orange juice to satisfy the heartiest appetites.

Twin Anchors Restaurant and Tavern – *1655 N. Sedgwick St., Old Town.* 🔥 ☎ *312-266-1616.* **$ Barbecue.** Beloved for its succulent, melt-in-your-mouth ribs, Twin Anchors has been a popular pub since its opening after Prohibition. (Frank Sinatra stopped here regularly in the 1960s.) The essential neighborhood joint, its relaxed and modest atmosphere makes a nice escape from upscale chic.

Wishbone – *1001 W. Washington Blvd., Near West Side. Closed for dinner Mon.* 🔥 ☎ *312-850-2663.* **$ Southern.** Have a heaping helping of hoppin' John or mix and match down-home side dishes with blackened catfish and chicken étouffée. Wishbone's colorful, lively dining room attracts an eclectic crowd, from kids to celebrities, and serves a hearty Cajun breakfast as well.

Where to Stay

One perquisite of Chicago's popularity as a convention town is its considerable number of hotels and motels, especially in the heart of the city. Downtown hotel rooms number over 27,000, and most of the major chains are represented. Chicago also boasts a delightful collection of boutique hotels that offer a more intimate milieu, most of them clustered along the Magnificent Mile, with a few newer additions in the Loop. *For general information about hotel chains in Chicago, see the* Accommodations *section in the back of this guide.*

The properties listed below were selected for their ambience, location and/or value for money. Prices reflect average cost for a standard double room (two people) in high season (not including any applicable city or state taxes). Room prices may be considerably lower in off-season, and many hotels offer discounted weekend rates. The presence of a swimming pool is indicated by the ⌇ *symbol.*

$$$$	over $300	$$	$75-$125
$$$	$200-$300	$	less than $75
$$	$125-$200		

Luxury

Allerton Crowne Plaza – *701 N. Michigan Ave., Magnificent Mile.* ✗ 🔥 ▣ ☎ *312-440-1500 or 800-227-6963. www.crowneplaza.com. 443 rooms.* **$$$$** The Allerton has served Chicago as a hotel since 1924, and a recent renovation nicely restores its original polish inside and out. Guest rooms are outfitted with marble baths and glow with warm wood tones and a rich palette of wall and fabric colors. Check out the view from the 25th-floor fitness center.

The Drake Hotel – *140 E. Walton Pl., Magnificent Mile.* ✗ 🔥 ▣ ☎ *312-787-2200 or 800-553-7253. www.hilton.com. 537 rooms.* **$$$$$** Since 1920, the Italian Renaissance-style limestone building at the top of the Magnificent Mile has been *the* address for visiting celebrities. Antique solid-brass candelabras and the original mahogany ceiling inset with hand-painted tiles set the tone in the lobby. Rooms, some overlooking Lake Michigan, combine floral fabrics with dark woods.

Hotel Inter-Continental Chicago – *505 N. Michigan Ave., Magnificent Mile.* ✗ 🔥 ▣ ⌇ ☎ *312-944-4100 or 800-327-0200. www.chicagointerconti.com. 844 rooms.* **$$$$** This Mag Mile classic began life as a men's club in 1929 and still retains many of the club's original decorative embellishments. Egyptian, Renaissance and Middle Eastern motifs ornament public spaces and ballrooms, and lavish majolica tile sets off the hotel's celebrated junior Olympic-size swimming pool. South tower rooms are furnished in elegant Biedermeier style and have the best views; those in the north tower tend toward a more modern look.

Hotel Monaco – *225 N. Wabash St., Magnificent Mile.* ✗ 🔥 ▣ ☎ *312-960-8500 or 800-397-7661. www.monaco-chicago.com. 192 rooms.* **$$$$** Two blocks from the Magnificent Mile, this boutique property was designed as the world traveler's 1930s Art Deco-style living room. In the oversized lobby, the registration desk is modeled after a classic steamer trunk. Whimsical amenities include an in-room pet goldfish on request, and your choice of lottery tickets or candy at turndown.

The Raphael – *201 E. Delaware Pl., Magnificent Mile.* ✗ 🔥 ▣ ☎ *312-943-5000 or 800-983-7870. 172 rooms.* **$$$$** Rustic Old World charm emanates from the beamed ceilings and arched windows of this small hotel located east of Michigan Avenue. Less showy than other Michigan Avenue boutique properties, the Raphael nonetheless offers a quiet stay in the heart of the city.

Regal Knickerbocker Hotel – *163 E. Walton Pl., Magnificent Mile.* ✗ ♿ 🅿
☎ *312-751-8100 or 800-222-8888. www.millenniumhotels.com. 305 rooms.*
$$$$ Transformed several times since its construction in 1927, the Knickerbocker has recently undergone a $35 million renovation. Its distinctive
cathedral-style windows and lit marquee welcome guests as they did in
Prohibition-era Chicago, and the breathtaking, 5,000sq ft Crystal Ballroom
(now used for meetings and special events) still echoes with the sounds of the
Jazz Age. Rooms are small but comfortable.

Silversmith Crowne Plaza – *10 S. Wabash Ave., Loop.* ✗ ♿ 🅿 ☎ *312-372-
7696 or 800-227-6963. www.crowneplaza.com. 143 rooms.* **$$$$** Tucked into
Jeweler's Row just feet from the elevated tracks, the beautifully appointed
Silversmith comes as an elegant surprise. Built in 1897 as a warren for jewelry
makers, the National Historic Landmark has been recently converted into a hotel
and renovated in turn-of-the-century Arts and Crafts style, complete with rich
oak paneling, glazed terra-cotta and Stickley furnishings throughout.

The Tremont Hotel – *100 E. Chestnut St., Magnificent Mile.* ✗ ♿ 🅿 ☎ *312-
751-1900 or 800-621-8133. 129 rooms.* **$$$$** Another inn in the English style,
the Tremont is named for a "luxury" hotel that served pioneer Chicago in 1838.
Its cozy lobby, complete with fireplace, welcomes guests with manor-house
ambience; likewise the bright rooms and suites. The Tremont House next door
offers furnished suites with kitchens.

Mid-Range

City Suites Hotel – *933 W. Belmont Ave., Lakeview.* ♿ 🅿 ☎ *773-404-3400
or 800-248-9108. www.cityinns.com. 45 rooms.* **$$$** City Suites inhabits a
neighborhood that bustles with street life day and night, crowded as it is with
restaurants, bars, nightclubs and even a tattoo parlor. Most of the units in this
Art Deco restoration are suites furnished with hide-a-beds and refrigerators,
and room service can be ordered from nearby Ann Sather restaurant *(see Where
to eat)*. The elevated train just west provides rapid transportation downtown.

Hotel Allegro Chicago – *171 W. Randolph St., Loop.* ✗ ♿ 🅿 ☎ *312-236-
0123 or 800-643-1500. www.allegrochicago.com. 483 rooms.* **$$$** Bold colors
and prints have transformed the North Loop theater district's 1926 Bismarck
Hotel into a stylish Hollywood set. The lobby's fluted glass and oak-paneled
walls are the backdrop for cobalt-blue velvet chaise lounges and red velour
sofas. Guest rooms feature eye-popping pink wallcoverings, melon-and-
magenta bedspreads and oval desks.

Hotel Burnham – *1 W. Washington St., Loop.* ✗ ♿ 🅿 ☎ *312-782-1111 or
877-294-9712. www.burnhamhotel.com. 122 rooms.* **$$$** Designed by Daniel
Burnham's architectural firm in 1895, the historic Reliance Building now houses
the fanciful Hotel Burnham, where original design elements blend with bold and
colorful interior stylings, including royal-blue velvet headboards and matching
cornices in the guest rooms. Located across from Marshall Field's, the Burnham
is also within walking distance of theaters, the Art Institute and the lakefront.

The House of Blues Hotel – *333 N. Dearborn St., River North.* ✗ ♿ 🅿 ☎ *312-
245-0333 or 877-569-3742. www.loewshotels.com. 367 rooms.* **$$$** Forget
English manor style and French country charm, the House of Blues Hotel aims
to rock your world. Flamboyantly decorated throughout, the hotel makes a
fitting partner for the exuberant House of Blues restaurant/nightclub next door.
Located along the Chicago River in landmark Marina City, the HOB complex
also includes a 36-lane bowling alley, boat charters, a health club, a wine bar
and an upscale steakhouse.

Majestic Hotel – *528 W. Brompton Ave., Lakeview.* ☎ *773-404-3499 or 800-
727-5108. www.cityinns.com. 53 rooms.* **$$$** In the vicinity of Wrigley Field
and steps from Lincoln Park and Belmont Harbor, this comfortable English-
style inn is nicely situated for North Side activities. Of the 53 units, 22 are suites
that include refrigerators, microwaves and wet bars.

Talbott Hotel – *20 E. Delaware Pl., Magnificent Mile.* ✗ ♿ ☎ *312-944-4970
or 800-825-2688. www.talbotthotel.com. 147 rooms.* **$$$** Snug, intimate and
decorated in an English fox-hunting theme, the tony Talbott features antiques
and two fireplaces in its wood-paneled Victorian lobby. Guest rooms and suites,
some with full kitchens, are simply but tastefully appointed in period reproductions. The hotel's overall tranquility transports guests far from the bustle of
nearby North Michigan Avenue.

The Whitehall Hotel – *105 E. Delaware Pl., Magnificent Mile.* ✗ ♿ 🅿 ☎ *312
944-6300 or 800-323-7500. 221 rooms.* **$$$** Just off the Mag Mile, this
venerable inn is among the original small hotels in the city, serving an elite
clientele since 1974. Today it retains its polish thanks to a 1994 renovation
that refreshed its English country manor atmosphere. The attentive staff pro-
vides personalized service.

he Willows Hotel – *555 W. Surf St., Lincoln Park.* ☎ *773-528-8400 or 800-*
'27-5108. www.cityinns.com. 55 rooms. **$$$** The Willows occupies a vintage
920s building just off busy Broadway. Recently renovated in 19C French
ountry style, the lobby is pretty in pinks and peaches. Though bathrooms are
mall, the rooms are restful, done in a soft pastel palette.

Budget

he Carleton of Oak Park Hotel and Motor Inn – *1110 Pleasant St., Oak*
'ark. ✗ & 🅿 ☎ *708-848-5000 or 888- 227-5386. www.carletonhotel.com.*
54 rooms. **$$** The Carleton, recently redecorated and enlarged with 42 addi-
ional rooms, offers pleasant accommodations convenient to downtown Oak
'ark and about 20 minutes from the Loop via the nearby elevated train.

he Essex Inn – *800 S. Michigan Ave., Grant Park.* ✗ & 🅿 ⛷ ☎ *312-939-*
'800 or 800-621-6909. 267 rooms. **$$** Though its rooms are basic, the Essex
ppeals for its good prices and convenient location along South Michigan
venue. Across the street, Grant Park makes a lovely front yard, and the hotel
s walking distance to the Loop, lakefront and Art Institute.

he Margarita European Inn – *1566 Oak Ave., Evanston.* ✗ 🅿 ☎ *847-869-*
'273. www.margaritainn.com. 44 rooms. **$$** Located 10mi north of the Loop
n suburban Evanston, the Margarita Inn is close to Northwestern University
nd steps to the elevated train to downtown. In addition to rooms with shared
nd private baths and several suites, the 1915 Georgian-style inn features an
legant Grand Parlor, a cozy English library and a rooftop sundeck in the sum-
nertime. **Va Pensiero**, an acclaimed Italian restaurant, is located downstairs.

Motel 6 – *162 E. Ontario St., Magnificent Mile.* ✗ ☎ *312-787-3580.*
www.motel6.com. 191 rooms. **$$** Comfortable and clean, this budget inn lives
p to its swanky location just off Michigan Avenue without pretension. While
he room décor and layout are basic motel fare, the small lobby sports marble
nd chandeliers. The on-site restaurant is the popular **Coco Pazzo Café** *(☎ 312-*
;64-2777) trattoria version of its pricier namesake down the street in River
Jorth. Homemade pastas and tender fried calamari steal the day here.

he Write Inn – *211 N. Oak Park Ave., Oak Park.* & 🅿 ☎ *708-383-4800.*
www.writeinn.com. 111 rooms. **$$** This suburban inn is located along a shady
tretch of residential street not far from local shopping, dining and trains to
he Loop. It offers a wide variety of rooms and suites decorated with 1920s
ntiques; the smallest feature Murphy beds, others offer sitting areas,
vhirlpools and kitchenettes.

Out on the Town

Useful Numbers *(pre-recorded information)*

Mayor's Office of Special
vents
☎ 312-744-3370

ine Arts Hotline
☎ 312-346-3278

azz Hotline
☎ 312-427-3300

PERFORMING
ARTS

Chicago provides a vari-
ty of music and enter-
ainment year-round.
Close to 100 theaters
ost dramas and musi-
als, ranging from trav-
ling Broadway produc-
ions to performances by
ighly acclaimed local
ompanies. Dance, sym-
hony and opera pro-
uctions are performed
t venues throughout
he city. Small clubs spe-
ializing in jazz, blues,
ock and country offer

© Kevin O. Mooney/Odyssey

first-class music in an intimate setting. Popular rock and alternative performe[] play in stadiums or convention centers in outlying areas. Summer brings t[] suburban **Ravinia Music Festival** as well as outdoor performances at parks a[] downtown plazas. For a detailed listing of events, call the **Mayor's Office of Spec[] Events** (☎ *312-744-3370*).

Music and Dance

Classical Music	Venue	☎
Chicago Symphony Orchestra	Symphony Center 220 S. Michigan Ave. (Loop)	312-294-300[]
Chicago Sinfonietta	Symphony Center 220 S. Michigan Ave. (Loop)	312-236-368[]
Chicago Opera Theater	Athenaeum Theater 2936 N. Southport Ave. (Lakeview/Wrigleyville)	312-704-841[]
Grant Park Symphony Orchestra *(mid-Jun–late Aug)*	Petrillo Music Shell (Grant Park)	312-742-476[]
Lyric Opera	20 N. Wacker Dr. (Loop)	312-332-222[]
Old Town School of Folk Music	909 W. Armitage Ave. and 4544 N. Lincoln Ave. (Lincoln Park/DePaul)	773-525-775[]

Rock/Pop		
Allstate Arena	6920 N. Mannheim Rd., Rosemont	847-635-66[]
Aragon Ballroom	1106 W. Lawrence Ave. (Uptown)	773-561-950[]
Double Door	1572 N. Milwaukee Ave. (Wicker Park)	773-489-316[]
Metro	3730 N. Clark St. (Lakeview/Wrigleyville)	773-549-020[]
New World Music Theatre	I-80 & Harlem Ave. (Tinley Park)	312-559-121[]
Skyline Stage	Navy Pier (Streeterville)	312-595-743[]
Star Plaza Theater	I-65 and US-30, Merrillville, IN	773-734-726[]
United Center	1901 W. Madison St. (Near West Side)	312-455-450[]

Dance		
Ballet Chicago	185 N. Wabash Ave., (Loop)	312-251-883[]
Hubbard Street Dance Chicago	1147 W. Jackson St. (Near West Side)	312-850-974[]
Joffrey Ballet of Chicago	70 E. Lake St., Suite 1300 (Loop)	312-739-012[]

Theaters and Performances

Theater in Chicago Guide, a free bimonthly publication available at major hote[] and visitor information centers, provides descriptions and schedules of pla[] currently being performed.

Theaters	Address	☎
Apollo Theater	2540 N. Lincoln Ave. (Lincoln Park/DePaul)	773-935-61[]
Athenaeum Theatre	2936 N. Southport Ave. (Lakeview/Wrigleyville)	773-935-686[]
Auditorium Theatre	50 E. Congress Pkwy. (Loop)	312-431-235[]
Briar Street Theatre	3133 N. Halsted St. (Lakeview/Wrigleyville)	773-348-400[]
Cadillac Palace Theater	151 W. Randolph St. (Loop)	312-409-290[]
Chicago Theatre	175 N. State St. (Loop)	312-443-113[]
Court Theatre	5535 S. Ellis Ave. (University of Chicago)	773-753-447[]
Ivanhoe Theatre	750 W. Wellington St. (Lincoln Park/DePaul)	773-975-717[]
Goodman Theatre	170 N. Dearborn St. (Loop)	312-443-380[]
Marriott Theatre	10 Marriott Dr., Lincolnshire	847-634-020[]

...ental Theater/ ...rd Center for the Performing Arts	24 W. Randolph St. (Loop)	312-902-1400
...ppet Parlor	1922 W. Montrose Ave.	773-774-2919
...yal George Theatre	1641 N. Halsted St. (Lincoln Park/DePaul)	312-988-9000
...icago Shakespeare Theater	Navy Pier (Streeterville)	312-595-5600
...ubert Theatre	22 W. Monroe St. (Loop)	312-977-1700
...eppenwolf Theatre Company	1650 N. Halsted St. (Lincoln Park/DePaul)	312-335-1650
...eatre Building	1225 W. Belmont Ave. (Lakeview/Wrigleyville)	773-327-5252
...ganic/Touchstone Theatre	2851 N. Halsted St. (Lakeview/Wrigleyville)	773-404-4700
...ctory Gardens Theatre	2257 N. Lincoln Ave. (Lincoln Park/DePaul)	773-871-3000

...ickets

...s some of the more popular events sell out months in advance, it is advisable ...buy tickets early. Full-price tickets can be purchased directly from the venue's ...ox office or from Hot Tix or Ticketmaster; major credit cards are usually ...ccepted *(a service charge of $1-$5 may be added to the ticket price)*, but not ...all locations. Licensed ticket agencies sometimes have tickets available when ...e box office is sold out but expect to pay a substantial service fee (up to 35%). ...he hotel concierge may be able to help secure tickets for a performance. ...ot Tix offers half-price tickets for selected events on the day of the show. ...urchases must be made in person *(78 W. Randolph St.; 163 E. Pearson St. ...: N. Michigan Ave. in Chicago's historic Pumping Station; and at Tower ...ecords; offices open Mon–Sat 10am–6pm, Sun noon–5pm; ☎ 312-977-...755)*. Ticketmaster *(charge by phone: ☎ 312-559-1212; recorded information: ...· 312-559-8989)* outlets are found at most locations of Carson Pirie Scott, ...ower Records and Blockbuster Music.

...IGHTLIFE

...ightlife in Chicago ranges from quiet, elegant hotel lounges to lively rock bars ...ong Rush and Division Streets or sultry blues and jazz clubs on the North and ...outh Sides. The city has also garnered an excellent reputation for its numer-...us comedy clubs, which have hosted the likes of John Belushi, Dan Aykroyd ...nd Bonnie Hunt. Consult the arts and entertainment sections of local newspa-...ers for a detailed listing of events. Some establishments have a cover charge ...r entertainment. Many bars and clubs serve food (menu may be scaled down ...· light appetizers after 10pm or 11pm). Since alcoholic beverages are served ...· nightclubs, proof of age is required to enter. Following is a list of clubs organ-...ed by type.

...lues Clubs	Address	☎
...ue Chicago	736 N. Clark St. (River North)	312-642-6261
...ue Chicago on Clark	536 N. Clark St. (River North)	312-661-0100
...L.U.E.S	2519 N. Halsted St. (Lincoln Park/DePaul)	773-528-1012
...L.U.E.S. Etcetera	1124 W. Belmont Ave. (Lakeview/Wrigleyville)	773-525-8989
...uddy Guy's Legends	754 S. Wabash Ave. (South Loop)	312-427-0333
...heckerboard Lounge	423 E. 43rd St. (Near South Side)	773-624-3240
...ouse of Blues	330 N. State St. (River North)	312-923-2000
...ingston Mines	2548 N. Halsted St. (Lincoln Park/DePaul)	773-477-4646
...omedy Clubs		
...omedy Sportz	2851 N. Halsted (Lincoln Park/DePaul)	773-549-8080
...nprovOlympic	3541 N. Clark St. (Lakeview/Wrigleyville)	773-880-0199
...ne Second City	1616 N. Wells St. (Old Town)	312-337-3992
...anies Comedy Night Club	1548 N. Wells St. (Old Town)	312-337-4027
...inner Theater		
...ommy Gun's Garage	1239 S. State St. (South Loop)	773-728-2828
...ony n' Tina's Wedding	230 W. North Ave. (Old Town)	312-664-8844

Jazz Clubs	Address	☎
Andy's	11 E. Hubbard St. (River North)	312-642-68C
Cotton Club	1710 S. Michigan Ave. (South Loop)	312-341-978
Dick's Last Resort	435 E. Illinois St. (Streeterville)	312-836-787
Green Dolphin Street	2200 N. Ashland Ave. (West Lincoln Park)	773-395-006
Jazz Showcase	59 W. Grand. Ave. (River North)	312-670-247
The Green Mill	4802 N. Broadway (Uptown)	773-878-555
Pops for Champagne	2934 N. Sheffield Ave. (Lakeview/Wrigleyville)	773-472-10C
Underground Wonder Bar	10 E. Walton Pl. (Magnificent Mile)	312-266-776

Nightclubs		
Excalibur Entertainment Complex	632 N. Dearborn St. (River North)	312-266-194
Red Dog	1958 W. North Ave. (Wicker Park)	773-278-10C
Wild Hare & Singing Armadillo Frog Sanctuary	3530 N. Clark St. (Lakeview/Wrigleyville)	773-327-427

Shopping

A world-class shopping mecca, Chicago attracts residents and tourists alike
its famous department stores, designer boutiques and trendy second-hand shop
not to mention its large flea market featuring live blues. The main shopping are
are clustered around downtown, but the various neighborhoods offer their fill
tiny stores stocked with used books, unusual crafts or ethnic fare. Most store
accept major credit cards and traveler's checks, but are reluctant to take out-o
state checks. Many shops extend their hours during the Christmas seaso
(typically starting in mid-November). The *Chicago Official Visitors Guide* (pul
lished quarterly by the Chicago Convention and Tourism Bureau) offers detaile
information on the types of shops, their locations and hours of operation.

MAIN SHOPPING AREAS

*Large department stores in downtown are generally open Mon–Fri 10am–7pr
Sat 10am–6pm & Sun noon–5pm; hours vary seasonally. Opening hours fe
smaller stores vary; call to check hours before you go.*

The Loop – Chicago's two largest department stores, **Carson Pirie Scott & Compar**
(1 S. State St.; ☎ 312-641-7000) and **Marshall Field & Company** *(111 N. State S*
☎ 312-781-1000) anchor the main shopping area along State Street. **Jewele**
Row *(Wabash Ave. between Madison & Washington Sts.)*, the center of Chicago
jewelry business, includes **Wabash Jewelers Mall** *(21 N. Wabash Ave.; ☎ 312-26.*
1757) and the 165 vendors of the **Jewelers Center at the Mallers Building** *(5 S. Wabas*
Ave.; ☎ 312-853-2057). **Booksellers Row** *(408 S. Michigan Ave.; ☎ 312-42*
4242) offers a vast selection of used books in excellent condition. The **Atriu**
Mall *(ground level of James R. Thompson Center, 100 W. Randolph St.; ☎ 31.*
346-0777) includes 30 retail stores and restaurants in its sun-lit atrium.

River North – Best known for its art galleries and boutiques, River North als
includes the **Jazz Record Mart** *(444 N. Wabash Ave.; ☎ 312-222-1467)*, whic
claims to be the world's largest jazz and blues record store. **Jay Robert's Antiqu**
Warehouse *(149 W. Kinzie St.; ☎ 312-222-0167)* houses 54,000sq ft of antiqu
furniture and housewares on three floors. Overlooking the river, th
Merchandise Mart houses **Shops at the Mart** on its first two floors *(22*
Merchandise Mart Plaza, at Wells St.; ☎ 312-527-7615), with more tha
50 food, specialty and apparel shops, including Crabtree & Evelyn and Coacl

Lincoln Park/DePaul – This district offers an eclectic assortment of antiqu
shops, funky boutiques and a branch of the Hollywood landmark music stor
Tower Records *(2301 N. Clark St.; ☎ 773-477-5994)*. Several used bookstore
line Lincoln Avenue north of Fullerton Avenue.

Hyde Park – This neighborhood is a bookworm's delight, offering numerou
bookstores, grouped around the University of Chicago and along E. 57th ar
E. 55th Streets., featuring new, used and hard-to-find books. **Harper Cou**
(5201-25 S. Harper Ave.; ☎ 773-363-8282) is an open-air mall consisting c
close to 20 specialty shops and restaurants.

Devon Avenue – *Between Western & California Aves.* The "Midwest capital c
gold dealers" contains nearly 20 jewelers selling mostly 22- and 24-karat go
jewelry. The heart of Chicago's Indian community, Devon also features India
restaurants, sari shops, and electronics stores.

Magnificent Mile—

CTA bus no. 151 ($1.50) makes a loop from W. Harrison & S. State Sts. to Walton St. & N. Michigan Ave. This section of North Michigan Avenue between Illinois and Oak Streets is *the prime shopping area of Chicago. It includes expansive malls, department stores (Marshall Field, Neiman Marcus, Saks Fifth Avenue) and some of the world's finest designer boutiques (located primarily on Oak St. between N. Michigan Ave. and Rush St.). The newest addition to the Magnificent Mile's upscale department-store lineup is Nordstrom (entrance on Grand and Wabash Aves.), which opened in September 2000.

Mag Mile Malls

For locations, see map opposite.

Chicago Place
☏ 312-642-4811

More than 50 shops, including Saks Fifth Avenue, Ann Taylor and Williams-Sonoma, as well as restaurants and a gourmet supermarket.

One Magnificent Mile
☏ 312-664-7777

Several upscale boutiques such as Chanel and Polo/Ralph Lauren.

Water Tower Place
☏ 312-440-3165

Some 125 shops and restaurants on 7 levels including Marshall Field's, Lord & Taylor and Laura Ashley.

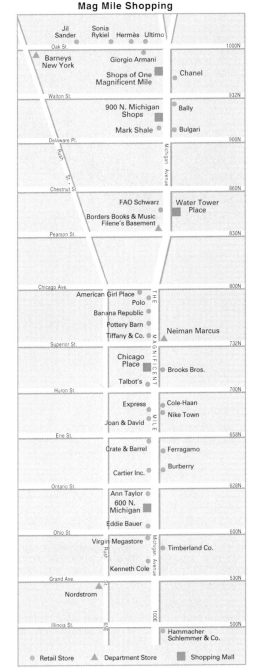

Mag Mile Shopping

600 North Michigan Shops ☏ 312-266-5630

Several stores including Marshall's and Eddie Bauer as well as restaurants and a multiplex movie theater.

900 North Michigan Shops ☏ 312-915-3916

More than 70 shops, including Bloomingdale's, Gucci and Jessica McClintock.

Art Galleries

In general, most commercial galleries open between 9am and 11am Tuesday through Saturday, and close at 5pm or 6pm; many close between exhibits. The *Chicago Gallery News (free, available at galleries and visitor centers),* published quarterly, provides a comprehensive listing of exhibits and their locations.

Chicago's **main gallery districts** are located in **River North** *(between N. Wells N. Orleans, W. Superior and W. Huron Sts.)* and **Michigan Avenue** *(between E. Oak and E. Ontario Sts.).*

Clusters of galleries can also be found on the **West Side** along North Milwaukee Avenue *(between N. Damen Ave. and N. Wood St.)*, on the **North Side** off North Lincoln Avenue *(between W. School and W. Division Sts.)*, and in **Evanston** along Sherman Avenue and Grove Street.

Maxwell Street Market

Canal St. between Taylor and 16th Sts. Entrance on Roosevelt and Canal Sts. Open Sun 7am–3pm. ☎ *312-922-3100.* This colorful, open-air flea market offers a mixture of antiques, collectibles, new and used merchandise, a live blues band and about 30 food vendors. Arrive early for the largest selection.

Sightseeing

VISITOR INFORMATION

Two free publications, the *Chicago Official Visitors Guide* and *Key This Week* offer information on events, attractions, shopping and dining. Both are available at visitor centers. A third publication, *WHERE Chicago*, is available in hotels

Chicago Office of Tourism Visitor Information Centers

Chicago Cultural Center:	78 E. Washington St., at Michigan Ave. *(open Mon–Fri 10am–6pm, Sat 10am–5pm, Sun noon–5pm; closed Jan 1, Thanksgiving Day & Dec 25;* ♿ ☎ *312-744-2400)*
Chicago Water Works:	163 E. Pearson St., at Michigan Ave. *(information booth open daily 7:30am–7pm; closed Jan 1, Thanksgiving Day & Dec 25).* A café and Hot Tix office are also located here
Illinois Market Place:	700 E. Grand Ave. on Navy Pier *(open Mon–Thu 10am–8pm, Fri–Sat 10am–10pm, Sun 10am–8pm).*

TOURS *Map p 13*

A variety of guided tours are available to the visitor. Below is a selection of the principal tours. For more information about tours of Chicago, access the Web site: *www.ci.chi.il.us/tourism/thingstodo/tours.html.*

Tours of the City

Trolley Tours – Offered daily by **Chicago Trolley Co.** *(year-round daily 9am–6:30pm, last pick-up at 5pm; $18, allows free reboarding;* ☎ *773-648-5000; www.chicagotrolley.com).* Visitors can board every 10-15min at any of the 16 stops located at major city attractions.

Carriage Tours – In general, horse-drawn carriages hold 4-6 passengers and tour route depends on passenger preference. Tours offered by **J.C. Cutters Ltd** *(Mon–Fri 7pm–1am, Sat 12pm–2am, Sun 1pm–1am; 30min; $35;* ☎ *312-664-6014)* originate at Michigan Ave. and Peason St. **The Noble Horse** tours *(Fri 8pm, Sat 5:30pm & 8pm, Sun 3pm; $30/30 min, $60/hr;* ☎ *312-266-7878)* start at the corner of Michigan Ave. and Pearson St.

Gangster Tours – **Untouchable Tours** offers a lighthearted and often silly look at Prohibition-era Chicago and the gangsters that ruled this city *(2hrs; depart from 610 N. Clark St. at Ohio Ave. Mon–Wed 10am, Thu 10am & 1pm, Fri 10am, 1pm & 7:30pm, Sat 10am, 1pm & 3pm, Sun 11am & 2pm; not offered Jan 1, Easter Sunday & Dec 25; $22; reservations recommended;* ☎ *773-881-1195)*

Architectural Tours

Chicago Architecture Foundation (CAF) – Founded in 1966, the Chicago Architecture Foundation is dedicated to preserving and increasing public appreciation of Chicago's architecture. Today the organization conducts more than 60 tours of Chicago's neighborhoods by foot, bus, boat, bicycle and elevated train. Tickets are available at CAF/Mercury Cruise Line ticket booth *(southwest corner of Michigan Avenue Bridge on the river level)* or from the two CAF Shop and Tour Centers: Santa Fe Building *(224 S. Michigan Ave.; open year-round Mon–Sat 9am–7pm, Sun 9:30am–6pm;* ☎ *312-922-8687)* and in the John Hancock Center *(874 N. Michigan Ave.; open year-round Mon–Sat 10am–7pm, Sun 10am–6pm;* ☎ *312-751-1380).* Cost of tours is discounted for CAF members. Advance ticket purchase is strongly recommended *(to charge by phone, call Ticketmaster,* ☎ *312-902-1500).*

A sampling of CAF tours is cited below; for a complete listing, call their recorded tour line (☎ 312-922-8687) or access their Web site (www.architecture.org).

Architecture River Cruise – This excellent cruise provides an in-depth study of the Loop's architecture as seen from the Chicago River (1hr 30min; departs from southwest corner of Michigan Avenue Bridge late Apr–early Jun Mon–Fri 11am, 1pm & 3pm, weekends on the hour from 11am–3pm; early Jun–Oct Mon–Fri on the hour from 10am–3pm; Oct Mon-Fri 11am, 1pm & 3pm, weekends on the hour from 10am–3pm; $21; ♿).

Walking Tours – **Historic Skyscrapers** examines the beginnings of the Chicago school of architecture through study of structures built between 1870 and 1935 (2hrs; departs from the Santa Fe Building Mar–Nov Sun–Fri 1:30pm, Sat 11am & 1:30pm; rest of the year daily 1:30pm; $10). **Modern Skyscrapers** looks at international, Modern and post-Modern structures (2hrs; departs from the Santa Fe Building Mar–Nov Sun–Fri 1:30pm, Sat 11am & 1:30pm; rest of the year daily 1:30pm; $10).

Loop Tour Train – Board the "L" for a new perspective on the Loop's architecture and discover the history of the early city and its elevated train system (40min; May–late Sept Sat 11:35am, 12:15pm, 12:55pm & 1:35pm; free; tickets must be obtained in advance at the Chicago Office of Tourism Visitor Information Center, 1st floor, Chicago Cultural Center, 77 E. Randolph St. at Michigan Ave.; directions provided when you pick up tickets).

River and Lake Cruises

Tours of the Chicago River and Lake Michigan offer panoramic views of the city's skyline and feature architectural and historical points of interest. In addition to the cruises listed below, in summer 2000 the city added two unique new ways of cruising the river: floating bikes mounted on surfboards accommodate up to three riders; Venice-style gondolas, complete with a serenading gondolier, accommodate up to six passengers. **RiverBikes of Chicago** operates on the south bank of the river at LaSalle Street (daily in summer during daylight hours; single bikes: $15/half-hour, $25/hr; tandem bikes: $40/hr; ☎ 773-348-9903). **Old World Gondolas** also operates on the south bank at Wells Street and Wacker Drive (Jun 14–Sept 10 Tue–Thu noon–8pm, Fri–Sat noon–9pm, Sun noon–6pm; $1/min/person for 6 passengers; $90/15min for private rides; by reservation only, ☎ 773-871-6666; information: ☎ 312-726-7574).

Chicago from the Lake cruises depart from River East Plaza, formerly known as North Pier (May–Oct daily 10am–4pm; 1hr 30min; reservations suggested; $19; ✗ ♿ 🅿 ☎ 312-527-1977).

Mercury Cruise Line tours depart from southwest corner of Michigan Avenue Bridge: Landmark Classic (May–Oct 1 daily 10am, 11:30am, 1:15pm, 2:30pm, 3:15pm, 7pm & 8:30pm; 1hr 30min; $14), Summer Sunset (May–Oct 1 daily 7:30pm; 2hrs; $16) and Skyline Special (May–Oct 1 daily 5pm & 9pm; 1hr 30min; $14). Arrive 1hr early to purchase tickets. For information: ☎ 312-332-1353.

All **Wendella** cruises depart from the northwest corner of the Michigan Avenue Bridge: River and lake cruises (mid-Apr–Oct daily 10am–8:30pm; 1hr 30min; $14; ✗ 🅿); Lake Michigan cruises (mid-Apr–Oct daily 7:30pm; 2hrs; $16; ✗ 🅿). Arrive 1hr early to purchase tickets. For information: ☎ 312-337-1446; www.wendellaboats.com.

© Carol Mallory/DPA

Tour Boats on the Chicago River

Shoreline cruises of Lake Michigan depart from Navy Pier *(May–Sept 30 dai* *10am–11pm; 30min; $9)*; from Buckingham Fountain in Grant Par *(Jun–Aug 31 daily 7:15pm–11:15pm; 1hr; $8)*; and from Shedd Aquariur *(May–Sept 30 daily 10:15am–6:15pm; 1hr; $8)*. For information: ☎ 312-222 *9328. www.shorelinesightseeing.com.*

Neighborhood Tours

Chicago Neighborhood Tours – Weekly half-day bus excursions, sponsored b the City of Chicago and Sears, explore the city's community cultural attractions Stops include landmarks, murals, cultural centers, theaters, museums and ar galleries. Participants also explore neighborhood shopping areas and taste loc cuisine. A different neighborhood, such as Chinatown, Bronzeville or Devo Avenue, is visited each week *(motor-coach excursions depart from Chicag Cultural Center, 77 E. Randolph St., Apr–Sept Sat. 10am, rest of the year Sa 1pm.; arrive 30min in advance for boarding; 4hrs; $30, includes light lunch advance purchase recommended; ☎ 312-742-1190).*

Self-guided Literary Tour

Site	Locatio
Fine Arts Building	Loo
Site of the "Little Room" 1890s literary gatherings	
Founding of Harriet Monroe's *Poetry* magazine in 1911	
Founding of Margaret Anderson's *Little Review* in 1914	
Chicago Board of Trade	Loo
Previous BOT building was the setting for *The Titan*	
by Theodore Dreiser and *The Pit* by Frank Norris	
4646 N. Hermitage Ave. (Ravenswood)	Uptow
Carl Sandburg lived on the second floor while writing *Chicago Poems*	
1958 W. Evergreen Ave. (Wicker Park)	Milwaukee Avenu
Nelson Algren lived on the third floor from 1959 to 1975	
Printer's Row	South Loo
Setting for Sara Paretsky novels	
47th St. and Drexel Blvd. to M.L. King, Jr. Dr.	Near South Sid
Setting for *Native Son* by Richard Wright	
and *A Street in Bronzeville* by Gwendolyn Brooks	
Union Stock Yards	Bridgeport/Canaryvill
Setting for Upton Sinclair's *The Jungle*	
University of Chicago	Hyde Par
Setting for novels by Saul Bellow, Pearl S. Buck, Phillip Roth,	
Robert Pirsig, Robert Herrick	
339 and 600 N. Oak Park Ave.	Oak Par
Birthplace and boyhood home of Ernest Hemingway	

CHICAGO FOR CHILDREN

Chicago for Children – *Sights throughout this guide of particular interest t children and students are indicated with* ▨ *symbol.* Many of these attraction offer special children's programs. The popular Chicago Children's Museum o Navy Pier features interactive exhibits designed for children under age 12. Mos attractions in Chicago feature discounted, if not free, admission to visitors unde 18 years of age. In addition, many hotels offer special family discount pack ages, and numerous restaurants provide a children's menu. Two annual events the **Taste of Lincoln Avenue Kid's Karnival** *(last weekend in July; Altgeld St. fror Lincoln Ave. to Halsted St.; ☎ 773-472-9046)* and the **57th Street Children's Boo Fair** *(late Sept; 57th St. between Kimbark & Dorchester Aves.; ☎ 773-536 8103)* are conceived especially for children. *Chicago Parent,* a free monthl newspaper, includes articles of interest to parents as well as an extensive ca endar of family-oriented events; it is available at major attractions and librarie throughout the area. To obtain copies by mail, write to: *Chicago Parent,* 14 S. Oak Park Ave., Oak Park, IL 60302; or call ☎ 708-386-5555.

Gateway Park, Navy Pier

Sports and Recreation

hicago's primary recreation area is an almost continuous span of public parks
ong the city's 30-plus miles of lakefront, including Lincoln, Grant, Burnham
nd Jackson Parks. The **Chicago Park District** maintains these parks, and well over
00 other recreational areas offering a wide range of activities including swim-
ing, archery and bocci ball *(information & maps: 425 E. McFetridge Dr.,
hicago, IL 60605, ☎ 312-742-7529)*. The **Forest Preserve District of Cook County**
rovides information about natural areas and facilities outside the city bound-
ies *(536 N. Harlem Ave., River Forest, IL 60305, ☎ 773-261-8400)*.

he Lake

wimming – Over 30 public beaches are scattered along Lake Michigan.
feguards are on duty from Memorial Day–Labor Day *(9am–9:30pm; South
each closes 8pm)*. Many beaches have refreshment stands and changing facil-
es; no alcoholic beverages are allowed *(for more information about Chicago's
ublic beaches, call ☎ 312-747-0832)*. The beaches listed below are presented
om north to south according to block numbers on **Lake Shore Drive**.

eaches	Block	Beaches	Block
oward St. Beach	7500N	Foster Ave. Beach	5200N
argo Ave. Beach	7432N	Montrose Beach	4400N
rvis Ave. Beach	7400N	North Ave. Beach	1600N-2400N
oyola Beach	7100N	Oak St. Beach	1000N-1400N
ogers Park	6700N	49th St. Beach	4900S
erger Park	6200N	57th St. Beach	5700S
ine Beach	5900N	South Shore Cultural Center	7100S

ishing – Lake Michigan abounds with various species of fish, including coho and
hinook salmon *(prime season May–Jun)*; brown, rainbow and lake trout *(prime
eason Jul–Aug)*; and yellow perch. Most charter boats depart from Burnham
ark Harbor *(southeast of Grant Park)*. A fishing license is required; one-day non-
esident licenses are available in fishing supply stores *(equipment rental may be
vailable)*. Smelt fishing runs from early April until mid-May *(after 6pm)* all along
e lake. Ice-fishing is permitted on area lakes when the ice is at least four inches
ick; contact the Forest Preserve District of Cook County *(☎ 773-261-8400)*
r more information. Onshore fishing *(prohibited May 15–Oct 15)* is allowed at
urnham and Montrose Harbors and at Jackson Park.

oating – The lake is a great location year-round for sailing and power boating.
ontact the Harbor Division of the Chicago Park District for temporary docking
cilities *(☎ 312-747-0737)*. **Sailboat rentals** (1-4 persons) are available through
e Chicago Park District at Montrose Beach and 63rd Street Beach *(late
ay–Labor Day Wed–Sun 10am–5pm; $45/2hrs; sailing proficiency necessary.
struction provided; ☎ 312-747-7684)*. Contact **Chicagoland Canoe Base** *(4019
, Narragansett Ave.; ☎ 773-777-1489)* for rentals and information about
aces to canoe or kayak.

Biking, Hiking an Jogging – Bike Way is paved 18.5mi lakefro path extending alor Chicago's shoreline. T path is also open t pedestrians and in-lir skaters. In additio 15 Chicago parks off dedicated bicycle path *(contact Chicago Pa District for info mation)*. For more info mation and a map bike routes in the are contact the **Chicagolar Bicycle Federation** *(4 S. Dearborn St Chicago IL 6060. ☎ 312-427-3325* Bike and in-line ska rentals are availab from **Bike Chicago** *(loc tions at Navy Pier North Avenue Beac Apr–mid-Oct, protecti gear provided; ☎ 31 755-0488)*. The **Chica Area Runners Associatii** provides maps and ii

Lakefront Recreation

formation about local races and routes *(203 N. Wabash St., Suite 110 Chicago IL 60601; ☎ 312-666-9836; www.cararuns.org)*.

Working Out – The following clubs allow nonmembers to use their faciliti (weight rooms, aerobics classes and pools) for a daily fee *($7-$15)*:

Club	Address	☎
Chicago Fitness Center	3131 N. Lincoln Ave.	773-549-8181
Chicago Hilton	720 S. Michigan Ave.	312-294-6800
& Towers Athletic Club	1320 W. Fullerton Ave.	773-477-9888
Lakeshore Athletic Club	441 N. Wabash Ave.	312-644-4880
	211 N. Stetson Ave.	312-616-9000

Many private fitness centers are open to guests of major hotels; check with th hotel's concierge. **YMCA** memberships are valid worldwide; call for closest recr ation center and available facilities *(☎ 312-977-0031)*.

Cross-Country Skiing – Extensive cross-country facilities in the Chicago are are available throughout the city to tourists and residents *(open Mon–F 2pm–9pm, weekends noon–5pm, weather permitting; rentals available at son facilities; Chicago Park District, ☎ 312-294-2200)*.

Ice-skating – Enjoy skating *(weather permitting)* among the skyscrapers **Daley Bicentennial Plaza** *(337 E. Randolph St.; Nov–Mar Mon–Fri 10am–10p weekends 10am–5pm; closed Thanksgiving Day & Dec 25; $1.50; rentals ava able; ☎ 312-294-4790)*; or take in superb views of the lake and city wh gliding at Navy Pier *(600 E. Grand Ave.; Nov–mid-Apr daily 10am–8pm, S til 7pm; rentals available; ☎ 312-595-5189)*.

Snowmobiling and Tobogganing – The Forest Preserve District of Coc County *(☎ 773-261-8400)* maintains five snowmobiling areas; courses a open when snow depth is over four inches. Snowmobiles must be registere with the Forest Preserve. Also contact the Forest Preserve for information abo toboggan runs in the Dan Ryan Woods and other locations *(many offer rental*

Tickets can be purchased at the individual venue or through **Ticketmaster** (☎ *312-902-1500*).

Sport/Team	Season	Home Stadium	☎ Information
Major League Baseball	**Apr–Oct**		
Cubs (NL)		**Wrigley Field**	773-404-2827
(*▣▣ Red Line to Addison or bus no. 22, or no. 152 express service to night games*)			
White Sox (AL)		**Comiskey Park**	312-674-1000
(*▣▣ Red Line to Sox-35th or bus no. 24 or 35*)			
Professional Football	**Sept–Dec**		
Bears		**Soldier Field**	847-295-6600
(*▣▣ bus no. 128 express service to games*)			
Professional Basketball	**Oct-Apr**		
Bulls		**United Center**	312-455-4000
(*▣▣ bus no. 20 express service to games*)			
Professional Hockey	**Oct–Apr**		
Blackhawks (NHL)		**United Center**	312-455-7000
(*▣▣ bus no. 19 express service to games*)			
Wolves (IHL)		**Rosemont Horizon**	847-390-0404

Cubs Game at Wrigley Field

© Robert Holmes

Navy Pier

Sights

THE LOOP ★★★

Brown, Green or Orange line to Adams, Red or Blue line to Jackson
Map pp 72-73

Source and center of Chicago, the Loop forms the heart of a commercial metrop
that invented the skyscraper and the department store. Culture, commerce and p
tics are focused in an area bordered on the north and west by the Chicago River,
the east by Lake Michigan and on the south by Congress Parkway. Originally a mu
swamp, today this bustling district is an outdoor museum of architecture and sc
ture girdled by a loop of steel elevated tracks.

Historical Notes

A Prairie Grows Wild – Chicago began as a frontier trading post at the intersect
of Lake Michigan and the Chicago River, hunkered in the shadow of Fort Dearbo
Set between the watersheds of the Great Lakes and the Mississippi, the site offe
the possibility of an inland waterway connecting New York to New Orleans, and
canal planners laid out the original Loop grid at the mouth of the river in 1830.
Illinois & Michigan Canal opened in 1848, followed immediately by railroads. So
Chicago became the largest railroad center and fastest-growing city in the wo
expanding from barely 4,000 people in 1837 to 30,000 in 1850 and then tenfolc
300,000 by 1870. The city's growth reflected the nation's growth, as products a
people passed through Chicago's formidable rail and shipping network, supply
lumber and steel to the emerging West and grain and meat to the established E
By the 1880s a ring of cable-car tracks linking neighborhoods to the downtown
created the "Loop" sobriquet, a nickname made official by the 1897 constructior
the Union Loop Elevated, connecting transit lines running north, west and south.

A City Reborn – On October 8, 1871, a devastating fire destroyed, in two days ti
the entire Loop. While the conflagration was a monumental tragedy, it was also
opportunity. Fortunately, the city's industry and continental rail connections had
burned, and its commercial future was never in doubt. Architects Daniel Burnha
John Root, Louis Sullivan, William Holabird and Martin Roche were drawn to Chica
by the prospect of rebuilding a metropolis. Skyrocketing land values encouraged ev
taller buildings that allowed for more rentable space on each parcel of land.
straight lines of the city's grid gave rise to rows of rectangular buildings set next
each other. Pioneering skyscrapers such as the Rookery, Monadnock, Marquette a
Reliance buildings illustrated an aesthetic that celebrated functionalism and hel
usher in the modern world. Chicago architects sank foundations into the swampy sc
developed windbracing and fireproofing techniques, and erected continuously hig
steel frames. They developed an artistry based on engineering that would be en
lated worldwide.
The 1890s witnessed the emergence of many of the city's cultural venues as it sou
to dispel its frontier, money-grubbing image. The Art Institute (founded in 187
Public Library and Opera provided stylish landmarks in the Loop, while the ne
wealthy were drawn by the shopping attractions of State Street's palatial departm
stores and the ostentatious Palmer House Hotel. Prior to the Great Fire, real est
investor Potter Palmer determined that State Street should replace Lake Street as
retail thoroughfare, and he lured Field, Leiter & Co. (later Marshall Field & Co.)
move their substantial dry-goods business to the street—then lined by a disparate c
lection of laundries and stables.
The new Loop claimed distinct areas—the Water Street Market fronted the river, wi
LaSalle and Clark Streets hosted banks, attorneys and government offices. La
Street's retail strength was dealt a permanent blow by the construction of the e
vated train, or "L," in 1897, while State Street grew rapidly, much to Palmer's bene
Wabash Avenue mixed retail with music businesses, and Michigan Avenue evolved in
a cultural boulevard stretching from the auspicious Auditorium Building to the gra
Public Library. The South Loop around the various train stations became a red-lic
district, while theater marquees lined Randolph Street on the north.

20C Development – The Loop thrived as the economic, political and cultural heart
Chicago for the first half of the 20C. **State Street** became "that Great Street" with ei
department stores, some a full block long. LaSalle Street became synonymous w
the financial district, a half-mile canyon of stock exchanges, banks and business
Michigan Avenue added Orchestra Hall, new offices and private clubs to its impr
sive facade overlooking Grant Park. The nature of the Loop began to change in
1920s as the famous 1909 Plan of Chicago was implemented. Grant Park v
redesigned as a Beaux-Arts promenade, the South Water Street Market was relocat
allowing for the creation of two-level Wacker Drive, while the Michigan Avenue Bric
spurred the development of the North Side.

n-rise construction continued until the Great Depression, and stunning Art Deco
landmarks like the Board of Trade Building dominated the skyline. The end of World
War II heralded drastic change: the new automobile culture, with its suburban housing
developments and shopping malls, threatened the vitality of an area defined by steel
rails. The Loop became the retail center for the urban poor, accelerating the decline
of State Street, which was being rapidly supplanted by North Michigan Avenue as the
principal commercial thoroughfare. While business and commerce continued to prod
the erection of new skyscrapers after 1955, the Loop lost many of its retail and entertainment functions and became a "daytime" environment. By the early 1970s the city
declared the North Loop "slum and blighted" and pushed for its redevelopment, a
move seen as a reaction to the African-American clientele of North Loop retailers and
theaters. State Street was transformed into a pedestrian mall in 1978, but retail
activity remained in a slump. In an effort to revive local commerce, State Street was
reopened to vehicular traffic in 1996; its sidewalks were transformed with Victorian-
style streetlights, subway entrances and decorative plantings.

Architecture continued to flourish. World-famous architects such as Helmut Jahn, Philip
Johnson and Cesar Pelli flocked to the "home of the skyscraper" to erect new office
towers along Wacker Drive in the 1980s, before the 1990 recession halted construction. Today the Loop strives to re-create its origins, encouraging residential and
institutional uses along the older commercial streets and continuing to attract tourists
with shopping, architecture and its new theater district. At the beginning of the 21C,
Mayor Daley is also encouraging the development of cafes, bars and walkways along the
Chicago River, in an effort to return to the city's waterway as a source of recreation.

⊔ WALKING TOUR: THE LOOP'S CORE *Distance: 3.3mi*

A walking tour of the Loop combines the vitality of a commercial hub with a wonderful collection of art and architecture, including the Chicago skyscrapers that
revolutionized architecture in the late 19C, towers rendered in the Art Deco,
International and post-Modern styles, and a panoply of modern sculpture. The Loop
bustles with pedestrians from the predawn opening of the stock, commodities and
options markets until early evening. *Along State Street a "cultural walk" describes
the street's history and architecture in colorfully illustrated panels on each block.*

*Begin at Congress Pkwy. and S. Michigan Ave. Note that sights located in the western
section of the Loop, including the Sears Tower, appear after the Walking Tour.*

South Michigan Avenue★ forms the eastern facade of the Loop, a mile of attractive historic buildings facing Grant Park and presenting an inviting front door to the City
on the Lake. Unfortunately, it is almost impossible to admire the detailing adorning
the high rises from the sidewalk. Several vantage points—including the front steps
of the Art Institute—on the east side of the avenue afford good views of the elaborate facades.

Auditorium Building – *430
S. Michigan Ave. Theater
may be visited by guided
tour (1hr) only; call ahead
for times. $4. Reservations
required.* ▯ ☏ *312-431-
2354.* This building
launched the career of architects **Dankmar Adler and
Louis Sullivan**. Influenced by
H.H. Richardson's Marshall
Field Wholesale Store (now
demolished), the Audito-
rium Building ranked as the
tallest and heaviest structure in Chicago when it was
completed in 1889. The pioneering multi-use building
was also the first con-
structed under electric
lights at night, and incorporated a 400-room hotel, a
17-story office tower and a
4,000-seat theater. The Auditorium also influenced the
design of the Congress
Hotel (1893, Clinton J.
Warren), located immedi-
ately south and originally
called the Auditorium
Annex.

Wabash Station, Lake Street

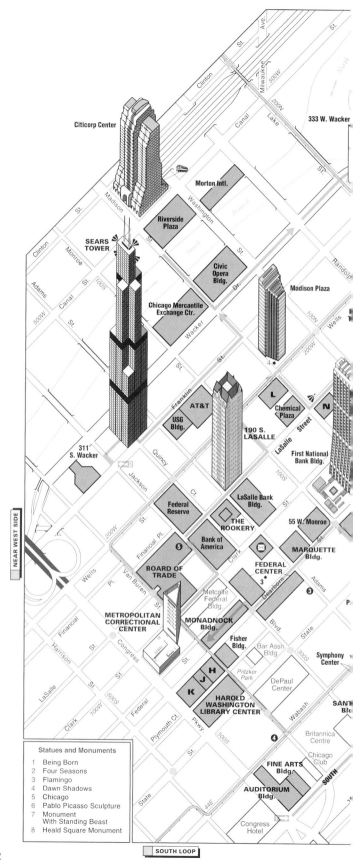

Citicorp Center

333 W. Wacker

Morton Intl.

Riverside Plaza

SEARS TOWER

Civic Opera Bldg.

Madison Plaza

Chicago Mercantile Exchange Ctr.

311' S. Wacker

AT&T

USG Bldg.

190 S. LASALLE

Chemical Plaza

L

N

First National Bank Bldg.

Federal Reserve

LaSalle Bank Bldg.

THE ROOKERY

55 W. Monroe

Bank of America

MARQUETTE Bldg.

BOARD OF TRADE

FEDERAL CENTER

METROPOLITAN CORRECTIONAL CENTER

MONADNOCK Bldg.

Metcalfe Federal Bldg.

Fisher Bldg.

Bar Assn. Bldg.

Symphony Center

Pritzker Park

DePaul Center

H

J

K

HAROLD WASHINGTON LIBRARY CENTER

SANT Bl

Britannica Centre

Chicago Club

FINE ARTS Bldg.

AUDITORIUM Bldg.

Congress Hotel

NEAR WEST SIDE

Statues and Monuments

1 Being Born
2 Four Seasons
3 Flamingo
4 Dawn Shadows
5 Chicago
6 Pablo Picasso Sculpture
7 Monument
  With Standing Beast
8 Heald Square Monument

SOUTH LOOP

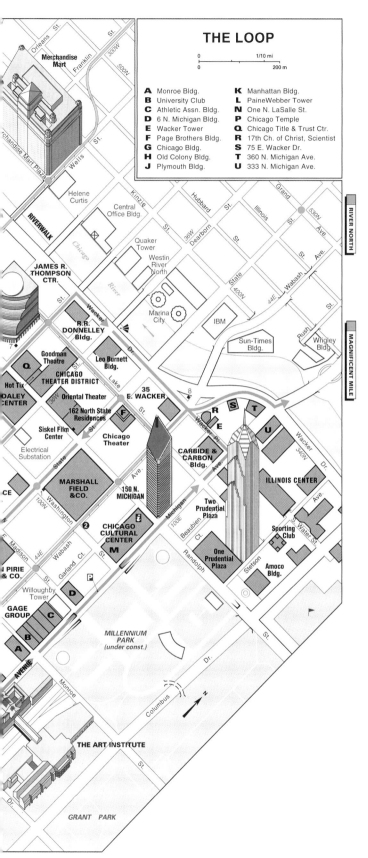

THE LOOP

0   1/10 mi
0   200 m

A Monroe Bldg.
B University Club
C Athletic Assn. Bldg.
D 6 N. Michigan Bldg.
E Wacker Tower
F Page Brothers Bldg.
G Chicago Bldg.
H Old Colony Bldg.
J Plymouth Bldg.

K Manhattan Bldg.
L PaineWebber Tower
N One N. LaSalle St.
P Chicago Temple
Q Chicago Title & Trust Ctr.
R 17th Ch. of Christ, Scientist
S 75 E. Wacker Dr.
T 360 N. Michigan Ave.
U 333 N. Michigan Ave.

RIVER NORTH

MAGNIFICENT MILE

Merchandise Mart

Orleans St.
Franklin
300W
500N

Helene Curtis

Central Office Bldg.

Kinzie St.

Hubbard

Illinois

Grand

590N

Ave.

RIVERWALK

Chicago River

Quaker Tower

Westin River North

Dearborn

36W

State

400N

Wabash

44E

Rush

St.

JAMES R. THOMPSON CTR.

Marina City

IBM

Sun-Times Bldg.

Wrigley Bldg.

R.R. DONNELLEY Bldg.

Wacker Dr.

Lake

Goodman Theatre

Leo Burnett Bldg.

35 E. WACKER

Q

Hot Tix

DALEY CENTER

CHICAGO THEATER DISTRICT

30W

Oriental Theater

162 North State Residences

Siskel Film Center

F

Chicago Theater

CARBIDE & CARBON Bldg.

R S T

E

U

Wacker

340N

ILLINOIS CENTER

Electrical Substation

State

MARSHALL FIELD &CO.

150 N. MICHIGAN

Ave.

Michigan Ave.

100E

Two Prudential Plaza

Ave.

Water St.

Sporting Club

CE

Washington

100N

CHICAGO CULTURAL CENTER

M

Beaubien Ct.

One Prudential Plaza

Amoco Bldg.

N PIRIE & CO.

Madison

44E

Wabash

Garland Ct.

Randolph

Stetson

St.

Willoughby Tower

P

D

GAGE GROUP

C

B

A

AVENUE

Monroe

MILLENNIUM PARK (under const.)

Dr.

Columbus

N

THE ART INSTITUTE

St.

GRANT PARK

Dr.

The design of the Auditorium Theatre *(50 E. Congress Pkwy.)* by engir Dankmar Adler is still considered an acoustic marvel: a young draftsman on project named Frank Lloyd Wright called it "the greatest room for music and op in the world—bar none." The Chicago Symphony Orchestra, headed by Theoc Thomas, first played at the Auditorium Theatre, eventually moving to the sma Orchestra Hall. Abandoned by the Civic Opera in 1929, the Auditorium would h been torn down but for its exceptional size and weight. It served as a USO ce during World War II, with bowling alleys installed on the stage. In 1946 **Roos University** converted the hotel and office areas for its use. The widening of Cong Parkway in the 1950s turned the southern bay of the first floor into a pedest arcade, destroying several rooms. In 1967 the Auditorium Theatre Council resto the theater, which now hosts major Broadway musicals and ballet. The facac a symphony of design, rising from rough granite to smooth limestone in a se of Romanesque arcades. Walk into the lobby to admire some of Sullivan's intri organic floriated design, as well as a small exhibit describing the building's his and construction.

Walk north on S. Michigan Ave.

★**Fine Arts Building** – *410 S. Michigan Ave. Open year-round Mon–Sat 8am–9 Sun 10am–4pm.* ✗ ⅊ ☎ *312-427-7602.* This 10-story structure (1885, Solo Beman) symbolizes the transition of South Michigan Avenue from a comme and residential street to an artistic and cultural center. The "Studebaker" na inscribed above the first floor indicates its original use as a wagon showroom 1898 Beman redesigned it as the Fine Arts Building, adding theater and stu spaces and altering the roofline to match the Auditorium Building. The stone terra-cotta structure, which features Romanesque windows, column capitals arched entrances, hosted several luminaries: architect Frank Lloyd Wright, Wil Denslow, who prepared his illustrations for *The Wizard of Oz* in the building, Harriet Monroe, whose *Poetry* magazine began here in 1911. From 1914 to 1 Margaret Anderson's radical literary journal, *The Little Review,* was published h introducing a reluctant America to James Joyce's *Ulysses.* Maurice Brown and B Van Volkenburg's influential Little Theater (1912-17) on the fourth floor he define 20C art theater across the country. The building still houses dance and m studios. Take the old-fashioned, manually operated elevator to the 10th floc view eight beautiful **murals** created by artists of The Little Room—a gatherin resident artists formed in 1892—including Frederic Clay Bartlett and R Clarkson.

The 1929 red Romanesque Revival Chicago Club *(corner of S. Michigan Ave. Van Buren St.)* mimics the original Burnham & Root building that collapsed du renovation in 1929.

Cross Van Buren St. and continue north.

At 310 South Michigan Avenue stands Britannica Centre, formerly the S.W. St Building, today home to the Encyclopedia Britannica Co. At night six 1,000-w light bulbs enclosed in a blue box illuminate the glass beehive adorning the r The imposing structure was erected one year after Chicago's 1923 zoning which allowed construction of buildings taller than 260ft, as long as setbacks w incorporated into the design.

Cross Jackson Blvd.

★**Santa Fe Building** – *224 S. Michigan Ave.* Formerly known as the Rail Exchange Building, this 1904 design by D.H. Burnham & Co., finely detaile pale terra-cotta, combines the structure of the Chicago school with the w Neoclassical ornament popularized by the 1893 World's Columbian Exposit Burnham was both architect and developer, moving into the building and ducing his famous 1909 Plan of Chicago here. Step in to see the two-story atri reminiscent of Burnham & Root's Rookery with its grand staircase, balustra mezzanine and elaborate metal light standards.

The not-for-profit **Chicago Architecture Foundation Shop and Tour Center** located ▮ offers some of the city's best neighborhood tours, as well as free lectures and t porary exhibits *(open year-round Mon–Sat 9am–7pm, Sun 9:30am–6pm; clc Jan 1, Easter Sunday, Thanksgiving Day & Dec 25;* ⅊ ☎ *312-922-8€ www.architecture.org).*

Orchestra Hall at Symphony Center – *220 S. Michigan Ave.* ☎ *312-294-30 www.chicagosymphony.org.* Cornerstone of Symphony Center is the 1904 Orc tra Hall, home of the world-famous Chicago Symphony Orchestra. The Georg style hall was planned by orchestra founder Theodore Thomas and completed a his death by D.H. Burnham & Co. In 1993 Daniel Barenboim succeeded the n Sir Georg Solti as conductor of the prestigious orchestra. Barenboim currently se as the Symphony's Music Director with Pierre Boulez as Principal Guest Conduc In 1997 a $110 million renovation and expansion were completed, which impro the main hall's acoustics and doubled the building's space to 291,000sq ft. The new space includes **ECHO**, an interactive music learning center on the ground floor, and an elegant new restaurant, **Rhapsody**, which serves innovative American cuisine in the elegant dining room or on a landscaped outdoor terrace.

Dominating the Grant Park side of South Michigan Avenue, between Jackson Boulevard and Monroe Street, is the imposing facade of the **Art Institute**. At the corner with Adams Street, look north to view **One Prudential Plaza** (1955, Naess & Murphy), the first high rise built after the Great Depression and the tallest in Chicago when it was completed. It is now dwarfed by **Two Prudential Plaza** (1990, Loebl, Schlossman & Hackl), with its dramatic needle-like spire and chevron roofline. Farther east, the **Amoco Building**,

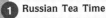

1 Russian Tea Time

Map p 73. 77 E. Adams St.
☎ *312-360-0000.*
Distinguished by red velvet furnishings, this elegant tea room located one block west of the Chicago Art Institute buzzes with the polite chatter of classical music lovers when the symphony or opera performs. Fine caviar and champagne are de rigueur in the evening as is tea in the afternoon. The restaurant also offers a complete menu featuring Russian, Uzbek, Ukrainian and Baltic delicacies.

ninth tallest in the world and Chicago's second tallest, was designed in 1973 by Edward Durell Stone and Perkins & Will. After a time, the thin marble sheathing began to warp, and the entire building was refaced with thicker North Carolina granite in 1990 at a cost equal to the original construction.

Cross Adams St. and continue north.

People's Gas Building *(122 S. Michigan Ave.)* is a massive Beaux-Arts high rise executed in 1910 by D.H. Burnham & Co. for the city's major natural-gas supplier. Here the steel framework characteristic of the Chicago school is almost entirely disguised with two-story granite Ionic columns, terra-cotta fretwork and stone lion heads.

Continue north to the corner of S. Michigan Ave. and Monroe St.

The **Monroe Building** (**A**) *(104 S. Michigan Ave.)* and **University Club** (**B**) *(76 E. Monroe St.)* were designed in 1912 and 1908 respectively by Holabird & Roche to cater to the eclectic tastes of the early 20C. The Monroe Building features Mediterranean columns, Gothic terra-cotta ornament and a gabled roof. Its narrow yet elegant L-shaped **lobby** incorporates vaulted ceilings and blind arcades of Rookwood tile. The Monroe was designed to complement the Gothic Revival University Club across the street, which also sports a gabled roof. The exterior of the private club is embellished with leaded-glass windows, protruding bays, and Gothic spires and gargoyles at the crown.

Cross Monroe St. and continue north.

Gage Group – *18-30 S. Michigan Ave.* Built for the Keith, Gage and Ascher millinery firms in 1899 by Holabird & Roche, this trio exemplifies the typical Chicago school facades that use a brick curtain wall to express the skeletal steel frame. In traditional construction, the walls supported the buildings. The Chicago school reversed architectural tradition by making the building (a steel frame) support the walls, which were draped on the iron skeleton like a curtain. Note the facade by Louis Sullivan at no. 18, where his typical flowery ornament enlivens the spandrels and explodes from the piers at the cornice.

Adjacent to the Gage Building, the **Chicago Athletic Association Building** (**C**) (1893, Henry Ives Cobb) draws attention by the interweaving Venetian Gothic trefoil arches adorning its richly varied facade. The 1929 Willoughby Tower *(8 S. Michigan Ave.)* applies Gothic ornament to an Art Deco facade.

Cross Madison St. and continue north.

6 North Michigan Building (**D**), executed in 1899 by Richard E. Schmidt, was the site of Montgomery Ward's nationwide mail-order business. Aaron Montgomery Ward performed a great service to Chicago when he sued to keep the lakefront (now Grant Park) free of buildings. Dedicated to the art of designing, the Chicago Athenaeum's **Museum of Architecture and Design** *(entrance on Madison St.)* presents five rotating exhibits a year.

Cross Washington St.

Chicago Cultural Center – *78 E. Washington St. Open year-round Mon–Wed 10am–7pm, Thu 10am–9pm, Fri 10am–6pm, Sat 10am–5pm, Sun 11am–5pm. Closed major holidays. Guided tours (1hr) leave from Randolph St. lobby Tue–Sat 1:15pm. ⚹ ⛨ ☎ 312-744-6630. www.cityofchicago.org/tour/culturalcenter.* This marvelous Neoclassical palazzo served as the city's first library when completed in 1897 after designs by Shepley, Rutan & Coolidge, who also designed the Art

Chicago Cultural Center, Stairway

Institute. Noteworthy elements include a smooth limestone facade, reces
windows and elaborate Renaissance moldings at the entrance, cornice and
conies. Step inside to admire the inlaid-marble grand stairway that ascends f
the Washington Street entrance to **Preston Bradley Hall★**, with its Tiffany stained-g
dome. Visit any Wednesday at 12:15pm and Preston Bradley Hall reverberates v
the classical sounds of the Dame Myra Hess Memorial Concert series. Another m
nificent stained-glass dome is located on the north end of the second floor.
A wide array of free public programs is offered here daily, including concerts, f
dance, lectures and art exhibits. This is also the home of the Chicago Departm
of Cultural Affairs, the Museum of Broadcast Communications and the **Chicago C
of Tourism Visitor Information Center** *(north side of building, 1st floor)*. A good p
to start a Loop tour, the information center features an exhibit on the history
the Loop and a 7min video tour of Chicago's "downtown neighborhood" in e
languages *(open year-round Mon–Fri 10am–6pm, Sat 10am–5pm, Sun noon–5,
closed major holidays; & ☎ 312-744-2400)*. The Landmark Chicago Gallery *(v
side of building)* exhibits photographs of historic buildings throughout the c

Museum of Broadcast Communications (**M**) – *Open year-round Mon–Sat 10am–4:30
Sun noon–5pm. Closed major holidays. ✗ & ☎ 312-629-6000. www.mbcnet.c*
Located on the ground floor of the Cultural Center, the museum is one of two
its kind in the country (the other is in New York City). The MBC Television Ce
(to the right of the Washington St. entrance) provides an opportunity to dc
news anchor's jacket and report news on video with a TelePrompTer *($19.95, c
includes a copy of the videotape; tapings are conducted every 20min)*. To the
of the entrance is the Radio Hall of Fame, which includes a radio studio and exh
celebrating famous radio personalities.

Behind the main staircase is the television gallery, with video loops illustrating g
moments in Chicago television history, such as the famous Kennedy-Nixon debate
1960. Early Chicago television personalities such as Studs Terkel and Dave Garro
are lionized here along with modern stars Oprah Winfrey and Siskel & Ebert.
second-floor archives *(closed Sun)* store 10,000 television programs, 50,000 hc
of radio programs, 2,500 newscasts and some 9,000 commercials, indexed on a c
puter catalog. *After locating your video or radio selection, you may use one of
26 study booths for a $3/day fee (free to MBC members).*

Cross Randolph St. and continue north on N. Michigan Ave.

The unique roofline of **150 North Michigan Avenue★** (1984, A. Epstein & Sons), sl
at a beveled angle and set at a 45-degree angle to the street, marks the enc
Michigan Avenue's Grant Park frontage.

Cross Lake St. and continue north.

Extending over 83 acres along the east side of North Michigan Avenue, **Ill
Center** *(between Michigan Ave., N. Lake Shore Dr., the river and Lake St.)* compr
more than a dozen buildings, grand in conception but muted and sterile in exe
tion. One of the world's largest mixed-use projects was first envisioned in the 19
for the air rights of the Illinois Central Railroad, which has run along the lakefr

since the 1850s. Built in the 1970s and 1980s, mostly by the successor firms of Mies van der Rohe, the complex includes hotels, offices, shops, apartments and the Illinois Golf Center, a nine-hole course reputed to be the first urban golf course. The small **Sporting Club** (1990, Kisho Kurokawa) is recognizable by its four white, framework towers that pay homage to Louis Sullivan and sport 17ft wind sculptures, called *Children of the Sun*, by Osamu Shingu.

Continue to Wacker Pl.

★**Carbide and Carbon Building** – *230 N. Michigan Ave.* This Art Deco skyscraper (1929, Burnham Bros.), inspired by Raymond Hood's American Radiator Building in New York, is faced with dark green terra-cotta accented with gold-leaf ornament, especially on the stepped-back tower. A two-story lobby features curvilinear and geometric ornament with incised carving characteristic of the Deco style.

Turn left on Wacker Pl.

Designed in 1928 for the Chicago Motor Club by Holabird & Root, **Wacker Tower** (**E**) (*68 E. Wacker Pl.*) is a good example of the Art Deco style, defined by setbacks,

② Heaven on Seven
Map p 73. 111 N. Wabash Ave., 7th floor of Garland Building. ☎ *312-263-6443.* Creole shrimp, crab cakes, po'boy sandwiches and gumbo are just a few of the New Orleans-style dishes served in this small but bustling lunchroom *(open for dinner only on 1st & 3rd Fri of the month).* Most entrées are served plenty spicy, but connoisseurs of Cajun heat use the bottles of Louisiana hot sauce on the tables to season their food. For a sweet ending, try a healthy serving of cinnamon-spiked bread pudding.
A slicker version of the original, **Heaven on Seven on Rush** *(600 N. Michigan Ave., between Ohio & Rush Sts., 2nd floor;* ☎ *312-280-7774)* serves lunch and dinner daily.

continuous piers and recessed windows that emphasize the vertical. The **lobby**★ features a 1920s transcontinental highway map by John W. Norton.

Visible just north of the river are the "corncob" towers of the Marina City complex.

Turn left on Wabash Ave., right on Lake St. and continue to State St.

This section of Lake Street is located beneath the elevated Loop railway, first erected in 1897 to connect the various railroad lines serving the central business district. Marking the southeast corner of State and Lake Streets, the **Page Brothers Building** (**F**) (1872, John Mills Van Osdel) features a cast-iron Italianate facade *(Lake St. side)* and is a rare survivor of the building boom that followed the Great Fire of 1871.

Turn left onto State St. and continue south.

One of the city's earliest and largest (4,000 seats) vaudeville movie palaces, the **Chicago Theatre**★ *(175 N. State St.)*, designed by Rapp & Rapp in 1921, is French Renaissance in inspiration. Its terra-cotta facade and multistory **lobby**★ were restored in 1985 after narrowly avoiding demolition.

At the northwest corner of State and Randolph Streets, the **Siskel Film Center** and **162 North State Residences** of the Art Institute of Chicago incorporate the facade of the Old Heidelberg restaurant (1934, Graham, Anderson, Probst and White) on Randolph and the 1924 terra-cotta Butler Building on State in a white concrete design (2000, Booth/Hansen Associate of Chicago). The oversized cornice and attic level with porthole windows contains art studios, while the ground level features retail stores and the school's famed Siskel Film Center.

Cross Randolph St.

★**Marshall Field & Company** – *Bounded by State, Randolph and Washington Sts. and Wabash Ave. Open year-round Mon–Fri 9:45am–7pm (Thu til 8pm), Sat 10am–6pm, Sun 11am–6pm. Closed major holidays.* ✗ ⅍ ◪*(fee varies).* ☎ *312-781-1000. www.marshallfields.com.* Occupying an entire city block, this building was constructed in several stages between 1892 and 1914 by D.H. Burnham & Co., combining the firm's structural engineering innovations with the Neoclassicism made popular by the World's Columbian Exposition of 1893. Marshall Field's career in commerce began in the dry-goods business with partners Potter Palmer and Levi Leiter. In the 1860s Palmer left to focus on real estate, and Leiter split off shortly afterwards. Field became the preeminent department store retailer, succeeding under the dictum "Give the Lady What She Wants." The richly embellished clocks that ornament the corners on State Street are Chicago icons. The interior contains over one million square feet of retail space and features a Tiffany favrile dome *(near State and Washington Sts.)* as well as a new atrium resulting from a $110 million renovation.

Virginio Ferrari's *Being Born* (**1**) sculpture *(corner of State and Washington Sts.)* celebrates both the city and the precision metalwork of the "tool and die" industry that sponsored it.

■ Looping the Loop

Most Chicagoans agree that the Loop is best explored on foot. However, the city offers some fun alternative methods of exploring the Loop.

By bus: Chicago Architecture Foundation proposes an overview of the city that includes a drive through the Loop. Or hop aboard a 🚌 no. 151 bus at Wacker Drive and Michigan Avenue, grab a window seat and enjoy the view *(the bus crosses the Loop, stops at Union Station, then returns to State St.).*

By boat: The best way to view the riverfront skyscrapers, river and lake cruises are available from several tour operators and provide a fascinating look at the Loop's architectural diversity.

By "L": The elevated Brown line (Ravenswood) circles the Loop, affording an intriguing, if noisy, glimpse of the bustling activity.

By train: Departing at the corner of Randolph Street and Wabash Avenue, this "chartered" free 40min train tour offers the same views as the "L" *(May–Sept, Sat 11:35am & 12:55pm).* Tickets are available daily at the Visitor Information Center in the Chicago Cultural Center.

★★Reliance Building – N. State St., at corner Washington St. Years ahead of its time, this building anticipated the glass and steel skyscrapers of Mies van der Rohe and the Second Chicago school of the 1930s through 1970s. In 1895, a decade after the invention of the skyscraper, **Charles Atwood** of D.H. Burnham & Co. realized the possibilities inherent in skeletal frame construction and designed the Reliance Building. The facade is almost entirely glass. Extremely narrow piers and spandrels between floors, featuring Gothic ornamentation in creamy white terra-cotta, reduce the solid exterior walls to a minimum. Projecting bays create a play of light across the facade and allow more light into the interior. Initially occupied by dentists and doctors, the structure was neglected for half a century before its 1999 restoration as the

122-room **Hotel Burnham** (☎ 312-782-1111; www.burnhamhotel.com). The new hotel retains many of the building's original elements, including the ornamental iron work elevator grills and the marble mosaic floor in the elevator lobby.

Continue south on State St. to Madison St.

The corner of State and Madison is the heart of Chicago's rectilinear street grid, with all addresses to the north reading "North," to the south "South," and so forth.

Facade of Carson Pirie Scott Store

All four corner buildings exhibit the typical "Chicago window." The rusticated brown **Chicago Building** (or at 7 West Madison Street (1904, Holabird & Roche) exemplifies an early skyscraper divided into a base, shaft and crown. Of note are the projecting bays of Chicago windows and the fancy cornice. In 1997 the office tower was rehabilitated as a dormitory for the nearby School of the Art Institute of Chicago.

★★★Carson Pirie Scott & Company – 1 S. State St. Open year-round Mon–Fri 9:45am–7pm, Sat 9:45am–6pm, Sun 11am–6pm; hours vary seasonally. Closed Easter Sunday, Thanksgiving Day & Dec 25. ✗ ♿ ☎ 312-641-7000. Designed by **Louis Sullivan** in 1899, this structure is considered his greatest work. Sullivan decreed that "form follows function," yet he was the consummate 19C ornamentalist, and his gift is nowhere more apparent than here. The upper stories are white terra-cotta plainly expressing the steel grid underneath, but the first two floors are bedecked with some of the most elaborate and plastic designs ever created by Sullivan. His ability to produce foliate ornament in three dimensions is best seen in the rounded corner, where the cast iron reaches out to create portholes that hover above the glass, making a massive building seem light and airy. In a sense, form was following function, as the ornament was designed to attract shoppers to the goods in the windows.

Cross Monroe St.

The **Palmer House Hilton** (1927, Holabird & Roche), located at the southeast corner of State and Monroe Streets, is the fourth of this name founded by real estate mogul Potter Palmer. The luxurious interior features a grand Beaux-Arts second-floor **lobby**★ and the Empire Ballroom.

Turn right on Monroe St. and continue to Dearborn St.

★**Inland Steel Building** – *30 W. Monroe St.* This elegant high rise (1958, Skidmore, Owings & Merrill) must have been an apparition when it opened, its shining stainless-steel facade surrounded by masonry buildings that were dark with soot. Bruce Graham designed a unique structural cage that supports the building outside of the wall plane, creating column-free floors. To achieve this, steel pilings were anchored 85ft deep into the bedrock, while the mechanical and elevator systems were placed in a windowless steel tower to the east. In addition to innovative engineering techniques, Inland Steel also pioneered the use of air-conditioning and dual glazing for windows. The lobby is graced by Richard Lippold's *Radiant I*, a three-dimensional web of steel rods and wires.

At Dearborn Street, look north to the gracefully rising concave facade of the 60-story **First National Bank Building**, designed in 1969 by Perkins & Will. The edifice has extremely wide bays sheltering a large bank on the lower floors and offices above. The popular plaza, known for its summer lunchtime concerts, surrounds the rectangular *Four Seasons* (**2**) mosaic created by artist Marc Chagall in 1974.

Walk south on Dearborn St.

The **55 West Monroe Building**, formerly the Xerox Centre (1980, C.F. Murphy Assocs.), sports the mirrored wall surfaces and curving facades favored by chief architect Helmut Jahn.

★★**Marquette Building** – *140 S. Dearborn St.* Considered one of Holabird & Roche's skyscraper masterpieces, this 1895 Chicago school design expresses the structural frame in the finely detailed terra-cotta and brick exterior. The piers project forward from the windows, creating a soaring grid best appreciated by looking up from the entrance. The corners are emphasized to suggest solidity. Four bronze panels above the entrance illustrate journal writings of French explorer-missionary Jacques Marquette, one of the first Europeans to visit the Chicago region. The hexagonal lobby features a stunning Tiffany glass **mosaic**★ by J.A. Holzer illustrating Marquette's journey in the Mississippi River basin, as well as bas-reliefs of early French explorers and Native Americans by Edward Kemeys.

Cross Adams St.

★★**Federal Center** – *On Dearborn St. between Adams St. and Jackson Blvd.* Designed by **Ludwig Mies van der Rohe** in 1964 and completed ten years later, this three-building complex is an excellent example of International-style architecture and urban

Flamingo by Alexander Calder

③ The Berghoff

Map p 72. 17 W. Adams St.
☎ *312-427-3170.* Founded
in 1898 by brewer Herman
Berghoff, this spacious
German restaurant is one of
the oldest operating taverns
in the city. The sauerbraten,
schnitzel and creamed
spinach draw huge lunchtime
crowds. The adjacent stand-
up bar (no seating), best
known for its bratwurst and
its potato salad, caters to
diners on the run. The
Berghoff sponsors a raucous
outdoor Oktoberfest
celebration every second
weekend in September.

space. The one-story post office is as tall
as the lobbies of the Dirksen and Kluczyn-
ski buildings, set at right angles to each
other across Dearborn Street. All three
buildings frame the beautiful plaza graced
by Alexander Calder's 1973 **Flamingo** (**3**),
which seems to suggest steel beams that
have leapt off the building to dance a
bright red ballet. Mies van der Rohe's
buildings appear stark and unadorned,
but their beauty depends on rigid adher-
ence to laws of proportion, and the edifices are ornamented by attached I-beams
that run up the facade like vertical ribs.

★★**Monadnock Building** – *53 W. Jackson
Blvd.* Behind the Federal Center rises a
long, narrow building defining the architectural revolution that saw bricks replaced
by steel. The northern half of the building
(1891, Burnham & Root) is the tallest masonry structure in Chicago. Walls 6ft thick
at the base support 16 stories plus an attic of bricks piled on bricks (the thickness
of the walls can be seen in the window openings on the ground floor). Peter and
Shepherd Brooks developed the structure, insisting on brick, which they thought was
more fireproof than the new steel technology. They also didn't want to pay for ornament. It must have shocked Victorian Chicagoans to see a "naked" building rising
in this section of the Loop. Architect John Wellborn Root said its design, flared at the
base and crown, was based on an Egyptian papyrus or the capital letter "I." Root's
skills are apparent in the muscularity of the bays that ripple out of the wall plane
along Dearborn Street. The southern half of the building (1893, Holabird & Roche)
is partially braced by a steel frame and features more traditional ornament.

Walk south through the lobby of the Monadnock Building.

The **interior**★ was painstakingly restored to its original design in the 1980s, including
replication of the mosaic floor, fragments of which are preserved beneath glass at
the north entrance and south elevators. The original marble ceiling and restored
marble walls are ornamented by cast-aluminum light fixtures and a staircase in
foliate forms reminiscent of the Rookery. The large interior shop windows provide
a second "street" for retailers and bring precious light into the corridor from outside.

Exit the lobby at Van Buren St., turn left and walk east.

Located at 343 South Dearborn Street, the Gothic-style **Fisher Building** (1896,
D.H. Burnham & Co.), inspired by the Reliance Building, is faced with light orange

④ Prairie Avenue Bookshop

*Map p 72. 418 S. Wabash
Ave.* ☎ *312-922-8311.
www.pabook.com.* Set into
a frame of white terra-cotta,
the double-height glass
facade of the bookstore
encloses 9,000sq ft
chockablock with new, used,
and rare books on every
aspect of building and
environmental design that
can easily ensnare the
architecture enthusiast for
hours. Dubbed the "best
architectural bookshop in
the world" by the *London
Financial Times*, Prairie
Avenue Bookshop was
established by Marilyn
Hasbrouck in 1961 as a
mail-order service. The shop
opened on Prairie Avenue in
the South Loop in 1974 and
operated there for two
decades before moving
to its present quarters.

terra-cotta that includes playful references to the owner's name in the form
of sculpted fish surrounding the edifice's
former entrance in the center of the Van
Buren Street facade.

Farther east, on the left, are the
Chicago Bar Association Building
(1990, Tigerman McCurry) with its
spindly top, and tiny Pritzker Park, designed after René Magritte's *The Ban-
quet*, housed at the Art Institute. Visible across the park, the block-long,
white terra-cotta facade of the DePaul
Center is a 1993 restoration of a 1912
Holabird & Roche department store.

★**Harold Washington Library Center** –
*400 S. State St., bounded by Van Buren
St., Congress Pkwy., and Plymouth Ct.
Open year-round Mon–Thu 9am–7pm,
Fri–Sat 9am–5pm, Sun 1pm–5pm.
Closed major holidays.* ☎ *312-747-
4999. www.chipublib.org.* Hammond,
Beeby & Babka won a competition to design Chicago's new library, a grandly
scaled 1991 design that announces its
public function with classical arcaded facades, ornamental garlands and an over-
achieving roofline of green metal and
glass with looming owls. The building's

rusticated base refers to landmarks such as the Auditorium and Marquette buildings. Inside, a mosaic mural on the sterile first floor memorializes the city's first African-American mayor, the building's namesake. Reading rooms fill floors three through eight, and a large skylit "winter garden" tops out the structure. The western facade is a post-Modern glass wall, reflecting the historic structures across the street.

Backtrack on Van Buren St. and cross Dearborn St.

Look south on Dearborn to admire a trio of late-19C buildings. The **Old Colony Building** (**H**) (1894, Holabird & Roche), at 407 South Dearborn Street, is the only downtown structure with rounded corners, a hallmark of the Victorian era. Located next door at no. 417, the **Plymouth Building** (**J**) (1899, Simeon B. Eisendrath) illustrates the use of Gothic ornament to illuminate high-rise towers. The **Manhattan Building** (**K**) (1891, William Le Baron Jenney), at no. 431, is an experiment in decoration, with polygonal and rounded bays, a granite base and a variety of ornament such as the grotesque faces that stare at passersby from the bottom of each protruding bay.

Continue west on Van Buren St.

★**Metropolitan Correctional Center** – *On Van Buren St. between Clark and Federal Sts.* Appearing almost two-dimensional, this unique concrete structure (1975, Harry Weese & Assocs.) resembles an old IBM punch card. The triangular layout affords an easily patrolled plan for the cells holding prisoners awaiting trial in the nearby Federal Center. The cells also dictate the narrow beveled windows, which can only be 5in wide without bars. Unless the inmates are in the rooftop recreation area, it is easy to forget the building's purpose.

Turn right on Clark St.

Dominating the lobby of the Metcalfe Federal Building *(77 W. Jackson Blvd.)* is a huge Frank Stella sculpture, *The Town's Ho Story*, visible from the street.

Turn left on Jackson Blvd.

Chicago Stock Exchange, detail

★**Chicago Board of Trade Building** – *141 W. Jackson Blvd.* Considered one of the city's best Art Deco skyscrapers, the 45-story Board of Trade (1930) was designed by Holabird & Root, successor to the Chicago-school firm of Holabird & Roche. Soaring limestone piers terminating in sculptures are balanced by recessed windows and terra-cotta spandrels. The pyramidal roof is capped by John Storrs' 32ft-tall aluminum sculpture of Ceres, the goddess of the harvest, and the clock in the center of the main facade is flanked by Father Time and a Native American cradling grain. The Board of Trade was founded in 1848 to regulate the trade of grain and commodities from Illinois and the Great Plains through Chicago to the eastern seaboard. In 1980 Helmut Jahn of C.F. Murphy Assocs. designed a rear addition that defers to the older building in scale and form despite its reflective surfaces. Jahn's addition includes a lovely 12th-floor atrium with a sensuous 1930 mural of Ceres by John W. Norton. The Board of Trade recently underwent a third expansion to the east. Completed in 1997, the new 60,000sq ft annex has four floors (equivalent in height to 12 stories) and is connected to the main building by a

⑤ Everest

Map p 72. 440 S. LaSalle St., in One Financial Pl. ☎ *312-663-8920. Reservations required.* Named for its 40th-floor perch atop the Chicago Stock Exchange, Everest commands a sweeping view of the city from its lofty dining room. Award-winning chef Jean Joho (also of Brasserie Jo) crafts the finest seasonal ingredients into mouth-watering creations, often adding accents from his native Alsace. Dine à la carte or sample several of Joho's favorite starters and entrées by ordering the *dégustation* menu.

bridge spanning a landscaped pedestria mall. The beautiful four-story **lobby** the main building is decorated with ge metric forms in a variety of marble nickel-plated brass and platinum.

From the visitors galleries for the agr cultural and the new 60,000sq ft fina cial **trading floors★** *(4th floor)*, visitors ca watch frenetic traders in brightly colore jackets use elaborate hand signals ar shouts to buy and sell options as well commodities *(open year-round Mon–8am–2pm; closed major holidays; 45m guided tours available, reservations r quired for groups of 3 or more;* ☎ *312-435-3590; www.cbot.com).*

Walk north on LaSalle St.

The **LaSalle Street** "canyon" stretches fro the Board of Trade to the river, its wa formed by banks and brokerage instit tions in a unity of architecture that b lies the competitive financial wor within. The **Bank of America Building** (192 and **Federal Reserve Bank Building** (1922 both designed by Graham, Anderson, Probst & White, frame the end of LaSa Street with classical grandeur. Ionic columns and an entrance pediment on the Ban of America are mirrored by a Corinthian portal on the Federal Reserve, the ensemb a fitting anchor for the LaSalle Street canyon. The Bank of America features a r stored second-floor banking hall with a coffered ceiling and huge **murals** by Jul Guerin, illustrator of the 1909 Plan of Chicago. In the small visitor center in th Federal Reserve you can ogle—but not touch—a million dollars in cash.

Continue north on LaSalle St. to Adams St.

As you pass Quincy Court on the left, note the Sears Tower looming before yo and the elevated train station a block west.

★★ The Rookery – *At the southeast corner of LaSalle and Adams Sts.* This 1888 stru ture is one of the earliest designs by Burnham & Root and the most impressi landmark rehabilitation in the Loop. The building's name comes from a tempora city hall erected here in 1871 that attracted pigeons and other birds. A playful re erence to this attraction is found in carved birds (rooks) on either side of th entrance. Noted for the richness of John Wellborn Root's design and detailing, th 12-story facade of red granite, terra-cotta and brick is a combination Romanesque Revival and Queen Anne elements, the former apparent in the larg arched entrance. Two-story columns frame the lower retail floors, while arcad organized around the protruding entrance bay characterize the upper floors.

The square building is organized around a large **light court★★**, a device that broug natural light to interior offices in the era before gas and electric illumination. No enclosed by a domed skylight, the light court is considered a work of art in i own right. The interior was remodeled in 1906 by Frank Lloyd Wright, wh covered Root's iron columns and staircases with white marble, incised and inla with gold leaf. One side of the column to the left as you enter the atrium is expose to reveal the original Root design. This rare commercial work of Wright featur Prairie-style urns framing the central staircase to the east. The west side is dor inated by a graceful eight-story spiral staircase. The 1928 elevator lobby by Prair school architect William Drummond includes whimsical elevator doors by Annet Cremin Byrne, which again play on the building's avian nomenclature. $103 million restoration in 1992 brought the building back to its full glory.

★ 190 South LaSalle Street – *At the northwest corner of LaSalle and Adams St* Internationally renowned architects come to Chicago to realize their own work ar to pay homage to the birthplace of the skyscraper. This 1987 building by Phil Johnson recapitulates Chicago's Masonic Temple (1892, Burnham & Root, demo ished in 1939) with its distinctive cross-gabled roof and elaborate iron crestin The elegant white marble **lobby** is distinguished by red marble pilasters and ove sized lanterns, surmounted by a gilded, vaulted ceiling. Art enlivening the lobb includes a 28ft steel sculpture, *Chicago Fugue*, by Anthony Caro.

Located across the street at no. 135, the **LaSalle Bank Building** (1934, Graham Anderson, Probst & White), erected by the estate of Marshall Field, was the last hig rise built during the Great Depression. The edifice stands on the former site of th Home Insurance Building erected by William Le Baron Jenney in 1884. Step insid the huge Art Deco structure to view the lovely two-story lobby featuring chevrone skywalks, fluted chandeliers and an elevator panel in the shape of the building.

Continue north on LaSalle St., turn left on Monroe St. and walk west.

Look west to view the 1988 **AT&T Corporate Center** *(227 W. Monroe St.)*, linked to the 1992 **USG Building**, both designed by Adrian Smith of Skidmore, Owings & Merrill. The complex reinterprets Art Deco and marks a return to architecture organized around a hierarchy of detail, with ornamented window spandrels and light sconces shaped like the spires atop the structure.

Turn right on Wells St. and continue to Madison St.

At the corner of Wells and Madison Streets stands **Madison Plaza** (1982, Skidmore, Owings & Merrill), distinguished by an accordion wall of mirrored glass and steel typical of 1980s architecture. The facade, which creates numerous corner offices, provides a touchstone for Louise Nevelson's sculpture *Dawn Shadows* (**4**), an intricate group of curving black forms. Marking the southeast corner of that intersection, **PaineWebber Tower** (**L**) *(181 W. Madison St.)* is another international contribution by Cesar Pelli, with extremely narrow bays and ribbing that dramatize its verticality. Colorful found-object sculptures by Frank Stella, *Loomings* and *Knights and Squires*, decorate the barrel-vaulted lobby.

Walk east on Madison St. to LaSalle St.

Chemical Plaza *(southwest corner of LaSalle and Madison Sts.)* features the original base of a 1912 building by Holabird & Roche surmounted by a sleek addition (1989) of blue and green aluminum and glass by Moriyama & Teshima. Designed in 1930, **One North LaSalle Street** (**N**) *(northeast corner of LaSalle and Madison Sts.)* draws the eye to its fifth-floor panels depicting French explorer La Salle, who is thought to have stayed here in the late 17C.

Walk north on LaSalle St. to Washington St. and turn right.

At the intersection of LaSalle and Washington, look back for an impressive **view** of the "canyon" culminating with the Board of Trade. The ornate City Hall/County Building *(bounded by Clark, Washington, LaSalle and Randolph Sts.)* was actually built in two sections, in 1907 and 1911, by Holabird & Roche. Huge, 75ft Corinthian columns (the tallest in the city) span the fifth to ninth stories.

Continue to the intersection of Washington and Clark Sts.

Chicago Temple (**P**) – *77 W. Washington St., at the southeast corner of Washington and Clark Sts. Sanctuary open year-round daily 7am–7pm. Sky chapel accessible by guided tour (30min) only, year-round Mon–Sat 2pm, Sun 9:30am & noon. Closed major holidays.* ☎ *312-236-4548. www.chicagotemple.org.* When completed in 1923 by Holabird & Roche, this edifice was the city's tallest building and remains the tallest church spire in the world at 568ft. The First United Methodist Church occupies the large, English Gothic-style sanctuary on the first floor, as well as the sky chapel, added to the steeple in the 1950s. Encompassing only 700sq ft, the tiny gem features lovely stained-glass windows and carvings on the oak walls.

East of the temple stands Joan Miró's celebrated *Chicago* (**5**) sculpture, resembling an elemental female form. A gift to the city from the artist, the 39ft statue was erected in 1981.

★ **Richard J. Daley Center** – *Bounded by Washington, Randolph, Clark and Dearborn Sts.* In 1965 Jacques Brownson of C.F. Murphy Assocs. designed this fine example of Miesian architecture, bold and muscular as the city it represents. Massive bays 87ft wide are joined by huge, cross-shaped beams that narrow as they rise to the top. Only three bays span the main facade of tinted glass and Cor-Ten steel, designed to weather to a bronze patina resembling rust. Rising 648ft, the 31-story structure was named for the late Richard J. Daley. Cor-Ten was also used to fabricate the untitled **Pablo Picasso sculpture** (**6**) in the plaza, which stirred controversy when unveiled in 1967 but has since become a beloved symbol of the city. The building houses courtrooms and offices, while numerous cultural events and a farmers' market *(Jun–Oct every other Thu, 7am–3pm)* take place in the plaza.

The **Hot Tix** booth, offering discount and full-price tickets to major shows, is located across from Daley Center at 78 West Randolph Street.

Continue north on Clark St. and cross Randolph St.

The unusual top of the **Chicago Title & Trust Center** (**Q**) *(161 N. Clark St.)*, built in 1992 by Kohn Pedersen Fox, suggests the bascule bridges over the Chicago River. The stately white terra-cotta facades of the landmark Harris and Selwyn theaters (1922, Crane and Franzheim) have been joined to form the new **Goodman Theatre** (2000, Kuwabara Payne McKenna Blumberg) at the northeast corner of Dearborn and Randolph. Established in 1925 as a gift to the Art Institute (in its former location on South Columbus Drive), the Goodman is considered the oldest residential theater in the US.

★★ **James R. Thompson Center** – *Bounded by Clark, LaSalle, Randolph and Lake Sts.* This unusual building, formerly the State of Illinois Center, was named for the Illinois governor who chose the 1985 design by architect Helmut Jahn. Today the center houses state agencies and a large lower-level food court. Note on the plaza Jean Dubuffet's *Monument With Standing Beast* (**7**), a fiberglass sculpture of cur-

■ Chicago Theater District

The North Loop's reign as Chicago's entertainment district dates to the late 19C when the Loop was a collection of five-story walk-ups. By 1879 the Central Music Hall stood at State and Randolph; it was joined 12 years later by Adler & Sullivan's skyscraper Schiller Theater (later renamed the Garrick), which rose between Clark and Dearborn. The construction of the Woods Theater in 1917 at Randolph and Dearborn was followed by a troupe of lavishly decorated vaudeville palaces in the Roaring 20s, including the Chicago, the Oriental and the United Artists theaters. By 1920 bright movie marquees lined Chicago's "Great White Way"—Randolph Street—promoting stars of stage and screen.

In the decades following World War II, the rise of television and the flight of city dwellers to suburbia began to bring the curtain down on Randolph Street. In the early 1960s the historic Garrick Theater (formerly the Schiller) was razed and replaced with a parking garage. By the 1970s the North Loop was beset by urban blight. Although preservationists saved the **Chicago Theatre** *(175 N. State St.; ☎ 312-443-1130)* after a struggle in 1986, other venues such as the Woods (1917-88) and United Artists (1928-89) were demolished.

In the late 1990s, local developer Lew Manilow realized his 20-year-old dream of a North Loop theater district with the renovation of the **Oriental Theater** by Ford *(now the Oriental Theater/Ford Center for the Performing Arts; 24 W. Randolph St.; ☎ 312-902-1400)* and the 1999 rescue of the **Palace Theater** by Cadillac *(151 W. Randolph St.; ☎ 312-409-2900)*. That same year, the district came full circle as the parking garage that had replaced the Garrick was torn down to create the new **Goodman Theatre** *(170 N. Dearborn St.; ☎ 312-443-3800; www.goodman-theatre.org)*. In 2000 the Siskel Film Center of The School of the Art Insititute added cinema to the collection of restored live theater venues. Today theaters in the historic district, touted in colorful banners that line Randolph Street from Michigan to Wells, offer performances ranging from classic dramas such as Arthur Miller's *Death of a Salesman* and August Wilson's *The Piano Lesson* to contemporary musicals like *Blast!*.

vaceous black and white forms. The building's exterior skin of glass and past panels seems ethereal when compared to the stone and steel buildings around and its form ignores the street grid to create a sense of dramatic entry. The shap is a post-Modern reference to the Classical domes of government buildings. A vis to the soaring **atrium★** is a must, since the building is all atrium, rising the f 17 stories with glass elevators to the beveled "dome within a dome." The effe of light filtering into the space creates a play of shadows that changes constantl The open office floors and glass skin have caused heating, cooling and noise pro lems, but few visitors pass up a chance to see this quirky monument.

Continue north on Clark St. and turn right on Wacker Dr.

Across the river to the east stand the Quaker Tower and Westin River North (fc merly Hotel Nikko) development, erected in 1987. Adjacent to the Marina Ci complex, the IBM Building forces its rectangular form into a curving riverfront sit

★**R.R. Donnelley Building** – *77 W. Wacker Dr.* Celebrated Barcelona archite Ricardo Bofill designed this 1992 office tower in his "Modern Classical" style wi a pedimented top and marble elements that suggest Greek and Roman temple The firm of DeStefano & Partners supervised construction of the 50-story stru ture, one of the last skyscrapers to be erected in the Loop in the 20C. The elega **lobby** in pure white marble from Thásos, Greece, features works by Catalan artist including a wonderful Bofill fountain, *Twisted Columns*, and the rocklike *Thre Lawyers and a Judge* by sculptor Xavier Corbero, set amid live bamboo.

Cross Dearborn St. and continue east on Wacker Dr.

At this point, take a moment to absorb the splendid **view★** east toward the Wrigle Building and Michigan Avenue Bridge. Erected in 1989 by Roche & Dinkeloo ar Shaw & Assocs., the **Leo Burnett Building** *(35 W. Wacker Dr.)* resembles a Prairi school column with its division into a base, shaft and capital. The corners protrud creating more corner offices. The gray granite facade's square windows are orn mented with chrome. Lobby sculpture includes a semifigurative bronze fountai *Rite of Spring*, by Bryan Hunt.

Cross State St. and continue east on Wacker Dr.

★**35 East Wacker Drive** – Reflecting historical themes popular in the mid-1920 this buff-colored terra-cotta high rise (1926, Thielbar & Fugard) is bedecked in profusion of Beaux-Arts detailing. Originally called the Jewelers Building (note th

"JB" initials carved in terra-cotta panels on the facade), it featured a car elevator until 1940 that allowed tenants to drive into the building. The top of the structure is distinguished by four large Neoclassical lanterns at the corners, artfully disguising water tanks, as well as a 17-story central tower capped by a dome housing a presentation room for architect Helmut Jahn. In the late 1920s the 37th through 40th floors were home to Al Capone's Stratosphere, a popular watering hole.

Adorning the island in the center of Wacker Drive, the **Heald Square Monument** (**8**) (1941, Lorado Taft and Leonard Crunelle) celebrates Haym Salomon and Robert Morris, financiers of the American Revolution. Both figures flank a statue of George Washington. Marking the corner of East Wacker Drive and Wabash Avenue is the round **Seventeenth Church of Christ, Scientist** (**R**) (1968, Harry Weese & Assocs.). White travertine marble, the prominent site and unusual form give the small building a large presence.

Bear left and continue east on Wacker Dr.

75 East Wacker Drive (**S**) (1928, H.H. Riddle), built by the descendants of Cotton Mather, is a pencil-thin Art Deco skyscraper sheathed in white terra-cotta.

Continue east on Wacker Dr. to N. Michigan Ave.

Distinguished by a curving Neoclassical entrance, **360 North Michigan Avenue** (**T**) (1923, Alfred S. Alschuler) is built on a trapezoidal riverfront site. The building's English Renaissance ornament is capped with a Greek lantern. Across the street rises **333 North Michigan Avenue** (**U**) (1928, Holabird & Root), a lovely Art Deco skyscraper with a dark granite base, stepped-back design and bas-reliefs that relate to the sculpted bridgehouses anchoring the Michigan Avenue Bridge. The building's architecture echoes the design proposed by Eliel Saarinen for the 1922 *Chicago Tribune* competition, which won second prize.

If you would like to return to Michigan Ave. and Congress Pkwy., walk south on the Grant Park side of Michigan Ave. for an interesting perspective of the different architectural styles lining the avenue.

⌷ WALKING TOUR: ALONG THE RIVER *Distance: 1mi*

Begin at the corner of Jackson Blvd. and Franklin St.

★★★**Sears Tower** – *233 S. Wacker Dr.* Tallest building in the world for over 20 years, this 110-story feat of engineering cuts an unmistakable profile on the city's skyline. At the time of construction from 1968 to 1974, the city did not require a zoning variance for the tower, allowing it to rise to an unsurpassed height of 1,454ft. In 1996 the tower was overtaken by architect Cesar Pelli's Petronas Towers in Kuala Lumpur, Malaysia, relegating the Chicago landmark to the rank of world's second-tallest structure—although the Sears Tower claims the highest roof, the highest occupied floor and the highest antennae.

Designed by architect Bruce Graham and chief engineer Fazlur Khan for Skidmore, Owings & Merrill, the tower comprises nine rectangular tubes, resting on more than 100 steel and concrete caissons anchored into the bedrock hundreds of feet below ground. These 75ft-high bundled tubes provide solidity to the tower by maximizing resistance to wind loads: two tubes end at the 50th floor, two at the 66th

> ■ Sears Tower: A Lesson in Size
>
> - Height: 1,707ft (including the antennas), as tall as 16 city blocks.
> - Weight: 222,500 tons, covered by 28 acres of black aluminum.
> - The tower has 103 elevators, one of which travels to the top at a speed of 1,600ft/min or 18mph.
> - Six automatic window-washing machines clean 16,000 windows eight times a year.
> - The tower contains enough phone wire to wrap around the earth 1.75 times and enough electrical wiring to run a power line from Chicago to Los Angeles.
> - About 12,000 people work here; another 5,000 to 11,000 visit the tower daily.
> - Even in high wind, the top of the tower never sways more than 6 inches.

floor, and three more at the 90th floor. Clad in black aluminum and bronze-tinted glass, the tower's structural skeleton required over 75,000 tons of steel.

Redesigned in 1985, the barrel-vaulted entrance on Wacker Drive is dominated by Alexander Calder's mobile **The Universe**, a collection of brightly colored forms turning and twirling.

Skydeck – ▦ *Enter on Jackson Blvd. between Wacker Dr. and Franklin St. Open year-round daily 9am–11pm. Last tickets are sold 30min before closing. The Skydeck may be closed occasionally due to high winds. $9.50. ⚒ ▣ ☎ 312-875-9696.*

www.the-skydeck.com. Your visit to the newly renovated Skydeck begins with a short film, *Over Chicago,* and a mutimedia elevator ride to the 103rd floor. Once at the top, you'll enjoy spectacular **views**★★★ of the city and the lake from the entirely glassed-in Skydeck. Touch-screen displays explain local landmarks in six different languages and the exhibit Chicago 101 relates Chicago history. Kids can discover the city through the new 4ft-high exhibit, Knee-High Chicago.

Exit Sears Tower on Franklin St.

Just south of the Sears Tower stands **311 South Wacker Drive** (1990, Kohn Pederson Fox), the world's tallest concrete frame skyscraper, built on speculation rights before the real estate depression of the 1990s. Planned as one of three buildings, the structure is topped by a huge illuminated crown resembling a circular fortress.

Continue north on Franklin St. to Madison St. Walk west to Wacker Dr. and across the bridge spanning the Chicago River to view sights to the west of the river.

Wacker Drive from the River

Formerly known as the Northwestern Atrium Center, the deep blue and silver **Citicorp Center** *(500 W. Madison St.)* rises like a giant jukebox, marking the intersection of Madison and Canal Streets. Another of Helmut Jahn's soaring atriums unites this combination commuter train station, retail arcade and office tower (1987), which takes its streamlined shape from 1930s "machine age" design.

Just east of Citicorp Center, **Riverside Plaza** (1929, Holabird & Root) was built for the now-defunct *Chicago Daily News.* The stately 26-story Art Deco high rise offers an expansive riverfront plaza, the first developed in Chicago. Built over active railroad tracks, this building incorporated ingenious foundations as well as vents for steam engines, a novelty at the time.

Visible to the north, the **Morton International Building** (1990, Ralph Johnson, Perkins & Will) is partly suspended over railroad tracks by means of an exposed rooftop truss that is reminiscent of the nearby bridges.

The bridge offers the best view of sights to the east of the river.

To the right, the **Chicago Mercantile Exchange** *(10-30 S. Wacker Dr.),* established in 1919 as the Butter and Egg Exchange, has evolved like the Board of Trade from commodities to the fast-paced world of futures and options. The "Merc's" twin towers (1983 and 1988, Fujikawa, Johnson & Assocs.) are linked by a windowless base that encloses two large free-span trading floors, open for public viewing from separate galleries. The frenetic activity on the floor is worth the visit *(open year-round Mon–Fri 7:15am–3:15pm; closed major holidays; 30min guided tours available; ✗ ও ☎ 312-930-8249; www.cme.com).* Some 3,000 people garbed in colorful jackets pack the large room. Here, eight transactions take place every second. The riverfront site has a modest walkway where the traders flock during lunchtime breaks.

To the left, the **Civic Opera Building** *(20 N. Wacker Dr.; 2hr backstage tours Feb 11, Mar 4 & Mar 11 at 11:30am; reservations required; ✗ ও ☎ 312-332-2244; www.lyricopera.org),* built by utilities magnate Samuel Insull to house both offices and the opera, combines Art Deco skyscraper design with a block-long Wacker Drive arcade that celebrates the classical origins of opera and theater. The building

(1929, Graham, Anderson, Probst & White) was dubbed "Insull's throne" due to its armchair-like appearance from the river. The former Civic Theater has been incorporated into a complete modernization of the Opera House. Opened in November 1929 with a performance of Verdi's *Aïda*, the theater still presents world-class opera performed by the Lyric Opera of Chicago.

Return to intersection of Madison St. and Wacker Dr. and walk north on Wacker Dr.

★ **333 West Wacker Drive** – This edifice (1983, Kohn Pedersen Fox) set a new standard for downtown development as it began the 1980s building boom. The design takes full advantage of the triangular site—a mere parking lot at the time—where the South Branch of the Chicago River diverges from the main channel. The green, mirrored-glass facade both suggests and reflects the river, with horizontal ribs that relieve the sheer height of the structure. When clouds play across it, the facade is stunning. The building's base has more traditional green marble and gray granite accentuated by louvered portholes, while the top folds the curving riverside facade into the flat walls of the Loop.

■ **Chicago's Riverwalk**

The redevelopment of the Chicago River east of Michigan Avenue has inspired the city to create a tree-lined pedestrian path along the south bank from Michigan Avenue to the lake. Beginning underneath Lake Shore Drive where the river meets the lake, the blue-trellised corridor passes the 170ft-long **Riverwalk Gateway** tile mural by Ellen Lanyon, which limns the history of the river in 16 narrative panels and 12 decorative panels. Along the north shore the walk leads to McClurg Court and Centennial Fountain, which emits a jet of water across the river every hour on the hour *(except 3pm & 4pm)* in summer. Besides affording fine **views** of Loop skyscrapers across the river, the esplanade passes such noteworthy landmarks as the new River East development *(south of McClurg St.)*, the River View condominiums (2000, DeStefano & Partners) on South Water Market Street, and Milton Horn's 1954 restored sculpture *Chicago Rising from the Lake* (at Columbus Dr.), representing the city's leading industries.

West of Wabash Street, riverwalk cafes share space with docking facilities for the many tour boats, gondolas, water bicycles and water taxis that have made the Chicago River the busiest urban river in the nation. The **State Street Bridge Gallery** *(enter through the Riverwalk at State St.; open May–Oct Mon–Sat 10am–7pm, Sun 10am–5pm; ☎ 312-744-6630)* offers a display explaining the history and function of Chicago's bascule bridges as well as changing exhibits of art and photography. Marking LaSalle Gateway Plaza three blocks farther west on the north side of the river is **Crossing**, a 25ft-tall steel sculpture by German artist Hubertus von der Goltz. The V-shaped sculpture is topped by a human figure symbolizing the citizen who will, in the artist's words, "contribute to the balancing and blending of the City of Chicago on the brink of the 21st Century."

Taking a Break along the Riverwalk

© Kevin O. Mooney/Odyssey

Notable for its masonry walls and four rooftop lanterns, **225 West Wacker Drive** *(located across Franklin St.)* was completed by the same firm in a post-Modern style six years later.

Across the river rises the massive **Merchandise Mart**, commissioned by Marshall Field & Co. in 1928 *(300 N. Wells St.;* ✗ ♿ 🅿*(fee varies);* ☎ *312-644-4664).* With 4.1 million square feet of space, the Mart is touted as the world's largest commercial building. Architects Graham, Anderson, Probst & White embellished their practical Art Deco design with simple geometric patterns incised and over-laid on the exterior. In the main lobby at the south entrance, murals by artist Jules Guerin depicting trading activities around the world presaged the Mart's current international status as a "world trade center." Joseph P. Kennedy purchased the Mart in 1945 and the Kennedy family owned it until 1998. A five-year renovation completed in 1992 included extensive exterior cleaning and the creation of a public retail mall, **Shops at the Mart**, on the first two floors *(open to the public year-round Mon–Fri 9am–6pm, Sat 10–3pm;* ☎ *312-527-7990).* Wholesale showrooms on the 13th floor have been opened to the public as well, but all other floors are closed to anyone but design professionals and authorized buyers.

Continue on Wacker Dr. and cross Wells St.

Located east of the Merchandise Mart, the red stone and green glass Helene Curtis Building was renovated from warehouse space to office building in 1984. Across LaSalle Street stands the Central Office Building (1914), topped by a clock tower.

Major Chicago thoroughfares are designated with a route number but are more commonly referred to by name:

I-55	**Stevenson Expressway**
I-290	**Eisenhower Expressway**
US-41	**Lake Shore Drive**
I-294	**Tri-State**
I-88	**East-West Tollway** *(toll road)*
I-94 *(north of 290)*	**Edens Expressway**
I-94 *(south of 290)*	**Dan Ryan Expressway**
I-90 *(north of 290)*	**Kennedy Expressway**
I-90 *(south of 290)*	**Chicago Skyway** *(toll road)*

MAGNIFICENT MILE★★★

bus no. 151
Map pp 94-95
Tourist Information: www.themagnificentmile.com

Champs Elysées of Chicago, this flower- and light-filled promenade along North Michigan Avenue is the city's most prestigious thoroughfare. Lined with exclusive shops and boutiques, luxury hotels, restaurants and premier residential and office high rises, the "Magnificent Mile" lies between Chicago's most important waterways, the Chicago River on its south border and Lake Michigan on its north. Just to the east, bustling Streeterville abounds in trendy restaurants and entertainment venues.

Historical Notes

From Mud Plain to Grand Boulevard – Chicago's first permanent settler, **Jean Baptiste Point du Sable**, built his cabin here in 1779, on an unpromising flat plain. In 1804 **John Kinzie**, a fur trader, situated his cottage on the north bank of the river close to the present site of the Equitable Building. Yet almost half a century later, when Chicago was incorporated as a city, the area remained a muddy patch of Lake Michigan sediment. By 1860 (the year Abraham Lincoln was nominated as the Republican candidate for president at the Wigwam a few blocks away), various mercantile establishments and ordinary two-story houses bordered the avenue, then called Pine Street. The Great Fire of 1871 leveled all of the buildings on the street except the Water Tower and Pumping Station, still standing proudly at Chicago Avenue.

By the turn of the century numerous businesses, including loft manufacturing establishments, warehouses, sign companies and taverns, transformed the street into a major traffic artery. The 1920 opening of the Michigan Avenue Bridge, which joined the south and north sides of the city, catalyzed an incredible building boom. Most of the landmarks on the avenue, including the Wrigley Building, Tribune Tower, Medinah Athletic Club, Lake Shore Bank, Woman's Athletic Club, Allerton Hotel, Fourth Presbyterian Church, Palmolive Building and the Drake Hotel were constructed during the decade that followed. A profusion of Art Deco and Neoclassical elements adorned the modestly scaled, limestone edifices, lending the avenue a sophisticated "European boulevard" look that would last until the 1970s. Although the Great Depression and World War II interrupted development, in 1947 Chicago developer Arthur Rubloff dubbed North Michigan Avenue "The Magnificent Mile," forecasting a commercial revival during the 1950s and 60s.

Retail Transformation – Construction of two extraordinary mixed-use complexes contributed to the retail boom of the 1970s that changed the face of Michigan Avenue. Erected in 1969, the landmark John Hancock Center ushered in a new era of skyscrapers along the avenue. Completed seven years later, Water Tower Place included one of the first and most successful vertical shopping centers in the US, and began a shift in retail focus from downtown State Street to the more glamorous Michigan Avenue location. The upward spiral continued through the 1980s and 90s as fashionable retailers multiplied each year, creating one of the most affluent shopping districts in the country. Recently, however, the slick and elegant image has been dealt a blow, as large-scale developers begin to invade the avenue, often demolishing historic structures to make way for mass-market shops. Long-time residents and architectural purists argue that the stores and their gaudy signage are gradually "cheapening" the area, transforming it into a "magnificent mall" of suburbia.

East of the Avenue – Immediately east of the Magnificent Mile lies **Streeterville**, an area originally settled in the 1880s by the infamous Capt. George Wellington Streeter. When his ship ran aground on a sand bar near present-day Chicago Avenue, Streeter built a causeway to the mainland and encouraged contractors to dump debris around his ship. The land grew to reach 180 acres and Streeter declared it the "District of Lake Michigan," separate from the city of Chicago and answerable only to the federal government. He and his wife battled police to a standoff, and his claim for independence wasn't dismissed from the courts until 1918. Most of the buildings east of Michigan Avenue are built on Streeter's landfill.

WALKING TOUR   *Distance: .8mi.*

Begin at the corner of N. Michigan Ave. and E. Wacker Dr.

★**Michigan Avenue Bridge** – *Corner of Wacker Dr. and N. Michigan Ave.* This monumental, double-leaf trunnion bascule, two-level bridge is the gateway to the Magnificent Mile. Like the seesaw for which it is named, the bascule is a kind of drawbridge counterweighted so that it can be raised and lowered easily. Built to designs by Edward H. Bennett (co-author with Daniel Burnham of the 1909 Plan of Chicago), the bridge was completed in 1920. Four corner bridgehouses, each almost 40ft in height, showcase bas-reliefs in Bedford limestone designed by J.E. Fraser and Henry Hering that celebrate important episodes in Chicago history. Michigan Avenue Bridge affords some of the most spectacular **views★★** of the gleaming Loop high rises towering over the river.

Walk north across the bridge on the west side.

★★ **Wrigley Building** – *400-410 N. Michigan Ave.* Set majestically on the north bank of the Chicago River, this sparkling edifice heralded the 20C development of the North Michigan Avenue business district. Designed by Graham, Anderson, Probst & White as the headquarters for William Wrigley, Jr.'s successful chewing-gum company, the structure was built in two stages (the 30-story south section in 1920 and the 21 story north section in 1924); the two towers are connected by an arcaded walkway at street level and on the 3rd and 14th floors. Modeled after Seville Cathedral's Giralda Tower in Spain, the structure represents a fine example of the French Renaissance style. The white terra-cotta cladding dazzles, especially at night when the building is illuminated. Chicagoans use the soaring, four-sided clock atop the south tower for time checks from several blocks away in every direction. A handsome little plaza between the two structures leads to a miniature park next to the Sun-Times Building.

Cross to the east side of Michigan Ave.

On the northeast bank of the Chicago River rises the **Equitable Building** at no. 401 (1965, Skidmore, Owings & Merrill; Alfred Shaw & Assocs.), a 40-story granite and glazed, bronze solar-glass office tower. Immediately north of the building, the Channel Garden, reminiscent of Rockefeller Center's Channel Gardens in New York City, offers a pleasant rest stop. Pioneer Court, a spacious plaza in front of Equitable's entrance provides a scenic outlook to the adjacent buildings and those on the avenue beyond. The plaza's sweeping stairway to the south leads down to **Riverwalk★** *(see Loop)* an esplanade extending along the north bank of the Chicago River.

Continue east along the promenade.

 Billy Goat Tavern

Map p 94. 430 N. Michigan Ave. (lower level). ☎ 312-222-1525. The gruff grill chefs at the Goat inspired John Belushi's famous "cheeseboorger, cheeseboorger, cheep, cheep, no Coke, Pepsi" skit from *Saturday Night Live.* Its proximity to the *Chicago Sun-Times* and *Tribune* offices makes this underground tavern a favorite with journalists, printers, delivery drivers and advertising executives. Framed newspaper clips and photos on the walls provide interesting slices of obscure Chicago history.

University of Chicago Graduate School of Business Downtown Center – *450 N Cityfront Plaza Dr.* Designed by Lohan Assocs. in 1992, this eight-level glass, steel and precast concrete structure features a glassed front facade overlooking the Chicago River and an angled back with cantilevered pods. Its stark, windowless western wall was dictated by the university, which did not want the architectural beauty outside to distract its students from their scholarly pursuits.

★ **NBC Tower** – *455 N. Cityfront Plaza Dr.* Reminiscent of New York's GE Building at Rockefeller Center, this 38-story Art Deco office tower (1989, Skidmore Owings & Merrill), topped by a 130ft steel spire, rises in a series of setbacks that strengthen its vertical progression. Limestone constitutes most of the building's skin except for the dark green precast concrete spandrels and the green, gray and black granite of its base.

The tower is set on the western edge of **Cityfront Center**, a 60-acre development extending east of Michigan Avenue and north to Grand Street that includes office hotel, entertainment, retail and residential development. The integration of this project with the surrounding city and the river provide a marked contrast with the stark monoliths of Illinois Center directly across the Chicago River.

Return to Michigan Ave.

★★ **Tribune Tower** – *435 N. Michigan Ave.* Corporate headquarters of the vast communications and sports empire held by the Tribune Company, this soaring, crenellated, Gothic-style tower (1925, Hood & Howells) was the first-place winner of the 1922 *Chicago Tribune* international competition to erect "the most beautiful and distinctive office building in the world." Adorned with floodlit flying buttresses, sculpted fleur-de-lis and numerous gargoyles and grotesques, the 36 story, 456ft limestone "cathedral of commerce" echoes the Butter Tower in Rouen, France, and the Tower of Malines in Meche-

Tribune Company publishes 11 newspapers, owns and operates 22 TV and 4 radio stations (Chicago-based WGN radio—World's Greatest Newspaper—broadcasts from a street-level, glass-enclosed studio in the building). In addition, it produces and syndicates information and programming, publishes books and information in print and digital formats and owns the Chicago Cubs baseball team.

len, Belgium. Fragments from more than 120 of the world's famous structures—the Parthenon, the Great Wall of China, Westminster Abbey, the Berlin Wall and Notre Dame Cathedral in Paris, among others—were collected by *Tribune* correspondents and have been embedded in the exterior walls of the building.

A richly ornamented, three-story arch adorned with a stone screen carved with figures from Aesop's fables marks the entrance to the **lobby**. This harmonious space, restored in 1990 by architect John Vinci, is known to journalists as the Hall of Inscriptions: A series of quotations expressing the ideals and obligations of the press is carved in its travertine marble walls. The east wall is dominated by a papier-mâché map of North America, constructed in 1925 by noted geographic sculptor George Robertson.

Guided tours (1hr) of the Chicago Tribune's Freedom Center printing facilities in River West (777 W. Chicago Ave.) are available year-round Tue–Fri 9:30am–1:30pm; closed major holidays; 1-week advance reservations required; children under 10 not admitted; ♿ 🅿 ☎ *312-222-2116.*

Cross Illinois St.

★**Hotel Inter-Continental Chicago** – *505 N. Michigan Ave.* ☎ *312-944-4100. www.interconti.com.* This eclectic 41-story building (1929, Walter W. Ahlschlager) was originally built as the Medinah Athletic Club for members of the Shriners organization. After the club closed in 1934, the building went through a succession of different owners until Inter-Continental Hotels purchased it in 1988. It opened as the Inter-Continental Chicago in 1990 following a $130 million restoration by Harry Weese & Assocs. In 1994 the hotel expanded to include its northern neighbor, the Forum Hotel Chicago, and is now contained in two towers connected by a glass lobby. Carved into the Indiana limestone facade, a large Egyptian-style frieze depicts builders parading in front of the pharaoh.

Inside the historic tower, public spaces are adorned with superb inlays of marble, intricately detailed bronze and brass trimming, murals and frescoes. Step through the heavy bronze doors to admire the ornate **entryway★** whose beamed ceiling is painted with colorful Celtic and Mesopotamian motifs—the lion, fish, eagle and peacock—representing the highest powers of nature. Marble stairways flank the arched greeting *Es Salamu Aleikum* (Peace Be to You) and are crowned with squat, Moorish-style columns sporting hooded, sleeping knights. The Hall of Lions *(2nd floor)*, King Arthur Foyer and Court *(3rd floor)*, the Spanish Court and the Renaissance Room Foyer *(both 5th floor)* have all been opulently restored. The 25-meter Olympic-size swimming pool on the 14th floor is the last remaining feature of the original Athletic Club (a 23rd-floor miniature golf course no longer exists). An onion-shaped dome and minaret atop the building complete the fantasy below (the dome was originally intended as a place for Shriners to dock their dirigibles, but the perpetual breezes of the Windy City thwarted that plan).

Across the street to the west stands the 16-story Art Deco **520 North Michigan Avenue** built in 1929 as the McGraw-Hill Building by architects Thielbar & Fugard, who had an office there. Clad in limestone on a granite base, the building displays a variety of exterior detail including sculpted mythological figures and ornamental panels. The limestone facade was completely dismantled and re-erected in 2000 on a new steel structure that houses a mall anchored by the **Nordstrom** department store, which fills a six-story Renaissance Revival building a block to the west. The store's glassy corner entrance at Wabash and Grand Avenues contrasts with the quoined corners and geometric incising of the buff concrete facade on Michigan Avenue.

Cross overpass spanning Grand Ave.

The intimate scale and decorative architecture of the five-story, Lilliputian gem at **543-545 North Michigan Avenue** (1929, Philip B. Maher) was originally constructed to house the luxurious Jacques dress shop. The sculptured female figures above each doorway, characteristic of the Art Deco style of the building, also served the practical purpose of attracting customers.

Cross Ohio St.

The four-story Lake Shore Bank at no. 605 (1922, Marshall & Fox), taken over by the **First National Bank of Chicago** in 1994, is noteworthy for its temple-like appearance and massive Corinthian columns. A recent renovation produced a new banking center on the second and third floors, while the first floor was given over to retail shops. On the west side of the street is the former site of 612 and 620 N. Michigan Avenue. After a bitter preservation battle, the historic structures fell victim to the wrecking ball—along with the Arts Club of Chicago, which featured an interior space designed by Mies van der Rohe—to make way for a nine-screen cinema complex and mall.

Continue north.

On the northwest corner of Ontario and Michigan Avenues at no. 626, the nine-story **Woman's Athletic Club** (1928, Philip B. Maher), one of the oldest, private athletic and social facilities for women in the US, provides a stately legacy of the avenue's

1920s understated, low-rise look. The Bedford limestone and pressed brick exterior, mansard roof, second-floor Palladian windows separated by carved ox skulls and the winged griffins in the seventh-floor niches reflect its French inspiration and the elegance of its interior. Upscale retail shops occupy the first floor on Michigan Avenue.

Its neighbor to the north, **Crate & Barrel** (1990, Solomon Cordwell Buenz & Assocs. at no. 646, makes a contrasting Modernist statement with the stark white aluminum and luminous glass of its exterior and the high-tech trappings of its interior. The northern curved corner of this flagship housewares emporium echoes the famed rotunda of Louis Sullivan's Carson Pirie Scott store on State Street.

Cross to the west side of Michigan Ave. and cross Erie St.

Terra Museum of American Art – *Entrance at 666 N. Michigan Ave. Open year round Tue–Sat 10am–6pm (Tue til 8pm), Sun noon–5pm. Closed Mon & major holidays. $7 (free Tue & 1st Sun of month). Guided tours (30min) available.* ♿ ☎ *312 654-2255. www.terramuseum.org.* Fitting snugly among the Magnificent Mile's retail emporiums, this modest museum presents a bite-size overview of over two centuries of American art history. Many major artists are represented, albeit by lesser-known works. Daniel J. Terra, appointed by President Ronald Reagan as ambassador for cultural affairs, founded the museum in suburban Evanston in 1980 to showcase his collection of 800 works. (In 1992 he opened a sister institution in Giverny, France.) In an effort to increase exposure, the Evanston museum moved to its present location in 1987, and occupies the top floors of 664 North Michigan (1927, Philip B. Maher) as well as the adjacent glass and marble edifice at no. 666. Erected in 1987 by Booth/Hansen & Assocs., the latter building contains the entrance lobby and a sweeping staircase connecting the four exhibit floors in no. 664. Works from the permanent collection displayed in the fourth- and fifth-floor galleries, highlight 19C portraiture, romantic landscapes and domestic scenes by artists such as John Singleton Copley, Thomas Cole, George Caleb Bingham, George Inness, William Merritt Chase and Winslow Homer. Also displayed are 200 works by Ashcan school artists Stuart Davis and Maurice Prendergast and Expressionists such as Reginald Marsh, Milton Avery and George Tooker. The museum frequently hosts traveling exhibits focusing on individual artists or themes, such as the American West. Lectures and educational programs round out the Terra's offerings.

Across the street to the east at no. 669 is **Nike Town Chicago** ▒▒, a five-level retail theater showcase for Nike's footwear and apparel collections *(☎ 312-642-6363, www.nike.com).*

② Garrett Popcorn Shop

Map p 95. 670 N. Michigan Ave. ☎ *312-944-2630.* The line that routinely winds out onto Michigan Avenue on weekends leads to Chicago's venerable popcorn shop, a local favorite since 1949. With four downtown locations, including the one next door to the Terra Museum, Garrett's retains a loyal clientele—including Oprah Winfrey and Roger Ebert—who swear that Garrett's caramel, cheddar-cheese or old-fashioned butter popcorn is the best around. Out-of-towners can order online: *www.garrettpopcorn.com.*

■ Chicago-style Pizza

Chicago undoubtedly ranks as one of the country's greatest spots for pizza. Pizza aficionados rave about the city's deep-dish pizza, sometimes called pizza-in-the-pan, a savory concoction of tomatoes, cheese, sausage and vegetables ladled over a thick, doughy crust. Over 2,000 restaurants serve a variety of this mouth-watering dish, with toppings ranging from the simple to the exotic, from mushrooms to clams and artichokes.

The dough remains an essential ingredient in preparing an old-fashioned deep-dish pizza. A mixture of water, yeast and flour is often embellished by adding sugar, cornmeal, oil and even milk. Once the dough has risen and been kneaded down, it is placed in a pan, pricked with a fork and baked at 475°F for about 5 minutes. Slices of mozzarella are then layered directly on the dough, followed by canned tomatoes seasoned with oregano, basil, salt and pepper. Fresh Parmesan is grated over the tomatoes. Next come the various meat and vegetable toppings. Finally, the pie is drizzled with olive oil and baked in a preheated 475°F oven until the crust is browned, about 30 to 45 minutes.

Set perpendicular to the avenue, granite **City Place** (1990, Loebl, Schlossman & Hackl) at no. 676 resembles a giant jukebox. Red vertical lines and pink spandrels provide a dramatic contrast to the smoky blue windows whose arrangement demarcates the varied purposes of the building—retail streetside with a hotel and offices above. The "bootlike" design with a lower mass at the sidewalk and a tower setback is typical of the skyscrapers built on the avenue in the 1980s and 90s.

Cross Huron St.

On the corner of Michigan Avenue and Huron Street, the 1924 **Allerton Hotel** was restored to its former Italian Renaissance glory in 1999 as the Allerton Crowne Plaza. The limestone and red tapestry brick "club hotel" is one of the Mag Mile's rare historic landmarks.

Chicago Place – *700 N. Michigan Ave. Open year-round Mon–Fri 10am–7pm, Sat 10am–6pm, Sun noon–5pm. Closed Easter Sunday, Thanksgiving Day & Dec 25. ✗ ♿ 🅿 ✉ 312-642-4811.* Distinguished by a varicolored two-story base in green and pink granite, this multi-purpose structure (1990, Skidmore, Owings & Merrill; Solomon Cordwell Buenz & Assocs.) also adopts the boot-shaped scheme. Eight floors of retail, including Saks Fifth Avenue and 50 other upscale shops, are topped by a 43-story residential tower setback to the west. Its windows are designed in the Chicago style, and its curved southern facade honors Sullivan's Carson Pirie Scott store. Step inside the huge **lobby** to view the 23ftx32ft Thomas Melvin murals depicting Chicago history. Soaring over the atrium is a barrel-vaulted roof whose skylights illuminate the charming garden and food court located on the eighth floor.

© Kevin O. Mooney/Odyssey

Shopping on the Magnificent Mile

Look north across Michigan Avenue at the **Neiman Marcus** store (no. 737) occupying the low-rise section of **Olympia Centre** (1986, Skidmore, Owings & Merrill), whose 63-story tapering office and residential tower looms over Chicago Avenue to the northeast. On the Sullivanesque arch over Neiman's main entrance, a whimsical glass panel replaces the keystone.

Cross Superior St.

730 North Michigan Avenue (1997, Elkus/Manfredi Architects, Ltd.) is a classical post-Modern building rendered as four separate facades. Tiffany & Company's refined Art Deco facade in lavender and gray anchors the southern end, followed by the Pottery Barn's Egyptian temple with modernized lotus columns and heavy yellow pylons. Next door, the machined industrial look of Banana Republic's black and buff stone facade is heightened by extruded steel details at the cornice, while Polo/Ralph Lauren's gray Florentine palazzo completes the north end. Around the corner, **American Girl Place** *(111 E. Chicago Ave.; ✆ 312-943-9400)* offers afternoon tea in addition to its popular historically inspired dolls.

Cross Chicago Ave.

Visions of another era, the **Chicago Water Tower**★ (1869, William W. Boyington) and **Pumping Station**★ (1866) stand like sentinels on the west and east sides of Michigan Avenue, solid reminders that they were the only two buildings in the area to survive the Great Fire. Both are built of Joliet limestone in the castellated Goth style. The still-operational Pumping Station houses a visitor information cent *(open daily 7:30am–7pm; closed major holidays)*. Horse-and-carriage rides alo the Magnificent Mile and environs, as well as double-decker bus and trolley tou *(see* Practical Information*)*, depart from the charming park adjoining the Wat Tower.

Just west of the Water Tower on Chicago Avenue and Rush Street, 67-story **Pa Tower** (2000, Lucien LaGrange) features streamlined details including Art De lanterns and setbacks, and a curved balcony and projecting loggia at the sixth flo overlooking the Water Tower. Here condominiums and the Park Hyatt hotel sha space with chic retail stores such as Armani.

The small downtown campus of Loyola University (Water Tower Campus) begi at the southwest corner of "little" Michigan Avenue and Pearson Street, at no. 820.

Continue north.

Occupying the former I. Magnin building *(830 N. Michigan Ave.)*, Filene's Basement, Victoria's Secret and Borders Books & Music advertise their wares in tall, red and pink aluminum letters plastered over the facade.

★**Water Tower Place** – *No. 835. Open year-round Mon–Sat 10am–7pm, Sun noon–6pm. Closed Easter Sunday, Thanksgiving Day & Dec 25.* ✕ ♿ ▣ ☎ *312-440-3166. www.shopwatertower.com.* Located on the east side of Michigan Avenue, this square-block complex (1976, Loebl, Schlossman & Hackl) salutes its neighbor, the historic Water Tower, in name only. The stark, almost windowless, whiteveined marble face it presents to the avenue accommodates a 12-story shopping complex and office space while a 62-story tower to the east houses the Ritz-Carlton Hotel and luxury condominiums. Its more than 150 shops, boutiques, services, restaurants and anchored by Lord & Taylor and Marshall Field, moved the center of retail action to this area from State Street downtown. A prominent tourist attraction, Water Tower Place is recognized as one of the most successful mixed-use projects in the US.

Cross Chestnut St.

★**Fourth Presbyterian Church** – *N. Michigan Ave. at Delaware Pl. Open year-round daily 9am–5pm. Closed major holidays.* ♿ ☎ *312-787-4570. www.fourth church.org.* Dedicated in 1914, this sanctuary is an elegant reminder of Michigan Avenue's character before the shopping malls and myriad tour buses. It was designed by Ralph Adams Cram, in association with Howard Van Doren Shaw, in the Gothic Revival style (Cram also designed the Cathedral of St. John the Divine in New York City). The church and parish house were fully restored and renovated in 1994. Al-

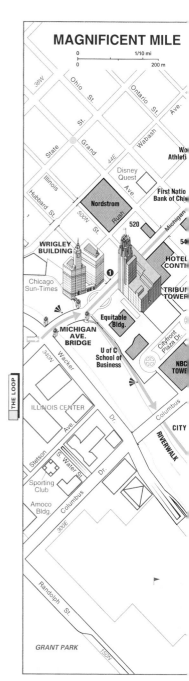

MAGNIFICENT MILE

Walton St.

Delaware Pl.

St.

36W

Walton St.

Cedar St.

11/20N

Lake Shore Dr.

Bellevue

40

Barneys
New York

Sonia
Rykiel

Hermès

Pl.

Oak Street
Beach

JOHN HANCOCK
CENTER

OAK ST.

900

Ave.

St.

Loyola University
Water Tower Campus

Rush

Chicago Ave.

44E

City Place

WATER
TOWER

Park
Tower

American
Girl Place

730

Chicago
Place

MAGNIFICENT

Neiman
Marcus

Nike Town
Chicago

te & Barrel

Allerton
Crowne Plaza

St.

Erie

St.

656N

Ontario

Ct.

Fairbanks

St.

STREETERVILLE

541

Ct.

400E

Ohio

Illinois

St.

McClurg

Grand

Ct.

Peshtigo Ct.

ENTER

RIVER EAST
PLAZA

Ogden Slip

ennial
ntain

FOURTH
PRESBYTERIAN

830

MILE

🕂

3

WATER
TOWER PLACE

One
Magnificent
Mile

DRAKE HOTEL

4

919

Walton
St.

1000N

Lake Shore Drive

Olympia
Centre

800N

PUMPING
STATION

Seneca
Park

Mies Van Der Rohe

Way

Delaware
Pl.

Pl.

900-910

860-880

Superior St.

MUSEUM OF
CONTEMPORARY
ART

Dewitt

Chestnut St.

Pearson

St.

Huron St.

Lake Shore
Park

Chicago
Ave.

Northwestern University
Chicago Campus

VA-Lakeside
Hospital

Lake shore
Place

Onterie
Center

LAKE SHORE DRIVE

Lake
Michigan

Ave.

Lake Point Tower

Ohio Street
Beach

Jane
Addams
Park

Milton Lee Olive Park

Gateway
Park

Streeter

Dr.

M

NAVY PIER

Chicago
Harbor

Stephen Graham/DPA

Chicago Water Tower and John Hancock Center

though originally built fo
wealthy and large cong
gation (the church sea
1,500), the interior is su
dued and somber. Staine
glass windows set high
the west and east wa
provide color and drar
and were designed
Charles J. Connick
Boston, while the int
cately painted **ceiling** is t
work of native Chicago
Frederic Clay Bartlett.
the base of the ceili
arches, 14 sculptured, li
size angels depicting mu
cians gaze down upon t
worshippers. The church
known throughout the c
for its Aeolian Skinn
organ, and concerts a
popular *(year-round A
12:10pm-12:45pm)*.
Outside, the charmir
cloister and fountain th
lie between the church a
its ivy-covered parish hou
provide a serene oasis.

*Cross to the east side
Michigan Ave.*

★★★**John Hancock Center** – *875 N. Michigan Ave.* Nothing represents Carl Sandburg
epithet for Chicago—"the city of big shoulders"—more than this 1,127ft skyscrap
(1969, Skidmore, Owings & Merrill). It is the third-tallest building in Chicago, t
sixth-tallest in the US and, because of its huge cross-bracing steel members, o
of the most recognizable in the city. Its 100 stories of black anodized aluminu
and tinted glass are divided between office and residential space.
The tower was constructed at half the cost of a building of comparable heig
thanks to engineer Fazlur Khan's efficient design. Applying the braced tube conce
to his structure, Khan developed an obelisk-shaped structural framework that fur
tions as a large-scale truss. Comprising some 46,000 tons of steel, the cross brace
columns and beams efficiently carry gravity and wind loads. The tapering tow
rises from a 265ft by 165ft base to a top floor measuring 100ft by 160ft, offeri
an interior space of 2.8 million square feet.
Wide steps descending into a large sunken **plaza** frame colorful planters and a w
waterfall. The plaza affords interesting views of the Magnificent Mile skyscrape
looming to the north and south. The **Chicago Architecture Foundation Shop and Tour Cen**
offers guided tours of the area *(open year-round daily 10am–7pm; closed Jan 1, East
Sunday, Thanksgiving Day & Dec 25;* & ☎ *312-751-1380; www.architecture.org*

The Hancock Observatory – *Open year-round daily 9am–midnight. $8.75.* ✗ &
☎ *312-751-3680 or 888-875-8439 (US only). www.hancock-observatory.co.*
During the 39 seconds that the elevators take to ascend to the 94th-floor obse
vatory, you almost feel airborne while experiencing panoramic **views**★★★ of the c
in every direction—particularly the spectacular eastern one of Lake Michigan. On
at the top, you can see Chicago from the new open-air Skywalk, poised 1,000
above the Mag Mile, and learn about the sites you are seeing through one of t
Soundscope talking telescopes.

Cross Delaware St.

Rising 871ft on the west side of Michigan Avenue, the 66-story **900 North Michig
Avenue** high rise (1989, Kohn Pedersen Fox) is best known for its anchor tena
Bloomingdale's, the Four Seasons Hotel and the four illuminated lanterns atop t
building. The spacious six-story atrium ringed by six levels of shops offers a retre
from the bustling streetscape.

The 37-story, 468ft **919 North Michigan Avenue** office building (1929) ascends grac
fully in a series of symmetrical setbacks topped by the now-dimmed 150
Lindbergh Beacon, whose two-billion-candlepower beam could be seen 500
away by airplane pilots. Sheathed in Bedford limestone above the first two ret
floors, which are clad in ornamental cast iron and metal, the edifice was initia
called the Palmolive Building for the company that commissioned Holabird & Ro
to design it as its headquarters. From 1967 to 1989 it was known as the Playbo
Building when the magazine's headquarters were located here.

Cross Walton St.

★**The Drake Hotel** – *140 E. Walton St.* ☎ *312-787-2200. www.hilton.com.* Listed on the National Register of Historic Places, this 537-room luxury hotel (1920, Marshall & Fox) built on landfill at the edge of Lake Michigan provides an elegant transition to the **East Lake Shore Drive Historic District**, which begins at its back door and marks the northeastern border of the Magnificent Mile. Covered in limestone, its plain exterior is unadorned except for a majestic colonnade on its northern face that looks out over Lincoln Park, Oak Street Beach and the lake. Its simplicity bespeaks the elegance of a grand hotel. Set on a rectangular base, the structure changes to an H-shape at the third floor to suit hotel room layouts. Step up into the dignified lobby and public rooms to admire the plush red velvet wall coverings, the wooden caisson ceiling and the elegant Palm Court.

Cross to the west side of Michigan Ave.

The northwestern border of this area is marked by **One Magnificent Mile** at nos. 940-980 (1983, Skidmore, Owings & Merrill), a 58-story mixed-use building comprising three hexagonal concrete tubes clad in rose-colored granite, which rise 57, 49 and 21 stories respectively. The three structures are joined together as a bundled tube to resist wind loads, a design originally conceived by engineer Fazlur Kahn and architect Bruce Graham for the Sears Tower.

Turn left onto Oak St.

★**Oak Street** – *Between N. Michigan Ave. and Rush St.* In a single turn one is transported from high-rise shopping flurry to a tree-lined streetscape reminiscent of New York's Upper Madison Avenue—sophisticated, but understated. This is a wonderful block for browsing or buying,

3 **Foodlife**
Map p 95. In Water Tower Place, mezzanine level. ☎ *312-335-3663.* Create an eclectic, healthful meal from the Chinese, Mexican, Middle Eastern, sandwich, burger and pizza stands housed in this bustling food court. At the entry, pick up a coded card and wooden tray and select entrées and drinks from a variety of stands. (The nutritional value of every item is clearly posted.) After you visit a stand, Foodlife staffers add the cost of your food to the electronic tally on your card; you pay the grand total when you leave. For those who prefer traditional restaurant service, the **Mity Nice Cafe** (at the back of the complex) offers comfort food and Amish fare.

4 **Palm Court**
Map p 95. In the Drake Hotel. ☎ *312-787-2200.* The potted-palm-dotted lobby of the Drake Hotel is a perfect spot to take a break after a shopping spree along Michigan Avenue or Oak Street. An elegant British-style high tea complete with scones, finger sandwiches and petit fours is served every afternoon *(reservations recommended Jan–Nov, not accepted in Dec).*

and each doorway heralds another upscale boutique: Hermès (no. 110), Sonia Rykiel (no. 106), Gianni Versace (no. 101), Jil Sander (no. 48) and others reflect the wealth of the Gold Coast neighborhood just to the north. At no. 40 a vintage 20-story apartment building erected in 1929 by Drake Hotel architect Ben Marshall conjures up images of a pampered past. Barneys New York (no. 25) anchors the western edge of this pleasant area.

★ **STREETERVILLE**

Bordered by Lake Michigan, the Magnificent Mile and the Chicago River, Streeterville exudes a cosmopolitan atmosphere enhanced by upscale residential high rises, the Museum of Contemporary Art and Navy Pier. The neighborhood is dominated by Northwestern University's Chicago campus—including its medical, dental and law schools and several hospitals of its McGaw Medical Center.

★**Museum of Contemporary Art** – *220 E. Chicago Ave. Open year-round Tue–Sun 10am–5pm (Tue & Wed til 8pm). Closed Mon, Jan 1, Thanksgiving Day & Dec 25. $6.50 (Tue free). Guided tours (1hr) available.* ✗ &. ▤ *($9/2hrs with museum validation)* ☎ *312-280-2660. www.mcachicago.org.* Founded in 1967, the museum presents a wide range of contemporary visual and performance arts by both well-established artists and those on the leading edge. In July 1996 the museum moved from limited quarters on Ontario Street to a two-acre site located between the historic Water Tower and Lake Michigan. (The museum's former location was the first building in the US to be wrapped by environmental artist Christo in 1969.) The new structure, the first in the US designed by Berlin architect Josef Paul Kleihues, features a 16ft-high staircase leading to a grand entrance framed by glass and aluminum panels. The building rises four stories, housing permanent-collection galleries, temporary exhibit space, a bookstore, and a ground-floor education

center with a 300-seat auditorium. On the main floor *(level 2)* facing La
Michigan, **Pucks at the MCA**—a collaborative effort with famed Spago chef Wolfgar
Puck—overlooks the one-acre sculpture garden.

The task of presenting the avant garde can be daunting, but the MCA attends pa
ticularly well to interpretation, attempting to make the works and movements
contemporary art accessible to everyone through thoughtful label writing, aud
programming and educational events. Exhibits, mounted on a rotating basis fro
the museum's 5,600-piece permanent collection, include works since 1945 by tl
likes of Marcel Duchamp, Max Ernst, René Magritte, Joan Miró, Jean Dubuffet ar
Andy Warhol. The collection is richly laden as well with pieces by Chicago ar
Illinois artists such as Ed Paschke, June Leaf, Leon Golub and Jim Nutt. The grou
floor is devoted to traveling exhibits (in summer 2000 the museum hosted
retrospective exhibit by conceptual artist Sol LeWitt). In the third-floor Video ar
Electronic Galleries you'll find works by film, video and multimedia artists, wh
the permanent collection—including new acquisitions by Ad Reinhardt, Jeff Koo
and Kara Walker—is displayed in the barrel-vaulted galleries on the fourth floc

541 North Fairbanks (formerly the Time-Life Building) – Harry Weese & Assoc
(1968) combined the traditions of the Chicago school—the exposed metal curta
wall, regular bay spacing and horizontal window emphasis—with the austere sir
plicity of the Miesian idiom in this 28-story office building. Two environmenta
correct and functional designs were incorporated into the building: the archite
chose bronze-tinted exterior glass to reflect the sun and reduce the need for a
conditioning. The interior elevator cabs were double-decked so that they cou
service two floors simultaneously during morning and evening rush hours (a
arrangement since discontinued).

Onterie Center – *446-448 E. Ontario St.* Completed in 1986 by architect Bruc
Graham and engineer Fazlur Khan, best known for their collaboration on the Sea
Tower and the John Hancock Center, this building is distinguished by concre
crossbracing expressed in blank window panels on each facade. A two-bay inse
notch runs the length of the south facade.

★**River East Plaza (formerly North Pier Chicago)** – *435 E. Illinois St. Open May–Sep
Mon–Thu 10am–8pm, Fri–Sat 10am–9pm, Sun & holidays 11am–6pm; Oct–Ap
Mon–Thu 10am–7pm, Fri–Sat 10am–9pm, Sun & holidays 11am–5pm;* ✗ ⓒ
☎ *312-836-4300.* Built originally as the Pugh Terminal Warehouse in 1905
North Pier Chicago was artfully rehabilitated in 1990 by Booth/Hansen & Assoc
to house office space on the upper floors and a 170,000sq ft retail and ente
tainment center on the lower. Under new ownership in 1997, the complex is no
called River East Plaza. It now houses a food court as well as interior shop
arranged around a central rotunda; further remodeling and the addition of mor
stores is planned for the future. Striking **views**★ of the city can be observed fror
the southern glass galleries or the dockside promenade. On the lower level yo
can purchase tickets for architectural and historical boat tours of the city *(depa
from River East Plaza May–Oct daily 10am–4pm; round-trip 1hr 30mir
commentary; reservations suggested; $19;* ✗ ⓖ ☐ *Chicago From the Lak
☎ 312-527-1977).*

★**Lake Shore Drive** – This thoroughfare bordering the lake is lined with an array c
high rises, several of which were designed by renowned German-born architec
Ludwig Mies van der Rohe (1886-1969).

★★**860-880 North Lake Shore Drive** – The completion of these apartment tower
in 1951 by Mies van der Rohe established his reputation as a master of Modernisr
and prefigured the design of steel-and-glass skyscrapers throughout the 1960s an
70s. Their prominent location, substantial scale and elegance of proportion wer
the first realization of steel-and-glass curtain wall designs that Mies had bee
developing for over 30 years. Here he used steel piers encased in concrete, an
created a strong vertical dynamic by attaching I-beams to the exterior between th
window frames. A transparent lobby space produces an elegant effect. The tw
buildings are angled toward each other and the street, providing many lake view
for the apartments. The success of these towers led to another commission two
years later at **900-910 North Lake Shore Drive**. Distinguished by dark glass and window
frames, these structures represent a more monochromatic design.

Lake Shore Place – *No. 680.* Visible from many places in the area is the blue pyram
idal roof of this office and residential complex, formerly known as the America
Furniture Mart (1926). The 30-story tower and its four corner tourelles are embe
lished with Victorian Gothic designs, including three-story arches and a
ornamental lantern at the top.

Lake Point Tower – *No. 505.* Lonely sentinel on the east side of the drive, this unusua
high rise was built in 1968 by Schipporeit-Heinrich, students of Mies van der Roh
who adapted an unexecuted 1920 design by the master. All of the exterior sur
faces of the Y-shaped tower are rounded, creating a flowing surface studded wit
vertical steel piers.

★★ NAVY PIER

🚇 *600 E. Grand Ave. at Lake Michigan. Open Memorial Day–Labor Day Sun–Thu 10am–10pm, Fri–Sat 10am–midnight. Sept–Oct Mon–Thu 10am–9pm, Fri–Sat 10am–11pm, Sun 10am–7pm. Nov–May Mon–Thu 10am–8pm, Fri–Sat 10am–11pm, Sun 10am–7pm. Shops & restaurants closed Thanksgiving Day & Dec 25.* ✗ ♿ 🅿 *($7.50-$17.50)* ☎ *312-595-7437. www.navypier.com.*

Designed by Charles S. Frost in 1916, the 3,000ft-long pier was the largest in the world at the time. With an upper level for passengers and streetcar tracks and a lower level for freight, it was an important terminal for several decades. Long freight sheds (since demolished) connected the Head House (now known as the Family Pavilion) to an auditorium building situated at the far end. The pier was used for naval training during World War II, and then by the University of Illinois until 1965, at which time it was affectionately known as "Harvard on the Rocks." Renovated in 1959 for the opening of the St. Lawrence Seaway and again in 1976, the pier fell into disrepair until 1991, when the city proposed a $190 million redevelopment plan, which foresaw the pier as an extension of McCormick Place Convention Center.

Today encompassing more than 50 acres of shops, eateries, gardens and attractions, the pier has regained its fame as one of the largest entertainment piers in the country. A bustling and festive place that draws throngs of fun-seekers, the pier features an IMAX theater, two museums, boutiques, restaurants and office space in its Family Pavilion. The pier is also the new home of the **Chicago Shakespeare Theater**, whose members perform here year-round in a 525-seat courtyard-style theater.

Carousel on Navy Pier

© Kevin O. Mooney/Odyssey

Adjoining the Family Pavilion to the east, the Crystal Gardens house an indoor tropical park, embellished with Arizona palm trees. At the center of the pier is Navy Pier Park, which showcases a 150ft-high **Ferris Wheel**, a musical merry-go-round and a 1,500-seat outdoor amphitheater called Skyline Stage. With its taut, sail-like roof, the popular venue rises above a one-story retail level. **Festival Hall**, a series of three-story structures designed for conventions, trade shows and meetings, connects the central area to the Terminals Building, with its splendidly restored ballroom. A seasonal beer garden welcomes weary strollers, who enjoy some of the city's best views of the lake and the famed skyline.

★ **Chicago Children's Museum (M)** – 🚇 *Open Memorial Day–Labor Day daily 10am–5pm (Thu 8pm). Rest of the year Tue–Sun 10am–5pm (Thu til 8pm). $6.50 (free Thu 5pm–8pm).* ✗ ♿ 🅿 *(discount with museum validation).* ☎ *312-527-1000. www.chichildrensmuseum.org.* Founded in 1982 as the Express-Ways Children's Museum, this three-story, hands-on facility is designed to activate the intellectual and creative potential of children from toddlers to pre-teens. Interactive exhibits invite youngsters to build bridges, appreciate grandparents, climb aboard a replica 1850 schooner, and create news broadcasts, all in a colorful environment monitored by trained supervisors.

Be sure to don a raincoat before entering **WaterWays**, to direct the world's most abundant resource through a system of rivers, locks and bridges. Prejudice and discrimination are explored in **Face to Face** *(not recommended for children under*

■ **Cruising Off Navy Pier**

From the south side of Navy Pier you can catch a variety of dinner cruises, charters (*Anita Dee I & II*; ☎ 773-281-1300; www.anitadee.com), speed boats, shuttles and the Pier's own four-masted schooner, *Windy (docked across from Riva Restaurant;* ☎ *312-595-5472)*. Following are some of the options:

Odyssey – This 700-passenger luxury liner offers brunch, lunch, dinner and moonlight cruises (☎ 800-947-9367; www.premieryachtsinc.com).

The Spirit of Chicago – Board this 600-passenger ship for brunch, lunch and dinner cruises featuring live entertainment and dancing (☎ 312-836-7899; www.spiritofchicago.com).

Seadog I, II, III & IV – Sleek, bright yellow speedboats, *Seadogs* provide 30min lakefront rides or 75min architectural river tours for up to 149 passengers (☎ 312-822-7200; www.premieryachtsinc.com).

UglyDuck – Chicago's newest passenger vessels, these 500-passenger yellow and white craft offers a variety of 2-3hr lake cruises, complete with DJ (☎ 630-916-9007; www.premieryachtsinc.com).

Shoreline Sightseeing – Operates daily lakefront and river tours from the southwest corner of Navy Pier (☎ 312-222-9328; www.shorelinesight-seeing.com). Shoreline also offers water-taxi service between Navy Pier and the Sears Tower (*southwest corner of Gateway Park & Adams St.*) and between the Pier and the Museum Campus (*Memorial Day–Labor Day daily 10:30am–6pm; $6 one-way*).

seven); exhibits here help kids identify offensive behavior and practice ways of responding constructively. Other popular permanent exhibits include Safe and Sound, designed to demystify children's fears about medical care; the Inventing Lab, where youngsters create their own flying machine; and the Info-Tech Arcade, a state-of-the-art television studio and computer lab.

★**Smith Museum of Stained-Glass Windows** – *Open year-round Mon–Th 10am–8pm, Fri–Sat 10am–10pm, Sun 10am–7pm.* ♿ ☎ 312-595-5024. Occupying an 800ft-long series of galleries along the lower level terraces of Festival Hall, this unique museum showcases more than 100 stained-glass windows. The majority of the windows were installed in Chicago between 1870 and the present. Both religious and secular windows are arranged by artistic style (Victorian, Prairie, Modern and Contemporary) and include national names such as Louis Comfort Tiffany and John LaFarge, as well as Chicago artists Ed Paschke and Roger Brown.

RIVER NORTH★

Brown or Orange line to State; Red line to Grand
Map p 105

Nestled in the crook between the Chicago River and its north branch, bounded by Rush Street on the east and Oak Street on the north, River North is an eclectic neighborhood of historic buildings, modern skyscrapers and churches that punctuate endless blocks of ordinary city. Site of Chicago's earliest industries, River North is today most famous for its art galleries, celebrity-owned restaurants and trendy clubs.

Historical Notes

From Factories to Flophouses – River North encompasses one of Chicago's oldest areas: Wolf Point, a small promontory around which the river turns north. Here in the 1830s early settlers, French-Canadian fur traders and Potawatomi Indians mingled at trading posts and taverns while small industries sprang up nearby. By mid-century, factories crowded the water's edge. Grain elevators, lumber mills, brick yards, tanneries and breweries bustled and spewed. Between the north and the main branches of the river, insalubrious shantytowns spread, housing laborers and their families. Waves of immigrants—Irish, Norwegians, Danes, Swedes and later Italians—settled south of Division Street, while in the blocks around Washington Square Park and just west of Michigan Avenue, Chicago's elite established an early North Side enclave.

In 1871 the Chicago Fire devastated shanties and mansions alike as it leapt the river and raged northward. Rebuilding began immediately, and the area re-emerged as a corridor of elegant homes flanking the eastern edge of a working-class neighborhood. By 1900 the blighted and lawless northwestern corner was known as Little Hell. As industry burgeoned, the population continued to increase. Around

World War I, the newest immigrants—blacks moving up from the South during the Great Migration—took their place in the melting pot that characterized this neighborhood.

In 1920 the completion of the Michigan Avenue Bridge ensured the destiny of that boulevard as the fashionable Magnificent Mile. Desirable neighborhoods along the avenue attracted wealthy residents from the blocks between Wabash Avenue and LaSalle Street to the west, leaving the old homes there to be subdivided into apartments and rooming houses. Washington Square Park, nicknamed "Bughouse Square," became the center of Chicago's bohemia, an open forum for soapbox orators, hobo poets and a parade of characters expounding on everything from Nietzsche to free love. Clark Street north of the river became the magnificent mile of

Rock 'n Roll McDonald's, Interior

© Kevin O. Mooney Odyssey

the demimonde, lined with flophouses, bars and dance halls. In the former Little Hell, massive urban-renewal efforts throughout the 1940s and 50s produced the controversial Cabrini-Green housing projects, now a sad reminder of good intentions gone awry.

A New Start with Art – In the 1970s art dealers frustrated by rising costs on Michigan Avenue sought less expensive gallery spaces. The deserted warehouses in the old industrial district south of Superior Street and west of Wells Street offered a perfect alternative, and they soon swarmed with artists, buyers and lookers. After a decade of prosperity, tragedy struck in 1989 when fire destroyed the entire block between Orleans and Sedgwick Streets south of Superior Street, consuming nine galleries. On its heels the economic downturn of the early 1990s caused several more galleries to close or leave, some for River West—the next reviving neighborhood to offer reasonable rents. Around 65 remain, however, sustaining River North's reputation as Chicago's center of contemporary art. This quarter seems also to be a favorite location for celebrity-owned restaurants and clubs. Popular spots, such as the Hard Rock Cafe, Harry Caray's and the Rain Forest Cafe, attract city folk, suburbanites and tourists like.

1 Ontario Street

Map p 105. Between Dearborn and Wells Streets, this neon-lit artery forms the hub of River North nightlife drawing hordes of tourists to such popular chain restaurants as the **Hard Rock Cafe** (*63 W. Ontario St.;* ☎ *312-943-2252*), **Rock 'n' Roll McDonald's** (*600 N. Clark St., at Ontario;* ☎ *312-664-7940*) and **Ed Debevic's** (*640 N. Wells St., at Ontario;* ☎ *312-664-1707*), a Chicago institution known for its sassy waitstaff, often dressed as characters from 1950s movies and TV shows. Ontario at Wells Street is also the new location of **Geno's East** (*633 N. Wells St.;* ☎ *312-988-2400*), Chicago's favorite deep-dish pizzeria, renowned for its two-inch-thick pies and its graffitti-splattered wooden booths. Call ahead and order your pizza, or be prepared to wait at least 30min for it to cook.

SIGHTS

River North covers a large area that can be divided roughly into six sections. Of most interest are the first three areas: the eastern corridor, stretching from the river to Pearson Street; the Washington Square neighborhood, primarily along Dearborn Street; and the gallery district concentrated around Wells, Orleans, Superior and Huron Streets. In addition, River North contains the Mart District, including the behemoth Merchandise Mart, the Ohio-Ontario corridor of trendy restaurants and the cathedral district, centering upon Holy Name Cathedral.

★EASTERN CORRIDOR 1.1mi

Located across the river from the Loop's bustling business district, this area offers a varied blend of architecture and purpose, including modern office buildings, 19C residences and religious edifices, that can best be appreciated on foot.
Begin at the intersection of N. State St. and Wacker Dr.

★**Marina City** – *300 N. State St.* From the river's edge rise the twin "corncob" towers of Bertrand Goldberg's prototype urban community. Revolutionary when conceived in 1959, the columnar apartment buildings were an attempt to encourage young professionals to resist the lure of the suburbs by providing not only living space but entertainment and services as well. Above the 18-story parking garages, pie-shaped units radiate from each tower's central core, where most of their load is borne. The cast-concrete construction and undulating surfaces of the towers contrast dramatically with the Miesian "glass boxes" so popular at the time.

Across State Street, for example, stands the **IBM Building★** (1971), the last American work of Ludwig Mies van der Rohe. Although still on the drawing board when the architect died in 1969, the edifice is quintessential Mies in its purity of form and function. Wrapped in a bronze-tinted curtain wall, its rectangular mass ascends from a spacious plaza.

Walk west along the river, then cross it via Dearborn St. bridge and continue to Westin River North; descend the stairs at the northwest corner of the bridge to the riverfront promenade and continue west.

An unlikely duo—**Quaker Tower** *(321 N. Clark St.)* and **Westin River North** *(320 N. Dearborn St.)*, formerly the Hotel Nikko Chicago—are connected by a riverbank promenade called Riverfront Park. Architects Skidmore, Owings & Merrill invoked the spirit of their own Lever House (built 30

Marina City and IBM Building

years earlier in New York) in the 35-story rectangular Quaker Tower (1987). The lines of the much smaller hotel (1987, Hellmuth, Obata & Kassabaum) next door seem soft by comparison. The serenity of the Westin's lobby is enhanced by the lovely riverside garden that it overlooks.

At the western corner of Quaker Tower, ascend the stairs to Clark St. and walk north; turn right on Hubbard St.

Courthouse Place (Cook County Criminal Courts Building) – *54 W. Hubbard S* Identifiable by its stern Romanesque Revival facade, this quiet professional buildin (1892) was for years the center of much judicial and journalistic hubbut Celebrated defense attorney Clarence Darrow defended Chicago murderers Natha Leopold and Richard Loeb here in 1924—saving them from the death penalty—

and journalists Ben Hecht and Charles MacArthur were inspired enough by the press room to write *The Front Page* in 1928. The courts moved out in 1929, leaving the building to the more mundane city agencies that occupied it until its renovation in the mid-1980s.

Walk east on Hubbard St. and turn left on State St.

The slab-like building at **515 North State Street**★ is Japanese architect Kenzo Tange's first Chicago work (1990). The razor-sharp, 45-degree angle that bisects the building on the west and the four-story cutout near the top lend the 30-story headquarters of the American Medical Association a most unusual profile.

Continue walking north on State St. to the intersection with Ohio St.

Built in three stages between 1894 and 1913, **Tree Studios** *(601-623 N. State St.)* were the inspiration of Judge Lambert Tree, who, as a prominent patron of the arts, wished to persuade artists to settle and work in Chicago by providing them an inexpensive place to live. Today artists continue to live and work in the historic studios.

Walk east on Ohio St. to Rush St.

★ **Disney Quest** – 🚇 *55 E. Ohio St. Open year-round Sun–Wed 11am–7pm, Thu–Fri 11am–10pm, Sat 10am–10pm. $34.* ✕ ♿ ☎ *312-222-1300. http://disney.go.com/disneyquest.* A shimmering facade of glittering color and stylized mouse ears anticipates the plethora of virtual reality and computerized arcade games inside Disney's "indoor interactive theme park." Designed with characteristic Disney bravura, this cavernous space is Las Vegas for kids, straddling the worlds of video arcade and amusement park. Your journey begins aboard the "cybrolator" where an animated elevator ride transports you to the third-floor Venture-Port. From here you can access all five floors of the "park," which is organized into four zones: Score!, Replay, Create and Explore. Each zone incorporates video or arcade games and at least one virtual ride. Design and ride your own roller-coaster on **CyberSpace Mountain**, where gravity poses no limitations. Compose your own melody and lyrics in **Song-Maker**, and take home your efforts on a CD. At the **Animation Academy** you can use digital sketchpads to create your own cartoons. Or hop on a life-size joystick and become a virtual pinball in **Mighty Ducks Pinball Slam**. All in all, the "rides" can induce almost as much vertigo as their real-time counterparts.

② ESPN Zone

Map p 105. 🚇 *43 E. Ohio St. Open year-round Mon–Thu 11:30am–midnight, Fri–Sat 11:30am– 12:30am, Sun 11:30am–11:30pm.* ✕ ♿ ☎ *312-644-3776. www.espn.go.com/espninc/zone.* Sports fans of all ages will revel in this digital-generation sports bar/arcade just west of Disney Quest. On the second floor, the 10,000sq ft **Sports Arena** offers a plethora of interactive sports and virtual-reality games ranging from bowling to car-racing to skydiving. The third-floor **Screening Room** is equipped with a 16ft video monitor surrounded by 36-inch monitors for the ultimate in multi-game viewing. (Couch potatoes will appreciate the comfy leather recliners with individual audio controls in the front row.) In the Studio Grill you can dine in replica ESPN studio sets while watching—what else?— ESPN sports.

Walk back one block west on Ohio St. to Wasbash Ave.

Medinah Temple, the curious mosque-like edifice at 600 North Wabash Avenue, was built by the Shriners in 1913 for fraternal meetings and ceremonials. Today it accommodates the annual Shriners Circus, as well as a variety of civic events. Textured brickwork and interlocking line designs around the doors and windows add to its exotic Arabian look. Its immense auditorium seats 4,200 *(guided tours available, reservations required; ☎ 312-266-5000).*

Walk north on Wabash Ave. to Erie St.

At the corner of Wabash Avenue and Erie Street stand two remnants of the gracious living that once characterized the eastern corridor of River North: the **Ransom R. Cable House**★ (1886, Cobb & Frost) at 25 East Erie Street and the **Samuel M. Nickerson House**★ (1883, Burling & Whitehouse), diagonally across the street. The two imposing residences display the Victorian tendency toward extravagance, stylistic eclecticism and mass. The Cable House, built by the president of the Chicago, Rock Island & Pacific Railway Co., exhibits the hallmarks of the Richardsonian Romanesque style, fusing a variety of architectural elements and design motifs into a uniform whole. Of particular interest are the turret, dormers, recessed windows, arches, surface decoration and steeply sloping slate roof. The rectangular symmetry of the Nickerson House is more traditionally Italianate. But the dark, brooding exterior belies the Baroque luxuriance of its renowned **interior**★, often referred to as the "marble palace." Samuel

3 Gold Coast Dogs

Map p 105. 418 N. State St. ☎ *312-527-1222.* The Chicago-style hot dog ranks with the deep-dish pizza as a source of local culinary pride, and this busy stand serves up some of the best in town. Though topping choices vary depending on individual taste, the basic architecture of the Chicago-style dog (also known as a "red hot") consists of a Vienna beef frank served on a poppyseed bun. Mustard, relish and onions are de rigeur, and tomatoes, pickle slices, cucumber, lettuce and both green and hot peppers are often added with a dash of celery salt. Ketchup, however, has no business on a red hot!

4 Jazz Record Mart

Map p 105. 444 N. Wabash Ave. ☎ *312-222-1467.* Impresario Bob Koester has been a fixture on the local scene for decades, and his commitment to and enthusiasm for jazz and blues make his record store one of the most popular in town. While the Mart's comprehensive selection of albums, CDs and cassettes includes everything from Bix Biederbeck and Thelonious Monk to Kenny G., serious jazz aficionados flock to the shop in search of vintage vinyl, imports and other rare recordings Koester and his staff are renowned for finding.

5 Pizzeria Uno and Pizzeria Due

Map p 105. Uno: 29 E. Ohio St.; ☎ *312-321-1000. Due: 619 N. Wabash Ave.;* ☎ *312-943-2400.* These sister restaurants located in converted Victorian mansions always rank at the top of local "best deep-dish" polls. Both restaurants are very popular on weekends, and the staff will take your pizza order before you sit down to help reduce your wait (which can run up to an hour). At lunchtime, Uno and Due offer express service, delivering an individual-size deep-dish pie to your table in 20 minutes.

Nickerson, president of the First National Bank when he commissioned the home clearly spared no expense. A dazzling mélange of woods, marbles, tile and glass decorates each room on the mansion's three floors. Nickerson House is now a lavish gallery space for the R.H. Love Galleries, who restored it in 1991 *(40 E Erie St.; open year-round Mon–Sat 9am–5pm; closed major holidays* ☎ *312-640-1300; www. artnet.com rhlove.html).* Next door at 50 East Erie Street, the incongruous facade of the **John B. Murphy Memorial Auditorium** (1926) looms over the sidewalk. Named for a prominent physician, the structure houses an auditorium-library for the American College of Surgeons.

Continue north on Wabash Ave. to Huron St.

★**Episcopal Cathedral of St. James** – *6. E. Huron St. at N. Wabash Ave. Visit by guided tour (30min) only; reservation required. Open Mon–Fri 10am–5pm. $25/group. Free guided tour first Sun of the month after the 11am service.* ☎ *312-787-7360. www.epischicago. org.* From the outside, this Victorian-style cathedral (1857, Edward J. Burling; 1875, Burling & Adler; restored 1985, Holabird & Root) appears typical of the Chicago churches built of local limestone around the time of the Great Fire. The original structure of 1857 was destroyed in the blaze; only the 1867 bell tower remains standing, still bearing telltale char marks. The Civil War memorial in the narthex also survived the fire and served as a temporary altar until the church could be rebuilt in 1875. The **interior**★ of the church is truly breathtaking; its meticulously restored stencilwork, originally applied in 1888, draws heavily on the naturalistic designs and colors of the Arts and Crafts movement.

Continue north on Wabash Ave. to Superior St. and turn left.

At the corner of Superior and State Streets, **Holy Name Cathedral** *(735 N. State St.)*, an impressive structure dating back to 1875, serves as the Cathedral of the Catholic Archdiocese of Chicago. Renovated twice in 1914 and 1968, the Gothic Revival edifice was the site of Pope John Paul II's 1979 visit to Chicago.

Return to Wabash Ave. and continue north to Chicago Ave.

At Chicago and Wabash Avenues, note the **Hotel St. Benedict Flats** (1882). These apartments were designed to attract upper-middle-class residents—an unprecedented concept since apartment living was then considered déclassé. To dispel that image, architect James J. Egan devised the facade to resemble attached row houses.

Continue north on Wabash Ave., turn right on Pearson St. and continue to Rush St.

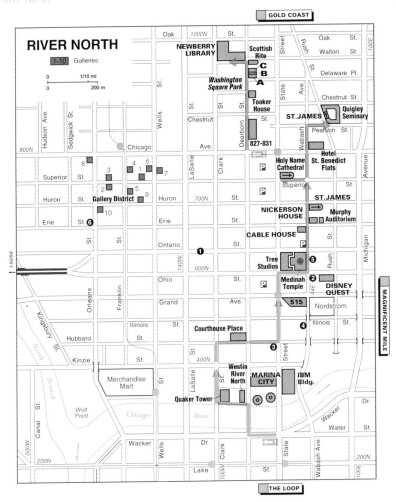

At 831 North Rush Street, the Gothic-style **Archbishop Quigley Preparatory Seminary** (1919), named for the archbishop dedicated to building Chicago's Catholic schools, bears testament to the heyday of Catholic architecture in the city. At the southwest corner, the **Chapel of St. James★**, modeled after Sainte-Chapelle in Paris, is noteworthy for its stunning windows *(open year-round Tue & Thu–Sat noon–2pm; closed Jan 1, Easter weekend & Dec 23-25;* ♿ ☎ *312-787-8625)*. Each window comprises 45,000 pieces of antique English glass that is truly "stained" (the glass, while molten, is mixed with pigment) and not merely painted.

Washington Square .25mi

The establishment of Washington Square Park in 1842 stimulated residential development in the neighboring blocks. Today the homes along Dearborn Street between Chicago Avenue and Maple Street give a sense of the area as it must have looked in the late 19C.

Begin at the intersection of Dearborn St. and Chicago Ave. and walk north.

North Dearborn Street – The row houses at **nos. 827-831** sport bas-relief portraits rescued from Adler & Sullivan's downtown Schiller Theater at its demolition in 1961. At no. 863 the **Robert N. Tooker House** was designed by William Le Baron Jenney and William A. Otis in 1886. But the Tooker name may be more famous for Tooker Place, the alley next door, where in later years, the denizens of bohemia flocked nightly to the Dill Pickle Club, located in a since-razed brick barn. Between 1916 and 1931 indigent artists, poets, playwrights and philosophers rubbed elbows and raised glasses here with thieves and gangsters, lawyers and professors.

The buildings in the next block north are owned by the Oriental Consistory (Scottish Rite Bodies), a Masonic lodge with headquarters at no. 915, the former **John Howland Thompson House** (**A**). Designed by Henry Ives Cobb and Charles S. Frost in

6 **Mr. Beef**

*Map p 105. 666 N. Orleans
St. ☎ 312-337-8500.*
Tonight Show host Jay
Leno put this place on the
map. He discovered it as a
struggling stand-up comic
working the nightclub circuit
and has been recommending
it to his Hollywood pals for
years. Don't go to Mr. Beef
just to catch a glimpse of a
visiting celebrity; go for the
Italian beef sandwiches,
consisting of a soft Italian
roll piled high with thinly-
sliced marinated beef
garnished with *giardinere*
(pickled peppers, celery and
spices). Variations on the
basic sandwich include "hot"
(topped with chili peppers),
"sweet" (with roasted red
and green peppers) and
"wet" (dipped in the beef's
juices).

1888, the mansion features a livel
roofline balancing the massive quality o
its rusticated sandstone surface. Th
1895 **George H. Taylor House** (**B**) *(no. 919*
is purely Georgian in style, while the ad
jacent **George B. Carpenter House** (**C**
(no. 925) combines massive stone wit
elegant, rounded bays. The **Scottish Rit
Cathedral** *(no. 929)* began life in 1867 a
Unity Church. The Great Fire destroyed a
but the church's Gothic limestone walls
and it was rebuilt in 1873 by the archi
tectural firm of Burling & Adler. Dankma
Adler, who established his reputation fo
superior acoustics with this commission
would go on to become Louis Sullivan'
partner and an expert in theater and au
ditorium design. The church was eventu
ally sold to the Oriental Consistory, whic
renovated the inside to meet its need
(not open to the public).

Walk west on Walton St.

Washington Square Park is Chicago's oldes
surviving park, donated to the city by de
veloper Orsamus Bushnell, who hoped i
would attract wealthy home builders t
his subdivision. Perhaps more famous a
"Bughouse Square," the park is sti
occasionally the site of speeches an
debates during the summer.

■ **River North Gallery District**

This bustling district in River North *(bounded by Chicago, Wells, Huron
and Orleans Sts.)* features more than 65 galleries devoted to contemporary and ethnic art; 19C and 20C American works; ceramics and furniture;
Chicago artists; photography; and a sampling of European paintings, sculpture and prints. On the first Friday of each month, in addition to special
"opening" nights throughout the season *(Sept–Jun)*, galleries sponsor concurrent evening receptions *(5pm–8pm; free)*, drawing Chicago art lovers
out for an evening of "gallery-hopping." *Most galleries are open Tue–Sat
10am–5:30pm (call to confirm). For schedules, call ☎ 312-649-0064 or
www.artline.com/associations.*

Following is a sampling of River North Galleries *(map p 105).*

Carl Hammer Gallery (6) – *740 N. Wells St.* ☎ *312-266-8512.
www.hammergallery.com.* Focuses on "outsider" and self-taught artists.

Carol Ehlers Gallery (8) – *750 N. Orleans St.* ☎ *312-642-8611.* 20C
masters and contemporary photography.

Carrie Secrist Gallery (3) – *300 W. Superior St.* ☎ *312-280-4500.*
Established and emerging contemporary art in all media.

Douglas Dawson Gallery (9) – *222 W. Huron St.* ☎ *312-751-1961.*
Ancient and historic art from Africa, Asia and the Americas.

Marx-Saunders Gallery, Ltd. (4) – *230 W. Superior St.* ☎ *312-573-1400.
www.marxsaunders.com.* Contemporary studio glass and sculpture.

Perimeter Gallery, Inc. (1) – *210 W. Superior St.* ☎ *312-266-9473.
www.perimetergallery.com.* Contemporary painting, sculpture, works on
paper and master crafts.

Printworks Gallery (2) – *311 W. Superior St.* ☎ *312-664-9407.*
Contemporary prints, drawings, photographs and artists' books.

Robert Henry Adams Fine Art (5) – *715 N. Franklin St.* ☎ *312-642-8700.
www.adamsfineart.com.* American Impressionist and Modern paintings,
drawings and sculpture pre-1945.

Roy Boyd Gallery (7) – *739 N. Wells St.* ☎ *312-642-1606.* Abstract
American works.

Zolla/Lieberman Gallery (10) – *325 W. Huron St.* ☎ *312-944-1990.
www.zollaliebermangallery.com.* The first gallery to come to River North, in
1975, showcases contemporary works by emerging and established artists.

★**Newberry Library** – *60 W. Walton St. Reading rooms open year-round Tue–Thu 10am–6pm, Fri–Sat 9am–5pm. Closed major holidays. Guided tours (1hr) available Thu 3pm & Sat 10:30am.* ♿ ❑*(fee)* ☎ *312-943-9090. www.newberry.org.* Established in 1887 with a bequest from merchant, banker and land speculator Walter L. Newberry (1804-68), this venerable institution ranks among the top independent research libraries in the country for scholars in the humanities. Its collections are impressive both in quality and quantity: 1.5 million volumes and 5 million manuscript pages include materials as diverse as a 1481 edition of Dante's **Divine Comedy** and a 17C Mexican manuscript on tree bark. Its map, music, American Indian and Midwestern literature holdings are unparalleled. Researchers come from around the country to use its genealogical resources. Architect **Henry Ives Cobb** designed the Spanish Romanesque edifice in 1893. A 10-story stack and storage wing by Harry Weese & Assocs. were added in 1982. For the casual visitor, a look around the lobby, with its tall ceilings, grand staircase, terrazzo floors and lovely reproduction light fixtures, imparts a sense of the building's grandeur. Rotating exhibits in the galleries located just off the lobby draw heavily on the collections, offering the non-researching public an opportunity to sample the library's treasures.

111 S. Michigan Ave. at E. Adams St.

bus no. 151

Map p 73 and plans pp 109, 114 and 120

One of the great museums of the world and the preeminent arts institution of the Midwest, the Art Institute of Chicago is a comprehensive center for arts education and exhibition. Its collections span 5,000 years of visual expression, drawing on the cultures of Europe, Asia, Africa and the Americas, and featuring works in a wide range of media. The museum's reputation is primarily based on its collection of Impressionist and post-Impressionist paintings, one of the largest and most important outside France.

Historical Notes

The Building – Founded in 1866 as the Chicago Academy of Design, the Art Institute was one of the first art schools in the US. Reorganized to incorporate a school and museum in 1879, this institution by 1887 occupied its own building two blocks south of its current location. The institute's board of directors, determined to create a world-class center for art education and exhibition, used the occasion of the World's Columbian Exposition of 1893 to construct a new facility. Architecturally intended to embody the cultural attainments of Chicago, the Neoclassical edifice countered the city's tough working-class reputation. The core structure, planned with its future as an art museum in mind, would be utilized by the World Congresses during the fair and then turned over to the Art Institute. It was the only World's Fair pavilion located off the fairgrounds of Jackson Park. Created by Shepley, Rutan & Coolidge, the building had initially been designed by architect John W. Root, who died before the construction began.

From the original 50,000sq ft of the Allerton Building, the Art Institute has expanded to over 400,000sq. ft. Coolidge & Hodgdon designed McKinlock Court (1924), the open-air garden to the east, today used for daily lunches and jazz concerts on Tuesday evenings during summer. Subsequent additions included the Goodman Theatre (1926) by Howard Van Doren Shaw; the Ferguson Building (1958) by Holabird & Root & Burgee, to the north of the Allerton Building; the Morton Building (1962) by Shaw, Metz & Assocs.; the Rubloff Building (1976) and a new facility for the School of the Art Institute by Skidmore, Owings & Merrill; and the Rice Building (1988) designed by Hammond, Beeby & Babka. Also of note is the reconstruction of Louis Sullivan's Trading Room from the Chicago Stock Exchange (1893).

The museum also houses many facilities for arts education, including a film center and study rooms for prints, textiles, architectural drawings and photographs. Opened 1992, the Kraft Education Center presents demonstrations of artistic techniques related to current exhibitions in the museum. The Ryerson and Burnham libraries were

■ Short On Time?

If you have only two hours to visit the Art Institute, spend them seeing the following masterpieces (listed in order of visit):

- **Thorne Miniature Rooms** *(Allerton, lower level, gallery 11)*
- **Archaic Chinese Jades** *(Allerton, 1st floor, galleries 131A-132)*
- **Tomb figures, Tang dynasty** *(Allerton, 1st floor, gallery 105)*
- **Mrs. Daniel Hubbard**, John Singleton Copley *(Rice, 1st floor, gallery 167)*
- **View of Cotopaxi**, Frederic E. Church *(Rice, 1st floor, gallery 170)*
- **The Child's Bath**, Mary Cassatt *(Rice, 1st floor, gallery 171)*
- **Rubloff Paperweight Collection** *(Rice, lower level, gallery 69)*
- **Augsburg Cabinet** *(Rice, lower level, gallery 71)*
- **America Windows**, Marc Chagall *(Rubloff, 1st floor, gallery 150)*
- **Ayala Altarpiece** *(Rubloff, 1st floor, gallery 157)*
- **Trading Room of the Chicago Stock Exchange** *(Rubloff, lower level)*
- **Architectural fragments** *(Allerton, 2nd floor, gallery 200)*
- **Mater Dolorosa**, Dieric Bouts *(Allerton, 2nd floor, gallery 207)*
- **The Assumption of the Virgin**, El Greco *(Allerton, 2nd floor, gallery 215)*
- **Old Man with a Gold Chain**, Rembrandt van Rijn *(Allerton, 2nd floor, gallery 216)*
- **Six versions of Stacks of Wheat**, Claude Monet *(Allerton, 2nd floor, gallery 206)*
- **Paris Street; Rainy Day**, Gustave Caillebotte *(Allerton, 2nd floor, gallery 201)*
- **A Sunday on La Grande Jatte—1884**, Georges Seurat *(Allerton, 2nd floor, gallery 205)*
- **Nighthawks**, Edward Hopper *(Allerton, 2nd floor, gallery 236)*
- **Mother and Child**, Pablo Picasso *(Allerton, 2nd floor, gallery 243)*
- **On the Threshold of Liberty**, René Magritte *(Allerton, 2nd floor, gallery 246)*
- **American Gothic**, Grant Wood *(Allerton, 2nd floor, gallery 236)*

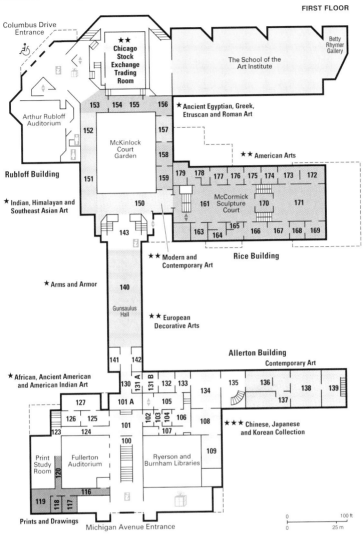

Columbus Drive Entrance

★★ **Chicago Stock Exchange Trading Room**

153 154 155 156

The School of the Art Institute

Betty Rhymer Gallery

★ **Ancient Egyptian, Greek, Etruscan and Roman Art**

Arthur Rubloff Auditorium

152

157

McKinlock Court Garden

158

★★ **American Arts**

Rubloff Building

151

159

179 178 177 176 175 174 173 172

★ **Indian, Himalayan and Southeast Asian Art**

150

McCormick Sculpture Court

161 170 171

143

163 164 165 166 167 168 169

★★ **Modern and Contemporary Art**

Rice Building

★ **Arms and Armor**

140

Gunsaulus Hall

★★ **European Decorative Arts**

Allerton Building

Contemporary Art

141 142

★ **African, Ancient American and American Indian Art**

130 131 A 131 B 132 133 134 135 136 137 138 139

127 101 A 105

126 125 102 103 104 106

123 124 101 107 108

★★★ **Chinese, Japanese and Korean Collection**

100 109

Print Study Room

120

Fullerton Auditorium

116

Ryerson and Burnham Libraries

119 118 117

Prints and Drawings

Michigan Avenue Entrance

0 ——— 100 ft
0 ——— 25 m

founded by Martin Ryerson, an art collector who donated his books on the fine and decorative arts, and by architect Daniel Burnham, whose architectural journals, drawings and letters formed the nucleus of the library collections.

Today the insitute's monumental Indiana limestone facade on Michigan Avenue reveals its relationship with the other Beaux-Arts buildings of the World Fair's "White City." The broad staircase, today one of the favorite people-watching and meeting places in the city, makes a suitably grand entrance. Inside the original building, a grand staircase leads to the galleries on the second level. Skylights restored as part of an extensive rehabilitation of the museum in 1987 heighten the drama of the space with a warm, natural light.

The Collections – The museum's seminal holdings flourished thanks to the enthusiasm of civic leaders whose wealth—derived from railroads, manufacturing, real estate and lumber—enabled them to amass personal collections. Their financial and material donations established the museum's reputation for large-scale, high-quality acquisitions. Among the earliest material donations to the Art Institute was the Henry Field Collection of 41 Barbizon school paintings. The museum made its first large purchase in 1894, acquiring the Demidoff Collection of 14 Dutch and Flemish masterpieces. Chicago's early art collectors reveled in their independence; they built their collections based on personal taste, in spite of criticism for ignoring expert advice. Because of this radical independence, by 1890 more collectors of French Impressionist and post-Impressionist paintings lived in Chicago than in Paris. Succeeding generations of Chicago collectors continued to challenge prevailing tastes and many of the museum's finest collections, including those of Asian, African and 20C art, have their roots in this determined acquisition style.

The Art Institute's prominent donors include Bertha Honoré Palmer, socialite wife
Potter Palmer, one of Chicago's most successful real-estate developers. Palmer esta
lished her role as collector and advocate of the Impressionists through her friendsh
with artist Mary Cassatt. Her bequest of the Potter Palmer Collection of
Impressionist paintings in 1922 helped secure the Art Institute's reputation in th
field. Lumber baron Martin Ryerson bequeathed an amazing 227 American an
European paintings, as well as drawings and Asian and European decorative arts,
the museum. The donations of Clarence Buckingham and his sister, Kate Sturg
Buckingham, featuring Chinese and Japanese prints, paintings, sculpture an
ceramics, form the foundation of the department of Asian art. A 1997 gift of 40
Indian, Himalayan and Southeast Asian pieces from the collection of James an
Marilynn Alsdorf has made the Art Institute's Asian holdings among the finest in th
US. The collection of avant-garde post-Impressionist paintings donated by Freder
Clay Bartlett in memory of his wife, Helen Birch Bartlett, includes many of the trea
ures of the museum, in particular George Seurat's *A Sunday on La Gran*
Jatte—1884 (1884-86). The Edwin and Lindy Bergman Collection, donated in 198
and 1991, brought the museum 78 significant paintings, collages, constructions an
works on paper by noted American and European Dada and Surrealist artists.

Principal Sections of the Museum

19C European Painting★★★
European Painting and Sculpture★★
Modern and Contemporary Art★★
American Arts★★
Chinese, Japanese and Korean Collection★★★
European Decorative Arts★★
Thorne Miniature Rooms★★
Chicago Stock Exchange Trading Room★★

African, Ancient American and American Indian Ar
Arms and Armor★
Ancient Egyptian, Greek, Etruscan and Roman Art
Prints and Drawings
Indian, Himalayan and Southeast Asian Art★
Photography
Architecture
Textiles

Collection highlights are indicated in colored boxes in the order of the visit.

Visiting the Museum

Open year round Mon-Fri 10:30am-4:30pm (Tue til 8pm), weekends & holiday
10am-5pm. Closed Thanksgiving Day & Dec 25. $8 contribution requested (fre
Tue). General introduction tour (1hr) Tue & Sat 2pm. ☆ ♿ ☎ 312-443-3600
www.artic.edu/aic.

Paris Street; Rainy Day (1876-77)
by Gustave Caillebotte

The main entrance is o
Michigan Avenue, acros
from Adams Street. You w
enter a foyer housing an i
formation desk and a ticki
booth, a checkroom and th
main gift shop, well stocke
with books, posters, decor
tive arts and a wide selectio
of beautifully crafted jewelry
The collections are displaye
in the Allerton Building and i
three major additions, Gur
nsfus Hall and the Rubloi
and Rice buildings to the eas
Buildings are connected onl
on the first floor. We sugge
you begin your visit at the
foyer information desk wher
you'll find schedules of tem
porary exhibits, lectures and
special events or tours. Jus
beyond the foyer is the gran
staircase, the point of depai
ture for the general introduc
tion tour. Recorded tours c
major special exhibits ar
available for rent near th
special exhibit areas. Certai
galleries may be closed (ask
at information desk) and spe
cific works of art may be ex
hibited in locations other thai
those indicated here.

■ **Raves for Monet**

From July 22 through November 26, 1995, the Art Institute of Chicago mounted a hugely successful retrospective. **Claude Monet: 1840-1926**. The blockbuster exhibit included 159 works by the French Impressionist painter, some of which had never been shown outside of France. Some 965,000 visitors attended the show, generating $389 million in economic benefits to the city. AIC membership soared to 158,000, surpassing for the first time the Metropolitan Museum in New York.

The Art Institute's regularly changing temporary exhibits draw from other sources as well as from the museum's own collections; supplemental lectures and demonstrations provide an in-depth experience of the work on view. In addition to special exhibits, the Art Institute offers a comprehensive program of classes for all ages, gallery tours, and films through the Film Center of the School of the Art Institute. *Check times and topics at the information desk.*

Around the Grounds – Don't miss the attractions found outside on the institute's grounds. At the main entrance, the bronze **lion** sentinels, cast by noted animal sculptor Edward Kemeys in 1894, have become popular symbols of the museum *(the lions have been temporarily relocated pending completion of construction on the Michigan Avenue steps)*. Located against the South Wing of the Allerton Building, Lorado Taft's monumental sculpture *Fountain of the Great Lakes* (1914) depicts the famed lakes as maidens, each pouring water into shells held by the others, representative of the lakes flowing into each other. The entrance arch to the Chicago Stock Exchange Trading Rooms is situated at the museum's Columbus Drive entrance.

Amenities – A favorite for outdoor summer dining, the **Garden Restaurant** serves a variety of light summer fare (sandwiches, pasta, salads). Both the restaurant and the **Court Cafeteria** are located in the lower level of the Rubloff Building. The more formal **Restaurant on the Park** offers elegant Continental cuisine, as well as a lovely view from the second floor. If you wish to dine without paying museum admission, use the secondary entrance facing Grant Park on Columbus Drive, south of Monroe Street.

19C EUROPEAN PAINTING
Galleries 221-226, 201-206, Allerton Building, 2nd floor.

The Art Institute's 19C European paintings form the heart of its prodigious body of works. Its collection of Impressionist and post-Impressionist paintings constitute one of the largest, most comprehensive and highest in quality outside France. Chicago collectors, in particular the Potter Palmers, Martin Ryersons and Frederic Clay Bartletts, began acquiring works by Monet, Renoir, Degas and Cézanne as early as the 1880s, and their gifts to the museum form the core of its holdings. The **Helen Birch Bartlett Memorial Collection★★** of post-Impressionist and early 20C masters on exhibit in gallery 205 comprises an imposing assemblage of painterly genius.

Neoclassicism, Romanticism and Realism – Out of the humanitarian ideals of the Enlightenment grew two major schools of artistic thought: Neoclassicism and Romanticism. In very different languages, both sought to express the idealism and nationalism of the new world order. Inspired by archaeological discoveries at Pompeii and Herculaneum in the mid-18C, the Neoclassicists—preeminently **Jacques Louis David**—viewed the quiet grandeur, heroic subjects and precise proportions of antiquity as fitting counterpoints to the petty dalliances of their Rococo predecessors. His superb draftsmanship and crisp, classical lines made **J.A.D. Ingres** the finest portrait painter of the era. Rejecting such precision, the painters of the Romantic movement reveled in a freer attitude toward brushstroke and color, relying on

Francisco Goya	*The Capture of the Bandit El Maragato by Friar Pedro de Zaldivia*, c.1806 (gallery 221)
Jacques Louis David	*Madame de Pastoret and Her Son*, c.1792 (gallery 221)
J.M.W. Turner	*Fishing Boats with Hucksters Bargaining for Fish*, c.1837 (gallery 222)
J.A.D. Ingres	*Amédée-David, The Marquis of Pastoret*, 1823-26 (gallery 222)
Eugène Delacroix	*The Combat of the Giaour and Hassan*, 1826 (gallery 222)
Jean-François Millet	*French Peasants Bringing Home a Calf Born in the Fields*, 1864 (gallery 223)
Gustave Courbet	*Mère Grégoire*, 1855-59 (gallery 223)

historic events and settings for their exoticism, drama and allegory. In a por
of Impressionism, **Eugène Delacroix**, master Romantic, declared, "I do not pain
sword but its sparkle." The treatment of atmosphere and light by Englishmen J
Constable *(gallery 222)* and **Joseph Mallord William Turner** is also prophetic. Tow
the middle of the 19C, a new movement grounded in reality began to emer
Forsaking classical ideals and romantic bravura, the Realists observed and record
the world around them. Inspired by **Camille Corot** *(gallery 223)*, their palette ten
to be dark, and, like **Gustave Courbet** and **Jean-François Millet**, their subjects were o
nary people.

Impressionism – The segue from Realism to Impressionism took place at the h
of **Edouard Manet**, who employed the dark tones and ordinary subjects of his c
temporaries to explore the opposition of light and shadow. Indeed, as it evolve

Two Sisters (On the Terrace) (1881)
by Pierre Auguste Renoir

Impressionism sought
define its subjects in ter
of their color and reflec
light, thereby dissolving
hard outlines that traditi
ally delineated the pain
form and, in the extrer
recasting subjects as
arrangement of colors a
light. The Impression
understood the epheme
nature of their quest a
painted rapidly to rec
moments in time with qu
brushstrokes that wo
give a spontaneous "
pression" of a scene.
They often worked o
doors attempting to c
ture the fleeting effects
sunlight, and the movem
acquired its name, coir
derogatorily by an un
pressed critic, from **Cla**
Monet's 1872 painting
pression, Sunrise. So rad
did these works seem
subject, palette and te
nique that they we
roundly rejected by the
establishment and refused admission to the annual exhibitions of the prestigi
Paris Salon. Undaunted, the Impressionists mounted eight of their own exhibiti
between 1874 and 1886, eventually gaining critical acclaim. From the smoky r
way stations and wintery grainstacks of Monet to the soft, summery aura of **Pie**
Auguste Renoir, the world as interpreted by the Impressionists was truly a colo
and luminous one.

Edouard Manet	*The Mocking of Christ,* 1865 (gallery 224)
Claude Monet	*Six versions of Stacks of Wheat,* 1890-91 (gallery 206)
Gustave Caillebotte	*Paris Street; Rainy Day,* 1876-77 (gallery 201)
Pierre Auguste Renoir	*Two Sisters (On the Terrace),* 1881 (gallery 201)
Edgar Degas	*The Millinery Shop,* 1879-84 (gallery 202)

Post-Impressionism – Because of its very nature and the diversity of its pra
tioners, the Impressionist phenomenon, though short-lived, opened the floodga
of artistic interpretation. Arising both out of and in opposition to its precepts,
artists of post-Impressionism pushed the formal aspects of painting in new er
tional, compositional, coloristic, symbolic and scientific directions. At the heart
the activity were several artists who had practiced as Impressionists, including F
Cézanne, **Paul Gauguin** and **Georges Seurat**. In general, they shared a desire to turn fr
the spontaneity of Impressionism to explore more enduring forms of expressi
Individually, each came to represent a different artistic vision. In rejecting
atmospheric realism of the Impressionists, these artists freed themselves to expl
new perspectives on color, symbolism, composition and form. Cézanne's intere
for instance, in structure and composition set him apart from the Impressioni
and strongly influenced Matisse, Picasso and the Cubist works of the n

A Sunday on La Grande Jatte—1884 (1884-86) by Georges Seurat

Vincent van Gogh	*The Bedroom*, 1889 (gallery 205)
Georges Seurat	*A Sunday on La Grande Jatte—1884*, 1884-86 (gallery 205)
Pablo Picasso	*The Old Guitarist*, 1903 (gallery 234A)
Paul Cézanne	*The Basket of Apples*, c.1895 (gallery 205)
Henri de Toulouse-Lautrec	*At the Moulin Rouge*, c.1895 (gallery 205)
Paul Gauguin	*Why are you Angry?* 1895-96 (gallery 234B)

generation, earning him the epithet "father of modern painting." Tahitian symbolism lends the work of Paul Gauguin a certain spirituality, and his bold planes of color bespeak permanence rather than impression. Seurat, in perhaps the ultimate departure, reduced his images to a near molecular level, only to build them up again using dot patterns of color. This technique, known as **Pointillism**, had its basis in the idea that points of color mixed more brilliantly in the observer's eye than did paint on the artist's palette. Other post-Impressionist directions can be seen in the work of **Vincent van Gogh**, **Henri de Toulouse-Lautrec** and **Alfred Sisley**.

★ EUROPEAN PAINTING AND SCULPTURE

Galleries 207-220, Allerton Building, 2nd floor.

This portion of the European painting and sculpture collection features work by masters from all of the major centers of artistic activity from the 15C to 1800. The art in these galleries takes religion, historic events, portraits, ancient myths, still life and landscape as its subjects, demonstrating the evolution of media and style from the early Renaissance through the Age of Reason. Small contemporary paintings, works on paper, and objects are installed in the connecting hallways.

Renaissance – As the Middle Ages came to an end after 1300, European arts and sciences flourished. The styles, subjects and media of Renaissance art vividly reflect the quickening quest for knowledge and an expanding curiosity about the world. Artists came to understand perspective, and flat landscapes of the Medieval era gave way to works with depth and dimension. Human faces took on an expressiveness, and subjects grew increasingly secular. Flanders, in present-day Belgium,

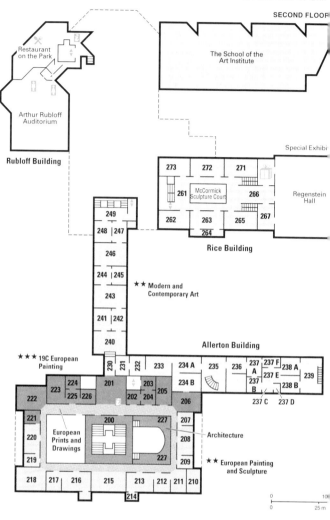

and Florence, Italy, burgeoned as artistic centers, developing distinctly differe
styles but trading influences. The Flemish discovered that oil, as a painting mediu
imparted to their work a translucent warmth missing in the bright and disti
colors of egg tempera, which remained popular in Italy for some time. Oil pa
made possible the rendering of nuance, and the northerners—**Dieric Bouts** and **H**
Memling *(gallery 207)* among them—became masters of depth and detail.
Florence, painters experimented with perspective and studied anatomy a
Classical sculpture, while in Siena **Giovanni di Paolo** and others continued to work
the flattened spatial field of their predecessors. In northern Italy, painters render
lush canvases; even their Biblical subjects assumed an increased sensuality, as
the works of **Sandro Botticelli**. Some artists of the High Renaissance like **Corre**
adopted Leonardo da Vinci's pyramidal composition and blending of light a
shade, experimenting with new ways to unify their works by softening the ru
of perspective and composition. Others, having mastered the human form, beg

Dieric Bouts	*Mater Dolorosa*, c.1475 (gallery 207)	
Giovanni di Paolo	*Six Scenes from the Life of St. John the Baptist,* c.1460 (gallery 208)	
Sandro Botticelli	*Virgin and Child with Angel*, c.1485 (gallery 208)	
Corregio	*Virgin and Child with the Young St. John the Baptist,* c.1515 (gallery 211)	
Tintoretto	*Tarquin and Lucretia*, c.1590 (gallery 211)	
El Greco	*The Assumption of the Virgin*, 1577 (gallery 215)	

to twist and manipulate it, working from intellectual preconception rather than observable reality. Called Mannerists, they took many cues from Michelangelo—whose influence can be seen in the works of both **Tintoretto** and **Titian** (gallery 211)—often producing large, dramatically lit works filled with complicated juxtapositions of humanity. With typical Mannerist zeal, **El Greco's** animated and elongated figures capture the essence of religious ecstasy, contrasting with the severe Sevillian styles of **Bartolomé Murillo** and **Francisco de Zurbarán** (gallery 215).

Baroque – Baroque painting would eventually encompass a variety of styles, but by 1600, the new realism that distinguished it from Mannerism was emerging. The often tortured forms of the 16C resolved themselves in the sharply illuminated, realistic tableaux of **Caravaggio** and the gentle luxuriance of **Peter Paul Rubens**. By contrast, **Nicolas Poussin** cultivated a heroic Neoclassicism based on the principles of geometry and a vision of the ideal landscape. Baroque style took another turn in Holland, culminating in the work of **Rembrandt**, whose masterful use of light, after Caravaggio, imbued his portraits with poignant realism. As the 17C waned, a stylistic ostentation inspired by the opulence and ceremony of the pre-Revolutionary court was becoming fashionable in France. Largely popular for their applications in interior design, ornate Rococo forms found expression in the fanciful portrayals of a pastoral world painted by **François Boucher**, **Jean Antoine Watteau** (gallery 219) and **Jean Honoré Fragonard** (gallery 219). The murals of **Giovanni Batista Tiepolo** (gallery 218) exuberantly epitomize both the decorative and artistic flamboyance of the Rococo. In the revolutionary atmosphere of the late 18C, however, artists rejected the Baroque and Rococo traditions as they had come to represent the hated exorbitance of the nobility.

Peter Paul Rubens	The Holy Family with St. Elizabeth and St. John the Baptist, c.1615 (gallery 212)
Nicolas Poussin	Landscape with St. John on Patmos, 1640 (gallery 213)
Rembrandt van Rijn	Old Man with a Gold Chain, c.1631 (gallery 216)
François Boucher	Are They Thinking About the Grape?, 1747 (gallery 219)
Antonio Canova	Bust of Paris, 1809 (gallery 220)

★ MODERN AND CONTEMPORARY ART

Paintings, sculpture and objects produced from 1900 to 1935 are arranged chronologically from gallery 234B to gallery 249, Allerton Building, 2nd floor. To continue with art produced from 1935 to 1980, retrace your steps to gallery 235 and continue to gallery 239, also on the 2nd floor of the Allerton; then descend to galleries 136-139, Allerton Building, 1st floor. Additional 20C works are contained in gallery 150, Rubloff Building, 1st floor; and in galleries 261-267, 271-273, Rice Building, 2nd floor.

The significant and diverse collection of modern art at the Art Institute encompasses American and European painting, sculpture and mixed media works produced since 1900. Second-floor galleries in the Rice Building house recent works but are sometimes occupied by temporary exhibits.

Early Modernism – Experimentation and progress into the abstract characterize much of 20C art. Artists turned from rendering what they saw to expressing what they felt and finally to creating "subjectless" works reliant only on themselves for meaning. The accelerating pace and increasing complexity of the industrial age hastened the process, constantly challenging artists to respond anew. The free use of shockingly bright colors earned a small group of painters led by **Henri Matisse** the name les Fauves ("the wild beasts") when they exhibited together in 1905. Largely concerned with the decorative qualities of color, the short-lived movement inspired reaction from **Pablo Picasso**. Like post-Impressionist Cézanne, Picasso experimented with representing three-dimensional forms on a flat surface. When he and **Georges Braque** (gallery 233) first dissolved the bonds of perspective around 1908, unfolding and flattening their subjects, the results were dubbed Cubism. The concept exerted a powerful influence on the course of modern art. The faceted works of **Juan Gris** (gallery 232-233) and the curvilinear forms of **Fernand Léger** (gallery 247) demonstrate further developments in the Cubist style. Meanwhile, artists in pre-World War I Germany were thinking along very different lines. As the Cubists searched for new ways to render form, the Expressionists turned inward for inspiration. From the prismatic, mystical visions of **Franz Marc** (gallery 240), to the spontaneous compositions of **Wassily Kandinsky**, the Expressionists charged their work with emotion, capturing spirit, if not form. It is not surprising that Kandinsky would be the first painter to create completely abstract canvases.

Contemptuous of these serious currents, a group of young artists in 1915 pr
moted an irreverant anti-art known as Dada (a randomly chosen French wo
meaning "hobbyhorse"). Using nonsense words, collages of chance materials a
"ready-made" objects, **Dadaists** like Marcel Duchamp, Man Ray and Max Er
(gallery 242) jabbed mercilessly at society. Spent by 1922, the remnants of Da
fit well into the growing Surrealist movement, which practiced an art governed
the subconscious mind. Unexpected juxtapositions, distortions of time and spa
and eerie dreamscapes haunt the works of Surrealist painters such as **Salvador**
(galleries 237A & 246). The Surrealist influence can be seen in the works of J
Miró and **René Magritte**, and even the folk fantasies of **Marc Chagall**.

Pablo Picasso	*Daniel Henry Kahnweiler*, 1910 (gallery 232) and *Mother and Child*, 1921 (gallery 243)
Wassily Kandinsky	*Painting with Green Center*, 1913 (gallery 240)
Henri Matisse	*Bathers by a River*, 1907-16 (gallery 233)
Joan Miró	*The Policeman*, 1925 (gallery 244)
Alberto Giacometti	*Spoon Woman*, 1927 (gallery 244)
Salvador Dalí	*Inventions of the Monsters*, 1937 (gallery 246)
René Magritte	*On the Threshold of Liberty*, 1937 (gallery 246)
Marc Chagall	*America Windows*, 1977 (gallery 150)

American Trends – Although Modernism evolved mainly in Europe, painters I
Georgia O'Keeffe and Joseph Stella helped to Americanize it. But the representatio
impulse was strong, and much early-20C American art developed along realis
lines, delighting in the American landscape, both urban and rural. Around 19
the new Realists began to look to city streets for inspiration, but the art esta
lishment, disturbed by their graphic realism, derisively dubbed them the Ashc
school. The lonely urban vistas of **Edward Hopper** owe a strong debt to the Ashc
school. In the 1930s American painters looked again at the landscape, this tin
celebrating the countryside in an overt rejection of Modernism. The uncomplicate
figurative styles of **Grant Wood** appealed to Americans beset by the Great Depressio
In dramatic contrast came Abstract Expressionism in the 1940s, a movement th
combined subjectless abstraction with the emotion of Expressionism. The Acti
Painting of Jackson Pollock *(galleries 234 & 238B)* epitomized the concept: T
artist dripped and hurled paint onto the canvas hoping to create patterns reflecti
pure emotion. **Willem de Kooning** worked his painted surfaces over and over to achie
the right effect, and the massive color fields of Mark Rothko *(gallery 139)* vibra
with intensity. Many consider this the first truly influential American movement,
typically large and energetic canvases reflecting something of the national psyc

Grant Wood	*American Gothic*, 1930 (gallery 236)
Georgia O'Keeffe	*Cow's Skull with Calico Roses*, 1932 (gallery 248)
Joseph Cornell	*series of boxed constructions*, 1935-69 (galleries 237 A-D, F)
Edward Hopper	*Nighthawks*, 1942 (gallery 236)
Willem de Kooning	*Excavation*, 1950 (gallery 239)

Beyond Abstraction – From its epicenter in New York City, the sweeping influer
of Abstract Expressionism stimulated considerable artistic action and reaction arou
the world. After 1950 a proliferation of movements pushed the bounds of art in
directions. Ad Reinhardt *(gallery 138)* tested the limits of nonreference with his sere
and subtle series of black surfaces, as did Ellsworth Kelly *(galleries 139 and 261)* w
his colored canvas shapes. Others such as Gerhard Richter *(gallery 136)* and Gec
Baselitz *(gallery 136)* turned from pure abstraction to explore the human figure and
Philip Guston *(gallery 136)* rendered forms, however macabre, with a cartoonish ed
and **Andy Warhol** manufactured his Pop Art portraits, chiding Americans for the
growing fascination with commercial culture. In California, Englishman **David Hockn**
and other artists turned out canvases drenched in Pacific light.

David Hockney	*American Collectors*, 1968 (gallery 138)
Andy Warhol	*Mao*, 1973 (gallery 136)
Gerhard Richter	*Woman Descending the Staircase*, 1965 (gallery 136)
Roy Lichtenstein	*Brushstroke with Splatter*, 1966 (gallery 138)

★★AMERICAN ARTS

Galleries 161, 163-179, Rice Building, 1st floor; galleries 158-159, Rubloff Building, 1st floor.

American galleries at the Art Institute exhibit furniture and decorative arts from the 17C, and painting and sculpture to 1900. Beginning with the simple household objects of Puritan New England, the collection chronicles the development of American taste.

Colonial America – Pilgrim-style furniture in gallery 164 shows the influence of Medieval forms and somber Renaissance design. Makers favored carving, turning, and painting for decoration, although little of the painting has survived. Decoration on a chest made in Connecticut gracefully blends the stylized design elements popular at this time. Furnishings in galleries 165-169 reflect an increasing refinement of form and finish that began with the William and Mary, or early Baroque, style around 1690. Pieces grew tall and elegant; high chests came into vogue. By around 1725 the curvaceous and sturdy cabriole leg distinguished the Queen Anne style, to which the Rococo Chippendale designers added claw-and-ball feet. American cabinetmakers introduced undulating fronts to desks and bureaus. Note the bombe-style Bostonian **chest of drawers** and the block front of the **desk**, *(both in gallery 167)* made in Norwich, Connecticut.

Colonial **silverwares** include arcane receptacles and containers: caudle cups, porringers and patch boxes for storing false beauty marks fashionable in the early 18C. Look for works by several fine Boston and New York artisans—Jeremiah Dummer and Edward Winslow among them. Cornelius Kierstade's **two-handled cup** in gallery 165 is a lovely example of early American Baroque design.

The New Republic – Post-Revolutionary Americans adopted English Neoclassicism, sometimes called Federal style in honor of the new republic. Examples of this slender style furnish galleries 168 and 169. Popularized in England by George Hepplewhite and Thomas Sheraton, the style tends toward fine proportions, clear lines and Classical motifs. Another Neoclassical movement known as Empire *(gallery 172)* came by way of Napoleonic France, its massive forms and heavy antique flourishes replacing the delicate shapes of Federalism.

American painting matured with the new nation. Colonial portraitist **John Singleton Copley** painted with volume and luminescence in contrast to the flat, primitive works of his predecessors. **Raphaelle Peale**, son of Charles Willson Peale *(gallery 168)*, became the country's first virtuoso still-life painter, while **William Sidney Mount** rendered his genre scenes of American life with a classical rigor. Soon the drama of light and a heroic sense of landscape captured the imaginations of American artists. Awed by the vastness of the continent, painters of the Hudson River school such as **Thomas Cole** and others, including **Frederic Edwin Church**, Albert Bierstadt and **George Inness** (to whom gallery 170 is largely devoted), exulted in the wonder of nature. For **Winslow Homer**, heroism came with human endeavor. And, with a different sense of grandeur, American sculptors of the 19C Hiram Powers, Daniel Chester French and **Lorado Taft** *(gallery 161, McCormick Memorial Court)* used Neoclassical allegory to describe the ennobling power of art and the glory of the young republic.

Lorado Taft	*Solitude of the Soul*, date unknown (gallery 161)	
John Singleton Copley	*Mrs. Daniel Hubbard*, 1764 (gallery 167)	
Raphaelle Peale	*Strawberries, Nuts, etc.*, 1822 (gallery 169)	
Thomas Cole	*Distant View of Niagara Falls*, 1830 (gallery 172)	
William Sidney Mount	*Barroom Scene*, 1835 (gallery 172)	
George Inness	*Catskill Mountains*, 1870 (gallery 170)	
Frederic Edwin Church	*View of Cotopaxi*, 1857 (gallery 170)	
Winslow Homer	*The Herring Net*, 1885 (gallery 171)	

Victorian Era – Furniture styles between 1840 and 1920 proliferated in a series of concurrent revivals, including Gothic, Rococo and Renaissance. Victorians delighted in their eccentric shapes, decorations and blends of materials. The rosewood **étagère** in gallery 173 represents in form, fabric and function the spirit of the Rococo Revival, and indeed, the excesses of the Victorian era. Silver of the period erupted with florid surface patterns. In gallery 171, Tiffany's magnificent Greek Revival candelabra and **punch bowl** shimmer with the opulence of the age.

Pieces in galleries 175 and 176 signal a shift away from the historicism and exorbitance of the Victorian era and a return to handcrafting. The strong Japanese influence on such "art furniture" can be seen in the lovely **side chair** and Tiffany **pitcher** in gallery 175. Born of the same ideals, works of the Arts and Crafts movement are exhibited in gallery 176 and upstairs in gallery 158.

American painting of the late 19C took many forms, informed by currents in Europe where several influential American artists studied, lived and worked. **James Abbott McNeill Whistler**, an expatriate since 1855, renounced realism to experiment with compositions of light and color, an effort even his titles reflect. The flattering high society portraits of **John Singer Sargent** contrast with the penetrating realism of **Thomas Eakins**. A protégée of Edgar Degas in France, **Mary Cassatt** bathed her intimate views of women and children in the light and color of Impressionism.
Galleries 178 and 179 feature folk, naive and vernacular arts and crafts, including Shaker furniture and a beguiling array of ship figureheads made between 1790 and 1860.

John Singer Sargent	*Mrs. George Swinton*, 1897 (gallery 175)
Thomas Eakins	*Mary Adeline Williams*, 1899 (gallery 171)
Mary Cassatt	*The Child's Bath*, 1893 (gallery 171)
James Abbott McNeill Whistler	*An Arrangement in Flesh Color and Brown (Arthur Jerome Eddy)*, 1894 (gallery 171)

20C – American furniture and decorative arts of the 20C continue a half flight up in galleries 158-159. Prairie school furniture inherited the aesthetic ethos of the British Arts and Crafts movement. Called by innovator Frank Lloyd Wright his "architectural sculpture," pieces like the **oak desk** of c.1909 echo in miniature the geometry of Prairie school buildings. The 1920s, by contrast, heavily influenced by the advent of Modernism, embraced the smooth streamlining of Art Deco. Inventive forms, industrial materials and minimal decoration characterize the post-1940 International style, which had its roots in the German Bauhaus. The molded **chairs** of Charles Eames *(gallery 159)* have become icons of this eclectic modern movement.

★★★ CHINESE, JAPANESE AND KOREAN COLLECTION
Galleries 101-109, 130-134, Allerton Building, 1st floor.

This part of the Art Institute's Asian collection covers nearly 5,000 years, from the Neolithic Age to the 20C, including works in stone, bronze, jade, paint and print, pottery and porcelain. Particularly strong in Chinese ceramics, the museum has also accumulated one of the most significant collections of woodblock print outside of Japan.

China – The geometric precision of the Neolithic **jade prisms** *(cong)* dating to the third millennium BC *(gallery 131A)* testifies to the craftsmanship of the earliest Chinese cultures as well as to their ancient reverence for jade. Indeed, the **Sonnenschein Collection of Archaic Chinese Jades★**, mounted in a wall case that spans the length of galleries 131A-132, illustrates the beauty of Chinese jade craft. Although difficult to work, jade was believed to possess life-preserving properties, making it the ideal material for the manufacture of grave goods.
Artifacts in galleries 131B and 132 date back to the Bronze Age, which began in China around 2,000 BC. A stunning array of bronze vessels made to contain ritual offerings of wine and food traces the beginnings of Chinese surface decoration from the tightly wound spirals of the Shang dynasty to the robust relief work of the Zhou. In gallery 131B, compare the 12C tripod **wine vessel**, or *jia*, with a pair of 9C **wine jars**, called *hu*. These variously shaped containers signified the social status of their owners and mark the height of Chinese bronze-working skill. Gallery 133 introduces works from early imperial China. As a growing middle class demanded less costly tomb furnishings of clay and wood, items like ceramic burial models—to make the deceased feel at home in the afterworld—became popular. Note the Han dynasty **pigsty and latrines**. *Mingqi*, or spirit objects representing mortals and animals to attend the departed, also illustrate this increasingly world view of the afterlife. A particularly evocative ensemble of carved wooden **tomb figures** dates to the 4-3C BC burials in the Kingdom of Chu. **Earthenware vessels** of the ? foreshadow the virtuosity of later Chinese ceramics.

The extensive **collection of ceramics★** in gallery 134 demonstrates the incredible profusion of styles, colors and techniques that characterizes Chinese pottery through 1,800 years, from the Han to the Ming dynasties. Kilns proliferated during the cultural flowering of the Song dynasty, and various wares came to be known by their places of manufacture. Note the celadon-glazed stoneware of Longquan, precious because it resembled jade, and the creamy white Ding ware, bound with metal to cover its unglazed edge. A group of **ceramic pillows**, by contrast, typifies the exuberant decorative style of the 10-11C Cizhou potters, whose work was intended largely for a popular audience. Among the Ming ware, ceramics made for

Highlights of the Chinese Dynasties:

Neolithic Period (5th millennium BC to 18C BC): an era of emerging regional cultures with distinct craft traditions in clay, stone, bone, basketry and textiles.

Shang dynasty (1766-1111 BC): transition to the Bronze Age accompanied by the rise of cities and rival clans. Invention of remarkable piece-mold technique for casting shapely bronze vessels, whose artistry is unmatched in other contemporary cultures.

Zhou dynasty (1111-221 BC): an unsettled period of statemaking, but increasing prosperity creates a market for objects of extreme technical refinement and splendor. Decorative patterns on stone and bronze become lavish and complex.

Qin dynasty (221-206 BC): established by the first emperor, this dynasty represents the beginnings of imperial China. The Great Wall is begun.

Han dynasty (206 BC-AD 221): a major dynasty, marked by expansion and the coming of Buddhism. The decorative dragon becomes prominent, along with layered and inlaid bronzework.

AD 221-264: three kingdoms split the empire.

Western Jin dynasty (AD 265-317): a nominal reunion in a time of rebellion and rivalry, this short-lived dynasty produced an early celadon-glazed stoneware.

Six Dynasties (AD 317-580): the celadon technique is refined.

Sui dynasty (AD 581-618): the empire is reunited and potters improve glazing techniques.

Tang dynasty (AD 618-906): a time of power and international prestige with a taste for splendor. Aristocratic burial rites become increasingly elaborate and tomb furnishings proliferate in quality and quantity.

Five Dynasties (AD 907-960): breakdown of the empire into individual states.

Song dynasty (AD 960-1279): humanistic age of extreme aesthetic richness renowned for fine and varied ceramics.

Yuan dynasty (AD 1279-1368): this Mongol dynasty favored blue and white porcelains to trade with Islamic nations.

Ming dynasty (AD 1368-1644): marked by a return to native rule, this classic age of blue and white wares featured a proliferation of glazing and decorating techniques.

Qing dynasty (AD 1644-1911): foreign rule under the Manchus introduced delicate ceramics of brilliant color and eggshell translucency.

emperor's use include a striking mid-16C **plate** in brilliant yellow (the imperial color) and blue. In spite of their diversity, the pieces share an exquisite integration of form and surface design. The abundant collection overflows into gallery 108, where delicate and colorful porcelain work of China's last dynasty is exhibited along with furniture and hanging scrolls.

Another highlight of the Chinese collection consists of the elegant earthenware retinue of Tang dynasty funerary statues in gallery 105; most are decorated with polychrome glazes known as *sancai*, or three-color. Dating from the 8C, they reflect the life and fashion among the aristocracy during this golden age. The **equine statues**, for instance, convey the imperial love of fine horses; note the matronly equestrienne and her elegant mount, particularly unusual because it is unglazed.

Korea – Long overshadowed in the West by Chinese wares, Korean ceramics blend Chinese and original elements. The pottery in gallery 106 demonstrates the artistry of Korean celadon-glazed stoneware, which the 12C Chinese are said to have admired. The pieces are

Tang Dynasty Tomb Figure

touched by whimsy; a 12C **celadon ewer** takes the shape of a smiling bird figu
Later Korean pottery, made by simpler techniques, became even more casual a
spontaneous.

Japan – Japanese Buddhist art is presented in galleries 102-104, designed to eve
the serenity of a Japanese interior. Buddhism—with its host of deities—began
replace Shintoism in Japan in the 6C, taking strong hold in the 8C when the Japane
embraced the religious culture of the Tang Chinese. The **Seated Bosatsu** (bodhisatt
was made at the new Japanese capital of Nara around 775 during a time of int
sive temple building and statue production. In contrast to his peaceful visage, ot
figures depict dramatic personifications of the guardians of Buddhist virtues a
laws—note the **Thunderbolt Deity** in the same gallery—who derive the force of th
emotional expression from fierce facial features and exaggerated poses.

The **Clarence Buckingham Japanese Print Collection★** occupies gallery 107. The don
original gift of 2,000 prints has grown to 12,000 produced over the last 40 yea
with an emphasis on the 19C. Because of their light sensitivity, exhibits char
every six weeks and are likely to include the 18C Kabuki portraits of Toshu
Sharaku, the vistas of Ando Hiroshige or the works of 19C master Katsush
Hokusai. In gallery 109, a subtle combination of painted screens, textiles a
pottery complements the room's interior, designed by architect Tadao Ando
convey a sense of Japanese spatial aesthetics.

★★ EUROPEAN DECORATIVE ARTS

*This section occupies 13 galleries arranged chronologically in four sections. Be
with gallery 140, Allerton 1st floor; then on to gallery 157, Rubloff 1st flo
Continue to galleries 60-61, 63-69, 71, Rice lower level. End the visit in gallery .
Rubloff Building, lower level.*

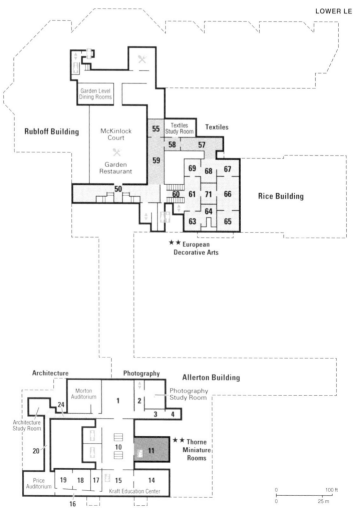

The institute's European Decorative Arts collection comprises a trove of household, ornamental and religious objects produced since 1100 and made more interesting by the wide variety in their materials and manufacturing techniques. To view the collection chronologically is a journey through the evolution of Western design and tastes.

The western end of the wall case in gallery 140 contains Medieval devotional objects in metal, ivory, wood and enamelwork. Seven pieces come from the Guelph Treasure of the Cathedral of St. Blaise in Brunswick, Germany; the most arcane are several reliquaries with transparent chambers still containing the relics of saints. The adjacent aisle cases include sculpture in stone and intricately woven chasubles in linen, wool and silk.

Farther on, an inventively decorated **wine cistern** (1553) highlights a considerable collection of Italian majolica, a tin-glazed, brightly painted earthenware. One of the prizes of the textile collection, a Spanish **retable and altar frontal**, adorns a freestanding panel across the aisle. This 1468 masterpiece of embroidered linen, silk and gilt metal-wrapped thread from the altar of the Cathedral of Burgo de Osma, catalogs an array of needlework styles and materials.

The wall case continues with German and Czech glass, vessels of all shapes and sizes, Dutch and English silver, and intricately carved wooden sculptures, including a fine Flemish boxwood *Corpus* of Christ dating to around 1650. Tableware from the 17-18C predominates at the end of the case, including plates, cups, salt cellars and pitchers, as well as a Chinese porcelain vessel transformed into a ewer with the addition of an English silver mounting (1610).

A shimmering exhibit of **European jewelry** (1450-1650) occupies part of the Alsdorf Gallery of Renaissance Jewelry *(gallery 157)*. Baroque pearls, devotional jewels and cameos, among other stunning pieces, illustrate the variety of techniques used in the production of jewels during the Renaissance period. The jewels are beautifully displayed and illuminated, many of them suspended so as to reveal both sides. In the adjacent space hangs the **Ayala altarpiece**, one of the largest intact Medieval altarpieces in America. Commissioned in 1396 to house a reliquary in the funerary chapel of a Castillian family, the work portrays various members of the family in scenes from the lives of Christ and the Virgin Mary.

Stairwell gallery 60 contains two wall boxes featuring 18C English porcelains. Pass through gallery 61 to the left and enter gallery 69 to view the **Rubloff Paperweight Collection★**, a superb assemblage of 1,000 glass paperweights dating from the 19C and 20C, manufactured by Baccarat, Clichy, St. Louis and others. The exhibit also presents a display on the making of "mushroom" and *millefiori* weights. Italian for "thousand flowers," millefiori involves encasing decorative glass canes in crystal for a kaleidoscopic effect.

Exhibits in galleries 68 through 61, arranged roughly by period and place of origin, include furniture as well as decorative items. Notable are the Mühsam Collection of engraved glass in gallery 68 and the Meissen porcelain **centerpiece and stand** (1737) in gallery 67. The amusing *Monkey Band* (1765-66)—a Meissen grouping of 15 clad music-making monkeys—reflects a contemporary fascination with simians. Marie Antoinette's **corner cupboard** (1785), which may have graced her two-room shepherdess' cottage on the grounds of Versailles, stands in gallery 64, and the famous Sèvres porcelain **Londonderry vase** (1813), originally commissioned by Napoleon in 1805, graces gallery 63. An unusual Florentine **chair** (1876) in gallery 61 boasts a cupid sleeping on each of its armrests. Gallery 71, located at the center of these galleries, features the stunning **Augsburg cabinet** produced in Nuremberg around 1640, a masterpiece of craftsmanship in ebony with inlaid ivory and carved wood relief.

Gallery 50, in the Rubloff Building, presents works from the late 1800s to the present, including striking examples of the British Arts and Crafts, Art Nouveau, Art Deco and Modernist movements. The **tall case**

Londonderry Vase (1813)

clock (1906) represents the ethos of the Vienna Secession movement, which rejected historicism and sought to blend the best of fine and applied arts in the creation of everyday objects. The collection also includes chairs designed by modern masters Marcel Breuer, Le Corbusier, Josef Albers and Ludwig Mies van der Rohe. A display of post-World War II furniture focuses on new materials and designs, with examples from Scandinavia, England, Italy and Austria (note the shapely English holly and hide chair).

★★THORNE MINIATURE ROOMS

Gallery 11, Allerton Building, lower level.

Of international renown, the 68 rooms in this unique collection, arranged in chronological fashion, display a gamut of interior decorative styles ranging from 13C Europe to 20C America. Some of these rooms re-create historic interiors, while others blend stylistic elements into typical, if imaginary, period arrangements. Naturalistic lighting and an occasional glimpse up a staircase or through an open door add to the realism of each setting, from a pre-Revolutionary Connecticut Valley tavern to a chic French library of the 1930s.

Mrs. James Ward (Narcissa Niblack) Thorne's childhood interest in miniature decorative objects began when her uncle, an admiral in the navy, sent her objects he found in his many ports-of-call. Mrs. Thorne (1882-1966) married the son of a founder of Montgomery Ward and Co. and traveled extensively, adding to the collection. Combining a love of miniatures with studies in the history of architecture and the decorative arts, Mrs. Thorne completed her first rooms in the early 1930s. Between 1937 and 1940, she hired skilled craftsmen to reproduce them in exceptional detail at a scale of 1in to 1ft. She even commissioned artists to paint the diminutive canvases that decorate the walls. Their technical excellence, delicate scale and charming variety lend the rooms a romantic sense of history. In 1941 Mrs. Thorne donated the rooms to the Art Institute, where they went on permanent display in 1954.

★★CHICAGO STOCK EXCHANGE TRADING ROOM

Rubloff Building, lower level; balcony access from gallery 153.

In its innovative structural design and ornamental detail, the old Chicago Stock Exchange (1893-94) was one of the most important buildings created by world-renowned architects Dankmar Adler and Louis Sullivan. In spite of intense efforts to save it, the structure fell victim to the wrecker's ball in 1972, but its entrance arch and Trading Room were carefully dismantled and preserved. The arch now stands outside the Art Institute's Columbus Drive entrance. The colorful Trading Room, reconstructed inside the Rubloff Building in 1977, features Sullivan's organic decorative scheme in painted stencils, plaster ornament and art glass. Photographer Richard Nickel, one of Chicago's earliest and most ardent preservationists, was killed when part of the structure collapsed as he was documenting the building's demolition.

★AFRICAN, ANCIENT AMERICAN AND AMERICAN INDIAN ART

Galleries 123-127, Allerton Building, 1st floor.

These galleries display an elite selection of artifacts representing the quintessential artistic traditions of Africa and ancient and native America. Ceremonial and festive objects are the focus of the small but choice installation of West African art in galleries 123 and 124. The masks, headdresses and sculptures in wood, ceramic and metal are arranged by culture and region, with many items from Ghana, Ivory Coast, Nigeria and the Democratic Republic of Congo. Note in particular the elaborately crafted works, such as the 13C Malian **kneeling figure** and the 20C Yoruba beaded **crown** festooned with birds, that well illustrate the complicated mythologies and symbolic systems of these cultures.

Mesoamerican and Peruvian objects occupy galleries 125 and 126, which display ceramics, jewelry, ritual implements and an outstanding collection of beautifully presented **Moche portrait vases** (100 BC to AD 500). Of particular historic importance is the commemorative **coronation stone of Moctezuma II**, which marked the ascendance of the last Aztec emperor in 1503.

Gallery 127 presents artifacts of the Plains Indians, including a Cheyenne war bonnet, beadworked clothing and accessories and a fascinating series of Comanche drawings from the 1880s. Also on exhibit are pre-Columbian ceramics from the southwestern US. Many of these pots were "killed" (note the holes) and buried with the dead; they illustrate the relationships between the community, nature and the spirit world. The human forms among the **cache of ritual figures** of New Mexico's Salado culture (14-15C) represent the spirits of the earth and sky. The ensemble relates to the interconnectedness of all life.

★ARMS AND ARMOR *Gallery 140, Allerton Building, 1st floor.*

The Harding Collection ranks among the most important collections of historic military arms and armor in the US. It is particularly strong in examples fabricated in Germany, Austria and Italy from the 14C to 17C, an era when armaments were as important for aesthetic and ceremonial purposes as for defensive or offensive reasons. Note the decorative richness of the later pieces, especially the gilded and etched steelwork of the 16C Italian armorers. The collection includes chain mail, plated armor and equestrian equipment, some designed for battle and some for tournament. Early weapons are represented by polearms, battle-axes, swords, maces, daggers and crossbows. A stately German two-hand sword (16C) stands as tall as a person. Historic firearms such as matchlock, flintlock and rare wheel-lock rifles with richly carved and inlaid stocks of wood and ivory, a set of 19C French dueling pistols and an ornate ivory-handled **Remington revolver** (1870) complete the exhibit.

★ANCIENT EGYPTIAN, GREEK, ETRUSCAN AND ROMAN ART

Galleries 153-156, Rubloff Building, 1st floor. For an electronic overview of the ancient world, spend a moment with Cleopatra, an interactive touchscreen located in gallery 153.

Egyptian ceramic vessels, mummy head covers, carved stone wall fragments and small art objects are exhibited in galleries 153, 154 and 154A. Most were found in tombs dating from 2600 BC through AD 200. Greek artifacts in gallery 155, from the Bronze Age to the Roman conquest, comprise works in stone, ceramic and metal, including jewelry, military helmets and coins. Among the collection of black- and red-figure vessels is a wine jar *(stamnos)* by an anonymous artist referred to as the Chicago Painter, because this is his signature piece. Produced in Periclean Athens, it represents the height of the red-figure technique.

The Theodore W. and Frances S. Robinson Collection of **antique glass** from around the Mediterranean occupies gallery 155A. These delicate bottles and ornaments in blown and core-formed glass are as remarkable for their longevity as for their beauty. Gallery 156A houses the Etruscan collection, which includes an incised bronze mirror (c.470 BC) and several lovely pieces of granulated gold jewelry, all testaments to Etruscan metalworking skill. A lifelike terra-cotta **votive head** represents a penchant for realistic funerary portraiture.

The Etruscans passed their love of the portrait bust on to the Romans, who applied the Greek figurative style to it to create a dynamic new form of sculptural portraiture, as in the marble **portrait of Hadrian** (AD c.100). A variety of Roman art—stone and bronze sculpture, fresco painting, jewelry, mosaic and glass—fills gallery 156. One case contains fine silver objects from the ship *Tivoli Hoard* dating from c.50 BC. These examples of late Republican craftsmanship were hidden, probably during time of war, and never retrieved by their owners. On nearby pedestals are sculptural fragments in relief and in the round from AD 1C to the 3C, and a fragment of a mosaic floor from the 5C.

Prints and Drawings

Galleries 202-226 and galleries of Modern and Contemporary art, Allerton Building, 2nd floor. Closed for renovation until summer 2001.

This collection includes some 69,000 works on paper from Europe and the Americas dating from the 15C to 20C. The Dutch and French Baroque are extensively represented with works by Rembrandt, Lorrain, Watteau, Boucher and Fragonard. The substantial 19C and 20C holdings include drawings by Goya, Turner, Delacroix, Daumier, Picasso, de Kooning, Miró and Johns. Because of their fragility, prints and drawings are exhibited on a rotating basis in the side galleries of the European Painting and Sculpture Collection and in the galleries of Modern and Contemporary art *(both in Allerton, 2nd floor).*

★INDIAN, HIMALAYAN AND SOUTHEAST ASIAN ART

Galleries 150-152, Rubloff Building, 1st floor.

Dominated by works associated with the Hindu faith, the collection of art in these galleries features sculptural reliefs, statuary, temple fragments and works on paper and cloth dating from AD 2C to the 19C, representing the gods, their servants and the forces of nature they control. In gallery 151, for instance, a bronze *Shiva Nataraja* of AD c.1000 presents the deity as the cosmic dancer who set the universe and the forces of life and death in motion. A pantheon of other Hindu deities, including the jolly elephant god Ganesha, populate the hall.

Other objects showcase the Buddhist heritage of India, the Himalayas and the Southeast Asian countries. The collection includes a range of freestanding representations of the Buddha in stone and bronze.

Photography

Galleries 1-4, Allerton Building, lower level; galleries of Modern and Contemporary art, Allerton Building, 2nd floor.

The photography department has amassed over 25,000 images dating from 1839 to the present and representing many of the world's most famous artists. The collection includes photos by Gustave Le Gray, Eugene Atget, Ansel Adams, Man Ray, Edward Weston, André Kertész and Diane Arbus. The Alfred Stieglitz collection, which includes images by Paul Strand, Edward Steichen, Stieglitz and others, forms an essential part of the museum's holdings. Works by 20C photographers are featured in the galleries of modern art, where they are installed along with contemporary paintings, constructions and books. Rotating exhibits occupy galleries 1-4.

Architecture

Gallery 200, top of the Grand Stairs; gallery 227, Allerton Building, 2nd floor; gallery 24, Allerton Building, lower level.

Chicago's best-known contributions to modern art have come in the field of architecture. Following the 1871 Fire, architects created a revolutionary approach to commercial architecture using steel-frame construction as the basis for the structural and aesthetic expression of a new building type—the skyscraper. The collection reflects the innovative work of the Chicago school and documents other architectural movements since the 18C. **Fragments★** of now-demolished buildings by such famous Chicago architects as William Le Baron Jenney, Daniel Burnham and Louis Sullivan encircle the second-floor balcony like pieces of ancient temples *(gallery 200)*. Represented by windows and other decorative elements are the designers of the Prairie school, led by Frank Lloyd Wright. Architects' works on paper (including Daniel Burnham's 1909 Plan of Chicago and blueprints for the entries in the 1922 *Chicago Tribune* competition) rotate in gallery 24, while gallery 227 features special architectural exhibits.

Textiles

Galleries 57-59, Rubloff Building, lower level; also in galleries of American Arts, European Decorative Arts and the Chinese, Japanese and Korean collection. Gallery 55 is a lecture, work and exhibit space within the Textile Department.

Presented in three temporary exhibitions each year, the museum's textile holdings span the period from 500 BC to the present, with objects from Africa, Asia, Europe and the Americas. The 15,000-piece collection includes woven and printed fabrics used as tapestries, wall hangings, quilts, clothing and religious vestments, as well as 20C fiber art. The only textile on permanent exhibit—made possible by special low-light levels in gallery 140—is the exquisite 1468 Spanish retable and altar frontal. Recent developments in fiber art are represented in works by Ed Rossbach, Lenore Tawney and Chicagoan Claire Zeisler.

SOUTH LOOP

Red line to Harrison or bus no. 29
Map p 125

Bordered by Congress Parkway, 16th Street, the lakefront and the South Branch of the Chicago River, this small neighborhood was taken over by industry after the Fire of 1871 and remained the grimy underbelly of the Loop's business district until its recent rebirth as a community of rehabbed loft buildings, new apartments and town houses. Today young urbanites frequent the various clubs, cafes and bookshops that have ensconced themselves in the historic structures along Michigan Avenue and Printer's Row, creating a lively, vibrant atmosphere. In addition to offering convenient access to Loop shopping, this district is only a hop, skip and a jump from the city's best museums in Grant Park and from the lakefront stadium Soldier Field.

Historical Notes

In the pedestrian city of the 1850s, Michigan and Wabash Avenues south of the Loop were lined with fine town houses and churches catering to the upper middle class. Following the 1871 fire, however, the wealthier classes moved away from the Loop to Prairie Avenue and the Near West Side. When the Dearborn Street railroad station was completed in 1885, the streets south of Van Buren between Wabash and LaSalle quickly turned into an industrial district. Attracted by convenient railroad access and narrow Dearborn Street lots that allowed more light into the buildings, printers moved in creating an international center for the printing industry. At the same time, hotels ea panded along South Michigan Avenue near the Illinois Central Railroad passenger station at Roosevelt Road.

The printing industry changed and moved out of the area after World War II. Many buildings were abandoned. Congress Parkway was widened in the 1920s and again in 1957, creating further separation from the Loop. State Street became a skid row area, and even South Michigan Avenue went into decline.

Two events led to the rebirth of the South Loop in the late 1970s. The first was the construction of the Dearborn Park community on vacant railroad land south of Dearborn Station. The second was the creation of the South Loop **Printing House Row Historic District** north of the station and subsequent rehabilitation of printing lofts as apartments and offices. Within 10 years almost every building in the district had been redeveloped and a new neighborhood was born,

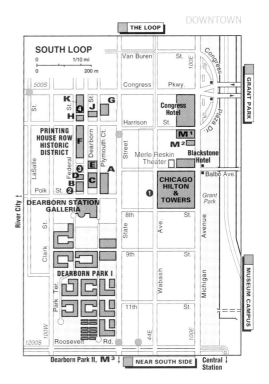

spreading west to the Chicago River with the 1986 construction of the River City apartments and marina. While State Street has not shed its seedy image, the 1986 renovation of the Chicago Hilton and Towers, and the creation of residential buildings on Wabash Avenue and in the Central Station development south of Grant Park have given the South Loop a new urbane character.

SIGHTS

Congress Hotel – *520 S. Michigan Ave.* This hotel was built in 1893 as the Auditorium Annex. The Clinton J. Warren design in limestone mimicked its namesake, the Auditorium Building, with arcaded windows and a third-floor balcony. Polygonal bays rib the facade, which was extended to the south in 1902 and 1907 by Holabird & Roche. Step inside the Congress Parkway lobby to see the lovely mosaic tile arches.

Known for its arts curriculum, especially broadcast media and photography, **Columbia College** occupies several South Loop buildings, including the Harvester Building at 600 South Michigan Avenue. The 1907 structure features a limestone base, red brick facade, and oversized brackets at the cornice. Today its ground floor houses a museum of photography.

Museum of Contemporary Photography (M¹) – *On Columbia College campus, 600 S. Michigan Ave. Open Sept–Jul, Mon–Fri 10am–5pm (Thu til 8pm), Sat noon–5pm. Closed major holidays.* ✗ ♿ ☎ *312-663-5554.* The only Midwestern museum dedicated exclusively to this visual art began in 1976 as the Chicago Center for Contemporary Photography. Since then, the museum has amassed an impressive permanent collection of 4,000 works by 460 contemporary American imagemakers, focusing on American photography since the 1959 release of Robert Frank's seminal work, *The Americans.* Masterpieces by Larry Clark, Diane Arbus, Aaron Siskind, Dorothea Lange and Irving Penn as well as temporary exhibits are featured on a rotating basis in the main gallery.

Spertus Museum (M²) – *618 S. Michigan Ave. Open year-round Sun–Thurs 10am–5pm (Thu til 8pm), Fri 10am–3pm. Closed Jan 1, Memorial Day, Jul 4, Labor Day & major Jewish holidays. $5.* ♿ ☎ *312-322-1747.* Located within the Spertus Institute of Jewish Studies, this small museum comprises some 6,000 pieces of Jewish art, making its collection the largest of its kind in the Midwest. Scholars from around the world come to consult the institute's 90,000-volume Asher Library, located on the fifth floor. The winding first-floor galleries house selections from the museum's permanent collection displayed in a series of small exhibits, each dedicated to a Jewish holy day or ritual. By juxtaposing objects from different eras and cultures, the displays highlight both diversity and tradition within the Jewish faith. Enclosed in a small, dark room, the **Zell Holocaust Memorial**

features videos, displays and an installation that lists Chicagoans' relatives who died during the Holocaust. Visitors can honor the dead by placing a stone atop a symbolic gravestone at the entrance to the memorial. The Spertus has hosted several important temporary exhibits, including Judy Chicago's Holocaust Project: From Darkness into Light; Biblical Images: Chagall and Tissot; and Being There: The Life and Works of Jerzy Kosinski.

① Buddy Guy's Legends

Map p 125. 754 S. Wabash Ave. ☎ 312-427-1190. Owned by blues guitar great Buddy Guy, this is one of the largest and most well-appreciated blues bars in town. Guy's status as a local legend ensures that the performers are top-notch (Eric Clapton gave several concerts here in 1994), and that visiting rock stars will sit in for impromptu jams (live music nightly).

The Rosenbaum **ArtiFact Center** 🎫 (*Open Sun–Thurs 1pm–4:30pm*) is located, appropriately, in the museum's basement. Dedicated to archaeology, this wonderful center for children features a mock excavation where kids can literally dig up reproductions of Jewish artifacts from different periods.

A mansard roof punctuated by dormers and white terra-cotta trim distinguishes the **Blackstone Hotel** (*626 S. Michigan Ave.*), designed in 1908 by Marshall & Fox in the Second Empire style. What the lobby lacks in size, it makes up for in style, with large chandeliers, curving staircases, marble balustrades and an ornate ceiling. Marshall & Fox also designed the French-inspired Blackstone Theater (*60 E. Balbo Ave.*) in 1910; the Blackstone is now the Merle Reskin Theater of DePaul University.

Erected in 1927 by Holabird & Roche, the 25-story **Chicago Hilton and Towers★** (*720 S. Michigan Ave.*) was at the time of its construction the largest hotel in the world, containing 3,000 rooms, an 18-hole rooftop miniature golf course and a hospital. French in inspiration, the design features a limestone base and cornice framing a red brick facade. The main lobby's ceiling is painted with clouds and angels bordered by ornate bands of gold and platinum leaf. Winding staircases on the left lead past a lion-head fountain to the grand ballroom. Known for years as the Conrad Hilton Hotel, the structure was renovated in 1986 and maintains its luxurious tradition.

The formerly run-down area around State Street and Roosevelt Road has been given new birth by the development of modern residential complexes. Organized around small interior parks and courtyards, the **Dearborn Park I** apartments and town houses

were built from 1979 to 1987 between State and Clark Streets north of Roosevelt Road. South of Roosevelt Road the newer town homes of **Dearborn Park II**, begun in 1988, exhibit more traditional urban design.

★**Dearborn Station Galleria** – *47 W. Polk St. Open year round Mon–Sat 8am–8pm. Closed major holidays* ✗ ♿ 🅿 *($2/hr)* ☎ *312-554-8100.* Loop skyscrapers rise to the north beyond the square tower of downtown's oldest surviving train station. Designed by Cyrus L.W. Eidlitz in the Romanesque Revival style, the 1885 building features red brick and stone with nicely detailed cornices and round-arched arcaded window and door openings. The original steeply gabled roof gave way to a third story following a 1922 fire. The train sheds were demolished in 1976 and the edifice renovated in 1985 to contain offices, shops and restaurants.

Chicago Historical Society (ICHi-05257)

1883 Poster

On the northeast corner of Plymouth Court and Polk Street, the **Lakeside Press Building★ (A)** *(731 S. Plymouth Ct.)* was designed in 1897 by society architect Howard Van Doren Shaw for the R.R. Donnelley Co., the world's largest commercial printer. Shaw's first nonresidential sports metallic bays surrounding a richly detailed entrance arch and a top story of semicircular windows alternating with stone medallions. Redeveloped as apartments in 1986, the building now serves as a dormitory for Columbia College.

★**Printing House Row Historic District** – *Along Dearborn St., between Polk St. and Congress Pkwy.* This stretch of late-19C and early-20C structures experienced a colorful history. First used by printing and other book-related industries, the buildings were eventually abandoned and some stood empty for years. In the late 1970s, architects Larry Booth and Harry Weese and industrialist Theodore Gaines realized the district's potential and began a massive restoration effort. Today the entire row has become a coveted residential area dubbed Printer's Row. At no. 720 stands the **Second Franklin Building★ (B)** (1912, George C. Nimmons), ornamented with colorful terra-cotta panels depicting the various steps in bookmaking. Redeveloped into residential lofts in 1988, the building also contains various shops.

Across the street, the **Donohue Building (C)** at no. 711 (1883, Julius Speyer) was redeveloped as commercial and residential lofts in the 1970s. A 1913 annex to the south continues the simplified Romanesque Revival style. Farther north, the red brick **Rowe Building (D)** (1892) at no. 714 was the first to be rehabilitated in 1978 and features a cast-iron entrance and Luxfer prisms on the staircase, which allow light to filter into the basement.

Grace Place (E) *(no. 637)*, a 1915 loft building, was renovated in 1985 by Booth/Hansen & Assocs. as a multidenominational worship space. Light floods the simple wood interior upstairs, streaming in from the circular skylight. The restoration of the once-abandoned **Transportation Building (F)** *(no. 600)*, a massive 1911 structure in light-colored brick, was crucial in securing the area's redevelopment. Today the building contains 294 apartments as well as restaurants and shops.

Visible to the right, on Plymouth Court, cantilevered balconies jut out from the side of the **Mergenthaler Linotype Building (G)** *(531 S. Plymouth Ct.)*. Built in 1886, the edifice was restored as luxury living spaces in 1980 by Kenneth A. Schroeder & Assocs. Mergenthaler invented the modern Linotype machine in 1884; within ten years all the daily newspapers were using it.

2 Gourmand Coffeehouse

Map p 125. 728 S. Dearborn St. ☎ 312-427-2610. Relax with a cup of gourmet coffee or a Ghirardelli hot cocoa in this friendly coffee shop. Quiches, soups, bagel sandwiches and several vegetarian dishes are available and the shop's muffins, cookies and breads are baked fresh every day.

3 Sandmeyer's Bookstore

Map p 125. 714 S. Dearborn St. ☎ 312-922-2104. The wooden floors will creak comfortably beneath your feet as you browse through Sandmeyer's aisles. The store stocks a thorough collection of fiction and poetry by local authors and books on Chicago history, but its main focus is the extensive travel section, which features guidebooks as well as creative works about life on the road.

4 Prairie

Map p 125. In the Hyatt on Printer's Row. ☎ 312-663-1143. The name of this highly acclaimed restaurant says it all: the furniture and decorations are inspired by Prairie school architect Frank Lloyd Wright, and the inventive menu features such regional Midwestern foods as buffalo, coho salmon, pheasant, duck and wild rice.

The **Pontiac Building★** (**H**) (no. 542), designed in 1891 by Holabird & Roche, exe plifies the firm's Chicago school design with its skeletal frame and brick sheath reminiscent of the contemporaneous Monadnock Building with bays that fl rather than project from the surface. At no. 537 the **Terminals Building** (**J**) (189 John M. Van Osdel & Co.) is an elegant design featuring a rusticated limest base below red brick Romanesque-style bays. The **Hyatt on Printer's Row** (**K**) no. 500 occupies three structures: two late-19C buildings and a modern northe addition designed by Booth/Hansen & Assocs. in 1987. The Old Franklin Buildi at no. 525 (1887, Baumann & Lotz) sports the iron windows and spandrels se in the Lakeside Press Building (on S. Plymouth Ct.).

Additional Sights

Central Station – East of Indiana Ave. between Roosevelt Rd. and 16th Although this new development south of Grant Park will not be completed decades, several homes have been occupied, including that of Mayor Richard Daley. The modern, Victorian-style town houses feature copper finials, turrets a window surrounds. Almost half of Central Station's projected 79-acre developme will be built on air rights over the railroad tracks located to the east.

River City – 800 S. Wells St. Revolutionary Chicago architect Bertrand Goldbe designed this 1985 development—his most famous since the similarly inspir Marina City executed 20 years earlier. Undulating walls ripple along the riverfr marina, while eyelid windows in the white facade suggest a futuristic space color

GRANT PARK★

Map p. 131

In Grant Park, Chicago's physical characteristics and urban personality converge. T city's 319-acre "front yard," located between Randolph Street on the north a Soldier Field on the south, marks roughly the midpoint in the swath of parks that tr Chicago's 30mi shoreline. From Lake Michigan on the east to Michigan Avenue on t west, the park is a segue from lakefront to bustling central city. Despite its chec ered history and sometimes haphazard development, the park exudes a sense of t grand urban landscape that turn-of-the-century city planners envisioned for Chicac Today, though bifurcated by busy streets, it offers tranquil corners, peaceful wat ways, picnic spots and lovely vistas of the city and lake.

Historical Notes

From Public Ground to Public Disgrace – In the 1830s, while selling land to finan construction of the Illinois & Michigan Canal, state commissioners designated a th strip of shoreline east of Michigan Avenue between Madison and Eleventh Streets

"public ground—a common remain forever open, clear a free of any buildings, or oth obstruction whatever." In t ensuing decades, Lake Park, it was then called, would be e croached upon by erosion fr Lake Michigan on the east an from the west, by city dwelle anxious to build on the prin real estate. In 1852 the cit promised the Illinois Centr Railroad the right to a trest just offshore in exchange for nancing the construction of breakwater. The narrow bas created between the railroa tracks and the park was filled with debris from the 1871 fir widening the land considerab and initiating a series of landfi that would eventually enlar the park to its present size. Railroad tracks, stables, an a mory, storage sheds, squatter huts and a city dump crowde the park grounds. In 1890 ma order magnate **A. Montgome**

Ward (1843-1913), whose offices overlooked this eyesore, decided he had had enough. For 20 years Ward battled the city and various private interests to clear and keep clear the lakefront park, basing his suits on the commissioners' original declaration. After a long and arduous fight, he prevailed, vilified by city officials who accused him of impeding progress.

A Formal Plan – In 1901 the park's name was changed to honor President Ulysses S. Grant, a resident of Illinois. In 1907 the first plans for formal development of the park were published by the Olmsted Brothers, whose architectural firm succeeded that of Frederick Law Olmsted. Their scheme, based on the gardens of Versailles, called for symmetrical divisions of the space defined by paths and allees of stately trees, promenades, formal gardens, fountains and sculpture. These landscaping principles worked nicely into Daniel Burnham's 1909 Plan of Chicago, which envisioned Grant Park as "the formal focal point, the intellectual center of Chicago." The actual execution of the design would take another 20 years, largely guided by the plan's coauthor, Edward Bennett. The Field Museum was given a home at the south end, and by the 1933-34 Century of Progress International Exposition, the park had assumed much of its modern form.

Since then, Grant Park has both suffered and profited from its central location. As a result of a 1919 city ordinance, the Illinois Central Railroad agreed to depress its tracks. The rise of the automobile brought the intrusion of major thoroughfares that inelegantly sliced through the park and eliminated much of its open plaza space. An underground parking garage skewed the plan again, although today, landscaping and recreational facilities above the garage help to mitigate its presence.

Southeast of Grant Park across Lake Shore Drive, an interesting parcel of land juts into Lake Michigan. This is the northern end of **Burnham Park**, which stretches the rest of its 598 acres south along the lakefront. In 1930, after 10 years of landfilling, the city created an offshore island, dubbed Northerly Island, intended to be the first in a manmade archipelago proposed in the 1909 Plan of Chicago. The Adler Planetarium took up residence on the northeastern corner of the island first; a bridge connected it to the mainland where Solidarity Drive is now located. The 1933-34 Century of Progress International Exposition spread from Northerly Island three miles south. After the exposition, plans surfaced to turn the island into an airport, and in 1945, it contended to become the home of the newly formed United Nations. Finally, in 1948, Northerly Island Airport opened to serve private air traffic. Its name was changed to Merrill C. Meigs Field in 1950 to honor a pioneer Chicago aviator. Today the number of flights in and out of Meigs has greatly declined. Plans have been approved to close the airport and return the land to a parklike setting in the next decade.

Practical Information

Getting There – Grant Park is accessible by several ▦ bus lines. The closest rapid transit stations are: Red or Blue line to Monroe or Jackson; Brown, Green or Orange line to Adams (☎ 312-836-7000). Limited underground parking is available on Monroe St.; metered parking is available on Columbus St.

Park Information – Visitor Center at Daley Bicentennial Plaza *(337 E. Randolph St.; open year-round Mon–Fri 10am–6pm, Sat 10am–5pm, Sun noon–5pm; ☎ 312-742-7650)* is located at the northern end of Grant Park between Columbus and Lake Shore Drives. Information by mail: Lakefront Region Office, South Shore Cultural Center, 7059 South Shore Dr., Chicago IL 60649 *(☎ 312-747-2474)*.

Recreation – Public sports venues located throughout the park include soccer fields, volleyball courts, softball fields, tennis courts and ice-skating at Daley Bicentennial Plaza. The park also houses Soldier Field, home of the Chicago Bears. A bicycle/running **path** runs along the lakefront. **Boat tours** depart near Buckingham Fountain at the Lake Shore Promenade and on the north side of Shedd Aquarium *(Shoreline Sightseeing; ☎ 312-222-9328)*. **Walking tours** of the park are conducted by the Chicago Architecture Foundation in summer *(☎ 312-922-8687)*.

Special Events – Musical performances at the Petrillo Music Shell include: free concerts during the **Grant Park Music Festival** *(mid-Jun–late Aug)*; the lively **Chicago Blues Festival** *(1st weekend in Jun)*; the three-day **Gospel Festival** also in June; and the Labor Day weekend **Jazz Festival**. Independence Day celebrations include fireworks over Monroe Street Harbor the evening of July 3, exploding to the music of the Grant Park Symphony. Held in late June into July, **Taste of Chicago**, one of the city's largest annual events, offers live music and an opportunity to sample the fare of restaurants from around Chicago. In late July, **Venetian Night** features a parade of decorated boats through Monroe Street Harbor, a concert and fireworks display.

Scheduled for completion in 2001, Millennium Park will fill the northwest corner of Grant Park, just north of the Art Institute. Bounded by Michigan Avenue, Columbus Street, Randolph Street and Monroe Street, Millennium Park will be a 25-acre "roof garden" built over a parking garage and a former railroad right-of-way. When completed, the park will incorporate an eye-catching Music Pavilion designed by world-renowned architect Frank Gehry, along with an ice-skating rink and a music and dance theater. *The construction of the park has temporarily re-routed traffic in that area.*

VISIT

Grant Park is divided roughly into large rectangles, each with its own character and purpose. Its center and visual focal point is Buckingham Fountain, which is aligned on an east-west axis with East Congress Parkway.

★**Grand Entrance** – The main entry to the park at Congress Parkway and Michigan Avenue retains only vestiges of its original grandeur. When built in 1929, its 100ft-wide staircase, flanked by two heroic equestrian statues—**Indians** *(The Bowman* and *The Spearman)* by Yugoslavian sculptor Ivan Mestrovic—welcomed visitors to the park. Burnham had envisioned an expansive plaza at the top of the stairs leading all the way east to the fountain. But by 1929 automobile traffic was already determining the shape of such spaces, and the plaza had evolved into a roadway. In 1956, with the Eisenhower Expressway under construction to the west, Congress was extended into the park, at the expense of the grand staircase, to link Lake Shore Drive with the new expressway. In 1996 the grand staircase and plaza were partly reconstructed to give a sense of the original design while retaining the roadways. Today the mounted Indians (**1** & **2**) remain, elegantly framing Buckingham Fountain to the east. Each bronze statue weighs 27,000 pounds and stands 17ft high.

Taste of Chicago Festival, Grant Park

Abraham Lincoln (The Seated Lincoln) – East of the grand entrance and one bloc north of Congress Parkway, *The Seated Lincoln* presides over the *Court of th Presidents*—a lonely post, since the other sculptures intended by park planner never materialized. Augustus Saint-Gaudens' Lincoln was cast in 1908 (a year afte the sculptor's death) and installed in the park in 1926. This work resembles Dani Chester French's figure in the Lincoln Memorial in Washington, DC since bot artists used as models the life masks of Lincoln taken by Chicagoan Leonard Vo in 1860.

★★**Buckingham Fountain** – Centerpiece of Grant Park, the Clarence Buckingha Memorial Fountain is truly a lakefront jewel. Donated to the city by philanthrop Kate Sturges Buckingham to honor her brother, the fountain was completed 1927 at a cost of $750,000. A $2.8 million restoration completed in April 199 returned the fountain to its original splendor. Architect Edward Bennett model it on the Latona Basin at Versailles, enlarging it to nearly twice the size of the original. Intended to represent Lake Michigan, the fountain pumps 1.5 million gallons from the lake, recirculating all but what's lost through spray and evaporation. Three basins of Georgia pink marble rise from a main pool that measures 280ft across; gargantuan carvings of seaweed and shells encircle the outside of each basin. In the large pool, four bronze sea horses, each 20ft in length, represent the states that border the lake.

As spectacular as its monumental scale are the water-and-light shows that emanate from the fountain throughout the summer. The fountain's 133 jets pump water at a rate of 14,000 gallons a minute, and the central jet shoots water skyward to 150ft. At night a carefully orchestrated **show of lights** plays off the cascading water to create a dazzling effect *(May–end Oct dusk–11pm; call ☎ 312-747-2474 to confirm)*. Once controlled entirely by hand, the choreography of water and light is today regulated by a computer.

Petrillo Music Shell – Originally located south of Buckingham Fountain at 11th Street, the first band shell was erected in 1931 in anticipation of the Century of Progress International Exposition. This "temporary" structure hosted nearly half a century of free musical entertainment. In 1935 James C. Petrillo, president of the musicians' union, saw park concerts as a way to employ musicians suffering the effects of the Depression. Working with the Chicago Park District, he used union funds to bring in the finest artists, including Lily Pons, Andre Kostelanetz, Yehudi Menuhin and Benny Goodman. Several orchestras, including the Chicago Symphony, appeared in the early years, and in 1944 the Grant Park Symphony was formed. The park district moved the popular venue to a new band shell at its present location in 1978.

Prairie Garden (Chicago Wildflower Works I) – In 1985, 1.5 acres above the Monroe Street parking facility were transformed into two oval plots of prairie wildflowers that bloom profusely during the summer months. A dramatic contrast to the formal plantings elsewhere in the park, the garden was at first the source of intense controversy, a "visual disaster" to some officials who lobbied to have it removed. Today, fully established and matured, the garden thrives thanks to the efforts of volunteers.

Soldier Field – At the southern end of Grant Park stands this famous athletic field, designed by

Holabird & Roche to harmonize with the Field Museum to the north. The formal dedication of the field, named to honor the soldiers of World War I, took place on the occasion of the 29th annual Army-Navy football game, on November 27, 1926. Soldier Field now serves as the home stadium for the Chicago Bears NFL football games.

MUSEUM CAMPUS★★★

McFetridge Dr. at S. Lake Shore Dr.   lots no. 146 (museum lots)
Map p 131

Re-routing the northbound lanes of Lake Shore Drive west of the Field Museum helped create this handsome 10-acre greensward, located just southeast of Grant Park. Known as the Museum Campus, the park unites in spirit and space Chicago's great triumvirate of natural-science museums, devoted to earth, sea and sky: the Field Museum of Natural History, the John G. Shedd Aquarium and the Adler Planetarium & Astronomy Museum. The proximity of these three museums provides them the opportunity to collaborate on outdoor as well as indoor programming, special events and concession sales.

The Museum Campus itself makes a pleasant place to picnic or stroll, through terraced gardens or along walkways bordering Lake Michigan, with great **views★★** of the Chicago skyline and the boats in Monroe and Burnham Park harbors.

Parking for the museums is located adjacent to the Field Museum and just south at Soldier Field *(access both lots via McFetridge Dr.)*. In summer, alternative methods of transportation to the Museum Campus include a free trolley system *(see Practical Information)* that runs along Michigan Avenue from Water Tower Park *(N. Michigan Ave. between Chicago and Pearson Sts.)* to the campus and a water taxi *(see Practical Information section at the end of this guide)* that ferries passengers back and forth from Navy Pier.

★★★ FIELD MUSEUM OF NATURAL HISTORY

1400 S. Lake Shore Dr. Plan p 136.

This world-class natural history museum commands a suitably grand presence at the south end of Grant Park. Indeed, there is nothing small about this institution. Nine acres of exhibit halls and over 20 million artifacts inhabit the vast Neoclassical edifice where collections, exhibits and public programs specialize in anthropology, geology, botany and zoology. Dinosaur bones, ethnographic materials and animal taxidermy are among the museum's traditional strengths; today all have been incorporated into modern interpretive exhibits.

Historical Notes

"A Grand Museum" – By the time work was begun on the present-day Field Museum in 1915, the institution already had a long history. Harvard anthropologist Frederick Ward Putnam was determined that the vast ethnographic and zoological collections he had amassed for display at the World's Columbian Exposition in 1893 would have a permanent home after the fair, envisioning for "this great city ... a grand museum of natural history." He enlisted the aid of Edward E. Ayer, a collector of Native

American artifacts, to persuade department store magnate Marshall Field to contribute the million dollars it would require to establish such an institution. That endowment funded the Field Columbian Museum, which was to be housed in the fair's Palace of Fine Arts in Jackson Park. Never intended as a permanent structure, the palace would not be suitable for long, and the Field soon required another home.

Before his death in 1906, Marshall Field hired architect Daniel Burnham to create a new natural history museum in the august Beaux-Arts style of the World's Columbian Exposition, bequeathing money to pay for and endow it. Burnham's vision of a museum in Grant Park raised a furor with advocates of a lakefront free and clear of building, and it wasn't until the Illinois Central Railroad offered a muddy and desolate parcel of land just south of the park that plans for the Field could be finalized. Begun in 1915, landfilling alone took a year to complete. The museum's doors finally opened in May 1921.

The Building – The monumental scale of the museum is at once awe-inspiring and exhausting. Burnham based the 706ft-long, colonnaded facade on the Ionic order, and even included caryatids modeled by sculptor Henry Hering on those at the Erechtheion on the Acropolis in Greece. Thanks to exterior conservation and an extensive cleaning in 1988, the crisp white Georgia marble cladding once again glows. The Field shares its front yard, a landscaped expanse that sweeps to the water's edge, with the John G. Shedd Aquarium.

© Kevin O. Mooney/Odyssey

A *Tyrannosaurus rex* Named "Sue"

The Collections – Equally grand in scale are the museum's collections of more than 20 million artifacts and specimens, only about four percent of which are on display in some 20 exhibits. Behind the scenes, millions of artifacts, many from the World's Columbian Exposition and others collected over years of field work or purchased from private collectors, serve as the basis for research projects and publications by scholars from around the world.

The Field's exhibits can be categorized into three groups: introductory exhibits, of special interest to children, presenting basic ideas in simple ways; comprehensive thematic exhibits, dealing with culture groups, botany, earth sciences and evolution; and resource centers, where visitors can extend their learning by doing research on their own. Some exhibits, notably in the Native American wing, are old and represent a more traditional, "study collection" approach—case after unvarying case of artifacts accompanied by very few labels.

Since the mid-1980s, as part of a $40-million, 10-year effort, many exhibits have been thoroughly renovated and now include computer and video elements, detailed interpretation and modern exhibit techniques. A reinstallation of the second-floor exhibit Moving Earth in the Earth Sciences hall was completed in 1997. Debuting in 1998, the Field's state-of-the-art fossil preparation laboratory affords visitors a chance to watch fossilized bones being prepared for exhibit. And Underground Adventure, opened in 1999, invites visitors to explore the world of subterranean animals and insects. The Field's latest acquisition—known as Sue—the world's largest, most complete and best preserved **Tyrannosaurus rex skeleton** found to date, was purchased at auction at Southeby's in 1997 for the incredible sum of $8.3 million by a consortium that included McDonald's and Disney.

The model of the brachiosaurus that once stood in Stanley Field Hall was moved to a new permanent home in O'Hare International Airport *(Terminal 1, Concourse B)* in order to make room for Sue. A new four-story-tall model of the brachiosaurus, made of weather-resistant fiberglass polyester resin, has been installed on the museum's northwest terrace, visible from Lake Shore Drive.

Visiting the Museum

Open late May-Labor Day 8am-5pm. Rest of the year daily 9am-5pm. Closed Jan 1 & Dec 25. $8 (free Wed). Additional charge for Underground Adventure and special exhibits. Guided tours (1hr) available Mon-Fri 11am & 2pm and weekends 11am & 1pm. ⅃ & ▯*($7)* ▥ ⬇ *312-922-9410, www.fieldmuseum.org).*

Since the museum offers enough to fill several days, visitors should focus on the subjects of interest to them by consulting the floor plan (available at the admissions desk) and the listing of daily special programs, activities and tours (posted at the admissions desk and on kiosks throughout the museum). Of special interest to children is the new exhibit Underground Adventure *(ground floor)*.

Visitors enter the museum via the 300ft-long, two-story Stanley Field Hall on the main level, location of the 6,000sq ft museum store (southeast corner) and the Corner Bakery *(northeast corner)*. The latter features cafeteria-style service and offers a variety of sandwiches, pizza, salads and pastries, as well as indoor and outdoor seating. For those wanting faster service, a McDonald's restaurant and vending machines are located on the ground level.

Main Level

The new star of Stanley Field Hall is **Sue**★★ (**A**), the 42ft-long *Tyrannosaurus rex* skeleton, which went on view at the museum in May 2000. Named for Sue Hendrickson, the fossil hunter who discovered the skeleton in South Dakota in 1990, Sue stands 13ft tall at the hip (the creature's gender is unknown, but there is evidence to suggest that this T-rex was female). When she roamed the earth, some 65 million years ago, Sue weighed seven tons. Sue's actual skull, which at 600 pounds is too heavy to be mounted on the structure that holds the skeleton, is displayed on the upper level; the skull in Stanley Hall is a lightweight cast.

Other displays in the hall, including a pair of taxidermied bull elephants (**B**), two Haida totem poles (**C**), and four 20ft New Guinean ceremonial masks (**D**) reflect the museum's interest in the development and diversity of life on the planet and the study of human cultures. Behind stately arches and columns on either side of the hall, exhibit spaces unfold deep into the symmetrical wings. Female statues (the work of Henry Hering) representing the four purposes of the museum—science dissemination of knowledge, research and recording—gaze down from each of the four upper corners of the hall.

West Wing – Beginning in the southwest corner of Stanley Field Hall, the lively exhibit entitled **What is an Animal?** presents a colorful array of animal life, from head lice to giant squid, arranged so that visitors can contrast and compare sizes, colors habitats, skeletons, survival techniques and other animal behaviors and characteristics.

Inside Ancient Egypt starts with a tour through the **mastaba tomb**★ of Unis-ankh, son of the last pharaoh of Dynasty V (2428-2407 BC). Part replica and part authentic this is the largest full-size reconstruction of a tomb outside Egypt. In the original chambers, tomb paintings are preserved under glass. A stairway leads to the roof for a good view into the tomb, and from here a spiral staircase winds down to the **ground level** of the museum, where the exhibit continues into the depths of the tomb burial chamber. The Field's strong collection of Egyptian **burial and mortuary artifacts** fills the following rooms with some 20 mummies, sarcophagi, papyrus scrolls and other funerary objects arranged by dynasty. Admire the tiny **diorama** illustrating the embalmer's art—a two-month process—before exiting through an ancient Egyptian marketplace, c.2450 BC.

The rest of the first floor of the west wing is largely devoted to mammals, birds and their habitats. In the **World of Mammals** and the **World of Birds**, hundreds of creatures are mounted in old-fashioned display cases. To this traditional approach have been added interpretive graphics, sound effects (such as bird calls) and environmental notes. The galleries in general show off to great advantage the elaborate taxidermy and dioramas—largely the legacy of Carl Akeley—for which the Field famous. Akeley, who worked at the museum between 1896 and 1909, was a sculptor and pioneer in the field of taxidermy and diorama creation, setting the standards for realism and detail that would inform those crafts for 50 years. His most recognizable work is the pair of bull elephants in Stanley Field Hall, but his **Four Seasons**★, on display continuously at the museum since its crafting in 1902, represents the height of his art. The four-part tableau depicts deer in their habitat throughout the year. It can currently be seen in **Nature Walk★**, an exhibit at the north end that takes visitors on a trek through woods, wetlands and other wild places. Interpretive labels engage viewers of all ages to reflect on what they see in each detailed diorama, or invite them to turn over a log for a peek underneath. To complement Nature Walk, **Messages from the Wilderness** employs dioramas to deliver timely messages about environmental issues and extinction.

At the center of the west wing is a kaleidoscopic exhibit entitled **Africa★★**. From the streets of Dakar, Senegal, decked out for the Muslim feast day of Tabaski (which celebrates an Islamic story of Abraham and Isaac), to the sand dunes of the Sahara, where the Tuareg people live and trade, this sweeping presentation investigates African politics, art, environment, wildlife, geography, commerce and family life by focusing on representative regions and peoples. Note especially the **ritual regalia★** and beautifully crafted tools of the Bamum people of Cameroon in the section on art and society. In conspicuous contrast, a segment on the slave trade compels visitors to walk through a re-creation of a dimly lit slave ship's hold and consider such remnants of slavery as shackles and a restraining collar. Blending words, videos and artifacts, this exhibit is designed to appeal to every age group. At its conclusion, a resource center offers books and other reference materials for further study.

Along the end of the west wing facing Lake Shore Drive is the **Rice Wildlife Research Station**, a large, comfortable space where visitors can use books, computer programs and other resources to study specific subjects. Next to the research station you'll find the **Lions of Tsavo**. These two preserved man-eaters, depicted in the 1996 film, *The Ghost and the Darkness*, killed and ate 140 railroad workers in East Africa in 1898.

East Wing – The galleries to the east of Stanley Field Hall are devoted to the culture groups of North and South America. With the exception of the **Pawnee Earth Lodge** (one of several full-scale dwellings reconstructed throughout the museum) and the section on maritime peoples, these exhibits represent a past generation of museum display techniques. The artifacts are no less stunning for it, however. Kachina dolls, ancient pottery and Pima and Papago basketry highlight exhibits devoted to the Indians of the North American West. The dense **Eskimos and Northwest Coast Indians★★** exhibit, opened in 1984, contains a seemingly exhaustive catalog of materials contrasting life on the Northwest Coast and in the Arctic. Especially impressive are a case of Northwest Coast **masks** and a forest of stately carved cedar **totem poles★** (most collected by anthropologist Franz Boas for the World's Columbian Exposition in 1893), which towers above the display.

Upper Level

At the top of the north staircase is **More About Sue**. Here you'll find the tyrannosaurus' real **skull** (**E**)—baring a mouthful of frighteningly large, sharp teeth—along with exhibits focusing on theories and speculation about how Sue lived and died.

East Wing – Ten years in the making, the three-part exhibit entitled **Life Over Time★** was an ambitious undertaking for curators and proves equally so for visitors. Divided into three major halls, the exhibit covers life before the dinosaurs, the reign of the dinosaurs, and life after their demise and into the Ice Age. Truly interested visitors can lose themselves for a day in these halls, but the exhibit challenges the casual observer because it is so dense with information and materials. Throughout the exhibit, video "newscasts" starring local broadcasters provide effective summaries of the events of each time period covered. The first part, **DNA to Dinosaurs**, offers a comprehensive look at the prehistory of the earth over 3.8 billion years, from primordial soup to the emergence of four-legged creatures, investigating along the way mutation, evolution, adaptation and extinction, the processes by which life comes and goes and changes on our planet. **Dinosaurs!★★**, the highlight of the exhibit, bridges the first and last sections with breathtaking skeletons (replica and genuine) of those enormous beasts: long-necked *Apatosaurus*, delicate flying *Pteranodon* and primeval-looking *Triceratops* among them. **Life After Dinosaurs** opens with a cleverly contrived multimedia presentation entitled **Fossil Lake Adventure★** about the scientific value of fossils. Fast-paced, entertaining and stagy, the balance of the exhibit covers the rise of mammals, particularly in the Americas, and concludes with the origins and evolution of the human species.

Outside the entrance to Life Over Time, the museum has set up the **McDonald's fossil preparation lab**, where Sue's 300-bone skeleton was cleaned and prepared for exhibition. From three sides, visitors can watch the painstaking process by which paleontologists clean and repair other fossilized remains.

In a completely different vein, the serene and beautifully crafted exhibit **Plants of the World★** occupies the southeastern corner of the second floor. Including models of a third of the world's plant species, it is the most complete botanical exhibit in existence. It succeeds in dazzling the visitor with the incredible variety of form, color and function among the world's plants. Made through a process pioneered by Carl Akeley

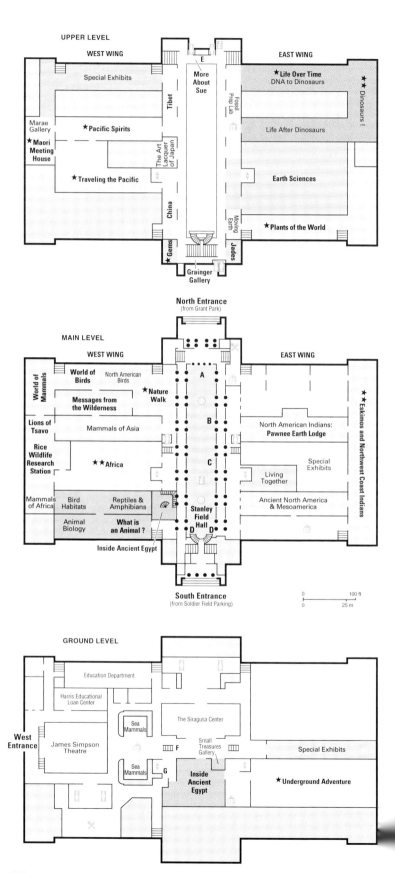

UPPER LEVEL

WEST WING   EAST WING

Special Exhibits

E

More About Sue

Tibet

Fossil Prep Lab

★ Life Over Time
DNA to Dinosaurs

★★ Dinosaurs!

Marae Gallery

★ Pacific Spirits

Life After Dinosaurs

★ Maori Meeting House

The Art Lacquer of Japan

★ Traveling the Pacific

Earth Sciences

China

Moving Earth

★ Plants of the World

Gems

Jades

★ Grainger Gallery

North Entrance
(from Grant Park)

MAIN LEVEL

WEST WING   EAST WING

World of Mammals

★ World of Birds

North American Birds

A

★ Nature Walk

Messages from the Wilderness

B

Lions of Tsavo

Mammals of Asia

North American Indians:
Pawnee Earth Lodge

Rice Wildlife Research Station

★★ Africa

C

Special Exhibits

Living Together

★★ Eskimos and Northwest Coast Indians

Mammals of Africa

Bird Habitats

Reptiles & Amphibians

Ancient North America & Mesoamerica

Animal Biology

What is an Animal?

Stanley Field Hall

D   D

Inside Ancient Egypt

South Entrance
(from Soldier Field Parking)

0 ____ 100 ft
0 ____ 25 m

GROUND LEVEL

Education Department

Harris Educational Loan Center

Sea Mammals

The Siragusa Center

West Entrance

James Simpson Theatre

Sea Mammals

F

Small Treasures Gallery

Special Exhibits

G

Inside Ancient Egypt

★ Underground Adventure

at the turn of the century, each model was meticulously formed of wax or plastic from molds of living plants. A single model may have taken two or three months to complete. Accompanying label text is no less detailed, describing fruits, flowers and leaves for family after family of plants. Interesting facts are highlighted, and visitors learn, for instance, that as members of the poison ivy family, cashews must be removed from the poisonous juices in their husks before they can be eaten.

The small **Hall of Jades** *(east wing)* is connected to the Hall of Gems *(west wing)* by the **Grainger Gallery**, which displays religious art from China and gold jewelry from around the world, along with selections from the Field's sizeable collections of meteorites and minerals.

West Wing – Tucked into a small gallery just west of the south staircase, the **Hall of Gems★** presents a shimmering collection of precious and semiprecious stones. Careful lighting in a darkened room brings out the best of the opals, moonstones, rubies, and others on display from among the museum's collection of 60,000. Don't miss the 5,890-carat **Chalmers topaz**. More mineralogy can be found in the **Earth Sciences** hall in the southeast section of the upper level.

The remainder of this side of the second floor is devoted to Asia and the Pacific. Small exhibits on **China** and **Tibet** showcase ritual and secular artifacts from those cultures. Particularly noteworthy are examples of Tibetan ceremonial paraphernalia—prayer wheels, wands, shell trumpets and the like—all forms unfamiliar to the Western eye, each exquisitely tooled and ornamented. Equally fascinating are the Tibetan anatomical and medicinal charts. By way of introduction, a video makes good use of historic footage of monastic life in Tibet.

Two full-scale exhibits focus on separate aspects of the cultures of Oceania: navigating the waters and ceremonial life. To evoke the essence of the islands, **Traveling the Pacific★** uses modern "stage settings"—a lava flow, a deserted beach—alongside traditional glass case displays. Hundreds of elaborately decorated artifacts related to canoes, canoe building and canoe ornamentation—including a wonderful assortment of paddles—form the core of the exhibit. Next door, **Pacific Spirits★** again draws on the museum's vast Oceanic collection to explore the religious beliefs of the peoples of Polynesia, Micronesia, Melanesia and New Guinea. The highlight of this journey around the Pacific is Ruatepupuke, an authentic **Maori meeting house★** that has been reconstructed here piece by piece. The only such meeting house in the Western Hemisphere, it is a sacred place to New Zealand's Maori people, and curators collaborated with Maori consultants to follow ancient protocols in its installation and reconsecration. The house, which dates from 1881, is 55ft long, 23ft wide and 15ft high, and represents both an ethnographic treasure and a work of art, as its intricate incised surfaces and complex carvings are unique to the Maori.

Ground Level

Aside from the continuation of the Ancient Egypt exhibit, this level holds special-exhibit galleries, classrooms and eating areas. Near the vending areas, note the sea mammals—narwhals, walrus, manatees, seals—cavorting in dioramas that line the walls.

In a case under the stairs sits the taxidermed **Man-eater of Mfuwe** (**F**), the largest man-eating lion on record. In 1991 this African lion claimed six victims in Zambia. Nearby you'll find **Bushman** (**G**), Lincoln Park Zoo's legendary gorilla, now preserved. Bushman captured the hearts of Chicagoans upon his arrival as a two-year-old orphan from the French Cameroons in 1930. He died in 1951 and has resided at the Field ever since.

A favorite with the younger set, **Underground Adventure★** simulates the creepy, crawly world beneath our feet. Before entering this subterranean scene, visitors first pass through a "shrinking chamber" where sound effects and mirrors create the impression that you have shrunk 100 times smaller than your normal size. Once the shrinking is complete, walk through the dark, narrow passages, the walls of which are laced with roots plunging down from plants aboveground and embedded with numerous creatures. Explore different zones to learn about the diversity of life underground, from bacteria to beetles. And watch out for moving critters, like the colossal crayfish and the giant grub-eating wolf spider. At exhibit's end are interactive displays that focus on managing our precious soil in the future.

★★ JOHN G. SHEDD AQUARIUM

📷 *1200 S. Lake Shore Dr. Plan p 140.*

Located appropriately at the very edge of Lake Michigan, the Shedd Aquarium is the world's largest indoor aquarium. Housing some 8,000 aquatic animals comprising 650 species—from tiny, jewel-like spiny lobsters to 1,500-pound beluga whales—the Shedd's exhibits and programs emphasize conservation and the environment. Its remarkable animals bring this message vividly to life.

Historical Notes

Ocean by the Lake – When John Graves Shedd, who rose from stock boy to chairman of Marshall Field & Co. between 1872 and 1926, donated $3 million for the construction of an aquarium in Chicago, he intended the structure to house "the greatest variety of sea life on display under one roof." Architects Graham, Anderson, Probst & White designed a fitting edifice to complement the stately Field Museum nearby. It opened in 1930, one of the last Beaux-Arts buildings in Chicago, and perhaps the final nod to city planner Daniel Burnham's vision of the "City Beautiful," an aesthetic outgrowth of the World's Columbian Exposition of 1893. The octagonal structure, clad in shimmering white Georgia marble, resembles at every turn a monument to Poseidon. Indeed, the sea god's trident surmounts the building's dome. The aquarium's nautical décor is among its most remarkable features: inside and out, repeating wave and shell patterns decorate doorways, cornices, tiles and pediments; bas-reliefs of elegant sea creatures embellish walls and even lighting fixtures mimic piscine forms. All blend into a delightful aquatic paraphrase of a Classical Doric temple. The building was awarded National Historic Landmark status in 1987.

Feeding Denizens of the Caribbean Reef

The aquarium is equally remarkable for its mechanical systems. Original plans called for the latest in materials, piping (75mi of it), water storage (enough for two million gallons—four times larger than any of that day) and environmental controls that made life in the aquarium's 200 exhibits possible. Salt water was imported by barge and train from Key West and the Gulf of Mexico until 1973 when the aquarium began mixing its own using water from Lake Michigan.

In 1991 the much-heralded 170,000sq ft oceanarium opened to the southeast of the original building to house marine mammals and an expansive replication of the endangered Pacific Northwest Coast ecosystem. Completed at a cost of $45 million, the addition (Lohan & Assocs.) is covered in marble peeled from the side of the old building now shared by the oceanarium. A broad "curtain of glass," its most distinguishing feature, barely seems to separate the interior from Lake Michigan. Inside, oceanarium planners created a habitat as close to nature as possible—down to the shape of the pools—after considerable study of the needs and behaviors of the animals that would live here.

Waters of the World – A pioneer in the re-creation of aquatic habitats, the Shedd is in the midst of transforming its old-fashioned stacked-rock tank environment into mini-ecosystems supporting not only fish but plants and microscopic life as well. This approach to aquatic exhibition makes habitats as handsome and interesting as their inhabitants. And, in keeping with the Shedd's focus on conservation, these habitats convey the importance of biodiversity and the interrelationships of species with each other and with their surroundings. Of particular interest are endangered and degraded environments; several displays offer visitors a look at ecosystems that may already no longer exist in the wild.

The aquarium is currently in the midst of executing a series of major renovations that began in late 1998 and will extend into the early 21C. To date, the rotunda has been restored and the centerpiece Caribbean Reef exhibit has undergone a face-lift. Galleries 1 and 2 in the main building re-opened in summer 2000 as **Amazon Rising** showcasing the diverse flora and fauna of the Amazon Basin, while illustrating how both animal and human inhabitants adapt to the ever-changing levels of the river. And a new **baby beluga** was born at the aquarium on July 15, 2000. Named Qannick (Inuit for "snowflake"), the newborn male weighed in at 125 pounds.

Planned for completion in 2002, a new underground wing to the south will house a 360,000gal habitat devoted to Indo-Pacific reef life, including fragile live coral and six types of sharks. Predictably, such expansion will intermittently close exhibit spaces in the aquarium over the next couple of years.

Visiting the Aquarium

Open Memorial Day–Labor Day daily 9am–6pm. Rest of the year daily 9am–5pm. Call to confirm hours. Closed Jan 1 & Dec 25. $15 for aquarium & oceanarium (aquarium free Mon). Guided tours are available daily Memorial Day–Labor Day 9:45am & 4:15pm; rest of the year daily 2:15pm. ✕ ♿ ☐ ($7) ⅲ ☏ 312-939-2438. www.sheddaquarium.org. During the summer, a water taxi operates between the aquarium and Navy Pier. ☏ 312-222-9328.

Morning is the best time to visit the Shedd Aquarium, especially in summer when a line is likely to form around the block by 11am. Early visitors can expect immediate admission to the oceanarium; those who come later often must wait to enter. No matter what time you go, the galleries seem to swim with children and school groups.

You'll find the **Go Overboard!** cafe and gift shop adjacent to the admissions desk off the main lobby. In the Oceanarium, **Soundings Restaurant** provides full table service, and the adjacent food court, **The Bubble Net**, offers pizza, burgers and sandwiches to go. Vending machines can be found on the ground level of the main lobby.

Main Building

Radiating from the central Caribbean Reef situated beneath the rotunda, six 90ft-long rectangular galleries flow one into the other here, each focusing on a different type of aquatic system. The darkened spaces contrast with the brightly lit tanks to provide optimum viewing.

Centerpiece of the main building, the 90,000gal **Caribbean Reef★** habitat underwent an extensive renovation in 1999, during which all the synthetic coral was recast in materials that are impervious to saltwater, and the life-support system was upgraded with state-of-the-art technology. The renovated exhibit also includes a 3,000gal reef-within-a-reef built into the original huge tank to facilitate the display of smaller fishes that might otherwise wind up as food for the larger species. Some 500 tropical fish inhabit the reef, from nurse sharks to parrotfish; new additions (as of May 2000) include yellow stingrays, Spanish hogfish and Caribbean spiny lobsters. Daily feedings by scuba-diving animal caretakers are engrossing; the divers narrate their actions underwater as they work.

Occupying 10,000sq ft of space in the south wing of the original building, **Amazon Rising: Seasons of the River★**, allows visitors to experience a year in the life of an Amazon floodplain forest. The journey begins as you are immersed in a humid tropical "forest," with rain falling behind you and the calls of myriad birds and insects echoing all around. Habitats (river beach, floodplain lake, forest) are stocked with some 250 species of animals, such as lungfish, piranha, bird-eating spiders, an anaconda and a two-toed sloth. Each environment is repeated to illustrate the different levels of the river during the year, from low-water season—when the river is only a few feet high—to high-water season, when the Amazon swells to a depth of 30ft and a breadth up to 40mi wide. Displays at the end of the exhibit reinforce the fragile interdependence of the organisms in this ecosystem and stress the global ramifications of human actions.

Continuing around the Caribbean Reef in a counter-clockwise direction, **Ocean Coasts** includes a Northwest Coast "surge zone," that teems with starfish and other tide-tossed life (the rushing tide is simulated by dump buckets above the exhibit that release 100gals of water every 15 seconds). Another popular denizen in this gallery is the giant Pacific octopus. A solitary nocturnal hunter, the giant octopus can grow to 30ft (from armtip to armtip) and weigh in at 100 pounds. Lively river otters stand out among the denizens of local waters contained in the adjacent gallery, **Illinois Lakes and Rivers**. Interpretive graphics and visitor-activated videos introduce the resident otters you can observe here.

In **Tropical Waters** flashlight fish dart and glow behind a darkened screen, and visitors wait patiently to see the alligator snapper turtle rise for air about once an hour. Next door, endangered and threatened species are showcased in **Asia, Africa and Australia**. In this gallery you'll find curious specimens ranging from the Australian lungfish, which possesses the ability to breathe through both lungs and gills, to the paddlefish, whose long, flat snout is covered with sensors to help it navigate and find food in murky waters.

Throughout the exhibit areas, a smattering of interpretive graphics with strong ecological overtones offers informative and sometimes humorous data on such diverse topics as fish senses and Chicago's changing shoreline.

★★ Oceanarium

In contrast to the darkened halls of the older building, light floods the airy and open oceanarium, one of the world's largest indoor marine mammal pavilions. A visit here amounts to a walk through a huge diorama, complete with living marine animals, that is a faithful reproduction in steel and epoxy—down to the last rock and pine needle—of a Northwest coastal ecosystem. Life along this coast lends itself particularly well to exhibit as the ranges of many marine mammals overlap here, and the Sitka spruce forest can be successfully simulated in an exhibit setting. Depicting this region also offers an unequaled opportunity to demonstrate the dynamics of an entire ecosystem, and an endangered one at that, as the harvesting of North American temperate rain forests proceeds at a devastating pace.

The self-guided stroll "along the coast" follows the edge of the oversized pools where **beluga whales**, Pacific white-sided **dolphins** and **harbor seals** carouse. Around each bend loom islands, a tide pool, a fault line and other geologic features. The wide expanse

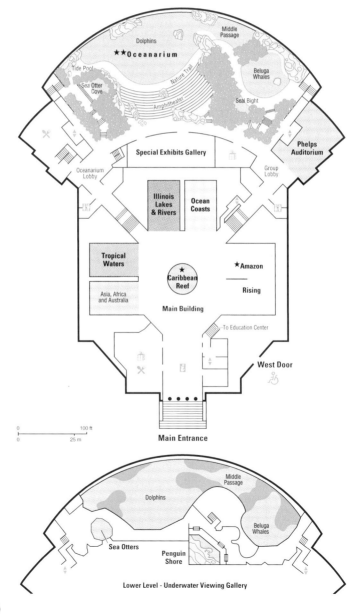

of Lake Michigan stretches beyond, a vista barely interrupted by the oceanarium's glass wall. Throughout the day, animal care specialists work in unscheduled sessions with the whales and dolphins to encourage natural behaviors, accustom the animals to human contact and provide them with play time. These sessions can be observed up close from the nature trail. Formal 15min demonstrations of natural behaviors are presented several times daily *(check presentation times at entrance)* and can be viewed from an amphitheater carved into the "rocks" above the pools. Demonstrators stress that the animals are not performing tricks but doing what comes naturally on hand cues from a poolside trainer. A "spy-hopping" dolphin, for instance, stands straight up on its tail for a better view above the water.

■ Fishy Facts

- A large Caribbean parrot fish excretes a ton of sand a year. Using two oversized front teeth, it nibbles on seagrass and scrapes algae; another set of teeth in its throat grinds up the coral it ingests.
- The Amazon River has more fish species than any other freshwater system on earth; each year the Amazon produces enough fish to fill a freight train more than 5,000 cars long.
- It takes two weeks for a pair of elegant shrimp to devour a starfish 100 times their size.
- Seahorses, and their relatives pipefishes and sea dragons, share an unusual trait: the males become pregnant and carry their developing young.
- At birth, Beluga whale calves weigh between 80 and 150 pounds and measure from 3.5ft to 5ft long.
- Adult electric eels 5ft to 7ft long produce enough electricity—600 volts—to stun a horse.

One level below the habitat, an **underwater viewing gallery** offers glimpses into the depths of the huge pools. **Penguin Shore** houses colonies of rockhopper, magellanic and gentoo penguins, three of the world's 17 penguin species. These creatures—found only in the frigid reaches of the Southern Hemisphere—are perfectly suited to their environment, combining the best of bird, marine mammal and fish. Strong "wings" allow them to "fly" through the water. Blubber and a complex layering of feathers keep them warm in water 70 degrees colder than their bodies. And their dolphin-like shape streamlines their swimming. The **sea otter** habitat can be viewed from both levels. These smallest of marine mammals lack the bulk and blubber their relatives rely on for keeping warm; instead, their dense fur must act as insulation. Clean fur is therefore essential, and the otters spend much of the day grooming. To an otter, an oil spill can be devastating. Three of the aquarium's otters were rescued from Alaska's Prince William Sound after the *Exxon Valdez* spill in 1989. A series of interactive exhibits presents topics related to marine mammals such as breathing and diving, beluga populations, locomotion through water, and otters and oil spills. One display explains the workings of the oceanarium, mechanical as well as human, and an intriguing video provides a look at the animals "after hours." One level above the oceanarium is the **Special Exhibits Gallery**, which presents changing exhibits on matters marine and maritime. The current exhibit is **Seahorse Symphony** *(until 2002)*, where you can see and learn about these astonishing creatures—whose numbers are dwindling at an alarming rate—and the animals related to them. In **Phelps Auditorium**, short multimedia programs on a variety of aquatic topics run continuously.

★★ ADLER PLANETARIUM & ASTRONOMY MUSEUM

1300 S. Lake Shore Dr. Map p 131.

Occupying a beautiful setting, the planetarium offers commanding **views**★★ up and down the lakefront. The oldest planetarium in the Western Hemisphere, the Adler is renowned for its fine collection of historic astronomical instruments and its splendid sky shows.

Historical Notes

Intrigued by a German device known as a Zeiss projector for re-creating the night sky on an enclosed dome, philanthropist **Max Adler** (1866-1952) decided in 1928 that Chicago ought to have one "to emphasize that under the great celestial firmament there is order, interdependence and unity." Adler, a retired officer of Sears, Roebuck and Co. (of which his brother-in-law Julius Rosenwald was president), donated $1 million to the city to establish a planetarium, and acquired a substantial collection of astronomical instruments for its museum. Architect Ernest A. Grunsfeld, Jr. designed a compact, Art Deco jewel for the dramatic setting at the

© Balthazar Korab

Adler Planetarium

tip of Northerly Island. When the planetarium opened in 1930, its modern style contrasted with the Beaux-Arts edifices that housed Chicago's other cultural institutions. Bronze bas-reliefs depicting signs of the zodiac punctuate the smooth reddish granite of the 12-sided, 3-tiered exterior. The whole is crowned by the dome of the original planetarium theater, where the facility's first Zeiss projector operated until 1970 (the theater is currently equipped with a Zeiss Mark VI projector).

The building was extended underground to the west in 1973, and a new entryway was added in 1981. In 1977 the **Doane Observatory** opened just east of the planetarium, offering the public a firsthand view of the heavens through its 20-inch cassegrain reflector telescope. The planetarium achieved National Historic Landmark status in 1987. A major renovation, completed in 1999, added a 60,000sq ft wrap-around addition to the old building and eliminated the 1981 entry. The addition contains two floors of exhibit space, one below street level and one above. The glass-enclosed upper level features interactive modules and telescope viewing areas. Exhibits are also housed in the original edifice, where visitors once again enter the planetarium through the main doors.

Visit

Open Memorial Day-Labor Day daily 9am-6pm (Thu & Fri til 9pm). Rest of the year Mon-Fri 9am-5pm (Fri til 9pm), weekends 9am-6pm. Closed Thanksgiving Day & Dec 25. $5 (free Tue). ⚓ ♿ 🅿 ($7) ☎ 312 922 7827. www.adlerplanetarium.org.

Gracing the grounds leading to the planetarium are several important sculptures. At the western end of Solidarity Drive (so named in 1980 by Mayor Jane Byrne at the request of the Polish community to honor Lech Walesa and the Polish labor movement) stands the **Tadeusz Kosciuszko Memorial (3)**, sculpted by Kasimir Chodzinski in 1904. Near the planetarium, a seated **Nicolaus Copernicus (4)** holds an open compass and a model of the solar system. Bertel Thorvaldsen cast the bronze original in Warsaw in 1823.

Henry Moore's 12ft working **Sundial (5)** (1980), which commemorates the "golden years of astronomy" from 1930 to 1980, is installed outside the glass-enclosed Galileo's restaurant on the building's north side.

Upper Level – Visitors enter on the upper level, the centerpiece of which is the **Sky Theater** where the Zeiss Mark VI star projector re-creates the twinkling night sky on the dome of the historic planetarium. Daily **sky shows★** *(check schedule at admissions desk)* focus on various aspects of astronomy, such as the fantastic findings of the Hubble Space Telescope, and the relationship between the orbits of the planets and human efforts at timekeeping throughout history. Lively narration accompanies the special effects created by the projector, making the program appeal to young and old alike. On Friday evenings the sky show includes a look at live or recorded images beamed in from the Doane Observatory's reflecting telescope.

Beside the theater, a mirrored passage called Space Walk simulates the vastness of the universe and leads to **Gateway to the Universe Gallery**. Here, displays reveal the nature of the universe in terms of light, mass, gravity and motion. Other galleries on this level investigate the planets of our solar system and the mysteries of the Milky Way galaxy through interactive exhibits.

Lower Level – A highlight of the recent renovation, the virtual-reality **StarRider®
Theater★★** *(entrance on lower level)* offers visitors an interactive voyage through
the universe using state-of-the-art computer projection technologies. Your simulated interplanetary journey might involve settling a colony—which you help
design—on Mars, or traveling back in time to watch our solar system form from
clouds of gas and dust.

Also on this level, the **History of Astronomy Gallery★** showcases the planetarium's extensive collection of historic astronomical, navigational, timekeeping, surveying and
measuring instruments. Case follows case of intricately decorated metal objects,
arcane and curious in appearance and name: orrery, astrolabe, compendium, eclip-
sometrium. Note in particular a remarkable assemblage of sundials in ivory, brass,
wood, silver and stone dating from the 14-18C. A model of a Medieval university
lecture hall allows visitors to don scholars' robes and pretend to be astronomy
students.

In the **Cosmology Gallery**, you can trace man's changing views of the cosmos from
the earliest theories of Copernicus and Galileo to the modern models provided by
the Hubble Space Telescope. Here you'll find a model of the giant wooden
Dearborn telescope (1789) with its 18.5in lens.

Adjacent to the StarRider® Theater, you can view a short presentation in the
Atwood Sphere. Inside this hollow, revolving metal sphere, the constellations are
visible via tiny holes in the metal through which light shines. A special-exhibits
gallery on the lower level rounds out the visit.

GOLD COAST ★★

Red line to Clark/Division or Intraste. LSI
Map p 146

This slice of Chicago's lakefront has been home to the city's most prominent and wealthiest citizens for over a century. Nestled between the nightlife district of Oak and Division Streets on the south and Lincoln Park on the north, the most expensive residential property in Chicago encompasses the towering apartment buildings of Lake Shore Drive and the quaint Victorian town houses of Astor Street. To the west LaSalle Street and Sandburg Village mark the transition to the recently gentrified Old Town Historic District, while the Magnificent Mile lies just a short walk to the south.

Historical Notes

Lifestyles of the Rich and Famous – The young city's moneyed classes first settled in the Prairie Avenue district south of the Loop. By the end of the 19C, they had relocated to the present-day Gold Coast. Two events contributed to the rise in fame of this patch of land located just south of Lincoln Park. In the 1860s the city's municipal cemetery—established on marshy swampland north of the city limits—was removed to create Lincoln Park, and in 1875 **Lake Shore Drive** opened, improving transportation to the area. Five years later the Roman Catholic Archbishop's lavish residence was built at North Avenue. And in 1882 **Potter** and **Bertha Honoré Palmer**, the city's real-estate king and society queen, erected an ostentatious mansion on Lake Shore Drive, striking the decisive blow in the battle to win the homes and haunts of Chicago's rich and famous. Abandoning Prairie Avenue en masse, the wealthy elite soon followed Palmer, who had wisely purchased much of the land, which quadrupled in value within a decade. Bertha Palmer entertained without pause, exhibiting her collection of French Impressionist works (later donated to the Art Institute) in the home's famed 75ft-long picture gallery. By 1900 the Archbishop had subdivided and sold his land as well, and the Gold Coast quickly filled with mansions and extravagant stone town houses, detailed in the popular styles of the period: Romanesque, Queen Anne and Beaux-Arts.

Return of an Era – Developers began to erect apartment high rises in the 20C, most featuring full-floor, 18-room units with servants' quarters and all the amenities of a private home. Many Victorian houses were razed in the 1920s, especially on Lake Shore Drive, as a rash of luxurious high-rise construction increased the density of the area without diminishing its prestige. While the Gold Coast was thriving, the area to the west of LaSalle Street was settled by working-class Irish, German and Swedish immigrants, followed by Italians. In 1929 Harvey Zorbaugh documented the contrast in *The Gold Coast and the Slum*, a benchmark in urban sociology.

Palmer's Lake Shore Drive "castle" was demolished in 1950 during another spate of high-rise development. More town houses were mowed down and replaced by hundreds of apartments with the most precious of Chicago commodities: a view of the lake. Urban redevelopment in the 1960s targeted the deteriorating area to the west by erecting Carl Sandburg Village along Clark Street from Division Street to North Avenue, initiating the gentrification of the nearby Old Town and Lincoln Park areas. In 196? Butch McGuire opened the first singles bar on Division Street, turning the southern edge of the Gold Coast into a raucous nightlife district, while a surgeon's stately home became Hugh Hefner's first Playboy Mansion. In 1973 the city designated **Astor Street** a landmark, and limited buildi

Gold Coast Town Houses

heights to help stem the high-rise trend and preserve the turn-of-the-century ambience. Four years later the entire Gold Coast, from North Avenue south to Oak Street and Dearborn Street east to Lake Shore Drive, was listed on the National Register of Historic Places, and in 1990 the city designated as landmarks the last seven houses on Lake Shore Drive. Today many mansions that had been divided into apartments are being restored as single-family homes, ushering in a new era of gentility and luxury in this parklike enclave.

WALKING TOUR *Distance: 2.3mi*

Tucked below the skyscrapers of the Magnificent Mile, the area exudes a sense of elegance and luxury. An early Sunday morning stroll is probably the best way to enjoy this lovely district, where stately town houses fronted by tiny, manicured lawns bring to mind visions of a bygone era. In the summer, end your walk by heading to popular Oak Street Beach.

Begin at Bellevue Pl. and Lake Shore Dr. and walk west.

Bellevue Place – This charming, tree-lined street exhibits an array of Victorian architectural styles. The handsome, three-story **Bryan Lathrop House** *(120 E. Bellevue Pl.)*, designed by McKim, Mead & White in 1892, created quite a contrast to the picturesque facades of Queen Anne and Romanesque Revival architecture dominating the Gold Coast in the late 19C. This Chicago landmark brought the comparatively sedate Georgian Revival to the area, and by 1900, it became the most popular style. Graceful, rounded bays frame a symmetrical brick facade with an expansive porch and Beaux-Arts detailing. A 1972 restoration by Perkins & Will replicated the original cornice. Built for a real estate magnate who helped found the Chicago Symphony Orchestra, the structure has housed the Fortnightly of Chicago, a women's literary club, since 1922.

Note the 1887 **Lot P. Smith House** at no. 32, a rare surviving home by Burnham & Root, and the looming, four-story, Georgian Revival Chandler Apartments at no. 33, designed in 1911 by Schmidt, Garden & Martin.

 Oak Street Beach

Map p 146. The most chic beach in Chicago is (appropriately) situated at the intersection of Oak Street and Michigan Avenue. In the summer, the tanned and toned soak up the rays and swim in the shadow of the Drake Hotel. To get to the beach (and the bike path that winds along the lakefront from Hyde Park to Hollywood Avenue), use the underground tunnels at Oak or Division Streets.

Turn right on Rush St.

The tiny, pie-shaped Mariano Park contains a 1900 pavilion designed by Birch Burdette Long, a student of Frank Lloyd Wright, and a new fountain (1998). The bustle of commercial Rush Street contrasts with the surprisingly quiet residential streets of the Gold Coast.

Turn right on Cedar St.

The 1920s high-rise boom in this tony area led to buildings like the Gothic-style **20 E. Cedar Street** (1924, Fugard & Knapp), which takes the lavish ornament and picturesque rooflines of a Gold Coast town house and stretches them out over 15 stories. The streetscape ranges from well-preserved Romanesque and Georgian Revival town homes to faceless modern high rises. The highlight of the street is the Romanesque Revival **60 E. Cedar Street** (1890, Curd H. Gottig), a confection of turrets, arches and protruding bays in rusticated Georgia marble. Note the lovely stained glass punctuating the facade.

Turn left on Lake Shore Dr.

Lake Shore Drive had witnessed $25 million worth of apartment high-rise development by 1928, mostly in the form of elegant structures such as no. 1120 (1926, Robert S. DeGolyer) and no. 1130 (1911, Howard Van Doren Shaw), one of the first cooperatives, featuring full-floor apartments and a Tudor Revival design with Medieval motifs. Marshall & Fox followed in 1913 with the luxurious **Stewart Apartments** *(no. 1200)*, in the Adamesque style with large bay windows. Look south for an impressive **view★** of the Drake Hotel and East Lake Shore Drive, a row of luxury high rises developed before 1929.

Turn left on Division St. and continue to Astor St.

Renaissance Condominiums – *1200 N. Astor St.* Originally the McConnell Apartments, this 1897 Holabird & Roche design is one of the earliest high rises in the area. Combining Victorian rounded corners with modern brick wall planes and massing, the structure is an excellent example of a Chicago school apartment building.

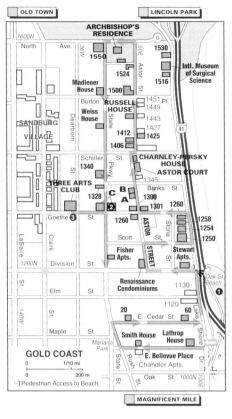

Turn right on Astor St.

Early high-rise apartments give way to quaint gray-stones with delicate wrought-iron railings and miniature front gardens on historic **Astor Street★★**, named for John Jacob Astor, whose American Fur Co. traded in the area before the settlement of Chicago. Note how the attached town houses are staggered along the angled street so that each facade projects forward as you walk north. While other wealthy neighborhoods boasted large lots, many Gold Coast mansions are squeezed into parcels only 25ft wide.

Turn right on Scott St. and left on Lake Shore Dr.

Four of the seven homes on Lake Shore Drive designated Chicago landmarks by the city in 1990 are located side by side in this block. The Carl C. Heisen House at **no. 1250** (1891, Frank B. Abbott) and Mason B. Starring House at **no. 1254** (1891, L. Gustav Halberg) are heavy Romanesque Revival structures that were joined in 1990 to create four luxury condominiums. Holabird & Roche designed the flowery Venetian Gothic home at **no. 1258** in 1898 for Arthur Aldis while the same firm exhibited Georgian restraint in 1910 at **no. 1260** next door.

Turn left on Goethe St. and right onto Astor St.

Philip B. Maher designed the nearly identical buildings at **1260** and **1301 N. Astor Street** in 1932. The sleek Art Deco towers retain the full-floor luxury of earlier apartment buildings; note the elegant canopy at no. 1260. Potter Palmer II and his wife occupied three floors in no. 1301 when it opened. The modern design at **no. 1300** (1963, Bertrand Goldberg) presents a sharp contrast with slender posts supporting the building above the automobile-oriented ground level.

★**James L. Houghteling Houses** (**A**) – *1308-1312 N. Astor St.* Designed in 1887 by John Wellborn Root of Burnham & Root, the three surviving houses have beautiful sculptural quality created by variegated massing and polychromatic wall treatments. A rusticated base of red sandstone supports tawny brick walls and metal bay windows, rising to a picturesque roofline of turrets, gables and dormers. Root himself lived at no. 1310 until his untimely death in 1891 during the planning of the World's Columbian Exposition. Root's sister-in-law, Harriet Monroe, lived here as well. Monroe was first in the country to publish works by Vachel Lindsay, Carl Sandburg and T.S. Eliot.

The Romanesque Revival row houses at **1316-1322 N. Astor Street** (**B**) were designed in 1889 for real estate mogul Potter Palmer. The walls of the houses gradually progress from heavy rustication to smooth surfaces. Note the huge Romanesque arch framing the entrance at no. 1322.

Cross Banks St. and continue north on Astor St.

More 1960s high rises on the left overwhelm tiny Victorians on the right, such as the multicolored checkerboard at 1345 N. Astor Street (1887, Treat & Foltz). William O. Goodman, who endowed the Goodman Theatre, lived at **Astor Court** *(1355 N. Astor St.)*, a stately Georgian mansion (1914, Howard Van Doren Shaw). A small courtyard is visible at the southern entrance behind a gate ornamented with golden door knockers in the shapes of hands holding apples.

★**Charnley-Persky House** – *1365 N. Astor St. Visit by guided tour (1hr) on Apr–Nov Wed noon, Sat 10am & 1pm. Rest of the year Wed noon, Sat 10am. Closed Jan 1 & Dec 25. $5 (free Wed). 2hr Sat tour of Charnley-Persky House* and Madlener House. $9. ☎ 312-915-0105. www.sah.org. **Frank Lloyd Wright** designed this 1892 home while in the employ of Adler & Sullivan. Wright, who immodestly called it the first modern building, managed to create a horizontal composition by employing his trademark Roman bricks and minimizing decoration. Sullivanesque ornament covers the protruding balcony and front door, while the limestone base and broad eaves hint at Wright's future work. The house has only 11 rooms organized around a central skylit stair; a kitchen is located in the narrow basement.

Cross Schiller St. and continue north on Astor St.

At the northeast corner of Schiller and Astor Streets, note the polychromatic stone treatments of the row houses, especially the greenstone at no. 38. The corner unit was given a Georgian facade at the turn of the century. On the west side, **1406 N. Astor Street** was built for steel scion Joseph T. Ryerson (grandson of philanthropist Martin A. Ryerson) in 1922 by David Adler, who excelled in French stylings. Adler added the slate mansard roof in 1931 to enclose a gallery exhibiting local memorabilia now housed at the Chicago Historical Society. The Thomas W. Hinde House at **no. 1412** boasts an unusual facade embellished with English Renaissance motifs and diamond-paned windows.

William D. Kerfoot gained fame in 1871 when his was the first Loop business to reopen the day after the notorious fire destroyed all of his real-estate holdings. The sign on his wooden shanty—now at the Chicago Historical Society—read, "W.D. Kerfoot. Everything gone but wife, children, and energy." By 1895 his energy afforded him the 8,000sq ft graystone Georgian at **1425 N. Astor Street**. Skyscraper pioneer William Le Baron Jenney and Sullivan collaborator J.L. Silsbee erected the adjacent Romanesque Revival homes at nos. 1427 and 1443 around 1890.

★**Edward P. Russell House** – *1444 N. Astor St.* Perhaps the most elegant Art Deco construction in the Gold Coast, the building (1929, Holabird & Root) features a facade of stone from Lens, France, a gently curved three-story metal bay with incised floral decoration and a carved panel depicting graceful peacocks. Delicate oval windows flank a door covered with grillwork.

The French Chateau style, ill-suited to narrow lots, was nonetheless attempted at 1449 N. Astor Street, while Howard Van Doren Shaw's John L. Fortune House *(no. 1451)* used a corner lot to accommodate the Jacobethan style that replaced the Georgian Revival around 1910.

Cross Burton St.

1500 North Astor Street – The huge Renaissance-style palazzo (1893, McKim, Mead & White) at the corner of Astor and Burton Streets was built by *Chicago Tribune* publisher and former mayor Joseph Medill as a wedding gift for his daughter Elinor Patterson. A two-story front porch supported by Doric and Ionic columns is flanked by orange Roman brick walls with elaborate terra-cotta trim and capped by a cornice and balustrade that exhaust the Classical vocabulary. Cyrus Hall McCormick II purchased the home in 1927 and employed David Adler to double its size. The addition is visible on the exterior of the structure, which became a school, and was then divided into eight $1 million condominiums in 1978.

Continue north on Astor St.

The rounded corner and brick facade of **1524 N. Astor Street** (1968, I.W. Colburn & Assocs.) harmonizes this modern high rise with the Beaux-Arts and Georgian town houses that first defined the block in the 1910s.

★**Residence of the Roman Catholic Archbishop of Chicago** – *1555 N. State Pkwy.* The oldest Gold Coast home (1880, Alfred F. Pashley), this Queen Anne fantasy in red brick with limestone trim is distinguished by 19 chimneys punctuating the roofline and an uncharacteristic expanse of surrounding land. The mansion was built prior to the rapid rise in real estate values in the 1880s and 90s.

At the edge of Lincoln Park turn left on North Ave., and left again on N. State Pkwy.

★**1550 North State Parkway** – When it opened in 1912, this Beaux-Arts apartment building set the standard for Gold Coast gentility with 9,000sq ft, 15-room apartments organized around expansive sun parlors. Its architect, **Benjamin Marshall** of Marshall & Fox, grew up rich and stayed rich by designing Chicago's most prestigious homes and hotels in the 1910s and 20s, including the nearby Drake Hotel. From its rusticated base to the large urns atop the balustrade, no. 1550 is a tour de force of white terra-cotta ornament and French grillwork with balconies overlooking Lincoln Park and the Archbishop's mansion.

Walk south on N. State Pkwy. and turn right on Burton Pl.

Albert F. Madlener House – *4 W. Burton Pl. Visit by guided tour only (2hrs; tour includes Charnley-Persky House). Apr–Nov Sat 10am & 1pm. Rest of the year Sat 10am. Closed Jan 1 & Dec 25. $9. ☎ 312-915-0105. www.ci.chi.il.us/land-*

marks/Madlener.html. An epochal 1902 work of Prairie school architect Hugh Garden, this mansion was built for a local brewer. Roman brick and coursed limestone create an austerity broken by the beauty of the **entrance★**, framed by oversize Prairie-style urns and wonderfully intricate coursing and grillwork. The former mansion is home to the Graham Foundation for Advanced Studies in the Fine Arts an architectural endowment.

Return to N. State Pkwy. and continue south.

The 1400 block of North State Parkway contains many lovely town houses, but the **George A. Weiss House** at no. 1428 (1886, Harald M. Hansen) garners the most attention with its pink Romanesque Revival stone facade, dramatic corner spire and a gabled chimney bay thrusting toward the street. Note the gargoyles and slate mansard roof.

Cross Schiller St. and continue south on N. State Pkwy.

A Queen Anne graystone with a prominent corner tower heralds a series of attached row houses at State and Schiller Streets. More stately town houses with English antecedents give way to the oversized but orderly French-inspired facade of **1340 North State Parkway**, designed in 1899 for surgeon George S. Isham by James Gamble Rogers, architect of Yale University. A steep slate roof is broken by three dormers surrounded by garlanded urns. These noble walls enclosed the after-dark lifestyle of *Playboy* magazine founder and Chicago native **Hugh Hefner** throughout the 1960s and 70s. The building was given to the School of the Art Institute of Chicago in the mid-1980s and served as classrooms and dorms until its 1993 conversion into condominium units. The famous Playboy Mansion underground pool and grotto were demolished in the rehabilitation.

A bit farther south, **1328 North State Parkway** presents a rounded glass-block corner with a deep, low entry into what are actually two homes on either end of a long narrow lot. Constructed in 1938 by Andrew N. Rebori, who designed the similar Frank F. Fisher Apartments, the buildings were joined into a single home and studio for artist Lillian Florsheim in 1956 by her son-in-law, architect Bertrand Goldberg.

Continue south to Goethe St.

Framing North State Parkway at Goethe Street are the **Ambassador East and West (C** two prestigious hotels that have catered to the Gold Coast for generations Booth 1 at Ambassador East's **Pump Room** was the most glamorous seat in town for entertainers and other luminaries from the 1940s to the 1970s.

Walk west on Goethe St. to Dearborn St.

At the corner of Goethe and Dearborn Streets, a stately brick palace surrounding an enclosed courtyard has provided living space for female art students since its opening in 1914. Designed by Holabird & Roche, the facade of the **Three Arts Club★** features large bas-relief sculpture and other eclectic ornamentation.

Return to N. State Pkwy. and continue south.

② The Pump Room

Map p 146. In the Omni Ambassador East Hotel. ☎ *312-266-0360.* In its heyday during the 1940s, this restaurant was the place to see and be seen for Chicago's swell set and visiting Hollywood stars. They undoubtedly came for the outrageous service: many dishes were delivered to patrons on flaming swords, and guests' dogs could dine in the adjacent Pup Room. While it's no longer the center of Chicago society, the Pump Room remains a charming, elegant restaurant. Don't miss the impressive gallery of photographs of celebrities in the bar area.

③ The 3rd Coast

Map p 146. 1260 N. Dearborn St. ☎ *312-649-0730.* Sip cappuccino or claret in this warm, comfortable coffeehouse and wine bar, which is open 24 hours a day. The clientele here ranges from well-dressed Gold Coast matrons to bohemian art students who board at the Three Arts Club across the street. Soups, sandwiches and salads are available as are several of Chicago's free arts publications.

Frank F. Fisher Apartments – *1209 N. State Pkwy.* In 1937 architect **Andrew Rebori** designed the white brick and glass-block Art Moderne facade leading 13 apartments organized around a very narrow atrium. Artist Edgar Miller, famous for his "handmade houses" on West Burton Place, contributed the facade's sculptural plaques.

Rows of late-19C Italianate and Victorian town houses frame North State Parkway south of Goethe Street, before giving way to the contemporary restaurants and noisy bars of bustling Division and Rush Streets.

Additional Sights

International Museum of Surgical Science – *1524 N. Lake Shore Dr. Open year-round Tue–Sat 10am–4pm. Closed major holidays. $6.* 🅿 ☎ *312-642-6502. www.imss.org.* Located on Lake Shore Drive in a landmark mansion (1917, Howard Van Doren Shaw), this museum features an idiosyncratic and sometimes bizarre collection of surgical instruments, art and artifacts devoted to the history of medicine and surgery. The museum was opened in 1952 by the International College of Surgeons, headquartered next door at no. 1516 and founded in 1935 in Geneva by Hungarian-born Chicago surgeon Max Thorek.

The collection is distributed over four floors. Highlights include a display on Civil War amputation illustrated with instruments, period photos and text conveying the enormity of the conflict *(1st floor)*. The "Hall of Immortals" *(2nd floor)* features 12 statues by Louis Linck and Edouard Chassaing, who also sculpted *Hope and Healing* on the front lawn. The 5,000-volume wood-paneled library here is an original interior feature of the house. Third-floor rooms focus on South American, Dutch, Egyptian and Canadian surgery. On the fourth floor you'll find a disquieting display of large "stones"—the kind that form in kidneys and gall bladders—and the primitive alloy tools used by the Incas for trephination (brain surgery), shown next to their patient's skulls.

Lake Shore Drive Mansions – *1516 and 1530 N. Lake Shore Dr.* Built of gray Indiana limestone in the Beaux-Arts style, these two mansions form bookends to the International Museum of Surgical Science. To the south the Edward T. Blair House *(no. 1516)* was designed by New York's McKim, Mead & White in 1914. Designed in 1916 by Benjamin H. Marshall, the Bernard A. Eckhart House *(no. 1530)* is now occupied by the Polish Consulate. Howard Van Doren Shaw's creation, now housing the museum, was modeled on Versailles' Petit Trianon at the client's behest.

OLD TOWN★

🚇 Brown line to Sedgwick and North
Map p 150

Vintage cottages and elegant row houses share tree-lined streets with modern apartments in this upscale residential neighborhood bounded by Division, Halsted and LaSalle Streets and Armitage Avenue. Bustling Wells Street, home to the renowned Second City comedy club and a variety of shops, bars and restaurants, cuts a colorful path through the charming Old Town Triangle Historical District north of North Avenue.

Historical Notes

German Broadway – In the 1840s and 50s, German immigrants began to settle just north of the city's border at North Avenue. These working-class families built modest homes and started their own businesses or took jobs as semiskilled laborers. Mostly Catholic, they established St. Michael's parish in 1852, and the church at Eugenie Street and Cleveland Avenue soon became the focal point of the German community. In 1871 their wooden cottages burned like kindling during the Great Chicago Fire, but immediately following the conflagration, "relief shanties" began to spring up. In no time, older residents had rebuilt their homes and, as factories crowded the banks of the Chicago River directly west, workers flocked to North Town, later called Old Town. In 1874 the city extended its strict fire ordinance to the community, forcing builders to abandon wood for more fireproof materials. Stone Italianate and Queen Anne row houses, as well as brick cottages and coach houses commingled with the older wooden structures, giving Old Town the variegated architectural look it retains today. By 1900, North Avenue—then known as the German Broadway—was alive with shops, bakeries, taverns and delicatessens. Surviving testaments to Old Town's German heritage include the House of Glunz wine shop at Wells and Division Streets and the Germania Club at North Avenue and Clark Street, which was built in 1888 as headquarters of the German Maennerchor singing club.

Century of Progress? – Growth of the community slowed in the early 20C as prewar buildings began to deteriorate. Impoverished neighborhoods to the west and south teeming with Eastern Europeans, Italians and African Americans pressed in on Old Town while the Germans moved north. By the late 1920s, the dilapidated tenements and boardinghouses southwest of Lincoln Park contrasted dramatically with the glittering Gold Coast to the east. Gradually, attempts were made to refurbish the blighted neighborhood. In 1927 a group of artists led by **Sol Kogen** and **Edgar Miller** bought run-down buildings along Carl Street (now Burton Place) and transformed them into fanciful Art Deco-style homes. Wealthy industrialist Marshall Field III tried his hand at urban renewal in 1928 by financing 10 five-story buildings on Sedgwick Street. Few poor families could afford the $35 to $63 monthly rents, however, and the managers let most of the flats remain vacant. In 1934 the Chicago Housing Authority's first effort to clean up the slum in western Old Town failed. When the CHA announced plans to clear 67 acres along Halsted Street, residents protested so vehemently that the city backed down. (Between 1943 and 1962, the CHA succeeded in establishing the huge housing project known as Cabrini-Green at the southern edge of Old Town.) In another form of urban renewal, the development of Carl Sandburg Village beginning in the 1960s along Clark and LaSalle Streets south of North Avenue heralded the influx of thousands of young singles and families.

A Community Reborn – By the late 1950s, Asian and Hispanic immigrants had joined the ethnic mix in Old Town, and inexpensive rents attracted artists and musicians. In 1947 a group of neighbors decided to raise money to spruce up a small park on Eugenie Street. They invited "anyone who painted, sculpted, wove or baked" to display and sell their work. The event evolved into the **Old Town Art Fair**, which today attracts artists from around the world and draws thousands of spectators every second weekend of June. The Old Town School of Folk Music opened in 1957 on North Avenue to preserve America's tuneful traditions and introduce music from around the world. (It has since moved to Armitage Avenue.) In 1959 comedians Paul Sills and Bernie Sahlins relocated their fledgling theater company from Hyde Park to Wells Street and renamed it "The Second City." The troupe, which performs comedy skits based on improvisation, earned rave reviews for its irreverent fast-and-loose style. Over the years The Second City has trained such great comic actors as Alan Arkin, Joan Rivers and its most famous alumnus John Belushi.

Old Town's "artsy" reputation and affordable housing made it a natural choice for the hippies of the late 1960s and early 70s. Political bookstores and psychedelic shops sprouted up all along Wells Street. As part of an urban-renewal project in the early 1970s, the city vacated broad Ogden Avenue from North Avenue to Lincoln Park— only 40 years after it had been slashed through the neighborhood. Housing developments for low-income families shared the newly vacant land with stunning single-family homes designed by Stanley Tigerman and other prominent Chicago architects. In 1976 the **Old Town Triangle**, bordered roughly by the former Ogden Avenue, North and Lincoln Avenues, was declared a Chicago Landmark District, and in 1984 the area was listed on the National Register of Historic Places, well-deserved recognition for the revived neighborhood.

WALKING TOUR *Distance: 1.4mi*

A walk through the Old Town Triangle offers a compact glimpse of Chicago's architectural history and gives a sense of the city's mid- to late-19C residential landscape, down to the narrow streets. Indeed, were it not for the high rises that loom on the perimeter of the neighborhood, it would be easy to lose track of the modern city.

Begin at St. Michael's Church between Hudson and Cleveland Aves.

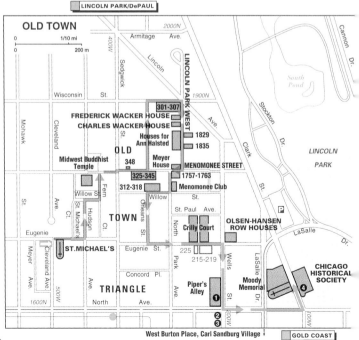

★**St. Michael's Church** – *Corner of Eugenie St. and Cleveland Ave. Open year-round daily 7am–7pm. Closed after morning mass on Jan 1, Memorial Day, Labor Day & Thanksgiving Day.* ⅍ ▯ ☏ *312-642-2498. www.st-mikes.org.* This is the third church building to serve St. Michael's parish since its formation in 1852. When the fire destroyed all but the east, south and west red-brick walls of the second structure finished in 1869, parishioners rallied to rebuild the interior in just a year's time. The steeple was added in 1888, and in 1913 an 8ft statue of St. Michael was placed in a niche high up on the facade. The church's ornate Bavarian Baroque interior is the result of years of renovation.

When exiting the church, walk east (right) to Hudson Ave., turn left on Hudson and continue to Willow St.

In temporal, architectural and cultural contrast to St. Michael's stands the **Midwest Buddhist Temple** *(435 W. Menomonee St.)* built in 1971. Its simple, pagoda-like lines and low profile evoke a Japanese shrine.

Continue east on Willow St., turn left on Fern Ct., right on Menomonee St. and cross Sedgwick St.

★**Menomonee Street** – This quaint street in particular evokes the essence of historic Old Town. The nine cottages on its south side, **nos. 325-345**, are good examples of the type built in the area during its original settlement, although they were constructed in the years immediately following the fire. These small wooden cottages could be erected in no time using "balloon framing," a Chicago building innovation partially accountable for the rapid growth and combustibility of the city. On the north side of the street, the tiny house at **no. 348** is a rare example of a fire relief shanty, one of 3,000 one-room dwellings donated by the Chicago Relief and Aid Society to families left homeless by the fire.

Proceed north on Orleans St. and turn right on Wisconsin St.

The brick row houses at **301-307 West Wisconsin Street** typify the Italianate style popular in late-19C Chicago. Incised sandstone lintels ornament their tall, narrow, bayed fronts.

Turn right on Lincoln Park West.

★**Lincoln Park West** – The well-to-do residents of eastern Old Town built their homes in the open land adjacent to the developing Lincoln Park. Completed in 1874, before the strict fire laws took effect, the ornate **Frederick Wacker House**★ at no. 1838 was built by a brewer who embellished its basic form with incised woodwork and other Victorian detail. Next door is the **Charles H. Wacker House**★ *(no. 1836)*, erected by Frederick's son Charles—the city planner for whom Wacker Drive was named—who relocated and remodeled his father's coach house in 1884. To the immediate south, a very different facade spans nos. 1826-1834, the **Houses for Ann Halsted**. These red-brick town houses were designed and built as rental property in 1884 and 1885 by Louis Sullivan and Dankmar Adler in a simplified Queen Anne style. They represent an early commission for Sullivan, a master of elaborate organic ornamentation, and his hand is especially evident in the terracotta stringcourses that top each unit. Across the street, note the handsome and well-preserved Italianate detail on **nos. 1829** and **1835**, both built around the mid-1870s. At the end of the block, the **Henry Meyer House** *(no. 1802)* dates from the same year. Although built as a farmhouse, the abode achieves a sophistication befitting this prosperous neighborhood through the simple decorative touches around its windows.

Henry Meyer House

151

Cross Menomonee St. and continue south on North Park Ave.

Nestled among the town homes and cottages of Old Town are garages and coach houses of the type seen at **1757-1763 North Park Avenue**. As Chicago's wealthy Gold Coast residents to the east acquired cars in the burgeoning age of the automobile, they built garages and lodgings for chauffeurs on the empty lots in Old Town. This example, which today houses the Old Town Triangle Association, was built for Philip D. Armour in 1915.

The **Menomonee Club for Girls and Boys** *(no. 244)* offers a nondescript wall along North Park Avenue, but the Willow Street facade erupts into an oriel of fanciful woodwork and stained glass, including a lovely etched-glass window reading "North End Bowling Club."

Turn right on Willow St. and continue to Orleans St.

Built in 1974, a century after Old Town's post-fire building boom, the row houses at **312-318 West Willow Street** represent the continuing effort to design efficient and comfortable city residences in close quarters. Architect Harry Weese modeled these multistory units on London row houses, adding garages at street level.

Turn left on Orleans St., left again on Eugenie St., and continue to Crilly Ct.

In 1885 developer Daniel F. Crilly bisected this block with a north-south street and spent the next 10 years erecting residential and commercial space around it. The centerpiece of his **Crilly Court Development** are the Queen Anne row houses (1885) that line the street's west side. The apartment buildings (1895) across the court bear Crilly's children's names above the entryways. Across Eugenie to the south are four Chicago cottages *(nos. 215-219 and 225)*, all built prior to 1874. Each has the characteristic high basement, steep front staircase and Italianate detail. The wall around no. 225 was added during its renovation.

Continue east on Eugenie St. to Wells St.

Across Wells Street, elegant and elaborate Queen Anne row houses flank the north side of Eugenie Street at nos. 164-172. A sharp contrast to the simpler Queen Anne houses in the interior of the Triangle, the **Olsen-Hansen Row Houses★** (1886) represent the style at its most flamboyant. Irregular rooflines, turrets and a variety of textures, materials and colors adorn the exteriors.

Turn right on Wells St.

Beginning with an existing bakery, architect Stanley Tigerman developed **Piper's Alley** as a multi-use mall between 1974 and 1977. Movie theaters, restaurants, ice cream shops and gift stores move in and out, but **The Second City** has prevailed at 1616 North Wells since 1959. The theater seems to transcend change in this neighborhood where so many other entertainments and diversions—from head shops to peep shows—have come and gone. Note the terra-cotta heads that ornament the facade; these German philosophers and poets were salvaged from Adler & Sullivan's downtown Schiller Theater when it was demolished in 1961.

Turn left on North Ave. for two blocks, then left again on Clark St.

A wide-open town like mid-19C Chicago attracted its share of evangelists and reformers. Among the revival movement's most powerful voices was that of Dwig

1 The Second City
Map p 150. 1616 N. Wells St. ☎ 312-337-3992. Scan the list of Second City "alumni" posted in the theater's lobby and you will find many familiar, famous names. Since the 1950s comic actors have come to The Second City to learn the art of improvisational comedy. Today the company's best students perform comedy revues featuring skits created from improv games. The scenarios in each show are the same every night, but the actors vary their performances based on feedback from the audience.

2 Up-Down Tobacco Shop
Map p 150. 1550 N. Wells St. ☎ 312-337-8505. Since the 1960s, this shop has featured fine smokes from tobacconists around the world. Hand-carved pipes, unusual lighters, chic cigarette cases and other smoking paraphernalia are available, and the store's helpful staff will recommend cigar- and pipe-friendly clubs and restaurants to the aficionado. Each year the shop sponsors a pipe-smoking contest; the winner is the one who can keep a pipe lit longest.

3 Zanies
Map p 150. 1548 N. Wells St. ☎ 312-337-4027. The oldest comedy club in the city, this well-worn venue has outlasted a dozen glitzier competitors. Name a stand-up comedian, and chances are he or she has performed at Zanies. The club usually features three comics a night: two up-and-coming performers and a well-known headliner.

Moody, who had come to Chicago in 1856. In 1893 he attracted more than two million people to his meetings at the World's Columbian Exposition. **Moody Memorial Church** *(1609 N. LaSalle St.)* testifies to his lasting influence on fundamental Christianity. Built in 1925, the brick edifice blends elements of Byzantine and Romanesque design, and is said to have been partially inspired by the Hagia Sophia in Istanbul.

Cross Clark St. to the Chicago Historical Society, where the walking tour ends.

★CHICAGO HISTORICAL SOCIETY

Sited at the southwestern corner of Lincoln Park, the city's first cultural institution reflects the evolution of history museums from storehouses of memorabilia to institutions actively engaged in making sense of history to a diverse audience. The society's collections and exhibits cover America until 1865 and Chicago since the arrival of explorers and settlers.

Historical Notes – Organized in 1856 by a group of prominent businessmen, the collections (then stored in the offices of one of the founders) were damaged in the Great Fire of 1871 and again by fire in 1874. In 1896 the society moved into a Richardsonian Romanesque structure designed by Henry Ives Cobb at Dearborn and Ontario Streets. In 1927 the society purchased the vast Gunther Collection of materials relating primarily to the Civil War. To house it, Graham, Anderson, Probst & White designed the institution's present home, a Georgian-style building completed in 1932. A 1971 addition on Clark Street doubled the original space. Aesthetic concerns and the need for yet more room in the 1980s inspired Holabird & Root to create the wraparound facade and the three-story rounded glass-and-steel atrium through which visitors now enter.

 Big Shoulders Cafe

Map p 150. In Chicago Historical Society. ☎ *312-587-7766.* Located in a sunny corner of the venerable institution, the cafe is a great place to stop during a walk through Old Town, a trek through the park or a visit to the society's museum. The cafe's light, healthy menu features a variety of salads, sandwiches and pasta dishes.

Visit

1601 N. Clark St. at North Ave. Open year-round Mon–Sat 9:30am–4:30pm, Sun noon–5pm. Closed Jan 1, Thanksgiving Day & Dec 25. $5 contribution requested. ✗ ♿ 🅿 ☎ *312-642-4600. www.chicagohistory.org.*

Artifacts representing the museum collections—architecture, manuscripts, paintings and sculpture costumes, prints and photographs, decorative arts—occupy a grid of niches on either side of the main lobby. The unexpected juxtaposition of such objects as the steering wheel from the ill-fated steamer *Eastland* and a grouping of Lava Lites makes this a lively display. The second floor houses the museum's highlights.

Second Floor – With an emphasis on interpretation, the permanent exhibits on this floor go beyond the traditional chronological approach. In the **American Galleries** on the right, the exhibit We The People: Creating a New Nation 1765-1820 examines the roles of ordinary Americans in the Revolution. Highlights include first printings of the Declaration of Independence and the Constitution, newsprint versions that most citizens of the period would have actually read. A House Divided: America in the Age of Lincoln uses the society's rich Civil War collection—including Lincoln's deathbed and John Brown's Bible—to explore the economic and social impact of slavery. On the left of the hall, six **Chicago History Galleries** illustrate themes in the city's growth: commerce, culture, public works, architecture, world's fairs and daily life. Here children can climb aboard the **Pioneer locomotive** 🔲, Chicago's first train and the society's largest artifact. Also of interest is Chicago's first fire engine, enlivened by bright red trim, purchased in 1835 and in service until 1860. These modern exhibits contrast revealingly with eight dioramas displayed in a small room just off the central hall. Created by WPA workers in the 1930s to represent moments in Chicago history, the beautifully crafted dioramas have themselves become artifacts of an earlier age of museum exhibition.

First Floor – A small exhibit entitled "Fort Dearborn and Frontier Chicago" offers an intimate glimpse into early-19C life in the lakeshore village, using personal artifacts, letters and daguerreotypes of Indians and the earliest settlers. Logs from the original Fort Dearborn form one wall of the exhibit.

At the south end of the museum, tucked away in the Big Shoulders Cafe, looms a re-creation of the massive archway that once marked the entrance to the Union Stock Yards. Its bas-reliefs of cattle and cowboys recount a closed chapter in Chicago's history.

ADDITIONAL SIGHTS

Several sights along LaSalle Street, south of North Avenue, are worth noting. The 1927 Art Deco renovations of Sol Kogen and Edgar Miller crowd the cul-de-sac that is **West Burton Place★**. This unusual collection of apartments began as Victorian houses that the two artists refitted with modern elements such as tile work, contemporary windows and mosaics.

In a complete change of visual scale, **Carl Sandburg Village** looms across LaSalle Street. This expansive agglomeration of high rises, town houses and ground-hugging apartment buildings that extends from North Avenue to Division Street was developed between 1960 and 1975.

A series of restored houses in the 1300 and 1400 blocks of LaSalle Street conjures up the elegant late-19C profile of this boulevard. A block farther south, at **no. 1211**, stands a fitting sentinel on the southern edge of Old Town. This 1929 hotel was renovated in 1981 as an apartment building. On its eastern and southern walls, artist Richard Haas has painted a trompe l'oeil entitled *Homage to the Chicago School of Architecture*. The work's primary elements include, at the top, a depiction of a Louis Sullivan window and, at the bottom, his golden doorway from the Transportation Building at the 1893 World's Columbian Exposition. Between the two, Haas painted an imaginary reflection of the Chicago Board of Trade Building, visible two miles south down LaSalle Street in the heart of the financial district.

LINCOLN PARK★★

Brown or Red line to Fullerton, or bus no. 22 or 36
Map p 157

Unlike so many urban areas whose waterfronts have been taken up by industry, Chicago provides its residents with unlimited access to the lake via its numerous lakefront parks. Among the finest of these is Lincoln Park. Belying its origins as a soggy cemetery, this sweeping expanse is today one of Chicago's most compelling landscapes. Stretching 6mi and 1,200 acres along the shoreline of Lake Michigan, from Ohio Street north to Ardmore Avenue, Lincoln Park trims the city's watery edge with a pleasant and peaceful greenbelt. Millions of Chicagoans flock here year-round to enjoy the zoo, conservatory, picnic groves, beaches and playing fields. At North Avenue, the park forms the northern edge of the affluent Gold Coast and at Clark Street, the eastern boundary of the lively Lincoln Park/DePaul neighborhood, where theaters, restaurants and shops abound.

Historical Notes

Back from the Dead – In typical Chicago fashion, Lincoln Park was the product of years of grass-roots activism, a rivalry with New York and copious amounts of landfill. In 1837 the Illinois General Assembly granted the city a large parcel of sand dunes and marshes, between present-day North Avenue and Webster Street, for use as a municipal burial ground. As development crept north toward this once remote location, the cemetery's new residential neighbors began to lobby for its closure and conversion into a greensward to be called Lake Park.
Formation in 1869 of several regional park boards charged with encircling the city with green space gave the North Side park movement its much-needed impetus. Inspired by Frederick Law Olmsted's Central Park in New York (begun in 1857) and by the beautifully landscaped cemeteries on the city's edge, the local citizenry, developers and civic leaders banded together and clamored for completion of their lakefront park. Work progressed slowly, since moving the thousands of corpses buried south of Menomonee Street—including Confederate dead from the prisoner-of-war stockade at Camp Douglas on the city's South Side—proved nearly impossible. Shifting sands, poor records and politics hindered the townspeople in their efforts to locate and identify all the graves, and still today, stray bones turn up during excavations in the area.

Northward, Ho – Renamed shortly after the assassination of President Lincoln in 1865, the park grew in stages between 1864 and 1957, at the hands of at least six landscape architects. One of the first sectors to take shape was the old cemetery, today the heart of Lincoln Park. Most corpses had been moved by 1875, and the park's naturalistic style began to emerge: winding pathways, flower beds and ponds, which landscapers **Swain Nelson** and **Olaf Benson** believed would enhance the park's lushness by reflecting the surrounding greenery. One by one, other elements of the modern park appeared: the zoo in 1868, Ridge Drive in 1878, the Lagoon in the 1880s. As the adjacent neighborhoods became more and more populous landfilling was begun to extend the park northward to Montrose Avenue by 1925, to Foster Avenue by 1936 and lastly, to Ardmore Avenue by 1957. Much of this portion of the park is landscaped with native plants, the work of Ossian C. Simonds and later, **Alfred Caldwell**, who also designed the serene Lincoln Park Rookery in the Prairie school style.

Practical Information

Getting There – Lincoln Park is accessible by several ▦▦ bus lines including no. 151 *(☏ 312-836-7000)*. Parking lots are located in the northern section of the park near Diversey Harbor or adjacent to North Avenue Beach in the southern section. Zoo parking is available along North Cannon Drive just south of Fullerton Parkway.

Park Information – Visitor Center is located at Lincoln Park Cultural Center *(2045 N. Lincoln Park West; open year-round Mon–Thu 9am–9pm, Fri 11am–7pm, Sat 8am–4pm, Sun 11am–5pm; ☏ 312-742-7726). Information by mail: Lakefront Region Office, South Shore Cultural Center, 7059 South Shore Dr., Chicago IL 60649.*

Recreation – Public sports venues (located primarily in the South Field, Waveland and Montrose areas of the park) include baseball/softball fields, basketball courts, soccer field and tennis courts. The Waveland area also features **archery** and a 9-hole **golf** course. A **bicycle/running path** runs along the lakefront. Miniature golf and a heated year-round driving range are located near Diversey Harbor.

Such extensive landfilling was not undertaken strictly for the recreational enjoyment of the populace, however. The development of Lake Shore Drive, which today cuts a swath up the lakefront from the south to north side, is closely linked with the history of Lincoln Park. The park's promenades and boulevards, designed for quiet strolls and leisurely carriage rides, had been conceived before the advent of the automobile. By the 1920s the park's bucolic atmosphere was in jeopardy as daily commuters began to overburden its thoroughfares and scenic routes. Lake Shore Drive, today an eight-lane highway, unrolled inexorably up the lakefront, sharing landfill with the park and posing new challenges for planners bent on maintaining a harmonious co-existence of parkland and expressway. Today some balance has been achieved on that score through pedestrian bridges and underpasses, and in recent years the drive itself has been softened by median landscaping. The rush of traffic seems not to affect the tremendous popularity of this pleasure ground, where throngs of visitors savor lake breezes against a stunning skyline backdrop.

WALKING TOUR *Distance: 2.8mi*

Begin on the east side of the Chicago Historical Society (1601 N. Clark St. at North Ave.).

Gazing out over the garden in front of him, Augustus Saint-Gaudens' **Standing Lincoln★** (1887) is a masterpiece of monumental art and likely the sculptor's finest work. Imbued with humanity and dignity, Lincoln seems on the verge of imparting a great thought. The exedra surrounding the statue was designed by architect Stanford White, with whom Saint-Gaudens often collaborated. Another of the sculptor's Lincoln statues resides in Grant Park.

Take the path heading northwest of the Lincoln statue.

On a small bluff rising behind the Chicago Historical Society stands the **Couch Mausoleum**, an anomalous reminder of the cemetery that once covered these acres. Deemed too difficult to move when the land was converted into a park, the tomb is the resting place of Ira Couch, proprietor of the Tremont House, Chicago's fashionable mid-19C hotel.

Continue under LaSalle St. and take the path northeast of the Franklin statue.

The only way to view the front of **Benjamin Franklin** (1896, Richard Henry Park) is on foot since he stands with his back to LaSalle Street. The playing fields to the east are generally alive with softball and other games on summer weekends and evenings.

Continue up Ridge Dr.

 North Avenue Beach

Map p 157. Access via overpass just north of North Ave. or via tunnel at North Ave. This broad stretch of sand is Chicago's volleyball mecca. In summertime, the Park District and several private clubs set up dozens of nets. Many courts are reserved for league play, but pick-up games are common. To organize your own game or outing, call the Park District six days in advance to rent a net, boundary line tapes and a ball.

The **Air and Water Show,** an annual festival of aviation and boating, takes place along the lakefront in late August and is best viewed from North Avenue Beach. Past shows have included exhibitions by precision military flight squadrons, acrobatic stunts performed in vintage planes and rescue drills executed by the Coast Guard and Chicago Fire Department.

At the crest of Ridge Drive (once a main north-south thoroughfare), a mounted **General Ulysses S. Grant** (**1**), the 1891 work of Louis T. Rebisso, surveys the park and Lake Shore Drive from atop a massive Romanesque base. Owing to the monument's height off the ground, it is best viewed from a distance rather than up close.

Continue on Ridge Dr., crossing over South Pond.

The splendid **view**★★ south from the bridge over **South Pond** breathes life into the city's epithet *Urbs in Horto* ("City in a Garden"). From here, downtown skyscrapers seem an afterthought to the park's towering trees.

Enter Farm in the Zoo, to the left.

★**Farm in the Zoo** – ▨ *1901 N. Stockton Dr. Open year-round daily 9am–4:30pm.* ♿ ▣*($7)* ☎ *312-742-2355. www.lpzoo.com.* This peaceful five-acre haven, a working farm constructed as part of Lincoln Park Zoo in the 1960s, offers city children a chance to commune with rural life. In five well-kept barns dwell cows, poultry, horses and other livestock. Demonstrations of butter churning, horse grooming and goat milking go on throughout the day *(times are posted).* Particularly interesting is the **Dairy Barn**, where cows are milked by hand and by machine, yielding 16 to 20 gallons of fresh milk daily, which goes to feed the other animals. Simple labels and interactive computers explain the milk-production process. In the **Poultry Barn**, fertilized eggs in all stages of hatching are on view in incubators. Lucky visitors might see chicks pipping, or breaking through their shells.

Exit farm to the west and head north on Stockton Dr.

To the west stands the Matthew Laflin Memorial, a three-story Renaissance Revival building financed in 1893 by the Chicago entrepreneur, who was disappointed he could not be buried in the park that was once a cemetery. The Lincoln Park Zoo renovated the building to house its administrative offices.

Walk across Stockton Dr. to the east.

★**Café Brauer** – *2021 N. Stockton Dr. Open Memorial Day–Sept daily 10am–5pm.* ♿ ☎ *312-742-2480.* Architect Dwight Perkins, whose other credits include several of the animal houses at Lincoln Park Zoo, designed this refectory in 1908 at the behest of restaurateurs Paul and Caspar Brauer. A striking example of the Prairie school style, it hugs South Pond with its main pavilion and two flanking loggias. Arts and Crafts details—chandeliers, tiles, mosaics and windows—lend the interior a suitably rustic charm. A popular gathering place until it closed in the 1940s, the cafe underwent a $4.2 million restoration in 1989 and today once again offers parkgoers a quiet spot to relax and enjoy a selection of salads and grilled sandwiches.

In a grove to the northwest of the cafe sits a bronze **Hans Christian Andersen** (**2**), sculpted by John Gelert in 1896.

Enter zoo along path north of Café Brauer.

★★**Lincoln Park Zoo** – ▨ *2200 N. Cannon Dr. Grounds open Memorial Day–Labor Day daily 8am–6pm (weekends & holidays til 7pm). Rest of the year daily 8am–5pm. (Zoo buildings open at 10am.)* ✗ ♿ ▣*($7)* ☎ *312-742-2000. www.lpzoo.com.* This wonderfully accessible zoo, convenient and free of charge, is best enjoyed in an afternoon of wandering. Founded with the gift of a pair of swans from New York's Central Park in 1868, the zoo has grown to encompass 35 acres, house over 1,000 animals and attract over 3 million annual visitors in the intervening years. Today the zoo's collection and agenda reflect its strong conservation mission. Twenty-nine of the zoo's species are endangered; interpretive graphics and labeling focus sharply on ecological issues.

Over the past decade, the zoo has meticulously renovated its historic exhibits—Primate House (1927, renovated 1984), Lion House (1912, renovated 1986), Bird House (1900, renovated 1986) and Sea Lion Pool (1889, renovated 1999)—adapting them to accommodate the realistic habitats typical of modern zoos while retaining their architectural charm and detail. Newer habitats, such as the Small Mammal-Reptile House (1997), the Great Ape House (1976), the Crown-Field Center (1979) and the Penguin and Seabird House (1981), burrow unobtrusively into landscaped hillocks, creating a pleasingly unobstructed terrain.

Visit – Entering the zoo from Café Brauer, note the **Waterfowl Lagoon** directly north. Although renovated twice—once in 1978 with the addition of the Flamingo Dome and again in 1996—the lagoon itself is one of the few remaining original elements of the park designed by Swain Nelson in 1865. It provides a lovely, naturalistic setting for local and migratory waterfowl. Farther along, a major center of zoo activity is the Lester E. Fisher **Great Ape House**★. Of particular interest here are families of endangered lowland gorillas, of which the zoo has birthed more than 40 since 1970. The zoo's most famous gorilla, Bushman, arrived in 1930 and lived 21 years to delight millions of visitors. (Today he is preserved and displayed at the Field Museum

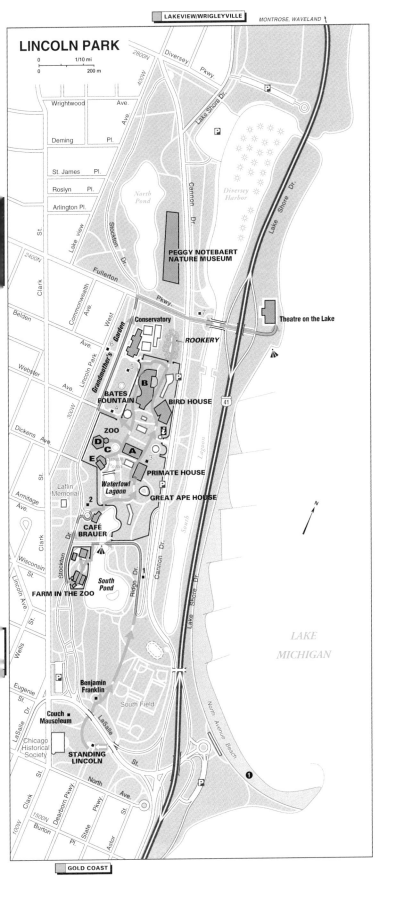

MONTROSE, WAVELAND

LINCOLN PARK

0	1/10 mi
0	200 m

Wrightwood   Ave.

Deming   Pl.

St. James   Pl.

Roslyn   Pl.

Arlington Pl.

North Pond

2800N

Diversey   Pkwy.

400W

Lake Shore Dr.

P

Diversey Harbor

Lake   Shore   Dr.

Lakeview   St.

2400N

Clark

Belden

Webster

Dickens   Ave.

Stockton   Dr.

Commonwealth   Ave.

West   Ave.

Lincoln Park West

300W

Fullerton   Pkwy.

PEGGY NOTEBAERT NATURE MUSEUM

Theatre on the Lake

7

Conservatory

Grandmother's Garden

ROOKERY

B

BATES FOUNTAIN

BIRD HOUSE

41

ZOO

D   C

A

E

PRIMATE HOUSE

Waterfowl Lagoon

GREAT APE HOUSE

Lagoon

South Lagoon

3

Armitage   Ave.

Clark   St.

Latin Memorial

2

CAFÉ BRAUER

Wisconsin   St.

Lincoln Ave.

Stockton Dr.

FARM IN THE ZOO

South Pond

Ridge Dr.

1

Cannon   Dr.

Wells   St.

LAKE MICHIGAN

N

Eugenie   St.

LaSalle   Dr.

P

Benjamin Franklin

South Field

Couch Mausoleum

Chicago Historical Society

LaSalle   St.

STANDING LINCOLN

North   Avenue   Beach

Clark   St.

100W

Dearborn   Pkwy.

North   Ave.

State   St.

Astor   St.

1500N

Burton   Pl.

P

1

The Helen Brach **Prima House★** shows off gibbor marmosets, mandrills a their relations in a rai forest environment. Ju northeast of the Prima House, note the **Eugene Fi Memorial (3)** (1922) sculptor Edward McCarta a gentle tribute to the ch dren's works of that Mi western humorist. The lar Kovler **Lion House (A)** fe tures the zoo's collection big cats, which are not docile as the ones cleverly incorporated into the exterior brickwork. The **McCormi Bird House★** presents a variety of avian species in intimate, sometimes open habita

At the far north end of the grounds, the **Rookery★** provides an interesting counte point to the Waterfowl Lagoon. Designed by Prairie school disciple Alfred Caldw in 1937, this wooded grove, planted thickly with native trees surrounding a lar pond, provides a tranquil enclave for zoo visitors and migrating birds alike. Inte pretive labels elaborate on bird-watching, migration patterns and the various speci that visit the rookery throughout the year. Low-slung, Japanese-style pavilions an stacked rockwork evoke the site's Prairie school inspiration *(the rookery can al be entered from the north off Fullerton Pkwy.; closed during inclement weathe* The return trail south passes the Regenstein **Large Mammal Habitat (B)**, housing pere nial favorites such as elephants and giraffes. Beyond the **Sea Lion Pool (C)**, the **Pritzk Children's Zoo (D)** incorporates a nursery behind large windows and an outdoor ga den. Docents offer kids of all ages a chance to hobnob with turtles, hedgehog parrots and other hardy creatures. Overlooking the restored Hope B. McCormi Swan Pond, the newest addition, the Regenstein **Small Mammal-Reptile House (** (1997, Coe, Lee & Robinson), bows to the traditional buildings with its brick e terior. Its domed southern section shelters an exhibit of the exotic ecosystems Asia, South America, Australia and Africa with representative species ranging fro koalas to crocodiles. The gallery section includes innovative displays of bat cave naked mole-rat tunnels and reptile habitats filled with native plants.

Exit the zoo at the west entrance and continue north to the Lincoln Pa Conservatory.

The approach to the Lincoln Park Conservatory is marked by a broad lawn dom nated by a formal garden nearly a block in length. South of the garden stan *Johann Christoph Friedrich von Schiller* (**4**), fashioned in bronze by Germa sculptor Ernst Bildhauer Rau in 1886. The traditionally styled statue of the Germa playwright and poet is a copy of one in Marbach, Germany. In the garden's cente the **Bates Fountain★** *(Storks at Play)* presents a joyful tableau of water play betwee storks, boys and fish *(covered in winter)*. The fountain (1887) is the work Augustus Saint-Gaudens and his assistant Frederick MacMonnies, although sin Saint-Gaudens was then busy on the *Standing Lincoln*, the credit for Storks at Pla goes largely to MacMonnies. Eli Bates, the Chicago lumber merchant for who

Western Lowland Gorilla

the work was named, left a bequest in his will for both the Lincoln statue and the fountain. A bust of **Sir Georg Solti** (**5**), renowned conductor of the Chicago Symphony Orchestra from 1969 to 1991, was dedicated north of the garden in 1987. To the west, across Stockton Drive, a bronze *William Shakespeare* (**6**) (1894) by William Ordway Partridge rests thoughtfully in the informal **Grandmother's Garden**.

© Doug Locke/DPA

Lincoln Park Conservatory

Lincoln Park Conservatory – *2400 N. Stockton Dr. Open year-round daily 9am–5pm.* ♿ ☎ *312-742-7736.* Modeled by architect Joseph Lyman Silsbee on London's Crystal Palace, the conservatory (1892) and its 15 propagating houses, greenhouses and gardens now cover three acres. Four main galleries in the glass and copper structure display extensive collections of orchids, palms, ferns and related flora, including a grouping of cycads, which are among the oldest-known plants. In the Show House, five major exhibits take place each year: chrysanthe-mums *(Oct 6–Nov 4)*; a poinsettia display *(Nov 24–Jan 6)*; azaleas and camelias in February; flowering bulbs in spring *(Apr 7–May 13)*; and tropical plants, such as bright hibiscus, in summer *(Jun 9–Sept 3)*. Many of the flowers that enliven Chicago's parks are germinated in the conservatory's greenhouses.

Continue north along Stockton Dr. to Fullerton Pkwy. Walk east on Fullerton and turn left (north) on Cannon Dr.

★**Peggy Notebaert Nature Museum** – ♿ *2430 N. Cannon Dr. Open Memorial Day–Labor Day daily 10am–6pm, Wed til 8pm. Rest of the year daily 10am–5pm, Wed til 8pm. Closed Jan 1, Thanksgiving & Dec 25. $6 (free Tue).* ⚄ ♿ ☎ *773-755-5100. www.chias.org.* Set along the lower end of North Pond, this sand-colored "cluster of wedge-shaped blocks" was designed by Ralph Johnson of Perkins & Will as "an abstraction of the dunes that used to cover the site." Opened in 1999, the museum houses six permanent exhibits on two levels; outside, the building is surrounded by seven different **gardens** highlighting native flora.

On the first level, the **Family Water Lab** features a 40ft interactive model of an urban river and a large stream table where visitors can place pipes and channels to direct water flow. Down the hall, a mock-up of a house in **City Science** *(continues upstairs)* introduces the fungus, mold, insects and mammals that secretly share our homes. Also on level one you'll find Environmental Central, a computer lab where students solve real-life problems such as dealing with drought, and the Children's Gallery (ages 3-8), where youngsters can participate in nature-related activities.

On level two, the humid walk-through **Butterfly Haven** flutters with some 20 local species of butterflies and moths. Here you can actually watch the fragile insects emerge from their chrysalides. Next door is an indoor **Wilderness Walk**, where dio-ramas re-create a Chicago prairie, savannah and dune as they existed 200 years ago. The museum also hosts occasional traveling exhibits.

Walk back to Fullerton Pkwy. and follow it east, across Lake Shore Dr.

On the north side of Fullerton Parkway stands Ellsworth Kelly's monolithic stain-less steel *I Will* (**7**), commissioned in 1981, the first new sculpture in Lincoln Park in 30 years. According to the artist, the work, bearing as its name Chicago's unofficial post-fire motto, represents the city as the birthplace of the skyscraper. Farther east, at the water's edge, the 384-seat **Theatre on the Lake** mounts ten productions each summer *(Jun–Aug;* ☎ *312-742-7995)*. The Prairie school building (1920) first served as the Chicago Daily News Fresh Air Sanitarium, located where tuberculosis patients might take full advantage of the lake's breezes. The **view**★ to the south from this vantage point imparts a real sense of the harmonious relationship between lake and city, nature and urban center.

LINCOLN PARK/DePAUL★

🚇 Brown or Red line to Fullerton, or bus no. 22 or 36

Map p 162

Hugging its namesake greensward to the east, the eclectic Lincoln Park/DePaul neighborhood is a checkerboard of lovely residential streets crisscrossed by lively commercial boulevards. From Armitage Avenue on the south to Diversey Parkway on the north, and west to Racine Avenue, the nucleus of Lincoln Park/DePaul is well suited to a pleasant day of walking, window-shopping and noshing. Evenings here draw colorful crowds attracted to the area's diverse offerings in music, food and theater.

Historical Notes

From Celery to City – Green Bay Road (present-day Clark Street) ran northwest through this territory along the marshy lakefront as early as the 1830s. To the west, German farmers established celery and other vegetable farms. By 1853 the land between North and Fullerton Avenues from the lake to the river had been annexed by the city, and the natural sprawl of the growing metropolis began to shape the area's development. Frame houses supplanted celery gardens, a horsecar line linked the area to downtown, and a public park began to unroll up the lakefront. The Great Fire in 1871 devastated the incipient neighborhood before burning itself out at Fullerton Avenue, but the area's location outside the city's strict new fire codes invited speedy recovery. As industry marched up the north branch of the river, German, Irish and Polish workers built cottages in the western reaches of the neighborhood. In a parallel progression to the east, well-to-do Germans commissioned fine homes along the edge of the increasingly lovely lakefront preserve known since 1865 as Lincoln Park.

Catholic Cornerstone – The Presbyterian Theological Seminary had located at Fullerton Avenue and Halsted Street in 1863. Surviving the fire, the seminary (later renamed McCormick in honor of its benefactor, the famous industrialist) attracted settlers to this distant corner of Chicago, spawned the establishment of several churches, and in 1882, even constructed row houses to let for income. Despite the seminary's influence, the more lasting effect on the neighborhood would be wrought by the Vin-

Biograph Theater (1934)

centian order, which founded St. Vincent de Paul parish in 1875 to serve the local Irish population. In 1898 the fathers established St. Vincent's College, from which would grow DePaul University, today a cornerstone of the Lincoln Park community.

Location, Location – Over the years the neighborhood continued to grow in both area and population. The blocks between Fullerton Avenue and Diversey Parkway were annexed by the city in 1889. Ethnic diversity increased as working-class Romanians, Greeks, Italians, Poles, Hungarians, Serbs and African Americans discovered the convenience and affordability of the neighborhood. However, new housing didn't keep pace with the swelling population and the existing buildings suffered from overuse. Except for the luxury residences east of Clark Street, Lincoln Park grew dilapidated.

The area's intrinsic advantages, however, served it well. Location, accessibility and a basic architectural soundness stimulated interest in the neighborhood, and conservation associations formed to encourage renovation efforts. In 1956 the community was designated an urban-renewal area. Rehabilitation, and the companion phenomenon dubbed "gentrification," proceeded so successfully that Lincoln Park today is one of Chicago's most desirable, attractive, high-priced—and congested—neighborhoods. In the late 1990s Lincoln Park has seen a resurgence in the construction of palatial residences, the likes of which has not been seen here since the early years of the 20C. A walk down Howe, Mohawk or Burling Streets north of Old Town reveals the elaborate limestone facades of dozens of new multi-story houses.

SIGHTS

Few of the residential blocks in the neighborhood will disappoint the visitor on foot, each one offering a variety of architectural and landscaping surprises. They are difficult to negotiate by car, however, as parking can be hard to find. The major commercial boulevards—particularly Armitage Avenue and Diversey Parkway, Halsted Street and the two diagonals, Lincoln Avenue and Clark Street—are chock-full of bookstores and boutiques, bars and bistros.

Lincoln Avenue and Clark Street slice the neighborhood roughly in pie-shaped thirds. To their west DePaul University serves as a major focus, and the surrounding blocks are known as the DePaul neighborhood.

DePaul University – Chartered in 1907 as DePaul University from St. Vincent's College, the campus grew outward from the limestone church buildings in the 1000 block of West Webster Avenue, where the Romanesque Revival **St. Vincent de Paul Church** (1897, James J. Egan) towers over the block. Today DePaul's 30-acre campus extends between Fullerton and Webster Avenues and Clifton and Halsted Streets. Major buildings face a pedestrian mall created in the 2300 block of Seminary Avenue in 1992. The concrete Brutalism style of the **Arthur J. Schmitt Academic Center** (**A**) and the **Harold L. Stuart**

■ Markers of a Dubious Past

Two neighborhood addresses figure prominently in Chicago's gangland history: 2122 N. Clark Street, the site of the garage (since demolished) where the St. Valentine's Day Massacre took place in 1929; and 2433 N. Lincoln Avenue—the **Biograph Theater**—where federal agents gunned down "public enemy number one" John Dillinger on July 22, 1934.

➊ Kingston Mines

Map p 162. 2548 N. Halsted St. ☎ 773-477-4646. Frequented by top-notch musicians and regular folk, this ramshackle blues club features live music until 4am *(5am on Saturday)*. Seven nights a week, two top local bands take turns playing on the club's two stages. The place fills up quickly, and at 2am fans pour in from B.L.U.E.S. across the street, so arrive early to get a good seat.

➋ B.L.U.E.S.

Map p 162. 2519 N. Halsted St. ☎ 773-528-1012. You feel like you can reach out and touch the performers in this tiny, smoky club. Quality players from across the city and a down-and-dirty atmosphere make this one of the most popular blues bars in town.

➌ Steppenwolf Theatre

Map p 162. 1650 N. Halsted St. ☎ 312-335-1650. John Malkovich, Laurie Metcalf and Gary Sinise are members of this acclaimed local troupe, which is renowned for the intensity of its performers as well as its impressive state-of-the-art theater. Steppenwolf presents five or six mainstage plays a year. Several workshop productions, staged readings and small-scale shows are mounted in the company's studio theater.

Center (**B**) *(2323 and 2324 N. Seminary Ave.)*, both designed by C.F. Murphy Assocs., contrasts with the more fitting brick construction of the **Richardson Library** (**C**) *(2350 N. Kenmore Ave.)*, completed in 1992 by Lohan Assocs.

DePaul acquired the land east of the elevated tracks from the Presbyterian Theological Seminary when it moved to Hyde Park in 1973. Embedded in the property is **Chalmers Place★**, a verdant block of privately owned town houses that were originally built by the seminary to generate income. An unembellished blend of Queen Anne and Romanesque Revival styling, their facades of smooth brown brick face each other with no-nonsense solidity on either side of a parklike square. The two freestanding houses at the eastern end of the square *(834 and 835 W. Chalmers Pl.)* were constructed in the 1880s for faculty members. Another series of row houses backs up to Chalmers Place along West Belden Avenue just south. These brick homes, the **McCormick Row Houses** (**D**) *(nos. 832-840, 844-858)*, built between 1884 and 1889, appear somewhat less heavy than their counterparts, with livelier rooflines, stained glass and decorative brickwork. Similar row houses also line the 900 block of Fullerton Avenue; the seminary originally built more than 50 in all.

Lincoln Avenue/Clark Street Area – Between Lincoln Avenue and Clark Street are some of the area's most interesting private homes, apartment buildings and churches. Along **Cleveland Avenue**, for instance, note the variety of styles and eras represented. At no. 2147, the **Leon Mannheimer House** bears the unmistakable decorative hallmarks of Louis Sullivan, whose firm designed it in 1884. Across the street at no. 2150, the **Walter Guest House** was remodeled in 1932 by the artistic hand of Edgar Miller, whose other Art Deco renovations grace West Burton Place. Incised chevrons embellish the expansive leaded-glass windows, and a close look at the front door reveals a frolic of Miller's favorite animals. In the next block, Bruce Graham of Skidmore, Owings & Merrill designed himself an impenetrable home at **no. 2215** in 1969 that reveals little of itself except its debt to the concrete hulks of the Brutalism style popular in the 1960s.

Several blocks north the **Ann Halsted House** (1883) at 440 West Belden Avenue is another Adler & Sullivan commission ornamented along its gable with the firm's signature lotus motif. **The Cobden** apartment building (1892, Charles S. Frost) spans 418 to 424 West Belden and bends around the corner along Clark Street, where the ground-level houses shops. The Belden Avenue facade is particularly interesting for its surface decoration, undulating bays and crowning gable. At 2325 North Clark Street, the whimsical **Reebie Storage and Moving Co.** warehouse was designed in 1923 in an unabashed celebration of the opening of King Tut's tomb in 1922. The two sentinel statues of Ramses II are said to represent the Reebie brothers; hieroglyphics below the right one read, "I give protection to your furniture!"

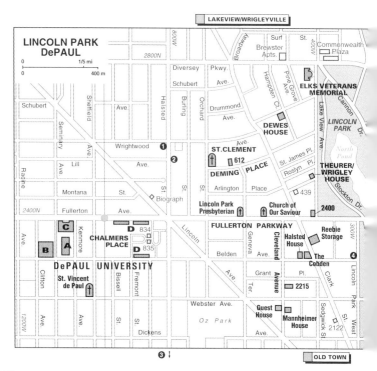

Since the 1880s **Fullerton Parkway★** between Clark Street and Lincoln Avenue has been a pleasant street of elegant homes, trees and gardens. Two hardy Romanesque-style churches dominate adjacent blocks, but blend genteely with their surroundings: the Episcopal **Church of Our Saviour** (1888) at no. 530 and the **Lincoln Park Presbyterian Church** (1888) at no. 600. Two blocks north, at Deming Place and Orchard Street, **St. Clement Roman Catholic Church★** (1918), constructed of smooth limestone with the twin towers and rose window of the French Romanesque style, underwent a thorough interior renovation in 1989 to restore the spectacular mosaics and murals of its Byzantine dome. Set back from the street, the houses along **Deming Place★** recall an elegant era; the oldest were built in the 1880s and 90s by successful German businessmen. A montage of elements from the Romanesque, Queen Anne, Gothic and Classical styles characterizes these residences. Note the Sullivanesque detail that trims the porch at **no. 612**.

④ Ambria

Map p 162. 2300 Lincoln Park West. ☎ *773-472-5959.* This elegant, romantic restaurant consistently ranks at the top of both critics' and diners' lists. Chef Gabino Sotelino (who also owns and manages the restaurant) prepares delicious, exquisitely presented French cuisine. To complement the chef's creations, Ambria boasts an extensive, award-winning wine list. Located across the lobby, the renovated dining room of the old Belden Stratford hotel houses **Un Grand Café** *(☎ 773-348-8886),* best known for its bistro atmosphere and classic French fare, including steak frites and onion soup topped with Gruyère.

Clark Street/Lakeview Avenue Area – East of Clark Street, high-rise apartment buildings of every description cluster along the edge of Lincoln Park, all vying for the best view of Lake Michigan beyond. The 30-story glass and steel structure at **2400 North Lakeview Avenue** (1963) is the last residential high rise to be designed by Ludwig Mies van der Rohe in Chicago. At no. 2466 the **Theurer/Wrigley House★** (1897) dominates the corner of Arlington Place. Italian Renaissance elegance swaddles its sturdy steel and concrete underpinnings, and a glimpse into the **solarium★** at the southwest corner hints at the decorative detail inside. Chewing-gum magnate William Wrigley, Jr. purchased the home from brewer Joseph Theurer around 1910. The Wrigley family occupied it until the 1930s when, supposedly, threats of kidnapping necessitated the move to a more secure apartment residence. The home lay virtually unused for 50 years until the specter of a high-rise replacement galvanized preservationists, politicians and developers to save it in the early 1980s. Other lovely homes line **Arlington Place** and, where it meets Clark Street, walkers are greeted by the cacophony of birdsong that emanates from the privately maintained bird sanctuary adjacent to no. 439.

The fairy-tale quality of the **Francis J. Dewes House★** (1896) at 503 West Wrightwood Avenue is perhaps exaggerated by the surrounding modern city. Crisp white Bedford limestone contrasts with a dark slate mansard roof and cast-iron railings. The house's zest, however, derives from its extravagant Baroque detailing, particularly the two disproportionate figures that flank the front door, and the elaborate variety of window decoration. Dewes was a German brewer who no doubt hired his architects, German Adolph Cudell and Hungarian Arthur Hercz, partly for their familiarity with European decorative traditions.

At 2750 North Lakeview Avenue, an entirely different architectural spectacle commands the corner at Diversey Parkway. The **Elks Veterans Memorial★** *(open mid-Apr–mid-Nov Mon–Fri 9am–5pm, weekends 10am–5pm; rest of the year Mon–Fri 9am–5pm; closed major holidays; contribution requested; ♿ 🅿 ☎ 773-755-4832; www.elks.org)* was completed in 1926 to honor Elks brethren who had served in World War I. It has since been rededicated to veterans of all succeeding American military conflicts. Inside the relatively sedate Neoclassical Indiana limestone exterior, not a square inch of wall, window or ceiling surface remains undecorated. In the rotunda and reception room, 26 varieties of marble and lavishly carved oak paneling dazzle the visitor, while gilded statuary, elaborate murals and art-glass windows illustrate the fraternal order's cardinal virtues of charity, justice, brotherly love and fidelity, along with other allegories.

A broad, bustling and colorful artery, Milwaukee Avenue has been the spine of a working-class immigrant community on the northwest side since its first settlement in the mid-19C. Historically Polish and currently Hispanic, the neighborhood extending from Chicago Avenue to Belmont Avenue remains a melting pot of diverse cultures and rich streetscapes, confirming Chicago's image as a city of neighborhoods and attracting a wide cross section of residents.

Historical Notes

A Growing Enclave – Lured by industries along the North Branch of the Chicago River, immigrant laborers from Germany began to settle the West Town neighborhood along Milwaukee Avenue following the revolutions of 1848, and the street became known as "Dinner Pail Avenue." Polish immigrants arrived in the 1860s and soon created St. Stanislaus Kostka parish near Division Street. While simple laborers' cottages mushroomed along the avenue, the area around Wicker Park, donated to the city by real estate developers Joel and Charles Wicker in 1870, became an enclave of grand mansions constructed by German and Scandinavian businessmen. As the number of Poles steadily increased, Germans and Scandinavians left, following the avenue north and west and establishing the migratory pattern for other immigrant groups. The development of the West Side Parks and Boulevard System—designed to ring the city with broad avenues and greenswards—after 1871 attracted many successful Norwegian and Swedish immigrants, who settled around Humboldt Park and Logan Square after the turn of the century. By 1900 more than eight Polish parishes filled the dense corridor, and over 5,000 families attended St. Stanislaus alone. Some 250,000 people, including Russian Jews, Ukrainians, Slovaks and Italians in addition to Polish residents, lived within walking distance of the intersection of Milwaukee and Ashland Avenues, dubbed the "Polish Downtown," home not only to local groups but also to all of the major Polish-American organizations in the nation.

Milwaukee Avenue Bookstore Window Display

Decline and Transformation – By the 1930s the lower portion of the Milwauke Avenue Corridor had fallen into decline. Chicago author **Nelson Algren** documented th sordid street life around Wicker Park in the 1940s in his novels and short stories. B the 1960s Hispanics, especially Puerto Ricans, were the dominant ethnic group i West Town and Humboldt Park, pushing other immigrants to the northwest to follow the pattern of migration established back in the late 19C. "Urban pioneers" began rehabilitating the Victorian mansions of Wicker Park and Logan Square in the lat 1970s, when both communities were listed on the National Register of Historic Place In the following decade, Wicker Park came to the forefront as an artists' mecca attracting galleries and theaters that had been priced out of Lincoln Park/DePaul an River West. Today the neighborhood is home to one of the nation's largest artist com munities.

DRIVING TOUR *Distance: 5.8mi (including 1mi walking tour)*

The tour covers a variety of ethnic neighborhoods and an eclectic mix of architecture, cultural sights and shops. Although long sections of the avenue resemble most urban streetscapes with nondescript buildings, discount warehouses and fast-food restaurants, the visitor will discover hidden gems lurking behind unassuming structures. The Wicker Park neighborhood has become the city's most popular nightspot, teeming with cultural venues and quirky boutiques ranging from the occult to the antique, and giving rise to several alternative bands, including the Smashing Pumpkins and Liz Phair.

Since this drive covers long distances, it is best to visit the area by car; however, we have included a walking tour of the Wicker Park neighborhood.

Begin at the intersection of Milwaukee Ave. and Augusta Blvd.

Polish Museum of America – *984 N. Milwaukee Ave. Open year-round daily 11am–4pm. Closed major holidays. $3. Guided tours (30min) available.* ♿ ▯ ☎ *773-384-3352. www.prcuofa.org.* Located on the upper floors of the Polish Roman Catholic Union of America headquarters, one of the oldest and largest ethnic museums in the US encompasses an extensive collection of fine arts and historical artifacts.

Sculptures and drawings by Stanislaw Szukalski (1893-1987) line the steps to the third-floor entrance. The main exhibit space is a two-story hall. Along the east wall stands a massive stained-glass piece, followed by Hussar armor and exhibits on Tadeusz Kosciuszko and Casimir Pulaski, heroes of the American Revolution. The west wall displays folk artifacts, crucifixes, silverware and wooden sculptures. Early-20C murals decorate the south wall, and cases at the north end exhibit costumes and church relics.

Outside the main room, an 8ft-long **sleigh★** carved from a single log in the form of a dolphin was given by King Stanislaus Leszczynski to Princess Maria, future wife of the Grand Dauphin of France, later Louis XV. A staircase lined with modern art leads to a gallery on the fourth floor, devoted to landscapes and portraits. A highlight of the museum is the **Paderewski Room★** *(2nd floor)*, which presents a large collection of artifacts from the life of the Polish pianist (1860-1941), including the living room where he spent his last years.

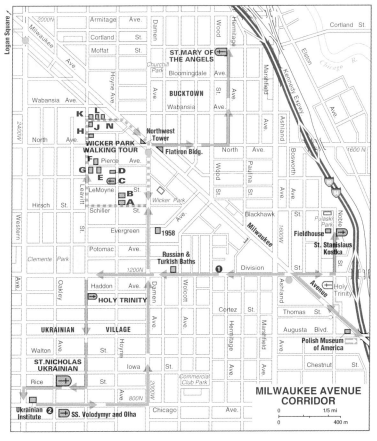

MILWAUKEE AVENUE CORRIDOR

1 Andy's Deli

Map p 165. 1737 W. Division St. ☎ *773-486-8870.* Dozens of sausages, breads, cheese and an assortment of knickknacks vie for shelf space in this cramped and bustling Polish delicatessen.

2 Sak's

Map p 165. 2301 W. Chicago Ave. ☎ *773-278-4445.* Aside from the nearby churches, this restaurant is one of the few places where you can experience the neighborhood's Ukrainian flavor. The menu features stuffed cabbage, borscht, sausages, potato pancakes and chicken Kiev. For a wide sample of Ukrainian cuisine, try the hearty family feast.

Continue northwest on Milwaukee Ave. to Division St. Turn right on Division St., then left on Noble St.

At 1255 Noble Street rises **St. Stanislaus Kostka Catholic Church**, a large brick structure covered with stucco. Following extensive community protest, the Kennedy Expressway was routed around the edifice, thereby saving the city's oldest Polish church (1877). Across the street, Pulaski Park is one of a series of green spaces developed in the 1910s to provide recreational facilities for the poor. Its most prominent feature, the 1912 **Pulaski Park Fieldhouse**, was designed by William Carbys Zimmerman and incorporates elements of the Tudor and Prairie styles. Visible to the south, the spires of Holy Trinity Roman Catholic Church *(1120 N. Noble St.)* tower over the neighborhood.

Return to Division St. and turn right.

The intersection of Milwaukee Avenue and Division Street marks the heart of the former Polish Downtown. West of the intersection, Division Street retains the urban seediness depicted by Nelson Algren in the 1940s. Just west of Wolcott Street, the **Division Street Russian & Turkish Baths** *(no. 1916)* still offer the old-world sauna treatment in a 1907 terra-cotta building *(open to men year-round Mon–Sat 8am–10pm, Sun 6am–10pm; $19; women are not allowed;* ✗ ▯ ☎ *773-384-9671).*

Turn left on Leavitt St.

The neighborhood of simple, red brick two-flats with neatly groomed lawns, located south of Division Street between Damen and Western Avenues, is known as **Ukrainian Village**. Built and settled by Ukrainian immigrants after 1900, especially Catholics from the Carpathian Mountains, the neighborhood's quiet streets and gardens still house Ukrainian families who frequent the Ukrainian shops and restaurants along Chicago Avenue. Local cultural institutions include the **Ukrainian National Museum** *(721 N. Oakley Blvd.; open year-round Thu–Sun 11am–4pm, Mon–Weds by appointment;* ☎ *773-421-8020; www.ukrntlmuseum.org),* which displays historic artifacts, folk costumes, ceramics and the famous Ukrainian *pysanky,* or decorated Easter eggs.

★**Holy Trinity Russian Orthodox Cathedral** – *1121 N. Leavitt St.* This tiny jewel designed by Louis Sullivan in 1899, combines his decorative aesthetic with the form of a rural Russian church. The tower topped by an onion dome is trimmed in yellow, while the building's walls are covered in white stucco. The edifice was constructed with a donation of $4,000 from Czar Nicholas II and became a base for Patriarch Tikhon, who was later beatified.

Turn right on Rice St. and continue to Oakley Ave.

At Oakley and Rice stands **St. Nicholas Ukrainian Catholic Cathedral★**, the mother church for Ukrainian Catholics in Chicago. The soaring structure features 13 domes symbolizing Christ and his disciples. Built in 1915 by architects Worthmann Steinbach & Piontek, St. Nicholas was restored in 1975 and glimmering mosaic were added in 1988.

Continue on Rice St. to Western Ave. Turn left on Western Ave. and left again on Chicago Ave.

At 2320 West Chicago Avenue stands the **Ukrainian Institute of Modern Art** *(open year round Wed, Thu & weekends noon–4pm; closed major holidays; contributio requested;* ♿ ▯ ☎ *773-227-5522).* Founded in 1971 and presenting works b artists of Ukrainian descent, the respected museum is located in a white one-stor building in the heart of the Ukrainian Village. Rotating exhibits occupy the larg gallery to the left of the entrance, while three connected galleries to the righ display the permanent collection of drawings, paintings, sculpture and multimed artworks.

Continue east on Chicago Ave.

In the 1960s the Ukrainian Catholic congregation was split by reforms of the sec ond Vatican council, and the traditionalists built a new edifice two blocks south c St. Nicholas Cathedral—**Saints Volodymyr and Olha Church** *(739 N. Oakley Ave.),* opene in 1975. Much simpler in design, the massive edifice is crowned by a huge go dome. Here services are still held in Ukrainian and worshippers follow the Orthodox (Gregorian) calendar. The arched mosaic above the entrance depicts Saint Volodymyr and his mother Olha blessing the Rus people in the Dnieper River in AD 988.

Drive east on Chicago Ave. and turn left on Damen Ave. Continue north to Schiller St. and park to tour the Wicker Park neighborhood on foot.

A small, 3-acre triangle, Wicker Park is lined with impressive stone Victorian mansions as well as early-20C apartment buildings along Schiller Street and Wicker Park Avenue. One block south, a plaque marks the three-flat building at **1958 West Evergreen Avenue**, where author Nelson Algren lived for three decades.

Walk west on Schiller St. and turn right on Hoyne Ave.

John H. Rapp House

A city and national landmark, the **Wicker Park★** neighborhood contains numerous mansions commissioned by prosperous German and Scandinavian immigrants in the late 19C. Occupying a spacious corner lot at the intersection of Schiller Street and Hoyne Avenue, the **John H. Rapp House★** (**A**) *(1407 N. Hoyne Ave.)*, built in 1879 by a wine merchant in the Second Empire style, sports a mansard roof, domed tower, elaborate wood brackets and trim, and a cast-iron porch and fence. Built in the 1880s for a Norwegian furniture maker, **no. 1427** (**B**) is an eclectic design reflecting Romanesque as well as Victorian detailing; note the workmanship of the wood and pressed-metal porch.

Cross LeMoyne St. and continue north.

The **Wicker Park Lutheran Church** (**C**) *(2112 LeMoyne St.)* was built in 1906 with granite salvaged from a brothel in the Levee. The pastor reportedly defended the material, saying the stones had "served the devil long enough, now let them serve the Lord." At **no. 1520** (**D**), golden hands rising from the stairs hold the banisters on the Second Empire mansion, built in 1886 for Russian lumberman Henry Grusendorf. Note the unusual double-gabled porch, with its intricate wood carvings, and the sculpted woman's head embellishing the facade.

Turn left and walk west on Pierce Ave.

The **Hermann Weinhardt House★** (**E**) at no. 2135 (1889, William Ohlhaber) defines ostentation with its unflinching use of architectural detail. The gabled roof is encrusted with pressed-metal bargeboards, and every element of the facade seems to drip with decorative forms in brick, metal or wood. The profusion of balustrades on the **John D. Runge House★** (**F**) at no. 2138 (1884, Frommann & Jebsen) helped advertise the owner's wood-milling firm. The home later served as the Polish Consulate and hosted a veranda concert by the Polish pianist Ignacy Paderewski in 1930. The Romanesque Revival **Theodore Juergens House** (**G**) at no. 2141 (1895, Henry T. Kley) features gargoyles and a third-floor ballroom.

Turn right on Leavitt St. and walk north to Concord Pl., one block past North Ave.

The two short blocks of Concord Place and Caton Street were developed by wealthy Scandinavians after 1890. Today their incongruous location behind discount shops and elevated rail tracks belies their former elegance. Built in 1893, **2156 West Concord Place** (**H**) features a conical tower and gabled dormer.

Continue north to Caton St. and turn right.

The large mansion at **2159 West Caton Street** (**J**) was erected two years earlier in the Queen Anne style. Norwegian merchant Ole Thorp developed Caton Street and lived in the large home distinguished by a domed turret at **no. 2156** (**K**) (1891, Faber & Pagels), where he reportedly entertained the Queen of Norway. The same architectural firm also designed **no. 2146 (L)**, a Romanesque Revival home in red brick with carved column capitals, and the pink sandstone and orange brick Queen Ann structure at **no. 2142 (N)**.

Turn right on Milwaukee Ave. and walk south to North Ave.

The heart of artistic Wicker Park is the intersection of Milwaukee, Damen and North Avenues, defined by the 12-story Art Deco **Northwest Tower** (1929, Perkins, Chatten & Hammond), centerpiece of the annual "Around the Coyote" tour of galleries and artists' lofts. The two-story terra-cotta **Flatiron Building** on the southeast corner of Milwaukee and North Avenues contains a bewildering array of restaurants, galleries and shops. In recent years coffeehouses, bookshops and antique stores have joined the discount furniture stores and fast-food restaurants lining Milwaukee.

■ Bookstores and Cafes

The artsy inhabitants of greater Wicker Park have mastered the art of hanging out, and this neighborhood's various haunts deserve a peek inside, if just for people-watching. Book-lovers should check out **Myopic Books** *(1468 Milwaukee Ave.; ☎ 773-862-4882)*, which has its own cafe and stays open until 1am; **Quimby's Bookstore** *(1854 W. North Ave.; ☎ 773-342-0910)* specializing in small press and underground magazines; and the **Occult Book Store** *(1561 N. Milwaukee Ave.; ☎ 773-292-0995)* for its works on witchcraft, tarot and all things eerie. Cafe culture in Wicker Park runs the gamut from bohemian/student to staid/banker. **Earwax** *(1564 N. Milwaukee Ave.; ☎ 773-772-4019)*—cafe on the first floor, video rental on the second—is the preferred meeting place for struggling musicians, while the neighborhood's well-dressed denizens frequent the **The Northside Cafe** *(1635 N. Damen Ave.; ☎ 773-384-3555)*.

■ Nightclubs

At night, people from across the city flock to the neighborhood's clubs and taverns. Originally a polka lounge, the **Rainbo Club** *(1150 N. Damen Ave.; ☎ 773-489-5999)* now claims varied performers including the likes of Tortoise, The Sea and Cake, and Joan of Arc. On the fringes of the Ukrainian Village, the **Empty Bottle** *(1035 N. Western Ave.; ☎ 773-276-3600)* books an eclectic mix of experimental jazz, hot local rock acts and bands on the brink of national renown. **Red Dog** *(1958 W. North Ave.; ☎ 773-278-1009)* is Wicker Park's dance club, where house and techno music rule. Decorated in kitschy Vegas-supper-club style, **Holiday** *(1471 N. Milwaukee Ave.; ☎ 773-486-0686)* caters to stylish martini drinkers. The **Double Door** *(1572 N. Milwaukee Ave.; ☎ 773-489-3160)* is the premier live-music venue in the area. The owners book bands that are just breaking onto the national scene and the small V-shaped room is a great place to see future stars up close.

Return to car along Damen Ave. Drive north on Damen Ave. and turn right on North Ave.; turn left on Hermitage Ave.

Located north of North Avenue between Milwaukee and Ashland Avenues, **Bucktown** was a largely Polish working-class community that experienced a sudden real estate boom in the late 1980s as hundreds of yuppies and artists moved into the quaint brick homes and quiet streets. Stately **St. Mary of the Angels Catholic Church★** *(185 N. Hermitage Ave.)* dominates the streetscape of Bucktown. The brown brick and white terra-cotta edifice, completed in 1920 by Polish Catholics in a Roman Baroque style, features a twin-towered facade with an elaborate portico, 9ft-high terra-cotta angels ringing the parapet, and a huge dome and cupola modeled on St. Peter's Basilica in Rome. Parishioners and neighbors led a successful five-year fund-raising effort that saw the church restored and reopened in 1992. The interior paintings and elaborate decoration well illustrate the exuberant Baroque style.

LOGAN SQUARE AREA DRIVING TOUR

Distance: 2.3mi. Map p 169.

Begin at the intersection of Milwaukee Ave. and Logan and Kedzie Blvds.

The **Illinois Centennial Monument (1)** (1918, Henry Bacon, architect and Evelyn Beatrice Longman, sculptor) marks the intersection of Logan and Kedzie Boulevards with Milwaukee Avenue. An eagle surmounts a fluted pillar that rises from a base ringed by marching Native Americans, French explorers, farmers and workers.

Turn right on Logan Blvd., on the frontage road, and continue to Washtenaw St.

The most beautiful stretch of Chicago's 28mi boulevard system is also the best place to view the city's finest **graystones**, houses that incorporate Romanesque-style stonework with Victorian and Neoclassical details in durable Indiana limestone. Stone stairs, turrets, battlements and stained glass lend many of these buildings a picturesque quality. The **John Rath House★** *(2701 Logan Blvd.)* is a Chicago landmark designed in 1907 by George W. Maher. Broad eaves and rectilinear forms of the Prairie style combine with Maher's distinctive flattened arches and floral motifs repeated in windows, brackets and doors. The porch seems carved out of the side of the house, set back to take advantage of the boulevard.

Turn left and return west on the frontage road of Logan Blvd. to Kedzie Blvd.

The **Apartments for John Gerson** (1909, Frederick R. Schock) at 2934-36 Logan Boulevard, feature a fascinating, bowed-arch doorway flanked by Prairie urns with Craftsman-style detailing. At 2614 North Kedzie Boulevard, the red brick Norwegian Lutheran Memorial Church, known as "**Minnekirken**" (1908, Charles Sorenson), boasts a large central tower and beveled edges that make the 30ft-wide building appear monumental.

Drive south on Kedzie Blvd.

More grand mansions line Kedzie Boulevard south of Logan Square, such as the 1897 **William Nowaczewski House** *(no. 2410)* with its elaborate porch, tower, gargoyles and stepped gables. Just south of Fullerton Avenue, the **Norske Club** *(no. 2350)* was designed in 1916 by Giaver & Dinkelberg as a lodge hall with dragonhead eaves that recall Norwegian architecture.

LAKEVIEW/WRIGLEYVILLE and UPTOWN

Map p 173

A dense residential district on Chicago's North Side lakefront, this popular area is known for its upbeat restaurants and theaters, and offbeat shops and nightclubs. Its most famous landmark, Wrigley Field, has lent its name to the northern part of Lakeview, which extends from Diversey Boulevard to Irving Park Road. Uptown stretches north to Foster Avenue. Lying between the two areas, Graceland Cemetery provides a unique slice of the city's history, art and architecture.

Historical Notes

A farming community settled by Germans in the 1830s, Lakeview began, as did its southern neighbor Lincoln Park/DePaul, as the celery basket of Chicago. Incorporated in 1857 the township was named for the 1854 Lake View House Hotel, a glamorous resort hotel built on the shores of Lake Michigan at present-day Grace Street. The late 19C witnessed the gradual transformation of the quiet lakefront community into a residential neighborhood, spurred by real-estate developers who offered cheap frame houses outside Chicago's fire district. Swedish immigrants followed the Germans to the remote area, working in steel plants, brickyards and tanneries along the Chicago River and relaxing in numerous beer gardens and saloons—for which Lakeview is still famous today. Incorporation into Chicago in 1889 and the completion of the elevated line in 1900 led to intensive development. The 1920s boom in population and construction spread north to the roaring nightlife district of Uptown.

The fledgling film industry produced hundreds of silent movies—starring the likes of Charlie Chaplin and Gloria Swanson—at the neighborhood's **Essanay Studios** before moving west to milder climes. Following the Depression years, Uptown fell upon hard times, losing its appeal as Chicago's entertainment district. With its stock of inexpensive apartments, the neighborhood became the "port of entry" for immigrants from Appalachia, the Far East, Latin America and even American Indian reservations.

By the 1960s much of the North Side was in decline, but the opening of several theaters, clubs and restaurants in the 1970s helped fuel intensive reinvestment. The neighborhood around historic Wrigley Field, promoted as "Wrigleyville" by apartment redeveloper Seymour Persky, attracted a young crowd in search of affordable digs. Large

① Argyle Street

Map p 173. Between Sheridan Road and Broadway, this bustling strip of Argyle Street is the focal point of Chicago's Southeast-Asian community. Take the time to browse among the dozen of Vietnamese, Laotian and Cambodian shops and restaurants, as well as numerous Thai, Chinese and Filipino establishments. Seafood, hearty soups and wrap-it-yourself cellophane-noodle dishes rank among the house specialties at **Nhatrang Restaurant** *(1007 W. Argyle St.; ☎ 773-989-0712)*. The Laotian **Cafe Nhu Hoa** *(1020 W. Argyle St.; ☎ 773-878-0618)* is known for its good food and budget-friendly lunch specials. Dried tamarind candy, pink pearl tapioca, leechee honey, fresh persimmons and other Asian delicacies fill the shelves of the **Viet Hoa Plaza** market *(1051 W. Argyle St.; ☎ 773-334-1028)*. **Vinh Tho** *(1112 W. Argyle St.; ☎ 773-275-2985)* offers herbal remedies and a wide assortment of medicinal teas.

Victorian homes on Hawthorne Place, Hutchinson Street and in the Buena Park area were restored. Gleaming high rises sprouted along the lakefront, which was gradually gentrified north to Irving Park Road.

Today Lakeview/Wrigleyville, home to the city's largest gay population, is best known for its plethora of entertainment options. Uptown retains a seedier image, exacerbated by many transient residents. Nonetheless, popular concert venues near Lawrence Avenue and Broadway, redevelopment of the Sheridan Park Historic District and the emergence of Chicago's Vietnamese Chinatown along Argyle Street have ended Uptown's decline. In addition, the Ravenswood and Lincoln Square neighborhoods located west of Uptown have experienced a surge in popularity, attracting a young and eclectic clientele.

SIGHTS

The far-flung sights in this area are best seen by car.

The southern section of Lakeview/Wrigleyville continues the genteel neighborhood feel of Lincoln Park/DePaul, with a densely built-up lakefront sheltering quiet residential streets. Of note here, the rusticated stone **Brewster Apartments** building *(2800 N. Pine Grove Ave.)* was designed in 1891 by Enoch Hill Turnock. This early high rise, distinguished by a rounded corner and rooftop penthouse, provides a vivid contrast to the stark aluminum **Commonwealth Plaza** *(330-340 W. Diversey Pkwy.)*, a Mies van der Rohe creation dating from 1956.

★**Hawthorne Place District** – *Between Broadway and Lake Shore Dr.* This landmark district of sprawling homes and gardens was developed as Lakeview' showpiece by Benjamin and John McConnell in 1883. Victorian mansions includ the **George E. Marshall House** (**A**) *(no. 574)*, completed in 1886 by Burnham & Root and the 1884 **Benjamin F. McConnell House** (**B**) *(no. 568)*, clad in shingles and clapboards. Dating from the 1890s, the Queen Anne **Herman H. Hettler House** (**C** *(no. 567)* owned by the adjacent Chicago City Day School, retains its original corne turret, curving veranda and stone foundation. The **John McConnell House** (**D** *(no. 546)*, built in 1885 for the developer and mayor of Lakeview, was extensivel renovated in 1993.

Just around the corner, at 3480 North Lake Shore Drive, stands **Temple Sholom**★, Byzantine-style octagon clad in yellow ashlar limestone that is covered with intr cate ornamentation. Designed in 1930 by the firm of Loebl, Schlossman & Demuth this large structure provides an elegant break in the seemingly unending wall lakefront high rises.

★**Wrigley Field** – *1060 W. Addison St.* ☎ *773-404-2827. www.cubs.com/wrigle* Built as Weeghman Field for the Cubs of the National League before bein occupied by the Cubs of the National League in 1916, this stadium (1914, Zacha Taylor Davis) is a North Side icon. Famous for its ivy walls and lovable losing team the stadium has a backdrop of turn-of-the-century three-flats rather than the usu sea of parking lots. Many of the adjacent buildings on Sheffield Street boast rooft clubs where members watch the game over the outfield walls. The communi stonewalled the addition of lights for night baseball until 1988.

★**Alta Vista Terrace** – *3800 block, between Grace and Byron Sts.* The city's fir protected landmark district was designed in 1904 by Joseph C. Brompton as single work of architecture. Each side of the street contains 20 homes mirror diagonally on the facing side. The Roman brick homes are 20ft wide and two st ries high, except for the four central, three-story limestone structures. Basica

Wrigley Field Stadium Entrance

Georgian in style, the homes nevertheless exhibit a rich variety of details from the Byzantine, Neoclassical, Gothic and Renaissance styles as well as colorful rooflines.

The street was built by the prolific neighborhood real estate developer **Samuel Eberly Gross** (1843-1913), whose inspiration came from his trips to London.

Graceland Cemetery – *Map p 172. 4001 N. Clark St. Open year-round daily 8am-4:30pm (office closed Sun). Closed Dec 25, July 4 and Labor Day.* 🅿 ☎ *773-525-1105. Site plan available at entrance.* One of Chicago's most evocative sites contains notable architecture and sculpture, marking the final resting places of many of the city's movers and shakers. The wealthy neighbors of Prairie Avenue and the Gold Coast, including the Palmers, Fields, McCormicks and Pullmans, are once again neighbors here, joined by renowned architects William Le Baron Jenney, Daniel Burnham, John W. Root, Louis Sullivan and Mies van der Rohe. Developed in 1860, Graceland received many reburials from the site of Lincoln Park. Its 119 acres were designed after 1883 in a picturesque, naturalistic style by Ossian Cole Simonds.

Lorado Taft sculpted the haunting *Eternal Silence* memorial for hotel owner Dexter Graves in 1909, and the heroic *Crusader* in 1931 for the grave of *Daily News* founder Victor F. Lawson. Louis Sullivan's masterful **Getty Tomb**★ (1890), designed for merchant Henry Harrison Getty following his wife Carrie Eliza's death, features intricate grilles (exhibited at the Paris Exposition of 1900), delicate acanthus leaf ornamentation, and windows in a round-arched composition of exquisite balance and plasticity. Sullivan's earlier **Martin Ryerson Tomb** (1887) takes the form of an Egyptian mastaba with a pyramid

2 Lincoln Square

Map p 173. This predominantly German neighborhood is located where Lincoln, Lawrence and Western Avenues converge. The stretch of Lincoln Avenue between Leland and Lawrence encompasses a pedestrian mall where German culture thrives, from the Stieff stuffed animals at **Timeless Toys** (*4740 N. Lincoln Ave.;* ☎ *773-334-4445*) to the Birkenstock shoes at **Salamander** (*4762 N. Lincoln Ave.;* ☎ *773-784-7463*). **Enisa's European Pastry and Cafe** (*4701 N. Lincoln Ave.;* ☎ *773-271-7017*) offers petit fours, tarts and cookies baked daily. Founded in 1875, the **Merz Apothecary** (*4716 N. Lincoln Ave.;* ☎ *773-989-9000*) stocks a huge selection of European and eco-friendly cosmetics as well as homeopathic herbs and remedies. Facing the square's small plaza, **Cafe Selmarie** (*2327 W. Giddings St.;* ☎ *773-989-5595*) serves mouthwatering pastries by day and exotic dishes by night. Whole smoked eels, homemade wursts and schnapps galore can be found at **Meyer Delicatessen** (*4750 N. Lincoln Ave.;* ☎ *773-561-3377*). Feast on a plate of sauerbraten and a stein of Stiegl at the boisterous **Chicago Brauhaus** (*4732 N. Lincoln Ave.;* ☎ *773-784-4444*), which features live German music nightly.

171

top in black polished granite. Daniel Chester French and Henry Bacon created the **Marshall Field Tomb** prior to their joint design of the Lincoln Memorial in Washington, DC. Socialites **Potter and Bertha Palmer** rest in two sarcophagi in a Neoclassical temple (McKim, Mead & White) overlooking a small winding lagoon dotted with an island where **Daniel Burnham** is buried. Brewer **Peter Schoenhofen's** tomb is a miniature pyramid guarded by a sphinx and a Victorian angel. **George Pullman's** Corinthian column and exedra by Solon S. Beman cover a maze of concrete and steel designed to prevent angry workers from

disinterring the railroad magnate. Sports legends buried here include boxing great Jack Johnson and National League founder William Hulbert, who lies beneath a large baseball.

St. Mary of the Lake Catholic Church – *4200 N. Sheridan Rd.* This 1917 design by Henry J. Schlacks draws on various churches in Rome, including St. Pudentiana for the dramatic campanile tower, and St. Paul's Outside the Walls for the main Neoclassical facade. The light terra-cotta facade and red tile roof reinforce the appearance of a Roman basilica.

❸ The Green Mill

Map p 173. 4802 N. Broadway. ☏ *773-878-5552.* Al Capone's crew used to hang out in this charming jazz club. The interior looks much as it did back in the 1920s and 30s. Owner Dave Jemilo books jazz acts seven nights a week, and the music plays until 4am (5am Saturdays). On Sunday evening, thick-skinned poets read their works to the rowdy-yet-discerning crowds who attend the infamous Uptown Poetry Slam competitions.

❹ Architectural Artifacts

Map p 173. 4325 N. Ravenswood Ave. ☏ *773-348-0622.* Baptismal fonts from crumbled churches and portraits of secret-society leaders are among the treasures (both architectural and decorative) that this store's owners have rescued from demolished buildings. The first floor features large furniture (antique sideboards, tables, mantels), tiles and smaller terra-cotta, iron and concrete pieces. A mishmash of signs, paintings and chairs can be found upstairs.

*★***Hutchinson Street District** – *Between Lake Shore Dr. and Hazel St.* Several designs by Prairie school architect George Washington Maher together with a range of eclectic, single-family homes provide a welcome diversion from the high-rise lakefront. The **Edwin J. Mosser House** (**E**) (1902) at no. 750 features oversized urns and a Sullivanesque entrance facing Clarendon Street. At no. 817, the two-story **Claude Seymour House** (**F**) (1913) is distinguished by banded leaded-glass windows, urns, a wide overhanging roofline, and Maher's signature flattened-arch entrance. Maher's 190C **Grace Brackebush House** (**G**) *(no. 839)* marks the integration of picturesque period revival elements with the horizontal emphasis of the Prairie school. The **John C. Scales House H**) *(no. 840)* resembles a Queen Anne home replete with shingles and round turrets. This 1894 Maher design experiments with volume in a manner similar to that of contemporary architect Frank Lloyd Wright.

Additional Sights

Uptown – Recalling the Roaring Twenties, the intersection of Lawrence Avenue and Broadway still features numerous large theaters and terra-cotta buildings from the era. The restored **Uptown National Bank** (1924, Marshall & Fox) at 4753 North Broadway us white terra-cotta in a stately Neoclassical composition with a curving corner entrance. Erected in 1925 by Rapp & Rapp, the once majestic **Uptown Theatre** *(4814 N. Broadway)* awaits renovation of its interior, seating almost 4,400. The 1926 Moorish-style **Aragon Ballroom** *(1106 W. Lawrence Ave.),* a former hot spot for ballroom dancing under a "starry sky" (the blue dome was adorned with stellar ornament), regularly hosts major rock-and-roll acts, as does the **Riviera Theatre** (1918, Rapp & Rapp) at 4746 North Broadway.

Ravenswood – Several structures along Hermitage Avenue are worth the trip to Ravenswood, a newly rediscovered residential area stretching to the west of Uptown. Erected in 1883, the distinctive **All Saints Episcopal Church** (**J**) *(no. 4550)* is a rare Chicago example of Stick-style architecture. Across the intersection, the grand Victorian **Wallace C. Abbott House** (**K**) *(no. 4605)* was built by the founders of Abbott Laboratories. At no. 4646 stands the **Carl Sandburg House** (**L**), a nondescript three-flat where the famous author composed his *Chicago Poems* in 1916.

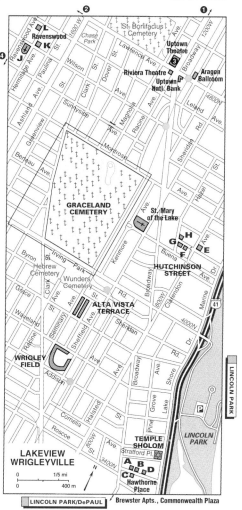

Located on the city's Far North Side, Devon (pronounced duh-VONE) Avenue (6400 block North) runs right through the hearts of Chicago's Indian and Jewish communities. West of Sacramento Avenue, several stores on the 2700 block West—including the **Russian American Book Store** *(no. 2746; ☏ 773-761-3233)*—feature signs written in Cyrillic and cater to Russian immigrants. The **Croatian Cultural Center of Chicago** *(no. 2845; ☏ 773-338-3839)* is located on the next block. Farther along the street, signs in Hebrew adorn dozens of businesses. Hundreds of books, journals, magazines and gifts are available at **Rosenblum's World of Judaica** *(no. 2906; ☏ 773-262-1700)*; across the street, **Hashalom Restaurant** *(no. 2905; ☏ 773-465-5675)* serves up kebabs and other Israeli dishes. The **Kol Tuv Kosher Foods deli** *(no. 2938; ☏ 773-764-1800)* offers Jewish specialties prepared under the supervision of the Chicago Rabbinical Council.

Walk east on Devon toward Oakley Street to admire beautiful silk and hand-embroidered fabrics hanging in the window of **Regal Sarees** *(no. 2616; ☏ 773-973-1368)*. Although dozens of restaurants mingle with jewelry stores, video-rental shops and markets, two stand out from the crowd: **Viceroy of India** *(no. 2518; ☏ 773-743-4100)*, renowned for its hearty buffet and **Moti Mahal** *(no. 2525; ☏ 773-262-2080)*, which serves the best nan bread in town.

NEAR WEST SIDE

Map p 175

Located west and south of the Loop, this neighborhood is bounded by the Chicago River on the east, 16th Street on the south, Ogden Avenue on the west and Kinzie Street on the north. Largely unscathed by the 1871 fire, it has faced other agents of change throughout its history. Encroaching immigrant communities eventually supplanted the "West Side Gold Coast" above Harrison Street, while the ethnic neighborhoods to the south have been neutralized over the years by various urban-renewal projects. However, through the layers of progress and blight peek the remnants of Chicago's old West Side.

Historical Notes

A Study in Contrasts – Bordering the South Branch of the Chicago River, the Near West Side attracted early settlers and was included, to Wood Street, in the incorporation of Chicago in 1837. The Irish arrived in the 1840s and 50s to work in the lumber mills, railroad yards and other riverside industries. Their frame cottages and barns crowded west to Halsted Street and south to Roosevelt Road, establishing the area as a port of entry for immigrants until well into the 20C. Meanwhile, mere blocks to the north and west, the city's merchant class built elegant homes along Washington and Ashland Boulevards. In true suburban fashion, developers widened and paved the streets, installed sewers and planted trees; horsecar lines provided transport to the central city. A multitude of churches and pretty Union Park, at Randolph Street and Ogden Avenue, added to the appeal of the neighborhood.

Such was the profile of the Near West Side, when, in 1871, a fire ignited in Mrs. O'Leary's barn on DeKoven Street in the heart of the Irish district. The blaze spread rapidly, consuming hundreds of wooden shanties along Clinton and Canal Streets, but jumped the river and headed northeast without damaging more of the West Side. Spared the flames, the neighborhood provided refuge for thousands of fire victims; the population soared to 200,000 and construction boomed. The wealthy continued to build fine homes along the northern boulevards, and to the south, new waves of immigrants settled in closely knit enclaves.

Land of Opportunity – By the end of the century, however, congestion, traffic and the spreading industrial city had emptied the exclusive residential sections of the West Side. In addition, violent labor protests frightened many well-to-do homeowners away. Events at Haymarket Square at Randolph and Desplaines Streets on May 4, 1886, hastened the process and changed forever the course of American labor history. Still the immigrants came, settling up and down Halsted Street into multiple communities, each anchored by churches, synagogues and other ethnic institutions.

By the 1890s thousands of Russian and Polish Jews had come to escape the intensifying pogroms in Europe. In the vicinity of Maxwell and Halsted Streets, they lived as they had in the Old World shtetls, abiding strictly by Orthodox ways. Many worked in the garment district along Jackson Boulevard; many were peddlers. The legendary **Maxwell Street Market** *(entrance on Roosevelt and Canal Sts.)*, crowded with kosher meat shops, bakeries and vendors of everything imaginable, resembled the open-air bazaars of European villages.

Just north, Italians teemed around Halsted and Taylor Streets in the largest Italian community in Chicago. The Delta near Halsted and Harrison Streets became the most populous Greek enclave in the US by 1930. In the midst of it all, Chicago's first settlement house, established by **Jane Addams** in 1889, provided a refuge from the slums where immigrants could learn American ways, celebrate their own national pride and participate in finding solutions to industrial problems. The renowned Hull-House served the community until the 1960s when the social service programs were relocated to other parts of the city to make way for the University of Illinois at Chicago Campus.

Urban Renewal or Upheaval? – The controversial campus was but one of many redevelopment projects to transform the Near West Side landscape in the last several decades. Beginning in 1938, a frenzy of construction resulted in the largest concentration of public housing in the city. In 1941 the state legislature established the Medical Center District just east of Ogden Avenue, recognizing a cluster of facilities that had been operating there since 1884 and opening the way for more. The Eisenhower Expressway, begun in 1954, cut a swath down the center of the Near West Side, and perpendicular to it, the Dan Ryan and the Kennedy Expressways devastated the neighborhoods in their paths. Still, remnants remain. Graystones along Jackson Boulevard echo the street's elegant era. Loft conversions in the garment district preserve the old warehouses. Although disrupted by the university, Little Italy prevails, complete with trendy trattorias along Taylor Street. Greektown thrives in the restaurants along Halsted Street north of Van Buren Street.

ost recently, African Americans and Mexicans have come to live on the Near West
de, replacing the Jews who moved west, and establishing their own ethnic enclaves.
he Maxwell Street Market was kept bustling—offering everything from hubcaps to
ot dogs—until it too was relocated in 1994.

SIGHTS

The far-flung sights on the Near West Side are best seen by car.

Certain pockets around the Near West Side have survived the hand of change.
Many of them seem incongruous in their settings now—the isolated mansion surrounded by vacant lots, the grand church hard by the expressway, the prep school
in the tough neighborhood—but the vigilant visitor will be rewarded by these unexpected glimpses into the neighborhood's past.

I-90/I-94 Corridor – East of the Kennedy Expressway (I-90) stands **St. Patrick's
Roman Catholic Church** *(140 S. Desplaines St.)*, Chicago's oldest extant church
building, erected between 1852 and 1856. The asymmetrical steeples were added
in 1885: the onion dome represents the Eastern Church, while the spire symbolizes the Roman Church in the West.

To the south, at 558 DeKoven Street, the **Chicago Fire Academy** fittingly occupies the
site of the infamous O'Leary barn where the 1871 Chicago Fire started. In front,
the tripartite **Pillar of Fire** (**1**), sculpted in bronze by Egon Weiner in 1961, commemorates the event.

★**Holy Family Church and St. Ignatius College Prep** – *1076-1080 W. Roosevelt
Rd.* This interesting pair of buildings creates an enduring West Side silhouette that
transcends the gritty city blocks around it. The church was the cornerstone of the
Irish community when it was built by the Jesuits in 1857. Rescued from demoli-

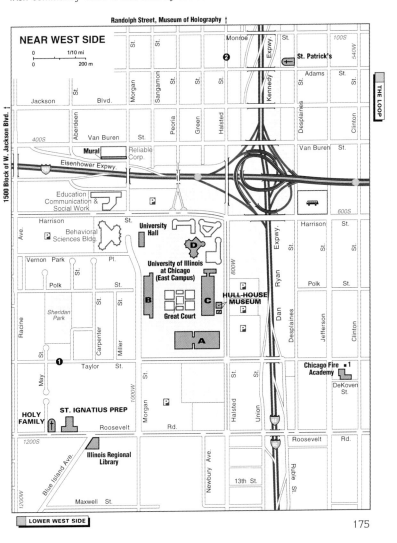

tion by fund-raising parishioners in 1990, the church today is undergoing met
ulous restoration. Next door, the elaborate Second Empire facade of the pr
school has been beautifully preserved *(visit by 1hr guided tour only, year-rou.
Mon–Fri 7:30am–5pm, Sat 9am–noon; closed major & academic holidays; 2-d
advance reservations required; & 🅿 ☎ 312-421-5900; www.ignatius.org)*. Bu
in 1870, the school offered students from all over the city the quality of a Jesu
education. Today more than 1,200 students come from every background an
neighborhood to take advantage of its rigorous curriculum.

Across Roosevelt Road stands the **Illinois Regional Library for the Blind and Physica
Handicapped** *(1055 W. Roosevelt Rd.)*, whose primary purpose is to serve as t
state's distribution center for Braille books and books on tape. The buildir
sheathed in boldly colored metal, sports a wonderful wavelike window incised alor
its Blue Island Avenue side. The work of Stanley Tigerman & Assocs., the stru
ture (1975) is designed for ease of access and use while displaying Tigerman
signature whimsy.

University of Illinois at Chicago (East Campus)

*The core of the campus is bounded by Halsted, Taylor, Morgan and Harrison S
A detailed campus map is posted in the lobby at University Hall, 601 S. Morg
St. ☎ 312-996-7000. www.uic.edu/homeindex.*

This inner-city campus has generated much controversy since it was first conceived
a commuter school to serve the throngs of students poised to enter college in the m
1960s. This location was proposed after a survey of 83 possible sites, and despite cc
siderable protest by the mostly Italian residents of the densely populated area, cc
struction began in 1963. The university's radical plan, devised by architect Walter

Netsch, Jr. of Skidmore, Owings & Merr
has long been debated. Netsch attempt
to create a campus appropriate to its c
setting and able to accommodate up
32,000 students—the current enrollme
is 25,000. But what seemed like a fittir
if dramatic, direction for the prototypi
urban university in the 1960s has tod
been acknowledged as cold, unmanag
able and at times downright inhuman. .
spired by the movement known as Brut.
ism, the hulking concrete and bri
exoskeletons of the buildings are punc
ated by slitlike vertical windows. Netsch i
cluded a layer of "express" walkwa
above those at grade level, all convergi
at the campus' center, where an outdc
amphitheater ringed by six lecture ha
with a common roof-deck formed an "
tellectual agora" for outdoor classes a
socializing. This Great Court proved to
inhospitably hot in summer ar
windswept in winter. Disintegrating co
crete, water seepage and security fea
contributed to the 1992 decision to r
configure it. As a result, the amphitheat
and elevated walkways have been dem
ished, and the lecture halls re-roofed.

The Campus – Greenery, colored sto
and wooden benches soften the op
plaza of the new **Great Court**, which offe
a pleasing visual break from the ha
lines of the surrounding buildings. T
Science and Engineering Laboratories **(A)** lie
the south, the **University Library** **(B)** to t
west and the **Chicago Circle Center** **(C)** (t
work of C.F. Murphy Assocs., the on
original structure not designed by Ski
more, Owings & Merrill) to the east. 7
the northwest stands the campus' and
"skyscraper": **University Hall**, the 28-sto
administrative center. Due north, t
brick **Architecture and Art Laboratories** (
represent Netsch's "field theory," an e
periment in rotated squares. Anoth

① Little Italy

Map p 175. The restaurants
lining Taylor Street (1000
block South) between
Halsted and Ashland Streets
bear witness to Chicago's
original Italian settlement
in the area. **Tuscany** *(1014
W. Taylor St.; ☎ 312-829-
1990)*, with its fresh, light
décor, yummy designer
pizzas and unorthodox pasta
dishes, attracts trendy
upscale crowds. Try **Mario's**
Italian lemonade and ice
sidewalk stand *(1066
W. Taylor St.; open
May–Sept)* for a refreshing
taste of the old
neighborhood. Cannoli
and other fresh-made Italian
pastries are available from
the **Pompeii Bakery** *(1455
W. Taylor St.; ☎ 312-421-
5179)*, which also serves
lunch and dinner in its casual
dining area. The king of
Taylor Street restaurants is
the popular **New Rosebud Cafe**
*(1500 W. Taylor St.; ☎ 312-
942-1117)*, renowned for its
excellent food served in
mammoth portions. Walk
three blocks north to
Tufano's—called the Vernon
Park Tap by regulars *(1073
W. Vernon Park; ☎ 312-
733-3393)*—a cozy dining
room tucked in back of a
well-worn barroom offering
wonderful homemade pastas
served family style.

major change on campus was the addition of dormitories at the corner of Halsted and Harrison Streets in 1988. Some 1,350 of the one-time commuter school's 25,000 students reside here. The multi-story dorms designed by Solomon Cordwell Buenz & Assocs. form the visual antithesis of the rest of the campus, with their warm, buff-colored brick sparsely decorated with delicate geometric designs.

The north side of campus offers a good view of Richard Haas' trompe-l'œil **supermural** across the Eisenhower Expressway. Ten tons of paint cover two city blocks along the west and south sides of the Reliable Corp. Building at 1001 West Van Buren Street. The colossal work depicts the Civic Center of Daniel Burnham's 1909 Plan of Chicago, which would have been located close to that spot, along with the city's modern skyline. The mural's medallions commemorate its historic role as a transportation hub.

★**Jane Addams' Hull-House Museum** – *800 S. Halsted St., on University of Illinois campus. Open year-round Mon–Fri 10am–4pm, Sun noon–5pm. Closed major holidays.* ♿ 🅿 ☏ *312-413-5353. www.uic.edu/jaddams/hull/.* Dwarfed by the surrounding campus buildings, the Hull-House Museum offers a glimpse into an important chapter in the history of American social welfare and reform. Founded in 1889 by pioneering social workers Jane Addams and Ellen Gates Starr, this settlement house became a focal point for citywide and national movements to improve living and working conditions of the nation's poor and disadvantaged.

Hull-House (1912)

A Life of Service – Jane Addams was born in 1860 near Rockford, Illinois, the youngest child of Sarah and John Addams. Among the first generation of American women to receive a college education, Addams was determined to make a contribution to society. Inspired by an 1886 trip to London's Toynbee Hall—the world's first social settlement dedicated to helping the poor through activity, culture and education—Addams returned to Chicago to launch a similar program with her college friend Ellen Gates Starr. Her success at Hull-House came in part from her willingness to "settle" among the immigrant poor on the Near West Side. Her method was to work with her neighbors to share experiences and find solutions to social and industrial problems. She became famous worldwide as a social reformer, suffragist, writer and pacifist, winning the Nobel Peace Prize in 1931. Hull-House achieved fame internationally as the birthplace of social work. Addams lived at Hull-House until her death in 1935.

In 1889 Addams and Starr moved into the house (1856) built by real-estate developer Charles J. Hull on the western outskirts of the city. Surrounded by diverse immigrant communities, industry, crowded tenements and sweatshops, Hull-House eventually grew to a complex of 13 buildings—among them Chicago's first public gymnasium, art and music schools and a cooperative residence for working women. In this spacious setting, Hull-House residents carried out their aggressive agenda of education, social service and reform. In 1963 a part of the Near West Side neighborhood was torn down to make way for the University of Illinois at Chicago. Of the original 13 buildings, the university retained the mansion and the Residents' Dining Hall, renovating and converting them into a museum. Hull-House's social

177

2 Greektown

Map p 175. Although the area first settled by Greek immigrants was destroyed by the construction of the Eisenhower Expressway and the University of Illinois at Chicago, many Greek restaurants, clubs, diners and shops remain along the stretch of South Halsted Street (800 block West) between Van Buren and Monroe Streets. The oldest restaurant, **The Parthenon** *(314 S. Halsted St.; ☎ 312-726-2407)*, boasts a huge menu with appetizer- and entrée-size portions of stuffed grape leaves, gyros, spanakopita and other Greek favorites. Religious statuettes, incense, candles and medicinal herbs and oils imported from the old country line the shelves of the **Athenian Candle Company** *(300 S. Halsted St.; ☎ 312-332-6988)*. **Roditys** *(222 S. Halsted St.; ☎ 312-454-0800)* is the spot for a boisterous evening of dining and drinking. At the north end of the strip, you'll find **Santorini** *(138 S. Halsted St.; ☎ 312-829-8820)*, an upscale seafood restaurant.

services were dispersed to locations around the city where the work is carried on today.

Visit – Today both museum buildings are open to visitors. The dining hall, built in the Arts and Crafts style in 1905, features a 15min slide show *(2nd floor)* providing information about Jane Addams and the philosophy behind the Hull-House settlement. Photographs of life at the settlement in the 1920s and 30s by Wallace Kirkland and a model of the original buildings are displayed here. The first floor has been restored to its 1905 appearance as a dining hall. Documents, photographs and other materials interpret the significance of this room and the influence of individuals who gathered here to shape US social policy during the first half of the 20C.

An attempt has been made to return the mansion, much remodeled over the years, to its earliest appearance. The two-story, brick Italianate exterior is topped by a cupola and surrounded by a white-columned verandah. The four rooms on the first floor are furnished and decorated in the Victorian style with many original pieces, including **Jane Addams' desk**, and they exude the homelike atmosphere that Addams herself cultivated. The setting belies the activity that once enlivened this space, always the business and social center of the settlement. News clippings, photographs, quotations and descriptive labeling convey a feeling for the daily life here.

North of the Eisenhower Expressway, two east-west streets several blocks apart epitomize the historic double image of the Near West Side. A panoply of Italianate, Queen Anne, Second Empire and Richardsonian Romanesque homes line the landmark **1500 block of West Jackson Boulevard** *(between Ashland and Laflin Streets)*. Built between 1871 and 1900, these residences recall the neighborhood's gilded era. Five blocks north, along **Randolph Street**, wholesale merchants supply fruits and vegetables, meat and poultry, flowers and other goods much as they have since the market opened in 1852. Trendy restaurants have also discovered the street, appreciating the huge spaces of its warehouses and loft buildings. To the east, the intersection of Randolph and Desplaines Streets marks Haymarket Square, scene of the 1886 labor disturbance

Museum of Holography – *1134 W. Washington Blvd. Open year-round Wed–Sun 12:30pm–5pm. Closed major holidays. $3. ☎ 312-226-1007.* Founded in 1976 to advance the science and art of holography, this museum encompasses four exhibit galleries that display items from the extensive permanent collection as well as changing exhibits of holograms by artists from the world over. Holograms are created through a complicated photographic process that records light waves reflected from an object illuminated with laser light on a light-sensitive medium. The three-dimensional effects can be dazzling since the process reproduces every blemish and nuance with molecular exactness.

■ United Center

Map p 11. The Near West Side is home to United Center, a sports venue for Chicago's basketball team, the Bulls, and hockey team, the Blackhawks. Erected at a cost of $175 million, the 1,000,000sq ft structure replaced the 1929 Chicago Stadium, which was torn down in 1994. The old Chicago Stadium gained fame for hosting the first football game to be played indoors in 1932, when a snowstorm forced the players inside. For information on sporting events at United Center, contact the center's Web site: *www.united-center.com.*

This industrial, working-class community of modest homes and grand churches is bordered on the south and east by the Chicago River, on the north by railroad tracks near 16th Street and on the west by Pulaski Road. Encompassing four neighborhoods—Pilsen, Heart of Chicago, Little Village and Lawndale—Lower West Side is today the center of Mexican culture in Chicago.

Historical Notes

The industrial district along the South Branch of the Chicago River was settled by immigrant Bohemians after the fire of 1871 and named Pilsen in honor of their homeland's second largest city. Between long hours of stacking lumber on the river edge and brewing Pilsener beer, the immigrants erected churches and social halls reminiscent of their native Bohemia. The already crowded district experienced a rapid expansion after the construction in 1854 of Blue Island Avenue, known as Black Road from the soot of the surrounding factories. Blue Island Avenue led to the McCormick Reaper Works at Western Avenue, where 35 percent of the nation's harvesters were built in the early 1900s. The neighborhood made headline news in the late 19C as labor strife rocked the area in 1877 and 1886. The "Battle of the Viaduct," where 30 workers were killed and 200 injured near 16th and Halsted Streets, took place here during the Great Railroad Strike of 1877. West of Damen Avenue, the district known as "Heart of Chicago" developed around the McCormick (later International Harvester) plant at 27th Street and Western Avenue. Here, enclaves of Germans and Poles, and later Italians and Jews, settled and worked in McCormick's factory. As the Bohemian immigrants prospered, they moved to the Lawndale community west of California Avenue, called "Czech California" by the early 20C, when Chicago had the third largest population of Czechs in the world after Prague and Vienna. The neighborhood produced Mayor **Anton Cermak**, and 22nd Street was renamed Cermak Road nine days after his 1933 assassination.

In the 1950s Pilsen became the entrepôt for Mexican immigrants in Chicago. In the ensuing decades they followed their Bohemian predecessors, moving west along the river, and by the 1970s, Czech California had been renamed *Pueblo Pequeño*, or "Little Village." The area continues to harbor Mexican and South American immigrants, who today make up close to 20 percent of the city's population.

SIGHTS

This area is best seen by car. Take the 18th St. Exit from I-90/I-94 and continue west along 18th St.

18th Street – The main thoroughfare in Pilsen, 18th Street (between Morgan Street and Ashland Avenue) is lined with 1870s and 1880s Second Empire commercial buildings distinguished by mansard roofs and elaborate window moldings. The limestone St. Procopius Church (1883), at Allport Street, faces the massive, Romanesque-style **Thalia Hall**, one of numerous community centers erected by Bohemians in the late 19C. At the intersection of 18th and Loomis Streets and Blue Island Avenue (southeast corner), immortalized in the Carl Sandburg poem "Blue Island Intersection," the **Rudy Lozano Branch Library** stands out with its lively frieze of decorative tile recalling pre-Columbian monuments in Mitla, Oaxaca. At Bishop Street, note the **Francis D. Nemecek Studio** *(1439 W. 18th St.)* with its corner tower and sloped skylight.

To the northwest, twin towers rising 185ft flank the Renaissance Revival facade of **St. Adalbert Catholic Church** *(1656 W. 17th St.)*, designed in 1914 by Henry J. Schlacks.

① Nuevo Leon

Map p 179. 1515 W. 18th
St. ☎ 312-421-1517. Named
for the area of Mexico where
the owners grew up, this tile-
decorated restaurant is
known for serving some of
the best food in Pilsen. The
menu ranges from tacos,
burritos and nachos to
less well-known Mexican
delicacies like *cesos* (beef
brains) and *menudo* (tripe
soup). Be sure to try one
of the dishes prepared with
mole sauce, which is flavored
with the surprisingly delicious
combination of chocolate and
hot peppers.

Mexican Fine Arts Center Museum

– 1852 W. 19th St., in Harrison Park.
Open year-round Tue–Sun 10am–5pm.
Closed major holidays. ♿ ☎ 312-738-
1503. www.mfacmchicago.org. The
largest institution of its kind in the US,
this respected ethnic center is best
known for its Day of the Dead (Nov)
exhibits featuring visiting Mexican artists
at work. Two large galleries sponsor activities ranging from fine arts exhibits by
such artists as Remedios Varos to performances and community meetings. A
new 33,000sq ft addition, scheduled to
open in spring 2001, will provide space
to display more of the permanent
collection as well as to host traveling exhibitions.

South of the museum and west of
Damen Avenue, the Heart of Chicago
neighborhood was settled by Germans
who erected **St. Matthew Lutheran Church**
(2100 W. 21st St.) in 1888, and **St. Paul Catholic Church** (2234 S. Hoyne Ave.) nine
years later.

Heart of Italy/Little Village – Extending south from 23rd Street, Oakley Avenue
boasts a small Italian district—called Heart of Italy—that draws its multi-ethnic
neighbors to a variety of intimate restaurants and cafes.
West of California Avenue, 22nd and 26th Streets form the busy commercial spine
of the Hispanic Little Village neighborhood. Colorful flags and banners flutter above
26th Street, known as **Calle Mexico**. Note the pink stucco arch (1987, Adrian
Lozano), topped by a red-tile roof, spanning the street between Albany and Troy
Streets.

NEAR SOUTH SIDE

Maps pp 186 and 187

One of Chicago's oldest areas extends from 16th Street south to Washington Park along the lakefront. Primarily African-American today, the area encompasses grand mansions on Prairie Avenue and Martin Luther King, Jr. Drive as well as poverty-stricken high rises lining the Dan Ryan Expressway. Marked by large swaths of urban renewal and pockets of gentrified historic homes, the Near South Side is full of the contradictions and color of a mature urban environment.

Historical Notes

From Prairie to Prairie Avenue – In 1835 New York merchant Henry Clarke acquired 20 acres of prairie land in the Near South Side and the following year he built a lakefront home at Michigan Avenue between 16th and 17th Streets, not far from the site the house occupies today. However, the area remained sparsely settled for several decades.

In 1852 politician Stephen A. Douglas developed a 70-acre lakefront tract north of 35th Street, which included the first University of Chicago, opened in 1859 (and closed in 1886). Douglas' famed 1858 debates with Abraham Lincoln led to his election as senator. During the Civil War, his widow donated land for Camp Douglas, which held prisoners of war. Douglas lies buried near his homesite in a massive stone tomb *(636 E. 35th St.)*.

When the 1871 fire destroyed the central city, Chicago's most prominent families moved south to develop a "Millionaire's Row" along Prairie Avenue between 16th and 20th Streets. On "the sunny street of the sifted few" lived industrial and commercial leaders Marshall Field and George Pullman, among others, in mansions designed by architects such as Richard Morris Hunt, Burnham & Root and H.H. Richardson. From 1872 to 1900 Prairie Avenue was the city's most fashionable address. In contrast, State Street between 16th and 22nd Streets became the notorious **Levee**, an area of saloons and brothels. A small African-American community occupied a thin belt of land on Federal Street south of 22nd Street (later called the Black Belt), while Irish Catholic and German Jewish immigrants developed prosperous middle-class communities along Grand and Drexel Boulevards.

Bootleg and Boogie – The establishment of four of Chicago's six major railroad terminals on the south side of the Loop after 1885 benefited the saloons, gaming dens and brothels of the Levee and drove many respectable families away from Prairie Avenue. The wealthy movers and shakers gravitated north to the Gold Coast, following Potter Palmer's lead. Finally, the Levee grew too outrageous even for the city, which shut it down in 1915. Throughout the Near South Side, residential uses gave way to warehousing and industry that pushed south from the train stations all the way to 22nd Street.

The 1920s witnessed the rise of bootlegging mobster **Al Capone** (1899-1947), headquartered in the Lexington Hotel, and the rapid expansion of the Black Belt, as the Great Migration of 1914-30 brought thousands of blacks to the area from the American South in search of jobs. By the late 1920s, a "black metropolis" thrived around 35th and State Streets, as African-American entrepreneurs built retail and service industries and black entertainers such as Louis Armstrong and Jelly Roll Morton turned Chicago into a renowned center for jazz and blues. As the Irish and German Jews settled farther south, middle-class blacks moved in and occupied the mansions and row houses of Grand Boulevard, while their poorer brethren filled the Federal Street slums, stretching from 22nd to 54th Streets.

Rebuilding – If decline hit the South Side first, so did renewal. Arriving in 1937, German refugee **Ludwig Mies van der Rohe** instituted a new campus plan for the Illinois Institute of Technology (IIT) that eliminated a half-mile stretch of slums along State Street, Wabash and Michigan Avenues south of 30th Street. By the 1940s Michael Reese Hospital and IIT began an urban renewal plan, which would replace acres of derelict housing with modern town houses and high rises. The redevelopment continued into the 1960s as middle-class apartments were erected along the lakefront north of 35th Street, and several public-housing high rises replaced the Federal Street slum. By 1966 industrial growth had caused the demolition of most of Prairie Avenue's once-proud mansions. Following a public outcry that year, the Glessner House was saved from the wrecking ball by the fledgling Chicago Architecture Foundation, and a Chicago Landmark District was created in 1979, preserving the remaining mansions. A pocket of homes untouched by urban renewal and known as The Gap has been restored by middle-class blacks, who are also maintaining the mansions along King Drive (former Grand Boulevard) and promoting the Black Metropolis Historic District in an effort to preserve the region's cultural and architectural heritage.

SIGHTS

It is best to tour the Near South Side by car. The Black Metropolis driving tour travels through a great variety of neighborhoods, not all of which will feel welcoming to the visitor. Travel on foot should be undertaken only by those familiar with the area. In addition to the driving tour, the Near South Side encompasses the Prairie Avenue Historic District and the Illinois Institute of Technology. Directions for each area are given from the Loop.

★PRAIRIE AVENUE HISTORIC DISTRICT

Drive south from the Loop on Michigan Ave., turn left at 18th St. and continue two blocks to Prairie Ave. (no through traffic).

Caught between the industrial wasteland south of the Loop and the mammoth McCormick Place Convention Center, the Prairie Avenue Historic District between 18th and 20th Streets preserves a sampling of Chicago's prestigious homes from the late 19C, highlighted by the city's two most historically significant house museums.

★**Henry B. Clarke House** – *1855 S. Indiana Ave. Visit by guided tour (1hr) only, year-round Wed–Sun noon–3pm. Closed major holidays. $6 ($11 for both Glessner & Clarke Houses). Tours depart from Glessner House.* ♿ ☎ *312-326-1480.* Built in 1836, this white clapboard home is considered Chicago's oldest structure. The spacious, two-story residence boasts a Doric temple entrance characteristic of the Greek Revival style; grand, 9ft-high triple-sash windows, tiny "frieze windows" and a central hall plan further illustrate the style. In the 1850s an Italianate cupola was added to the cross-gabled roof. The sturdy mortise-and-tenon timber frame construction has allowed the house to be moved twice—in 1872 and 1977.

Inside, period furnishings, artifacts and faithful reproductions of floor, wall and window coverings represent the Clarkes' occupation of the home from 1836 to 1872. Completed in the 1850s, the southern parlors exemplify the Italianate style with brilliant ceiling medallions, pocket doors and a Chickering piano. The upstairs bedrooms feature a marvelous sleigh bed and coal stove along with period toys, china and samplers. The basement contains a reconstructed kitchen and an exhibition gallery displaying photographs, artifacts and models that document the building's history and restoration.

★★**John Jacob Glessner House** – *1800 S. Prairie Ave. Visit by guided tour (1hr, only, year-round Wed–Sun 1pm–4pm. Closed major holidays. $6 ($11 for both Glessner & Clarke Houses).* ☎ *312-326-1480.* Designed by **Henry Hobson Richardson** in 1886, the Glessner House revolutionized domestic American architecture with its open floor plan and unadorned Romanesque facades. Richardson, whose work influenced that of both Louis Sullivan and Frank Lloyd Wright, combined Medieval Renaissance and American Colonial elements in designing the exterior. The fortresslike house turned its back on the street to focus on an inner courtyard making it the first modern urban home. At the time, its spare exterior shocked

John Jacob Glessner House

many Prairie Avenue inhabitants. The house was commissioned by Glessner, a manufacturer of farm implements who lived on the tony Near West Side until the Haymarket Riot occurred there in 1886, spreading fear of labor anarchy and spurring Glessner to move to Prairie Avenue.

The **interior★** is organized in an L-shape around a sunny southern courtyard. Heavy beamed ceilings (Richardson purposely bowed the beams to create an antique appearance) and a wealth of Arts and Crafts details, including wall and tile patterns by William Morris and furniture by local artist Isaac Scott, exemplify the Medieval motif. Over 80 percent of the items displayed were originally owned by the Glessners, and restoration has been guided by their profuse documentation and period photos of each room. Focal point of the house, the **library** contains a large sampling of the Glessners' extensive book, print and ceramics collections. In the music room, note the Steinway piano in a Francis Bacon case. The second-floor hall features a walnut Isaac Scott bookcase with Gothic arches and buttresses. The main bedroom has been exactingly restored down to the William Morris tiles, draperies, upholstery and carpet.

Across Prairie Avenue stand the **Kimball House** *(no. 1801)* and **Coleman-Ames House** *(no. 1811)*, both now headquarters of the US Soccer Federation. In 1896 railroad magnate George Pullman, wary of any more "modern" houses on Prairie Avenue, convinced piano and organ manufacturer W.W. Kimball to hire his architect, Solon S. Beman. The result is a highly ornate French Châteauesque house with crested turrets and elaborate carvings in limestone. The more restrained Coleman-Ames House was designed in 1886 by Cobb & Frost in the Romanesque Revival style.

To the south, the street leads past plaques depicting homes demolished before the Chicago Landmark District was created in 1979. Within the Hillary Clinton Memorial Park near Clarke House stands an 1893 **statue (1)** commemorating the 1812 Fort Dearborn Massacre. Also open to the public is the first floor of the 1870 **Elbridge Keith House** *(no. 1900; open year-round Wed–Fri noon–7pm, weekends noon–4pm; closed major holidays; 1hr guided tours available, reservations required; www.womanmade.org; ☎ 312-328-0038)*, where the Womanmade Gallery exhibits contemporary art. The derelict **Marshall Field, Jr. House** *(no. 1919)* still awaits restoration of its 44-room grandeur.

Farther west on Michigan Avenue, **Second Presbyterian Church** (1874) was designed by James Renwick and features Tiffany stained-glass windows.

Around the corner from Glessner House—and a million miles from the bygone gentility of Prairie Avenue—the **National Vietnam Veterans Art Museum** houses a powerful collection of more than 700 works by over 130 veterans of the war in Southeast Asia *(1801 S. Indiana Ave.; open year-round Tue–Fri 11am–6pm, Sat 10am–5pm, Sun noon–5pm; closed major holidays; $5; ☎ 312-326-0270; www.nvvam.org; due to the graphic nature of much of the art, this museum is not recommended for children)*. While intensely personal, the paintings, drawings and sculpture, poetry, prose and photographs speak universally to the horrors of war and its effect on mind, body and memory. Still a work in progress, the building provides an appropriately restrained backdrop for the exhibit. Note the strong figurative paintings by Ned Broderick (a founding member of the museum) and Richard Yohnka. Displays of military equipment, such as a Russian AK47 and a Chinese 122mm rocket launcher, lend a chilling dimension to the emotionally charged works that fill this museum.

 The Velvet Lounge
Map p 186. 2128 1/2 S. Indiana Ave. ☎ 312-791-9050. Blink and you'll miss this wonderful little club, which offers excellent jazz Thursday through Sunday nights. Acclaimed saxophonist Fred Anderson owns the place and plays in the legendary Sunday night jam sessions. During the annual Chicago Jazz Festival, players from around the world gather here for impromptu concerts.

BLACK METROPOLIS DRIVING TOUR *Distance: 8.1mi*
Drive south from the Loop on Michigan Ave. to 21st St.

This tour cuts a path through various South Chicago neighborhoods documenting black history in the city, and ends at a museum that pays tribute to African-American culture.

The former **Chess Records Studio** *(2120 S. Michigan Ave., between 21st and 22nd Sts.)* is an unassuming building (1911) sporting a 1957 storefront. Chuck Berry recorded "Johnny B. Goode" in this studio that helped define rhythm and blues with legends such as Howlin' Wolf, Bo Diddley and the Flamingos. The building is being refurbished by the Willie Dixon's Blues Heaven Foundation, which the song-writer/bassist established before his death in 1992, as an archive of Chicago Blues music, a revamped studio, and offices for the foundation.

Continue south on Michigan Ave.

Known as "Automobile Row," a series of early automobile showrooms (1910-30) are now primarily warehouses. Colorful terra-cotta facades reveal the logos of one-time brands such as Packard, Premier and Hupmobile, as well as survivors like Chevrolet. The Mediterranean-style **Chicago Defender Building** *(southwest corner of Michigan Ave. and 24th St.)* originally housed the Illinois Automobile Club.

Turn right on 24th St.

★**Quinn Chapel African Methodist Episcopal Church** – *2401 S. Wabash Ave. Open year-round Mon–Fri 10am–6pm, Sat by appointment only. Guided tour (20min) available, reservations required.* ⬧ ▯ ☎ *312-791-1846*. This lovely limestone chapel (1892, Henry Starbuck) was built by blacks before they constituted a sig-nificant portion of the population. The site, at the time located in a middle-class white neighborhood, was purchased by a fair-skinned member of the congrega-tion who could "pass" for white, thereby avoiding community opposition.

Continue west on 24th St., turn left on State St., and then left on 26th St.

26th Street passes underneath the Jackson Park elevated train line, the oldest in Chicago. Opened in 1893 to link the Loop with the World's Columbian Exposition, the line was known as the "Alley L" since its right-of-way was carved through back alleys. Located east of Michigan Avenue are the Mercy Hospital and Medical Center and Michael Reese Hospital, institutions created a century ago by the Irish Catholic and German Jewish communities respectively.

Turn right on Martin Luther King, Jr. Dr.

This boulevard is dominated on the east by the **Prairie Shores** and **Lake Meadows** devel-opments extending south to 35th Street. These tall, white and blue-green pastel buildings, set at an angle to the street, were planned as integrated middle-class housing in a massive, and largely suc-cessful, urban-renewal effort. To the east at 31st Street, note the **Olivet Baptist Church**★, built as First Baptist Church in 1873 by Wilcox & Miller. The edifice is now home to one of Chicago's oldest African-American congregations, which dates back to 1853.

Turn right on 31st St. and left immedi-ately on Calumet Ave.

The cluster of Victorian houses south of 31st Street was named The Gap because it was untouched by urban renewal ef-forts to the north, west and east. In the 1980s the restored homes earned land-mark status as the **Calumet-Giles-Prairie District** ★. Of note on Calumet Avenue are several lovely Romanesque Revival gray-stones on the left, a Victorian-style build-ing (1887) by Adler & Sullivan at **no. 3141**, as well as limestone row houses on the right, such as **nos. 3144-48**. South of 32nd Street on the left stand the only row houses designed by Frank Lloyd Wright, the landmark **Robert Rolosom Houses** ★ *(nos. 3213-19)*, built in 1894

② **The Clique**

Map p 186. 2347 S. Michigan Ave. ☎ *312-326-0274.* This three-story nightclub caters to Chicago's upscale African Americans. Stand-up comics, jazz combos and singers entertain in the posh, first-floor lounge. Gyrate to house music upstairs on the club's spacious dance floor. Keep an eye on the surrounding balcony for celebrities watching the action from the exclusive VIP area. Dress sharp, especially on weekends when the bouncers pick and choose who gets in and who stays on the sidewalk.

just after Wright left the office of Adler & Sullivan. Sullivan's influence is seen in the large, foliate, terra-cotta panels around the center of the uncharacteristically tall and narrow gabled facades. At no. 3322, the **Clarence Knight House** (1891) is a unique composition by Flanders & Zimmerman in orange stone and Roman brick.

"Then there was the fabulous city in which Bigger lived, an indescribable city, huge, roaring, dirty, noisy, raw, stark, brutal; a city of extremes: torrid summers and subzero winters, white people and black people, the English language and strange tongues, foreign born and native born, scabby poverty and gaudy luxury, high idealism and hard cynicism! A city so young that, in thinking of its short history, one's mind, as it travels backwards in time, is stopped abruptly by the barren stretches of wind-swept prairie! But a city old enough to have caught within the homes of its long, straight streets the symbols and images of man's age-old destiny, of truths as old as the mountains and seasons, of dramas as abiding as the soul of man itself."

Richard Wright, *How Bigger Was Born,* 1939

Continue south on Calumet Ave., turn right on 35th St. and then right again on Indiana Ave.

Seven buildings located on or near 35th Street comprise the recently created **Black Metropolis Historic District**, which commemorates the cultural flowering during the Great Migration. As the community grew, it developed its own commerce, industry and culture, isolated by racism from the rest of the city. These buildings are unique because many were not inherited from other ethnic groups, but financed and built by African-American capital.

One of the seven buildings is located at **3435 South Indiana Avenue**, a three-story buff brick structure that served as headquarters of the *Chicago Defender* from 1921 to 1960 and today houses the Second Ward Regular Democratic Organization. Founded in 1905, the influential African-American newspaper is credited with starting the Great Migration; rousing editorials, written by Robert Sengstacke Abbott, extolled Chicago's opportunities, calling for a "New Exodus."

The **Pilgrim Baptist Church**★ *(open during services only)* has existed at the southeast corner of 33rd Street and Indiana Avenue since 1926, but the present landmark edifice was designed 36 years earlier by Adler & Sullivan for Chicago's oldest Jewish congregation, K.A.M., founded in 1846. Adler's skill at designing auditoriums and Sullivan's irrepressible decorative talents combined—as they had in the Auditorium Building—to create a stunning assembly space.

To the west lies the campus of the Illinois Institute of Technology.

Pilgrim Baptist Church, Interior

Bob Thall

Turn right on 33rd St. and right on Giles St.

Giles Street was named after Lt. George Giles of the "Fighting Eighth," a black regiment formed from the community at the turn of the century. The **Eighth Regiment Armory** (1915) stretches on the left side of Giles Avenue south of 35th Street. This landmark of the Black Metropolis was restored in 1999 as Chicago Military Academy, the only public high school offering military-style education in Chicago.

Turn left at 35th St. and continue to Martin Luther King, Jr. Dr.

Grand Boulevard was developed in the 19C as an elite residential area, part of a 28mi ring of city boulevards. Known later as South Parkway, it was renamed in 1968 for the late Dr. Martin Luther King, Jr. **Victory Monument** (1928, Leonard Crunelle), the first dedicated to African-American soldiers, honors those of the "Fighting Eighth" who fought in World War I.

Turn right on King Dr., staying to the right to drive along the frontage road of the boulevard.

At no. 3624, the **Ida B. Wells House**★ was named a National Historic Landmark in 1973 in honor of the civil rights leader who lived here from 1919 to 1929. Wells, one of the first to document lynching in the US, moved to Chicago in 1893 to continue a lifelong crusade against racism and sexism. The 1889 Romanesque Revival home features a pressed-metal corner turret. Built in 1886 the **Charles H. Nichols House**

③ Checkerboard Lounge

Maps pp 186 and 187. 423 E. 43rd St. (valet parking available) ☎ *773-624-3240.* In the 1950s, 43rd Street was lined with nightclubs; today, only this popular joint remains. The South Side's preeminent blues club presents live music four nights a week. A wall of memorabilia honors Muddy Waters—who brought the Mississippi Delta Blues to Chicago—and other local blues legends.

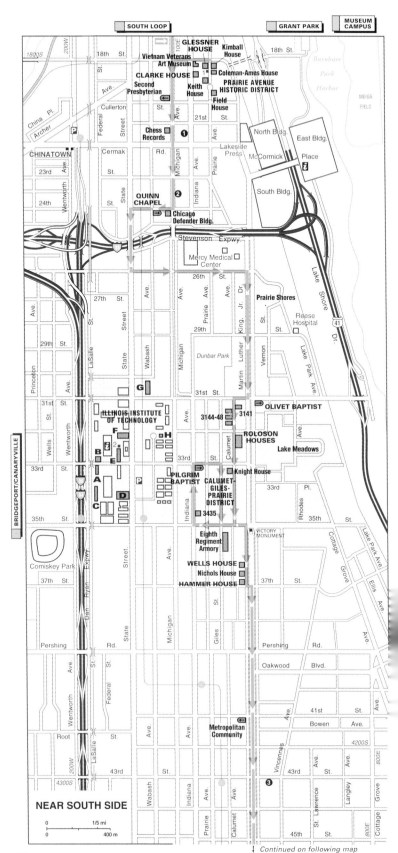

NEAR SOUTH SIDE

0 1/5 mi
0 400 m

Continued on following map

(no. 3630) is distinguished by rough-faced Romanesque arches enlivened by Queen Anne oriels. The orange brick and brownstone **D. Harry Hammer House** ★ *(no. 3656)* pounds the corner of 37th Street with massive ostentation. Exuberant detailing in terra-cotta, copper and stained glass enlivens this 1885 design by William W. Clay.

Continue south on the main roadway of King Dr.

At the southwest corner of 41st Street stands the **Metropolitan Community Church** (1891, John T. Long), originally 41st Street Presbyterian Church, a Romanesque Revival edifice featuring a large corner tower and gabled facade. 43rd Street bears the honorary name of legendary blues artist Muddy Waters, who lived to the east on Lake Park Avenue.

Just south of 46th Street, the **Mt. Pisgah Missionary Baptist Church** ★ occupies the large Sinai Temple designed by Alfred Alschuler in 1910. At 49th Street, note the Renaissance-style towers of **Corpus Christi Church** (1916), noted for its high-quality stained glass by the F.X. Zettler company of Munich.

At 51st Street, a large equestrian statue of **George Washington** (1904, Daniel Chester French and Edward Clark Potter) marks the entrance to Washington Park.

Turn left on 51st St. and continue to Cottage Grove Ave.

Provident Hospital of Cook County, to the left, one of the first founded by and for blacks, was established in 1891 by Dr. Daniel Hale Williams, who on July 9, 1893, became the first physician to perform successful open-heart surgery.

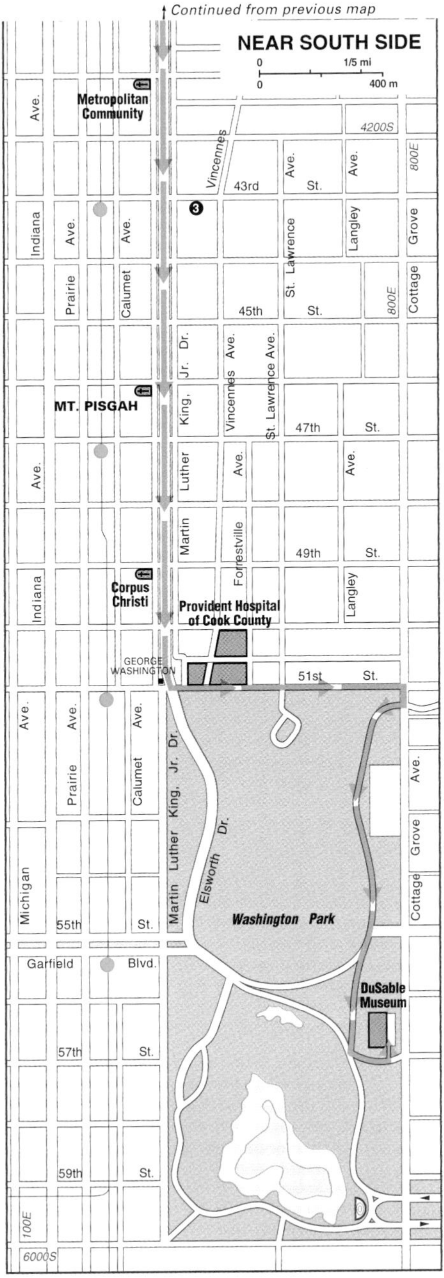

Turn right on Cottage Grove Ave. and right again immediately on Payne Dr., which enters Washington Park.

Designed in 1871 by Frederick Law Olmsted and Calvert Vaux, **Washington Park** is connected to its southern neighbor, Jackson Park, by the Midway Plaisance. The vast, 100-acre meadow covering the park's northern section was originally mown by sheep, kept in the park for this purpose.

Bear to the left at the fork at 55th St. to access the DuSable Museum.

DuSable Museum of African-American History – *740 E. 56th Pl. Open year-round Mon–Sat 10am–5pm, Sun noon–5pm. Closed Jan 1, Thanksgiving Day & Dec 25. $3 (free Sun).* ♿ 🅿 ☎ *773-947-0600. www.dusablemuseum.org.* Founded in 1961 by Dr. Margaret Goss Burroughs in her home, this cultural and historical museum now occupies a former park administration building (1910, D.H. Burnham & Co.). The modern Harold Washington Wing, added to the structure's south side in 1992, houses educational and cultural programs that supplement permanent and traveling exhibits on African-American life and history.

↑ *Continued from previous map*

NEAR SOUTH SIDE

0   1/5 mi
0   400 m

HYDE PARK/KENWOOD

UNIVERSITY OF CHICAGO

187

■ **Chinatown**

Every major city in the US seems to have a Chinatown. Located at the inter-section of 22nd and Wentworth Streets, Chicago's dates from the 1910s, when Chinese immigrants filled in a tiny neighborhood between the Black Belt on the east, Irish and Italian communities to the south and an indus-trial area to the north and east along the South Branch of the river. By the 1920s Chinese architectural forms appeared in the district, which has become a popular dining destination for locals and tourists alike.

The entrance arch spanning Wentworth Avenue was erected in the 1970s and features giant ideograms, dragons and other traditional designs shel-tered by red-tile rooftops. Buildings of interest along Wentworth include the **Puitak Center** (formerly the On Leong Merchants' Association Building) at no. 2216, with its prominent corner pagodas, balconies and colorful terra-cotta tile decoration. **Woks 'n Things** (no. 2234; ☎ 312-842-0701) sells its namesake pans along with a wide variety of cookware, as well as a fasci-nating assemblage of intricate vegetable- and cookie-cutters. The **Emperor's Choice Restaurant** (no. 2238; ☎ 312-225-8800), with its green and white terra-cotta facade enlivened by twisted snake columns, serves everything from egg rolls to spicy ducks' feet, while **The Mandar Inn** (no. 2249; ☎ 312-842-4014) specializes in Mandarin cuisine.

On the first floor of the old wing, you'll find a time line of African-American history from the slave trade to the civil rights movement through exhibits that rotate every six months. An exhibit of art and artifacts, assembled from the museum's perma-nent collection, includes works by 20C painter Archibald Motley and 20C sculptor Joseph Kersey. The second floor hosts traveling exhibits. The museum maintains an active theater and cultural agenda (call for schedule and tickets).

★**ILLINOIS INSTITUTE OF TECHNOLOGY (IIT)** Map p 186.

Drive south from the Loop on State St. to 33rd St., turn left and park in the IIT Visitor Parking Lot.

Unique in both design and curriculum, IIT fills a campus that largely realizes the plan of master Modernist **Ludwig Mies van der Rohe** (1886-1969), who came to direct the institute's architecture school in 1937 after fleeing Nazi Germany. The institute, formed in 1940 by the merger of the Armour and Lewis Institutes, has garnered an international reputation for excellence in the fields of tech-nology and design. Today the institute enrolls more than 6,000 students, who attend classes on the 120-acre campus (bounded by 30th St. on the north, the Dan Ryan Expwy. on the west, Michigan Ave. on the east and 35th St. on the south).

In 1999 Dutch architect Rem Koolhas—known for his deconstructivist, collage-style buildings—won an international competition to design a new campus center, thus sowing the seeds of potential conflict between Mies van der Rohe's orderly design of the landmark campus and Koolhas' sassy post-Modernism. The future campus center, which will straddle and enclose the elevated train in a steel tube, is slated for completion in 2002.

Visit – Stop at the information center in Hermann Hall, 3241 S. Federal St., for brochures and self-guided tour maps (open mid-Aug–late May Sun–Wed 8am–mid-night, Thurs–Sat 8am–1am; rest of the year Mon–Thu 7am–8pm, Fri–Sat 8am–5pm; closed academic holidays). ☎ 312-567-3075. www.iit.edu. Located at Federal and 33rd Streets, the **Main Building★** (**A**) (1891, Patton, Fisher & Miller) epitomizes the Romanesque Revival style; note in particular the lower stories faced in rough brownstone, the red-brick upper floors, the windows framed with round arches and the gabled dormers punctuating the roof. Across 33rd Street stands the simpler **Machinery Hall** (**B**), erected 10 years later by the same firm.

Mies' first construction for the institute, the 1943 **IIT Research Institute Materials Technology Building** (**C**), illustrates the central principle behind his campus design: a "module" of 24ftx24ftx12ft "blocks" that comprise both the buildings and the spaces between them. This concept has been thoroughly carried out—almost all the campus buildings employ the module in structures of steel, concrete, glass and pale yellow brick. There is said to be only one curving wall on the entire campus! Headquarters of IIT's architecture school, **S.R. Crown Hall★★** (**D**) is the capital achievement of both the campus and Mies van der Rohe, eloquently expressing his philosophy of design, materials, purpose and proportion. Calling it a "representa-tional building" on campus, Mies here abandoned his "module" to create a simple glass-walled pavilion housing a singular space 220ft wide, 120ft deep and 18ft high. The 1956 structure appears to hover above the ground, its flat roof suspended from four huge I-beams that wrap around the building. Entered on floating travertine steps, the building defines space by its structure, stripping away ornament without losing the humanizing effects of proportion and enclosure.

The three-story concrete and brick **Wishnick Hall** (**E**) (1946, Mies van der Rohe) became the standard for academic buildings on campus. Just north of this hall, note the George Segal statue, *Man on a Bench* (**2**). Farther north stands **Alumni Memorial Hall** (**F**) (1946, Mies van der Rohe), framed in steel with large glass windows. Here, as in many other Miesian campus buildings, the yellow bricks form a skin over the frame, but pull back at the corners to hint at the building's true skeleton.

At Wabash Avenue, the **Keating Sports Center** (**G**) (1966, Skidmore, Owings & Merrill) seems set upon an invisible podium, but its walls are sheer glass, hiding the structural steel beneath. **Carr Memorial Chapel** (**H**) is the only church designed by Mies. Known as the "God box," this nondenominational chapel features a glass facade on the east and west, and brick walls on the remaining sides.

BRIDGEPORT/CANARYVILLE

Red line to 35th St.
Map p 191

Dotted with churches, this small neighborhood of quiet streets and modest bungalows is flanked to the west and south by large industrial concentrations occupying the site of the former Union Stock Yards district. Settled by Irish canal workers in the 1830s, the community became the focal point of Chicago politics in the 20C.

Historical Notes

From Canal Town to Cow Town – In the 1830s the small trading post of Hardscrabble, located at the south fork of the South Branch of the Chicago River, mushroomed with construction of the Illinois & Michigan Canal, which connected the Great Lakes to the Mississippi River. Irish workers settled the town north of 31st Street and renamed it for the port area around the Ashland Avenue Bridge. Grain elevators and lumberyards developed on the river edge as thousands of immigrants harvested the prairies of Illinois and the forests of Michigan. In 1853 Bridgeport was annexed to the City of Chicago.

Slaughterhouses that had sprung up in the 1840s along the South Fork of the river were consolidated in 1865 into the great Union Stock Yards, which supplied meat to the world for over a century. Gustavus Swift, Philip Armour, Arthur and Charles Libby and other meat

"...men and women and children bending over whirling machines and sawing bits of bone into all sorts of shapes, breathing their lungs full of fine dust, and doomed to die, every one of them, within a certain definite time."
Upton Sinclair, *The Jungle*, 1906

barons pioneered the refrigerated railcar, and made their fortunes in the industry that earned Chicago the nickname of "hog butcher of the world": in 1892 alone, 2.5 million cattle and 5 million hogs were slaughtered in Chicago, and some 30,000 people worked in the stockyards. The districts of Canaryville, south of Bridgeport, and Back of the Yards, to the west, filled with insalubrious, crowded tenements, while the South Fork of the river became known as "Bubbly Creek" for the gases released by the decomposing animal carcasses floating along it. The area literally stank, drawing the attention of urban reformers such as **Upton Sinclair**, whose 1906 book *The Jungle* exposed the horrors of the industry and led to the adoption of the Pure Food and Drug Act. In 1905 the nation's first industrial park, the Central Manufacturing District (East District), was created at 35th Street between Morgan Street and Ashland Avenue, adding more manufacturers to the sooty environs.

Rise of the Political Machine – Italian, German, Polish, Lithuanian and Slovakian immigrants piled into the neighborhood as the century progressed, but the clannish Irish remained dominant through their rapid integration into the public service, which they parlayed into an effective political organization in the early 20C. In 1933 Bridgeport native Ed Kelly was appointed mayor following the assassination of Anton Cermak. A Bridgeport politician would hold the office until 1979, providing employment for and preserving the isolation and segregation of the community. Mayor for 21 years, political "Boss" **Richard J. Daley** lived his entire life on Lowe Avenue. His son Richard M. Daley is the fifth mayor hailing from Bridgeport, although he has resided in the Central Station development since 1993. The community's power has gradually declined with the dismantling of the city's political Machine. Chinese Americans, spilling over from neighboring Chinatown, and Mexican Americans, who moved in after World War II, now comprise a large portion of increasingly polyglot Bridgeport, which retains a quiet, small-town ambience.

3 Healthy Food

Map p 191. 3236 S. Halsted St. ☎ 312-326-2724.
Traditional folk art decorates the walls of this pleasant restaurant. The menu offers a mix of Lithuanian specialties, vegetarian entrées and good, old-fashioned American home cooking. Try the *kugelis* (potato dumplings filled with meat) or *blynais* (pancakes served with sour cream), then finish your meal with a slice of delicious, fresh pie.

SIGHTS

To visit sights in Bridgeport, drive south on I-90/I-94 and exit at 31st St. Continue west to the intersection with Halsted St.

Busy, urban **Halsted Street** forms the commercial heart of the community. The more prosperous section of Bridgeport lies to the east along streets such as Emerald and Lowe, lined with early-20C brick homes, bungalows and newer ranch houses. The oldest section occupies the northern triangle, anchored by Archer Avenue, while the area west of Halsted boasts numerous churches and narrow houses inhabited today mainly by Hispanics, Poles and some Lithuanians along Lituanica Avenue.

One of Chicago's oldest roads, **Archer Avenue** was built in 1836 by Col. William Archer to supply the Illinois & Michigan Canal. Italianate storefronts at **nos. 2727** and **2731** and a pre-fire cottage at **no. 2815** suggest the canal era. The old canal was partially replaced by the Sanitary & Ship Canal and the Chicago section later filled in for the Stevenson Expressway. Today, the giant trailer-truck warehouses flanking the expressway serve as way stations for goods shipped via rail, road or water. The huge barges plying the Sanitary & Ship are direct descendants of the narrow canal boats that first made Chicago a commercial power.

Burnham & Root designed the **Immanuel Presbyterian Church** *(1035 W. 31st St.)* in 1892; today it houses a Buddhist school. To the west, on Aberdeen Street, stands the **Monastery of the Holy Cross** *(3109 S. Aberdeen St.)*, formerly Immaculate Conception Church and Rectory, built in 1909 for German Catholics. One of the finest of Bridgeport's numerous Catholic churches is **St. Mary of Perpetual Help★** (1892, Henry Englebert), distinguished by its massive copper dome towering over the neighborhood. Located at 1035 West 32nd Street, the church occupies most of the block.

The Art Moderne **Valentine Boys & Girls Club** *(3400 S. Emerald Ave.)* was designed in 1938 by Childs & Smith. The terra-cotta entrance flanked by totem poles combines Pacific Coast Indian motifs with the sleek fluted chevrons and glass block of the International style.

Visible to the east are the bright blue rafters of the new **Comiskey Park** (1991 Hellmuth, Obata & Kassabaum). At **3536 South Lowe Avenue** stands the home of Mayor Richard J. Daley (1902-76); a police car still stands guard in front of the large but unassuming red brick bungalow (1939).

Union Stock Yards (c.1905)

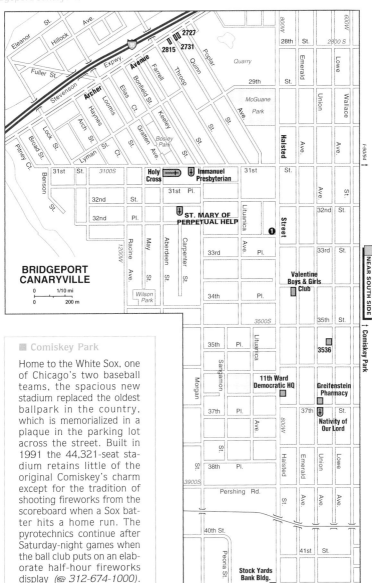

Comiskey Park

Home to the White Sox, one of Chicago's two baseball teams, the spacious new stadium replaced the oldest ballpark in the country, which is memorialized in a plaque in the parking lot across the street. Built in 1991 the 44,321-seat stadium retains little of the original Comiskey's charm except for the tradition of shooting fireworks from the scoreboard when a Sox batter hits a home run. The pyrotechnics continue after Saturday-night games when the ball club puts on an elaborate half-hour fireworks display *(☏ 312-674-1000)*.

The intersection of Union Avenue and 37th Street boasts two structures of merit. At the southeast corner stands the recently restored **Nativity of Our Lord Church** (1868), where Daley's funeral was held in 1976. The **Greifenstein Pharmacy** *(northeast corner)* has been in the same family for a century. Its classic drugstore paraphernalia includes large stoppered flasks, carved wooden screens and myriad advertising knick-knacks. Schaller's Pump *(3714 S. Halsted St.)* is an old-time Chicago tavern (1881) sited across the street from the **11th Ward Regular Democratic Headquarters**, the heart of the Machine that ran Chicago politics for most of the century. Popular legend states that political decisions were made in the smoky back rooms of Schaller's.

Drive south on Halsted St., past Pershing Rd. to visit sights in Canaryville.

At the corner of Exchange Avenue and Halsted Street, note the **Stock Yards Bank Building** (1924, A. Epstein), patterned after Philadelphia's Independence Hall. At 850 West Exchange Avenue, the **Union Stock Yards Gate★** (1879, Burnham & Root) is the sole reminder of the once flourishing industry. A steer head surmounts the large central arch, which marked the entrance to the livestock pens. The stockyards closed in 1971 and the site is now an industrial park. Farther south at 4220 South Halsted Street, the **International Amphitheater**, one of Chicago's premier convention halls for 40 years, hosted the infamous 1968 Democratic National Convention. Since the development of McCormick Place, it has fallen into decline.

Located at 4501 South Lowe Avenue, **St. Gabriel Church★** (1887, Burnham & Root), a masterful red-brick and stone Romanesque Revival design, features a square corner tower with lancet windows and massive triangular gables that seem to reach from earth to spire. The Canaryville parish has remained Irish Catholic since its founding in 1880 by Father Maurice J. Dorney, known as "King of the Yards" for ministering to packinghouse workers.

UNIVERSITY OF CHICAGO★★

Bus no. 6 (Jeffrey Express)
Map p 194

A bastion of scholarship, the University of Chicago (U of C) has spent its first century as a world leader in research and education. Called "the teacher of teachers," one in seven alumni works in education and a great number of them serve as college or university presidents or provosts. The 4,000 undergraduates and 8,000 graduate and professional students live in a world apart from the hustle and bustle of Chicago, a division reinforced by a unique physical setting covering 190 acres of Hyde Park, 8mi south of the Loop.

Historical Notes

Instant Tradition: Rockefeller Builds the University – Built on land donated by Marshall Field, the University of Chicago was founded in 1890 by the American Baptist Educational Society and oil magnate **John D. Rockefeller**, whose initial $600,000 drew $1 million from Chicago business leaders. Armed with a strong academic vision and Rockefeller's ample purse, President William Rainey Harper gathered scholars from leading schools, creating a first-rate faculty that included eight former university presidents.

Rockefeller continued to contribute—$35 million over 25 years—and pronounced the university "the best investment I ever made in my life." University of Chicago opened on October 1, 1892, not with ceremony or celebration, but by starting classes at 8:30am. Within 10 years, it was one of the nation's leading research universities.

University of Chicago from Midway Plaisance

The architecture was steeped in academic history. Trustees insisted that architect **Henry Ives Cobb**, famous for Romanesque Revival buildings such as the Newberry Library, use a late-English Gothic style, which they considered ennobling. Cobb designed 18 buildings, then passed the baton to the architectural firm of Shepley, Rutan & Coolidge. Gothic remained the style used by U of C architects until 1940. Borrowing liberally from Oxford and Cambridge, Cobb's cloistered quadrangular plan (one of the first used at an American university) guided subsequent development: four city blocks form the main campus, which is divided into six small quads grouped around a seventh central quadrangle.

The Life of the Mind – Despite its Baptist roots, the university was quite progressive, admitting women and minorities from the start. It was also rigorous: Harper established a two-year "common core curriculum," mandating that each undergraduate complete course work in physical sciences, social sciences, biology and the humanities, a program still firmly in place. Within two decades of the university's birth, U of C physicists had measured the speed of light and made other important breakthroughs in physics. By the 1920s the university's social scientists had invented modern sociology and developed the first community colleges.

From Football to Physics – In addition to academics, the university also became known for its Big Ten football team coached by Amos Alonzo Stagg, whose record of victories was surpassed only recently. The "Monsters of the Midway" dominated in the 1920s and premiered the huddle and the forward pass. The first Heisman Trophy was awarded in 1935 to U of C running back Jay Berwanger. Charismatic Robert Maynard Hutchins became president in 1929 at age 30 and instituted numerous reforms during his 22-year

---

■ Nobels at the U of C

Sixty-nine Nobel prize winners have been faculty, students or researchers at the U of C—more than at any other university. Twenty-three of the prizes have been in physics, 19 in economics, 14 in chemistry, 11 in physiology or medicine and 2 in literature, including novelist **Saul Bellow**.

The first American Nobel laureate in science was the university's **Albert A. Michaelson**, who received the award in 1907 for measuring the speed of light. Physicists **Robert Millikan** and **Arthur Compton** won in 1923 and 1927 for their pioneering work in quantum mechanics. **James Dewey Watson**, a 1962 winner, co-discovered the structure of DNA.

The school is best known for its economists, eight of whom have brought home the famed prize during their tenure as faculty members. **Milton Friedman** won in 1976. The most recent awards went to **Merton Miller, Ronald Coase, Gary Becker, Robert Fogel** and **Robert Lucas**, who won in 1990, 1991, 1992, 1993 and 1995.

University of Chicago may well boast, but its Nobelists would rather study than bask in glory. When physicist **James Cronin** won the Nobel Prize in 1980, he was asked to hold a 10am press conference. "I can't do it then," he said, "I've got a 10 o'clock class." Impressed by his dedication, the university spokesman asked what class he was teaching. "No, no," Cronin protested, "I'm not teaching a course. I'm taking Chandrasekhar's graduate course on the theory of relativity." **Subrahmanyan Chandrasekhar** won the Nobel three years later.

---

tenure. He and Mortimer Adler created a system of teaching based on the "Great Books" that is still a national model. Hutchins abolished football in 1939 because he felt it detracted from scholarship. In 1942 the unused football stands concealed the Manhattan Project laboratory of physicist **Enrico Fermi**, whose team of physicists achieved the first self-sustaining, controlled nuclear reaction. The top-secret project was the most significant step in the development of the atomic bomb and nuclear energy.

Maintaining Tradition – The university underwent a brief period in the 1930s as a hotbed of radicalism and was engaged in urban-renewal programs in the 1940s and 60s. In 1969 football returned (NCAA Division III) to U of C, and radical students occupied the Administration Building, but none of these events changed the rigorous curriculum. During the 1970s and 1980s President Hanna Gray avoided the overspending trend and maintained faculty and academic standards despite an endowment one-third the size of Harvard's. In the 1970s the university began its dominance in economics, while maintaining leadership roles in physics, sociology and Near Eastern studies. The tradition of interdisciplinary inquiry established by Harper continues today with Law School professors borrowing concepts from the university's Nobel laureate economists. The Medical School remains in the forefront of research while developing important medical techniques, especially in cancer and brain research.

WALKING TOUR *Distance: 2mi*

Maps and information are available at the University Visitors Information Desk on the 1st floor of Ida Noyes Hall (1212 E. 59th St.; open 8am–5:30pm Mon–Fri). Campus tours are available for incoming students. ☎ 773-702-1234; www.u chicago.edu.

Begin the tour at Ida Noyes Hall, 59th St. and Woodlawn Ave.

While walking through campus, watch for the innumerable gargoyles and bas-reliefs that adorn the buildings, depicting everything from invertebrate fossils to American presidents.

Ida Noyes Hall (A) – Built in 1915 (Shepley, Rutan & Coolidge) as a women's center in a Tudor Revival style, the hall is noteworthy for its finely detailed interior, in particular the beamed ceilings, wood-paneled parlors, original furnishings and a dramatic central staircase with carved monkeys on the handrails. The mural in the third-floor theater depicts "The Masque of Youth" enacted at the building's dedication. DOC Films, the oldest college film society in the US, shows films daily in the Max Palevsky Cinema. Several student organizations share the building with a pub, pool and dance studio.

Cross Woodlawn Ave. to Rockefeller Chapel.

The mile-long Midway Plaisance, designed by Frederick Law Olmsted in 1869, connects Washington and Jackson Parks and was the site of commercial side-shows during the 1893 World's Fair. Legend has it that the gargoyles on campus were designed to deter midway patrons from frequenting the university.

★ **Rockefeller Memorial Chapel** – *Open year-round daily 8am–4pm. Closed major holidays and for special events; call to confirm hours.* ♿ ☎ *773-702-2100. http://rockefeller.uchicago.edu.* Completed in 1928, the chapel was designed by Bertram G. Goodhue Assocs. and named for its donor in 1937. At 207ft, the structure remains the tallest building on campus. Embodying true Gothic principles, the brick and limestone edifice has little structural steel. The arches carry the weight of the vaulting, while the buttresses help withstand the outward thrust of the walls. Foundations 80ft deep support 32,000 tons of wall, tower and roof.

The 43ft-high nave windows composed of tracery glass in muted tones contrast with the bright cinquefoil window above the altar, added in 1979. Tall proportions draw the eye heavenward to the colored, glazed Guastavino tile ceiling, revealed in a 1988 restoration. The elaborate chancel with its organ pipes, pulpit and carved oak choir seats creates a sense of pomp for the four annual graduation ceremonies. Outdoor summer concerts feature the tower's 72-bell carillon *(late Jun–early Aug Sun 6pm)*, while other productions showcase the 103-stop E.M. Skinner organ.

Continue north on Woodlawn Ave. to 58th St.

Argentinian-born Rafael Vinoly won an architectural competition to design the new **Graduate School of Business Center** (**B**) located just south of Robie House. The center replaces a 1958 dormitory designed by Eero Saarinen.

★★ **Robie House** – *Northeast corner of Woodlawn Ave. and 58th St. (See description at the end of University text.)*

Walk west on 58th St. toward University Ave.

Chicago Theological Seminary (**C**) – Dating from 1857, this is the oldest of a cluster of seminaries in Hyde Park. The 1926 edifice (Riddle & Riddle) is composed of two wings connected by a skywalk. Visit the lovely **Hilton Memorial Chapel**

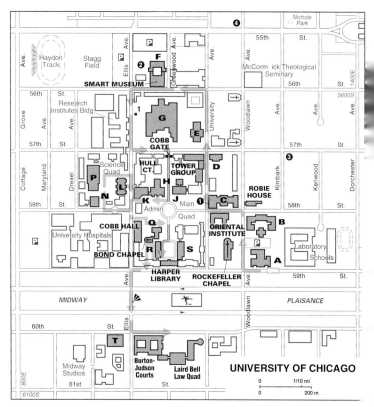

(1st floor; open year-round Mon–Fri 7am–3pm; closed major holidays; ♿ ☎ 773-752-5757) and the cloisters beneath the Lawson Tower. Scholars prize the Seminary Co-op Bookstore for its outstanding selection in the humanities and social sciences.

★★**Oriental Institute** – *1155 E. 58th St. at University Ave. After undergoing an extensive restoration, the Egyptian and Persian galleries are now open year-round Tue–Sat 10am–4pm, (Wed til 8:30pm), Sun noon–4pm. Closed Mon & major holidays. The remaining three galleries are scheduled to re-open in succession over the next several years.* ♿ ☎ *773-702-9514. www.oi.uchicago.edu/OI.* Dedicated to the study of languages, history and cultures of the Ancient Near East, this research institution is the premier authority in the dating and identification of archaeological artifacts. Its museum contains one of the world's choicest collections of Near Eastern art and antiquities. The majority of the items in the collection have been uncovered by the institute's own archaeological excavations. Since its

 Seminary Co-op

Map p 194. In Chicago Theological Seminary, lower level. ☎ *773-752-4381.* This huge, underground bookstore offering close to 100,000 volumes caters to more highbrow tastes than its sister store, 57th Street Books *(1301 E. 57th St.).* The staff is renowned for tracking down obscure and out-of-print books: in the unlikely event that they cannot locate something for you, they will happily search for it and ship it to you.

inception, the university has been a center for Near Eastern studies. Its first president, William Rainey Harper, taught Semitic languages and in 1896 set up an Ancient Near East museum close to his offices in Haskell Hall. **James Henry Breasted**, the first American to earn a PhD in Egyptology, led the university's initial field expedition to Iraq in 1904 and began excavating Egyptian and Nubian temples a year later. In 1919 he created the Oriental Institute, funded by John D. Rockefeller, Jr. Breasted was the expert sought by archaeologists in 1922 to positively identify the tomb of Tutankhamen. In 1931 the museum/research institution moved into its permanent home, designed by Mayers, Murray & Phillip in the Art Deco style. Researchers from the institute continue to excavate numerous sites and publish the definitive dictionaries of Assyrian, Demotic (Egyptian) and Hittite languages.

Collections – With more than 75,000 registered artifacts, the institute boasts extensive collections covering the Egyptian, Assyrian, Mesopotamian, Anatolian, Palestinian and Persian cultures, featuring not only tomb treasures but also domestic items such as tools, cookware and sculptor's models.

At the entrance to the recently renovated 4,000sq ft **Egyptian Gallery** looms a colossal, 18ft-high statue of King Tut. Inside, artifacts illustrate Egyptian funerary rituals with a mummy and sarcophagus from 3600 BC and an impressive collection of "tomb servants," tiny clay dolls intended to serve the deceased in the afterlife. Daily life in ancient Egypt is depicted through papyrus scrolls and furnishings, clothing and games dating back to 3000 BC.

Huge black sculptural pieces from King Xerxes' palace in Persepolis dominate the **Persian Gallery**, which claims the best collection of artifacts outside Iran. Arranged chronologically, exhibits here trace 8,000 years of Persian history from fragile 6800 BC ceramics found in Susa to 10C AD Islamic pottery. The gallery also features an excellent display highlighting the development of writing and a host of rare items excavated before the Iranian revolution.

At University Avenue, look south to the pointed Gothic spires of Foster, Kelly, Green and Beecher Halls, completed as women's dormitories in 1893, and now housing the Psychology Department. The 1971 Albert Pick Hall for International Studies suggests Gothic verticality with stonelike facing and lancet windows.

Walk north on University Ave.

★**The Tower Group** – *West side of University Ave.* Located north of Eckhart Hall (1930, Charles Z. Klauder), the Tower Group (1903, Shepley, Rutan & Coolidge) anchors the northeast corner of the main quadrangle. **Leon Mandel Hall**, a theater and assembly hall, imitates the campus chapel with its arched windows and tracery. Mitchell Tower, modeled on Oxford's Magdalen College bell tower, contains the Alice Palmer bells used for the Medieval art of "change ringing." Below the tower is Reynolds Club, a student center inspired by Oxford's St. John's College. Hutchinson Hall's design came from Oxford's Christ Church Hall and is noted for its grand dining hall featuring a hammer-beam ceiling, paneled walls, massive stone fireplaces and portraits of benefactors, including Rockefeller, Harper and Martin A. Ryerson.

The distinguished, red brick **Quadrangle Club** (**D**) *(southeast corner of University Ave. and 57th St.),* designed in 1922 by Howard Van Doren Shaw, serves the university faculty and their guests.

Cross 57th St. and continue north on University Ave.

2 Court Theatre

Map p 194. 5535 S. Ellis Ave. ☎ *773-753-4472.* Renowned for its excellent productions of Shakespeare's and Molière's works, the Court ranks with the Goodman and the Steppenwolf as one of the best theaters in the city. Its artistic board corrals Chicago's top caliber actors, production designers and directors for its five or six annual productions *(season runs fall to spring).*

Bartlett Dining Commons (E) – *Northwest corner of 57th St. and University Ave.* This 1904 gymnasium (Shepley, Rutan & Coolidge) features a striking, romantic mural by the donor's son, Frederic Clay Bartlett, and a stained-glass window depicting Ivanhoe winning a tournament. The building was renovated in 1999 as a dining hall. Built in 1932, the Crown Field House *(northwest corner of University Ave. and 56th St.)* now serves as a student gymnasium.

Continue north to 56th St. and turn left; walk west to Greenwood Ave.

The **Cochrane-Woods Arts Center (F)** (1974) contains the Art History Department and the Smart Museum. Sculptures by Richard Hunt, Henry Moore and Pomodoro frame the garden outside the entrance to the one-story, boxlike museum designed by Edward Larrabee Barnes.

★**David and Alfred Smart Museum of Art** – *5550 S. Greenwood Ave. Open year-round Tue–Fri 10am–4pm (Thu til 9pm), weekends noon–6pm. Closed Thanksgiving Day & Dec 25. Guided tours available Sun 1:30pm.* ✗ ⅙ ☎ *773-702-0200. http://smartmuseum.uchicago.edu.* Opened in 1974 and named for the founders of *Esquire* magazine, this small jewel of a university museum holds 7,500 pieces spanning 5,000 years. The Smart Museum rotates its permanent collection among the four major galleries surrounding the central Gray Special Exhibition Gallery, where the museum sponsors six to eight traveling exhibits a year.

Visit – Ranging from Greek kraters and Roman mosaics to contemporary art, the surprisingly diverse collection excels in late 19C and 20C painting, sculpture and decorative art contained in the **Landes Gallery of Early Modern Art**. Here Austrian constructivists such as Kokoschka and Archipenko signify turbulent modernity while primitive sculptures by Lipchitz and others are juxtaposed with native African folk art, from which the sculptures draw their inspiration. Paintings by Dove, Davies and du Bois lead to the decorative arts section, where furnishings, ceramics and metalware by the likes of Tiffany, Mackintosh, Rookwood and the Weiner Werkstätte give a good sense of the design revolution of the early 20C. Frank Lloyd Wright's dining room table and chairs from Robie House illustrate his attempt to create a "room within a room" by the use of high-backed chairs and corner posts with lanterns. The final section of the Landes Gallery highlights postwar Modernists, including a substantial collection of Abstract Expressionist works and pieces by Mark Rothko and Henry Moore.

In the **Arts of Asia Gallery** you'll find Shang dynasty bronze tripods, T'ang terra-cotta funerary figures, and contemplative silk and paper paintings from China, Japan and Korea. The **Old Master Gallery** hosts revolving displays from the museum's ample collection of Medieval and Renaissance works featuring masters such as Lorenzetti and Bramantino, along with religious icons and altarpieces, and sculpture and painting from the late Baroque and Neoclassical periods.

The **Contemporary Gallery** heralds the city with Chicago Imagists Ed Paschke, Karl Wirsum and Roger Brown, many of whom exhibited their work in the Hairy Who at the Hyde Park Arts Center where the colorful and disturbing Imagist movement began in the late 1960s. The tiny adjoining Bernstein Gallery features prints and drawings from Dürer to German Expressionists.

Continue west on 56th St., turn left at Ellis Ave. and walk south.

The three-ton bronze massiveness of **Nuclear Energy (1)**, a 1967 sculpture by Henry Moore, marks the site where Enrico Fermi's team of 41 scientists split the atom on December 2, 1942.

On the right, the Research Institutes Building connects to the Science Quadrangle by a skywalk across 57th Street.

Turn left on 57th St.

Hitchcock Hall *(southeast corner of 57th St. and Ellis Ave.)* was listed on the National Register of Historic Houses for its 1902 "Prairie Gothic" design by Dwight Perkins, who meshed the horizontal Prairie style with the vertical Gothic. Hitchcock and adjacent Snell Hall are the only dormitories remaining on the Main Quadrangle.

Continue east on 57th St.

Joseph Regenstein Library (G) – This massive structure holds most of the university's 5.7 million texts and 7 million other volumes. Two of its seven stories of open book stacks are below ground. The 1970 design by Walter A. Netsch, Jr.

(also responsible for the University of Illinois at Chicago) used irregular massing, vertical emphasis and setback to relate to the campus.

Continue east on 57th St. to Cobb Gate, on the right.

A gift to the university from architect Henry Ives Cobb, the ornate **Cobb Gate**★ (1900) leads into the main quadrangles. Tradition holds that the climbing gargoyles represent students struggling from their first year of college to eventual fourth-year triumph at the apex.

Gargoyles Guard Cobb Gate

★ **Hull Court** – This courtyard designed in 1897 by Henry Ives Cobb consists of the botany, anatomy, zoology and physiology buildings, joined by pleasant arcades. John C. Olmsted designed the romantic Botany Pond—allegedly the preferred site for marriage proposals—and Hutchinson Court.

Walk south through the quad.

The **Kent Chemical** (**H**) and **Ryerson Physical Laboratories** (**J**) (1894, Henry Ives Cobb) exhibit full-blown Gothic ornament, peaked dormers, crocheted finials and crenellated towers. West of Kent Hall is the **Jones Laboratory** (**K**) (1929, Coolidge & Hodgdon). A first-floor exhibit documents the weighing of plutonium in Room 405 on September 10, 1942, by Dr. Glenn T. Seaborg. To the left is the Administration Building (1948).

Walk west and return to Ellis Ave.

The University of Chicago Hospitals occupy 18 buildings covering 14 acres between 58th and 59th Streets. The largest teaching hospital in the nation is also the largest provider of indigent care in Chicago. At 58th Street is the University Bookstore (1902, Shepley, Rutan & Coolidge), distinguished by its red brick and arched windows.

Walk west on 58th St., past the bookstore, and turn right into the Science Quadrangle.

I.W. Colburn's 1969 **Henry Hinds Laboratory for the Geophysical Sciences** (**L**) and 1973 **Cummings Life Science Center** (**N**) play with Gothic ideas in limestone and red brick. The 40 red brick chimneys of Cummings ventilate laboratories requiring 20 fume hoods per floor. At the center of the quad, the four-story **John Crerar Library** (**P**) (1984, Hugh Stubbins Assocs.) holds thousands of scientific and medical texts. Step inside to view *Crystara*, an aluminum and Waterford crystal sculpture by John David Mooney, which refracts light into the atrium. The terraced glass walls of the Samuel Kersten, Jr. Physics Teaching Center (1985; Holabird & Root, Harold H. Hellman) facing the Science Quadrangle contrast with the more traditional limestone facade on Ellis Avenue.

Return to Ellis Ave., walk south to the Administration Building and reenter the main quadrangles.

★ **Cobb Hall** – Classes began October 1, 1892, in this building (1892, Henry Ives Cobb) named after Silas Cobb (no relation). Freshmen still take their "common core" courses here. The top floor of the oldest campus building houses the **Renaissance Society** contemporary art gallery *(room 418)*, well regarded for its progressive exhibits *(open Oct–Jun Tue–Fri 10am–5pm, weekends noon–5pm;* ♿ *(weekdays only);* ☎ *773-702-8670; www.renaissancesociety.org).*

197

Continue east toward the center of the quadrangle.

On the right is **Swift Hall** (**Q**) (1926, Coolidge & Hodgdon), home to the Divinity School, sited here to represent the centrality of religion to all fields of study.

Walk south toward Harper Memorial Library.

U of C students are known for their bookish nature. The university recently banned "Sleep Out," a spring ritual that saw hundreds of students camping here overnight in order to secure places in popular classes.

On the right, **Haskell Hall** (**R**) (1896, Henry Ives Cobb) housed the Oriental Institute until 1931. A simple roofline accommodated gallery skylights. Today it is the Department of Anthropology. On the left, **Stuart Hall** (**S**) (1904, Shepley, Rutan & Coolidge), modeled on King's College in Cambridge, houses parts of the Business School. Note the eclectic array of carved animals protruding from the facade.

★**Harper Memorial Library** – *Open Sept–Jun Mon–Thu 9am–1pm, Fri 8am–5pm, Sat noon–5pm, Sun noon–1pm. Rest of the year Mon–Fri 9am–5pm. Closed major holidays.* ♿. Distinguished by two massive, square towers, the library (1912, Shepley, Rutan & Coolidge) anchors the south end of the quadrangle and presents an impressive facade to Midway Plaisance. Bridges connect the library to reading rooms in Haskell and Stuart halls. Visit the main reading room on the third floor to admire the vaulted ceilings, huge chandeliers and stone screens carved with the insignia of universities from both hemispheres. To the east stands the Social Sciences Research Building (1929, Coolidge & Hodgdon).

Walk through the archway in Haskell Hall and head north.

★**Bond Chapel** – *Open year-round Mon–Fri 8:30am–5pm. Closed major holidays.* ♿. This delicate gem (1926, Coolidge & Hodgdon), covered with ivy and sculpture, is connected by a covered cloister to Swift Hall. Its intimate interior is noted for its Charles Connick stained glass, elaborate wood carvings and a hammer-beamed ceiling with polychrome angels. The frieze of beatitudes ringing the space conceals heating grates to warm the body as well as the soul. The chancel window facing the entrance represents the entire New Testament.

③ 57th Street Books

Map p 194. 1301 E. 57th St. ☎ 773-684-1300. Help yourself to a cup of complimentary coffee and wander through this well-stocked bookshop. Though the store is part of the huge Seminary Co-op, 57th Street Books features a selection geared toward general interest rather than academic pursuits. The intelligent, helpful staff encourages browsing, and kids can play with toys set out for them in the children's section.

④ Jimmy's Woodlawn Tap

Map p 194. 1172 E. 55th St. ☎ 773-643-5516. Known as Jimmy's after the owner, this dimly lit tavern is the off-campus hangout for U of C students. Frazzled graduate students unwind at the Woodlawn Tap talking theory and university politics into the wee hours. Jimmy's prices are low, beer selection good and the bartenders are friendly, so drop by and drink in the relaxed academic atmosphere.

Walk south to the Classics Quadrangle.

Gates, Blake and Goodspeed Halls (1892, Henry Ives Cobb), originally men's dormitories, are now classrooms. The Classics Building (1915, Shepley, Rutan & Coolidge) and Wieboldt Hall (1928, Coolidge & Hodgdon) complete the serene ambience of the quadrangle.

Walk through the arch and continue south across the Midway.

From 1906 to 1936 sculptor **Lorado Taft** lived and worked with students in the Midway Studios located one block east at 60th Street and Ingleside Avenue. Taft, the most prominent Midwestern sculptor at the turn of the century, developed the rambling studios as a Renaissance-style *bottega*, or informal arts school. He completed his greatest works here, including the *Fountain of the Great Lakes*, gracing the Art Institute's South Wing, and the *Fountain of Time* (on the Midway at Washington Park). The studio, a National Historic Landmark, is still used by university artists.

Look back across the Midway for an expansive **view★** of the main quadrangles. The **School of Social Service Administration** (**T**) *(southwest corner of Ellis Ave. and 60th St.)* was designed by master Modernist Ludwig Mies van der Rohe in 1965, in his familiar rectangular, glass-and-steel style. Located just east, across Ellis Avenue, the **Burton-Judson Courts** (1931, Zantzinger, Bori & Medary) were the first university buildings erected south of the Midway. These dormitories feature a square tower, an interior quadrangle and simplified Gothic styling.

Walk east on 60th St. to the Law School.

Four buildings compose the **Laird Bell Law Quadrangle**, designed by Eero Saarinen & Assocs. in 1959 as part of his master plan for the campus. The six-story D'Angelo Law Library is flanked by two long and low buildings holding classrooms and offices, organized around a large reflecting pool. A circular assembly hall and courtroom mark the eastern end.

★★ROBIE HOUSE

Seemingly floating on the corner of 58th Street and Woodlawn Avenue, this quintessential Prairie school home by Frank Lloyd Wright is the one that made him world famous and helped "break the box" of traditional architecture. Built as a private residence, it was saved from the wrecking ball at the eleventh hour, housed the University of Chicago Alumni Association for 30 years, and is now being operated in conjunction with the Frank Lloyd Wright Home and Studio Foundation, which is supervising an intensive restoration.

Robie and Wright – The house was commissioned by Frederick Robie, a rich, young inventor and heir to a bicycle and automobile firm. Robie's ideas for his home caused architects to mutter that he wanted "one of those damned Wright houses"—so he hired the iconoclastic Wright. The Robies lived in the house only from 1910 to 1911, when the firm went bust and the marriage dissolved. It was sold to the Taylor family, who resided in the house for 11 months, and then to the Wilber Marshall family. In 1926 the Chicago Theological Seminary occupied it as a dormitory and dining hall, accelerating its deterioration. Saved from demolition in 1957, the house was donated to the university in 1963 and designated a National Historic Landmark that same year. In 1995 the university entered into an agreement with the Frank Lloyd Wright Home and Studio Foundation to renovate Robie House into a house museum, a process expected to cost some $3.5 million and last 10 years.

Visit

5757 S. Woodlawn Ave. Visit by guided tour (45min) only, year-round Mon–Fri 11am, 1pm & 3pm, weekends 11am–3:30pm (every 30min). Closed Jan 1, Thanksgiving Day & Dec 25. $8. ☏ 708-848-1976. www.wrightplus.org.

Viewed from the exterior, the house is composed of intersecting rectangular volumes that alternately lead and fool the eye, dissolving the borders between interior and exterior and creating fluid spaces. Horizontal emphasis is found not only in the roofs, dramatic balconies and banded windows, but also in Wright's trademark long Roman bricks.

Although Robie House is three stories high, the cantilevered eaves and roofline make it appear shorter. Wright violated the block's 35ft setback by setting the house back, but extending the porch—and thus the living area—into the front yard. Robie's desire for both natural light and privacy is evidenced by the windows, which conceal the interior by stained, leaded patterns while admitting natural light.

The unusual designs are said to represent geometric versions of Midwestern foliage. Wright preferred casement windows that hinge on the side since the act of pushing them open created interaction with nature.

As in most Wright homes, the entrance is hidden under a deep overhang.

© Robert Frerck/Odyssey

Leaded Window, Robie House

199

Robie House, Living Room

Wright challenged the idea that a facade should be designed around an entrance, preferring a "pathway of discovery." The foyer is deliberately cramped, forcing the visitor to proceed immediately to one of the living spaces.

The guided tour begins in the home's three-car garage, which now functions as a gift shop, and focuses on the main living area upstairs—a **living room** and **dining room** separated and united by a grand hearth. The space is striking, lit by sidewalls of art glass and a rectangularly coved ceiling studded with a series of sphere-in-square "moonlights," another characteristic Wright motif. Wood trim reinforces the dramatic horizontal flow of the space.

By designing furniture and built-ins and leaving little empty wall space, Wright limited the ability of owners to change his design. Apocryphal stories have the architect reappearing at the house to ensure that the furniture was not rearranged. The finest furniture in the Robie House, the dining-room set, is preserved at the Smart Museum.

The tour continues to the ground floor playroom and billiard room once occupied by the offices of the University of Chicago Alumni Association.

HYDE PARK/KENWOOD ★

Map p. 202

An island of stability on Chicago's impoverished and embattled South Side, this racially integrated, middle-class community is closely identified with the cerebral University of Chicago and the popular Museum of Science and Industry. Bordered by Lake Michigan on the east, Washington Park on the west, 47th Street on the north and 61st Street on the south, Hyde Park/Kenwood also encompasses renowned architectural landmarks, sweeping greenswards and an array of shops and eateries. Once the site of the gleaming "White City" of World's Fair fame, Hyde Park/Kenwood remains a cosmopolitan and sophisticated neighborhood, well worth exploring.

Historical Notes

Suburbs "in Horto" – Paul Cornell envisioned a quiet residential suburb when he purchased 300 lakefront acres south of Chicago in 1852 and named the area Hyde Park. He lured the Illinois Central commuter train in 1856, barred industry in 1861 and helped create the South Parks Commission in 1869, which hired renowned landscape architect Frederick Law Olmsted to design Jackson and Washington parks. To the north dentist John Kennicott had purchased eight acres near 43rd Street in 1856 and named his suburb Kenwood, subdividing it into large, 50ft-wide lots. By 1874 it was hailed as the "Lake Forest of the South Side" for its large Italianate and Shingle-style mansions. Both communities were conservative and exclusive. They soon established the separate township of Hyde Park and began fighting annexation to the City of Chicago.

As public transportation improved in the 1880s, apartment buildings and commercial strips began to transform Hyde Park into an urban neighborhood. New residents in favor of annexation to the city outvoted their tony neighbors in 1889 as the entire town from 39th Street to 138th Street became part of Chicago. In 1891 Hyde Park was chosen as the site of the **World's Columbian Exposition**, fostering the completion of Jackson and Washington parks and ending the neighborhood's exclusivity. Simultaneously, the University of Chicago was built just north of the Midway Plaisance. The two events forever changed the destiny of the community.

View from Promontory Point

The World's Fair brought an avalanche of real estate development as hotels, apartment buildings and shops sprang up to cater to the 27 million visitors during the summer of 1893. The University of Chicago grew just as quickly, and Hyde Park became a bustling area comprised of a large university, fashionable residential hotels and vibrant commercial strips on 47th, 53rd and 55th Streets. The 1910 opening of the Kenwood "L" train increased Kenwood's density, and a streetcar line on 47th Street created a split between North and South Kenwood. By the 1920s the crowded Black Belt pushed toward Kenwood, setting off racial conflicts that continued for 20 years and divided largely black North Kenwood from mainly white South Kenwood. While it declined economically, Hyde Park blossomed culturally with jazz and blues clubs, a major artists' colony and a comedy troupe that eventually became The Second City.

Town and Gown – In 1949 neighbors created the Hyde Park/Kenwood Community Conference, and three years later, the University of Chicago organized the South East Chicago Commission to fight urban decline. As the birthplace of modern sociology, the university held a critical role: U of C scholars studied their declining neighborhood and developed guidelines for urban renewal. These studies were formalized into the Federal Housing Act of 1954, and when federal funds were released in 1955, it was no surprise that Hyde Park/Kenwood qualified for the largest urban-renewal project in the nation. More than 900 acres of buildings were demolished over the next decade, including almost every bar and nightclub on 55th Street. The south side of 47th Street was stripped of retail, so it could act as a buffer against the deteriorating North Kenwood community. Shopping centers replaced mansions on Lake Park Avenue and apartments on 53rd Street. Cottages with porches gave way to town houses oriented around interior courtyards. The radical surgery worked: the University of Chicago abandoned thoughts of leaving the city, the neighborhood maintained its integrated middle-class character and the economic decline sweeping the South Side leapfrogged over Hyde Park/Kenwood. Today one of the nation's most successful models for integration, the community remains a part and parcel of the university, which has helped shape its destiny.

DRIVING TOUR Distance: 9.3mi

Begin at the intersection of Drexel Blvd. and 51st St. (Hyde Park Blvd.).

Drexel Square's restored **Drexel Fountain** (**A**) is the oldest monument in the boulevard system, dedicated in 1883 by the sons of financier Martin Drexel. To the west lies Washington Park, designed in 1869 by Frederick Law Olmsted.

Drive north on Drexel Blvd.

Drexel Boulevard separates Kenwood from Washington Park and was one of Chicago's most fashionable streets from 1880 to 1930. Today large courtyard apartment buildings share the street with mansions from the horse-and-carriage era. On the east side, the Classical Greek temple facade of **Operation PUSH** (**B**) *(950*

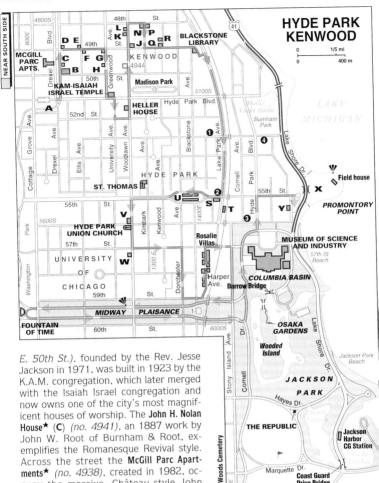

E. 50th St.), founded by the Rev. Jesse Jackson in 1971, was built in 1923 by the K.A.M. congregation, which later merged with the Isaiah Israel congregation and now owns one of the city's most magnificent houses of worship. The **John H. Nolan House★ (C)** (no. 4941), an 1887 work by John W. Root of Burnham & Root, exemplifies the Romanesque Revival style. Across the street the **McGill Parc Apartments★** (no. 4938), created in 1982, occupy the massive, Château-style John McGill mansion (1890, Henry Ives Cobb). At 49th Street note the **Martin A. Ryerson House (D)** (no. 4851), erected in 1887 in the Richardsonian Romanesque style, with its large stone verandah and coach house.

Turn right on 49th St. and continue east to Ellis Ave.

To the left at 4848 South Ellis Avenue stands the **Gustavus Swift House (E)** (1898, Flanders & Zimmerman), an exuberant Renaissance palace befitting the meat packer's imperial wealth. Across Ellis Avenue, on the southeast corner, the large 42-room **Julius Rosenwald House (F)** (4901 S. Ellis Ave.) was built for the Sears Roebuck & Co. chairman in 1903 by Nimmons & Fellows.

Continue to Greenwood Ave. and turn right.

On the southwest corner of 49th Street and Greenwood Avenue (no. 4900), note the **Henry Veeder House★ (G)** (1907, Howard Van Doren Shaw), a free interpretation of Neoclassical architecture. The variety of grand mansions along Greenwood Avenue recalls the elegance of the Gold Coast in the more expansive setting of Kenwood. Respect for the past disappears in the design of the **Ernest J. Magerstadt House★ (H)** (no. 4930), an important 1908 work by Prairie school architect George W. Maher. A wide, flat roofline, banded windows and a broad porch display the Prairie style, while columns adorned with poppies provide a motif that Maher repeats in the leaded-glass windows.

The Byzantine dome of **K.A.M.-Isaiah Israel Temple★★**, a masterful 1923 work by Alfred S. Alschuler, rises on the northeast corner of Hyde Park Boulevard. The synagogue's minaret (which actually disguises a smokestack) and the multicolored brick walls are based on a Palestinian precedent from 2C AD. The interior is renowned for its acoustics and features a Guastavino tile dome.

Turn left on Hyde Park Blvd., the dividing line between Hyde Park and Kenwood, and then right on Woodlawn Ave.

The **Isidore Heller House**★ *(5132 S. Woodlawn Ave.)* is an 1897 work by Frank Lloyd Wright that illustrates the emergence of his distinctive Prairie style. Wright achieved a horizontal effect on the vertical home by aligning windows under low-slung eaves and using brick banding and a frieze by sculptor Richard W. Bock. Like all of Wright's Prairie homes, the house has an open interior plan and eschews a front door for a "pathway of discovery."

Continue on Woodlawn to 52nd St. and turn right. Turn right on University Ave., right again on Hyde Park Blvd. and left on Woodlawn Ave.

To the right is **Madison Park**, an exclusive residential area set around a private boulevard, laid out in 1883 by John Dunham but not fully developed until the apartment-building boom of the 1920s. Past 50th Street, on the left, note the 1916 brick mansion at no. 4944, once inhabited by heavyweight boxer Muhammad Ali. On the northeast corner of 49th and Woodlawn stands the **Elijah Muhammad House** (**J**) *(no. 4855)*, erected in 1971 in a Mediterranean Modern style for the Nation of Islam leader. The home, which faces four smaller versions built for his sons on the west side of the street, features huge doors, stained-glass windows and a red tiled roof. The mansion is now occupied by controversial Nation minister Louis Farrakhan. To the north, on the west side, is the **James Douglas House** (**K**) *(no. 4830)*, a 1907 Howard Van Doren Shaw design that helped establish the Georgian Revival style in Kenwood. The neighborhood's oldest home is the **Christopher B. Bouton House**★ (**L**) (1873), a large, wooden, Italianate mansion located at no. 4812.

Turn right on 48th St. and right again on Kimbark Ave.

This block is unique in Chicago for its adoption of the Shingle style, although stone and brick are also used in deference to Chicago's climate. The **George Miller House** (**N**) *(no. 4800)*, an 1888 design by George Garnsey, was copied from an 1874 H.H. Richardson house in Newport, Rhode Island. Across the street at no. 4801, the **Joseph H. Howard House** (**P**) (1891, Patton & Fisher) uses pink slate shingles in a picturesque composition of turrets and dormers.

 Valois

Map p 202. 1518 E. 53rd St. ☎ *773-667-0647.* The sign outside this cafeteria-style diner reads "See Your Food." If you eat at Valois (pronounced "vuh-loys"), you'll see plenty more than the roast beef, baked chicken, greens and casserole on your tray. Here factory workers rub elbows with professors and professionals, and the resulting conversations make for great eavesdropping. When the restaurant is crowded, customers sit wherever there's room, so prepare to dine—and converse—with strangers.

 Hyde Park Co-op

Map p 202. 1526 E. 55th St. ☎ *773-667-1444.* Founded in 1932, this is one of the oldest cooperative grocery stores operating in the US. The co-op moved into a building designed by I.M. Pei in 1959 and is now open to the public. Its deli and bakery counters are good places to grab a quick snack or to stock up for a picnic on one of the university quads or on Promontory Point.

Turn left on 49th St. and continue to the intersection with Kenwood Ave.

On the northwest side of the intersection stand two of Frank Lloyd Wright's secret commissions, built in 1892 while he still worked for Adler & Sullivan: the **George W. Blossom House** (**Q**) *(4858 Kenwood Ave.)* and the **Warren McArthur House** (**R**) *(4852 Kenwood Ave.)*. Like his Oak Park "bootlegs", these homes are traditional in style, but Wright's restless creativity is visible in windows that sit below wide eaves and open interior plans.

Continue on 49th St. toward Lake Park Ave.

The **Blackstone Branch, Chicago Public Library**★ (1902, Solon S. Beman) typifies the Neoclassical style inspired by the 1893 World's Columbian Exposition, with its dome, acanthus leaves and pedimented temple entrance. In fact, Beman's design is a copy of his own Merchant Tailors Building at the fair.

Drive south on Lake Park Ave. and turn right on 55th St.

55th Street forms the heart of the Hyde Park/Kenwood Urban Renewal plan, which transformed the street from a jazzy nightlife district into a modern residential strip and shopping mall. The **University National Bank**★ (**S**) (1929, M. Louis Kroman), on the southwest corner of 55th Street and Lake Park Avenue, was built as an automobile showroom, its facade enlivened with playful terra-cotta roadsters, dashboards, engines and wheels. Farther south at 5529 Lake Park Avenue is the **Hyde Park Historical Society** (**T**), located in a tiny cable-car station *(open year-round weekends 2pm–4pm;* ☎ *773-493-1893).*

Looming ahead on 55th Street are the twin 10-story towers of I.M. Pei's **University Apartments (U)**, built in 1961 and known locally as "Monoxide Island" because the roadway circumscribes the high rises. Modern two- and three-story town houses face the island and line adjacent streets.

Continue west on 55th St.

At the northwest corner of 55th Street and Kimbark Avenue, **St. Thomas the Apostle Catholic Church★** *(open year-round daily 8am–5pm, see office secretary for admission; ▣ ☎ 773-753-7423; http://members.aol.com/stachurch)* is a revolutionary 1924 design by Barry Byrne, an apprentice of Frank Lloyd Wright and the first American to design a European church (The Church of Christ the King in Cork, Ireland). Byrne used unusual massing, narrow windows and scalloped terra-cotta ornament by Alfonso Ianelli to obliquely reference Gothic forms. The interior features a column-free sanctuary measuring 95ft by 125ft, with the altar pushed into the nave—anticipating Vatican II reforms four decades later. Stations of the cross by Alfeo Faggi complete this modern interpretation of a traditional building.

Continue west on 55th St. and turn left on Woodlawn Ave.

Many of the large homes on Woodlawn are owned by the University of Chicago, fraternal associations or theological schools that have clustered in Hyde Park. The massive, Queen Anne **Theodore Rice House★ (V)** (1892, Mifflin E. Bell) at the northwest corner of Woodlawn Avenue and 56th Street has colorful pink and gray tiles and a wide porch. Across 56th Street, the Romanesque Revival-style **Hyde Park Union Church★** (1906, James Gamble Rogers) features orange sandstone and stunning Tiffany and Connick stained glass. South of 57th Street on the west side stands the **Edgar Johnson Goodspeed House (W)** *(5706 Woodlawn Ave.)*, a 1906 Arts and Crafts-style home by Howard Van Doren Shaw.

Turn left on 57th St. and pass a small commercial area. Turn right on Dorchester Ave., left on 59th St., then left on Harper Ave. at the Illinois Central Railroad viaduct.

This quaint street provides insight into Hyde Park's early development, its small lots filled with Queen Anne and Shingle-style homes. The street was a planned community called **Rosalie Villas★**, designed in 1883 by Solon S. Beman, who was the architect for nos. 5832-34 and no. 5759. Other architects followed the same vocabulary of wood clapboard siding, shingles and cutout ornament.

Turn right on 57th St., and right again on Stony Island Ave., heading south to the Midway Plaisance. Follow the Midway Plaisance west, then double back at the Fountain of Time and follow the Midway eastbound until it intersects with Cornell Dr.

The open, grassy expanse of the **Midway Plaisance★** belies the raucous carnival atmosphere of the 1893 World's Columbian Exposition. While the term "midway" is still applied to carnival sideshows, its namesake now serves as the city's broadest boulevard and a foreground for the university. Designed in 1869 by Frederick Law Olmsted and Calvert Vaux as the connecting link between Washington and Jackson Parks, the Midway was intended to have a central canal linking the lagoons of the two parks. Although the center of the Midway is depressed below grade level, the water link was never implemented. The **Fountain of Time★★**, a monumental 1922

Fountain of Time by Lorado Taft

sculpture by Lorado Taft, anchors the western end of the Midway at Washington Park. A curving wave of humanity rises and falls as the solitary hooded figure of Time watches in passive solemnity. Inspired by these lines from Austin Dobson, "Time goes, you say? Ah, no!/Alas, Time stays, we go ...," the sculpture took 14 years and a 4,500-piece mold to complete.

Taft designed a complementary *Fountain of Creation* for the other end of the Midway, but it was never built. Instead, an equestrian sculpture (1) of a black knight, St. Wenceslaus, sculpted by Albin Polasek and dedicated to Czechoslovakian nationalist Tomas Masaryk, occupies the intended site. The drive around the Midway offers some of the best **views**★ of the Gothic facades of the University of Chicago.

Turn left (north) on Cornell Ave. Follow Cornell as it curves in front of the Museum of Science and Industry, and turn left on S. Hyde Park Blvd. Continue to 55th St. and turn right. Park in the lot at the eastern end of 55th St. and walk to Promontory Point via the pedestrian tunnel under Lake Shore Dr.

Jutting into the lake, the small **Promontory Point**★ was designed in 1937 by Alfred Caldwell, a student of Jens Jensen. Caldwell even supervised a restoration in 1987. The entrance is marked by the **David Wallach Fountain** (**X**), a drinking fountain designed for people and their pets, topped by a bronze of a resting doe. At the far end of "The Point," a stone **Field House** (1937) takes the appearance of a light-house with its circular tower. The **view**★★ north to the Loop is spectacular. At 5530 South Shore Drive are the **Promontory Apartments** (**Y**), the first high rise by Ludwig Mies van der Rohe. Completed in 1949 in concrete and glass, these apart-ments prefigured Mies' steel and glass apartment towers built on North Lake Shore Drive four years later.

JACKSON PARK

E. 56th to 67th Sts., Stony Island Ave. to Lake Michigan.

Located 8mi south of the Loop and stretching along Lake Michigan's shore-line, the park's 600 acres of playing fields, lagoons and lush vegetation began as a wasteland of sand dunes and scrub marshes.

Renowned landscape architect Frederick Law Olmsted's 1870 plan for the park was only partially implemented when he redesigned and completed it for the World's Columbian Exposition in 1893, using Lake Michigan and a series of la-goons and formal ponds as the organiz-ing principle. Following the fair's demoli-tion, Olmsted's sons redesigned it again in 1895. Despite the ravages of time, several Olmsted landscapes and turn-of-the-cen-tury structures survive today.

Visit

Open year-round daily dawn–11pm.

A highlight of the park is the gleaming, 24ft-high statue **The Republic**★ by Daniel Chester French, cast in 1918 from a scale

❸ Piccolo Mondo

Map p 202. 1642 E. 56th St. ☎ *773-643-1106.* The wide, arched windows of this Italian restaurant afford a pleasant view of Jackson Park and the facade of the Museum of Science and Industry. Spool spaghetti and sip Chianti in the candlelit dining room, or grab a sandwich and salad at the gourmet deli counter.

❹ Hyde Park Art Center

Map p 202. 5307 S. Hyde Park Blvd. ☎ *773-324-5520.* A spacious corner of the Del Prado apartment building houses a good-size gallery and a handful of studios for ceramics, painting and crafts classes. The gallery mounts about three shows a year often featuring prominent Chicago artists.

model of the original 65ft sculpture that stood in the Court of Honor during the 1893 fair. The only sculpture in Jackson Park, it was regilded in 1992 and stands on the site of the fair's administration building.

Wooded Island, one of the original features of Jackson Park, was designed as a natural area and rookery by Olmsted and is known today as the Paul H. Douglas Nature Sanctuary. More than 300 bird species have been spotted here, with some two dozen varieties nesting on small islands Olmsted designed for that purpose in the east and west lagoons. At the north end of Wooded Island lie the **Osaka Gardens**★, a modern replica of a landscape created during the 1893 fair by Japan, which replicated the *Ho-o-den* or "Phoenix Temple" at Uji, near Kyoto. In the traditional Japanese garden style, rocks, flowers, shrubs, decorative lanterns and pavilions are arranged to provide a succession of contemplative views *(to access Osaka Gardens: turn right toward Jackson Park at eastern end of the Museum of Science and Industry parking lot; continue to small parking area overlooking the Columbia Basin).*

North of Wooded Island is the **Columbia Basin**★, designed by Olmsted as a romantic reflecting pond for the Palace of Fine Arts, now the Museum of Science and Industry. Wooded Island, the east and west lagoons and Columbia Basin are the only landscapes that survive from the 1893 fair. To the east, the **Clarence Darrow Bridge** is named for the famous attorney who defended the Pullman strikers in the 1890s and the teaching of evolution in the 1924 Scopes Trial. The **Coast Guard Drive Bridge** at Marquette Drive is a rough-faced stone bridge (1904), ornamented with gargoyle-like sculptures of hippopotamuses, alligators and other water creatures. The former **Jackson Harbor Coast Guard Station**, a quaint 1906 Shingle-style boathouse, was restored in 1992 as the South Pier restaurant.

A half-mile south of the park stands the **South Shore Cultural Center★** *(71st St. and South Shore Dr.; open year-round Mon–Fri 10am–6pm; Sat 9am–5pm; closed major holidays; &. 🅿 ☎ 312-747-2536)*, an elegant former country club (1916, Marshall & Fox) that is now part of the Chicago Park District. A broad entrance colonnade leads to a Mediterranean structure framed by square towers topped by red tile roofs. The blue and white Renaissance interior boasts massive ballrooms, oak-paneled meeting rooms and a dazzling solarium that host classes, community events and private functions.

OAK WOODS CEMETERY

Designed in the monumental and picturesque 19C tradition by Adolph Strauch, this 183-acre cemetery hosts a diversity of occupants ranging from Confederate soldiers to mayors, governors and industrialists.

Visit

Enter off 67th St. at Greenwood Ave. Open year-round Mon–Fri 8:30am–4:30pm, Sat 9am–3pm. Guided tours (45min) available, two-week advance reservations required. 🅿 ☎ 773-288-3800. The office will provide a free map and listing of notable grave sites and monuments.

■ The 1893 World's Columbian Exposition

Following on the heels of the successful centennial exhibit in Philadelphia in 1876, the 1893 World's Columbian Exposition heralded another American city's debut on the world stage. In a spirited battle to host the fair, Chicago outbid three other cities—New York, Washington, DC and St. Louis—claiming the best amenities and the largest funds (over $10 million were pledged by 1890). That same year, President Benjamin Harrison signed a bill that provided for "celebrating the 400th anniversary of the discovery of America by Christopher Columbus, by holding an International Exhibition of the arts, industries, manufactures and the products of the soil, mine and sea, in the City of Chicago."

Covering over 650 acres along present-day **Jackson Park** and the **Midway Plaisance**, the grounds encompassed some 200 buildings erected at a cost of $30 million by such esteemed architects as John W. Root, Daniel Burnham, Charles Atwood and Louis Sullivan. Under the masterful hand of landscape artist Frederick Law Olmsted, several lagoons, three miles of canals and elaborate gardens appeared, lending the fair a Venetian look. From its opening day on May 1, 1893, to its close in October, the exposition attracted some 27 million visitors and awed them with its architecture (the largest structure, the Manufactures and Liberal Arts Building, encompassed 40 acres of gallery space and its 1,687ft-long roof was pierced by 11 acres of skylights) and attractions, including the world's first Ferris wheel towering above the spires of the University of Chicago and the infamous "Little Egypt" dancing the hootchie kootchie in the "Street of Cairo" exhibit. Fair officials quipped that it would take more than three weeks of walking some 150mi to take in all exhibits.

Uniform in design, the fair's structures reflected the grandiose Neoclassical style. At night, enormous floodlights (a first at the time) illuminated the buildings, creating a sparkling, white, fairylike atmosphere, and the complex was soon dubbed the "White City." The event had an enormous impact on American architecture, spawning the "City Beautiful" movement and marking a return to monumental Classical architecture. Several cities, including Washington, DC and Cleveland, Ohio, later called on Daniel Burnham's skills to create grand, spacious downtown areas.

Within a few years, most buildings—erected on iron and wood frames and clad with "staff," an amalgam of plaster, cement and fiber that had the appearance of white stucco—had been destroyed by fire and vandalism. The only structure remaining today is the Museum of Science and Industry, formerly the **Palace of Fine Arts**.

Rows of tiny white tombstones, cannons and a statue of a Civil War soldier mark the Soldier's Home Lot, while a sculpture of Abraham Lincoln stands at the Grand Army of the Republic Lot. Neither Union burial equals the grandeur of the **Confederate Mound**★ at the southern end of the cemetery, where some 6,000 Confederate prisoners of war are buried in concentric trenches under a massive obelisk surmounted by a statue of a defeated rebel. Four cannons guard the corners, while marble tombstones number the nameless Union guards who also died at Chicago's Camp Douglas, where the greatest killers were smallpox and cholera. More than 4,000 of the deceased are named on the monument erected in May 1895 with elaborate ceremony and 100,000 in attendance.

Distinguished by a red granite marker, the **Jesse Owens monument**, adjacent to the Lake of Memories, is one of the most impressive tombstones; note the stylized Olympic urns flanking the monument. The gray granite **Mayor Harold Washington grave** commemorates the long political career of the city's first black mayor. Among the others buried here are Hyde Park founder Paul Cornell, University of Chicago founding president William Rainey Harper, baseball pioneer Cap Anson and nuclear physicist Enrico Fermi.

MUSEUM OF SCIENCE AND INDUSTRY★★★

57th St. at S. Lake Shore Dr. 🚌 bus no. 6 (Jeffrey Express)
or bus no. 10 (weekends)
Map p 202

Part amusement park, part trade show and part museum, this cacaphonous hall of wonders and widgets is one of Chicago's most popular attractions. Located since 1933 in the only building left standing after the World's Columbian Exposition of 1893, the museum contains more than 2,000 exhibits that cover 14 acres spread over three floors. Dedicated to presenting science, industry and technology to the public in an entertaining way, the museum's hands-on displays invite visitors to push, pull, compute and enjoy.

Historical Notes

The Building – Perhaps the grandest structure at the World's Fair of 1893, the Palace of Fine Arts represented the essence of that great Beaux-Arts extravaganza. Designer **Charles B. Atwood** of D.H. Burnham & Co. left no Neoclassical reference unmade by combining elements from the Parthenon and other temples on the Acropolis along with ancient Roman forms. (The versatile Atwood would later design the strikingly modern Reliance Building in the Loop.) The sprawling edifice, encircled by 276 columns, extends 1,145ft across the front and contains 650,000sq ft of exhibit space. Its two wings, east and west, echo the central pavilion in a rigorous Ionic symmetry. At its rear, the Columbia Basin (North Pond), traversed by gondolas during the 1893 fair, laps at the building's south steps.

Born Again – Much has happened to the palace since its glory days at the World's Columbian Exposition when it housed works of art from around the world. In its second life as the home of the Field Museum, it slipped into such disrepair as to be dubbed a "scaly, wormy pile." Its condition resulted not from poor maintenance, but rather from the ephemeral materials of its construction, which were never intended to outlive the fair. By 1920, when the Field Museum moved to its new Grant Park facility, the palace's walls, made of brick covered with "staff," a flimsy compound of plaster, cement and hemp, had seriously decayed. It stood forlornly empty in Jackson Park for several years until a marriage of ideas and resources came to pass. Public sentiment to save the building was strong, since it was a remnant of the beloved fair and an unexcelled example of American Neoclassicism. At the same time, philanthropist **Julius Rosenwald**, who had made millions as chairman of Sears, Roebuck and Co., felt Chicago could benefit from a "hands-on" industrial museum like the Deutsches Museum he had seen in Munich, Germany. He would eventually contribute over $7 million to the project.

In 1926 the idea of using the old **Palace of Fine Arts** took root and plans for the complicated renovation got under way. After stripping the moldering plaster skin away from the building's brick and iron skeleton, crews fortified the walls using limestone on the outside and marble on the inside. Fragile skylights were eliminated; 200,000 pounds of copper sheathed the domes. Sturdy stone columns and caryatids replaced their deteriorating predecessors around the facade. Architects gave the interior an Art Moderne look, a most appropriate backdrop for the march of modern technology and science and an acknowledgment of the Century of Progress International Exposition planned to open in 1933 along the lakefront. A portion of the new Museum of Science and Industry (MSI) debuted simultaneously: the revered Palace of Fine Arts would see another World's Fair.

An Invitation to Industry – Times were hard for the museum during the Great Depression. Support was difficult to come by; exhibits remained sparse and restoration incomplete until 1940. The main attraction of those years was the "Coal Mine," its actual bituminous walls so convincing that visitors often wondered where they might place their orders for coal. The Century of Progress Exposition left the museum with two legacies: many of its exhibits made their way into the collection, and the man who had masterminded the successful two-year pageant, **Major Lenox Lohr**, was hired on as president. In 1940 Lohr, a practiced promoter and showman, left the presidency of the National Broadcasting Company to energize the struggling museum. Injecting life, color and controversy into the serious business of science and technology, Lohr began to shape the modern institution. He invited industries to underwrite, develop and maintain exhibits; he hired architects to enliven the halls; he startled visitors with displays on pregnancy and the human body and he added entertainment to the museum's agenda.

A Continuing Challenge – Lohr remained in charge until his death in 1968. During those years, the museum amassed an amazing array of oddities and wonders, including the U-505 Submarine, Colleen Moore's miniature Fairy Castle, the world's largest model railroad and the world's fastest car. At the same time, the corporate presence grew ever stronger as more and more exhibits carried company logos and transmitted overt and subliminal messages to thousands of daily visitors.

That legacy has bequeathed the museum a continuing challenge: how to weave these disparate parts into a meaningful and evenhanded whole. The master plan introduced in 1990 addressed that concern. The initial effect of the plan was to establish an admission fee in 1991. (Entrance to the museum had always been free.) Reassessing everything from parking to programs, the plan consolidated the museum's exhibits into six thematic "zones"—human body, transportation, communication, energy and environment, space and defense, and manufacturing. A 1,500-vehicle underground parking facility completed in 1998 is disguised as a six-acre park in the museum's front yard. The subterranean construction houses the **Great Hall**, the entrance to the museum, as well as the renovated 197ft **Pioneer Zephyr train**—featured in a new guided tour. Known as the "Silver Streak," the Pioneer Zephyr broke the world's record for speed and non-stop distance in 1934 when it traveled from Denver to Chicago is 13hrs, 5min. A scale model of the Saturn-bound Cassini Probe, a museum store and a visit-planning center are also located in the Great Hall.

Palace of Fine Arts, South Facade

Visiting the Museum

Open Memorial Day–Labor Day daily 9:30am–5:30pm. Rest of the year Mon–F 9:30am–4pm, weekends 9:30am–5:30pm. Closed Dec 25. $7 (free Thu) or $13 h museum admission & Omnimax Theater. & (§7) 773-684-1414. www msichicago.org.

The museum complex comprises the Henry Crown Space Center, the Great Ha entryway (underground garage) and three floors within central, east and west pavilion The floors are connected by four color-coded stairwells off the rotunda of the centra pavilion; there are also stairs in the east and west pavilions. Elevators and escalato are located near the main entrance. East of the central pavilion, the Crown center joined to the pavilions by a hallway accessible from the ground floor; the center al can be accessed by a separate outside entrance (on 57th Dr.).

he throes of its reorganization, the MSI remains a difficult space to negotiate effi-
ntly. Recently installed color-coded signage eases navigation. Pick up a floor plan
you enter the Great Hall from the underground garage. Staff are on hand in the
t-planning center to help you decide the sequence of your visit; also available
e are Omnimax and timed tickets for the Coal Mine, the U-505 Submarine and
Idea Factory, a must for young children *(through age 10)*. Waits in excess of an
ur are not unusual for these attractions on weekends and Thursdays (when admis-
n is free). Flight simulators in Navy: Technology at Sea also attract a crowd.

ove the Great Hall entryway on the parking-garage level, the three floors of the
seum are connected by four symmetrical stairways that flank the central rotunda.
ch has been painted a different color to help orient visitors. Elevators are located
he red stairwell. Powered by sunlight, a **solar fountain** in the yellow stairwell meas-
s the intensity of the day's sunshine. A huge sculpture bearing the **periodic table of
nents** hangs in the green stairwell. Below the second landing of the blue stair-
ll, a **Foucault pendulum** swings through its unceasing rounds with comforting
ularity, a sure sign that the earth continues to rotate. Among the enduring curiosi-
s of the MSI are the human-body sections, a mainstay of the museum since 1943,
display in the upper level of this stairwell. The **Big Idea** museum store is across
m the ticket booth in the Great Hall.

enities – MSI features five restaurants, four of which are on the ground floor. The
eteria-style **Century Room** offers healthy entrées, made-to-order sandwiches and
ads. Flanking the cafeteria are **Café Spectrum** (burgers, grilled-chicken sandwiches
d salads) and **Pizza Hut**. Located in the Henry Crown Space Center, **Astro Café**
ves sandwiches, fries and frosties with outdoor seating in summer. You'll find
igan's Ice Cream Parlor at the end of the Yesterday's Main Street exhibit on the first
or. All eateries are generally open 11am–4pm. A vending area is located across
m Pizza Hut.

Ground Floor

The MSI excels in its collections of **vehicles**; displayed in various corners and corridors are groupings of wagons and carriages (all in beautiful repair), classic and
racing cars, ships and fire-fighting equipment.

Henry Crown Space Center – Located east of the main building, this 36,000sq ft
hall features space-related exhibits, a theater, a museum shop and a cafe. The
Omnimax Theater offers a truly sensational experience: its 76ft-high screen nearly
engulfs the audience, absorbing them into the film, while the throb of the sound
track transport the action nearly palpable. Story lines transport viewers to such spectacular settings as the depths of the ocean and the outer reaches of space (new
films are introduced about three times a year). The theater presents two 40min
films, shown several times a day *($8 or $13 museum/Omnimax combination ticket)*.
Exhibits on space exploration and travel include the **Apollo 8 command module★**, the
first vessel ever to circle the moon in 1968. An open hatch reveals the cramped
interior, but most evocative is the pockmarked surface of the pod, which is covered
with the scars of space travel. Also on display are an Apollo Lunar Module trainer
used in the 1995 movie *Apollo 13*, and a model **space shuttle** where visitors can
experience the sensations of liftoff and space travel.

U-505 Submarine – *Tour guides take 15 people into the ship every 15min. While
you are waiting, you can browse through a brief history of the war in the Atlantic
and look at objects removed from the submarine. Free timed tickets may be
required if lines are long.* This icon of the museum seems as popular now as when
it arrived in 1954. Captured off the coast of French West Africa in 1944, the
German reconnaissance vessel was the first enemy warship apprehended by the
US Navy since 1815. Cipher books found aboard enabled American cryptographers
to crack a code used to track ships.
Designed to house 56 enlisted men and 4 officers, the U-505 is 252ft long, 37ft
high at the conning tower, 22ft wide at the widest point, and weighs 1,120 tons
when loaded on the surface (1,232 tons when submerged). It travels underwater
at 4.5mph (7.5 knots); on the surface, its speed can reach 13.8mph (19 knots).
An amazingly complicated array of switches, controls, tubes and hardware crowds
every inch inside the sub, punctuated by tiny but efficient living and working quarters. Indeed, the interior of the sub is as much a testament to the human spirit as
it is a wonder of science and industry. So small are the spaces that sailors were
required to be no taller than 5ft 7in in height. When leaving the submarine, take
a look through the periscope for a view of Jackson Park. Displays at the exit
describe the vessel's capture and eventual move to Chicago.

Nearby, the **Energy Lab** features simple and colorful hands-on experiments that
demonstrate the ways various forms of energy are produced and converted ther-
mally, mechanically, electromagnetically and also chemically.

Fairy Castle – An exhibit of a very different stripe is this miniature castle, whose
place at the museum is largely a sentimental one. The gift of silent-movie actress
Colleen Moore in 1949, the diminutive castle and its jewel-encrusted furnishings
took seven years to complete when they were fashioned to her specifications in
the mid-1930s. Measuring 9sq ft, the castle contains some 200 pieces of furni-

ture and over 1,000 miniatures; it is even equipped with electricity and runn
water (although finding a plumber to work on the small scale has proven pr
lematic).

Idea Factory – *Entry by free timed ticket available at exhibit entrance. Chil*
must be accompanied by an adult. A colorful and durable space with many mov
parts, this 8,000sq ft gallery is sure to delight young children (infants through
10) and their parents. Activity areas grouped according to age invite little ones
have fun pushing, pulling and experimenting under the guidance of staff membe
A moat snakes around the room, circulating bright spongy puzzle pieces dispen
from a clever Rube Goldberg-type contraption.

Long an MSI favorite, the Circus exhibit next door showcases the museum's col
tion of 22,000 miniature circus figures carved by Roland Weber over a 33-year per

Main Floor

★★**Coal Mine** – *Allow 20min for the tour, not including any wait. Free timed tick*
may be required if lines are long. This exhibit, recently renovated, has thrilled v
itors since the museum opened in 1933. From the top of the 60ft "headfram
(which visitors must climb to access the mine), an elevator operated by a gu
plunges in semidarkness to what seems like a great depth, but which is actu
only to the ground floor. *(The experience can be frightening to small childre*
The "mine" itself has walls composed of replica bituminous coal, and the gu
demonstrates the grind and groan of the authentic mining equipment on disp
In the "safety room," the guide describes the use of safety lamps to detect meth
gas in the mine, creating a contained explosion to illustrate the point. Then a r
in the rattling caged car of a mine train moves the tour along. A trip into this s
terranean world inspires awe at the difficult life of the coal miner.

Yesterday's Main Street – For a brief respite, stroll down this Main Street fc
nostalgic re-creation of 1910 Chicago. At the very end of the street, a nickelod
theater shows silent films, while Finnigan's Ice Cream Parlor serves sodas a
sundaes amid an old-fashioned décor.

★**Transportation Zone** – The first-completed thematic zone in the new muse
exhibit scheme takes up the eastern portion of the large East Court Hall as v
as the second-floor balcony. This is an exhibit of juggernauts and superlatives
steam engine called Buchanan's 999, for instance, broke the record in 1893
achieving a speed of 112.5mph. The *Spirit of America*, a specially designed
powered automobile, was driven by Craig Breedlove to smash the 500mph la
speed barrier in 1964. A minutely detailed **O-gauge model railroad**★ (7mm=1ft) ta
up 3,000sq ft in the middle of the hall. It is the largest in the world, built in 19
and revamped in 1988 to reflect Santa Fe Railroad's departure from the passen
business. Visitors can watch state-of-the-art computerized railroad traffic-cont
ling from the booth at the far end. The star of the exhibit is undoubtedly the Uni
Airlines **Boeing 727**★ that is cantilevered from the second-story balcony. It is a th
to stand beneath its highly polished underbelly and the impressive starboard w
that stretches out 50ft. At designated times throughout the day *(check sched*
when you buy your ticket) the gleaming craft becomes the center of a **light**
sound show intended to evoke a fantasy of movement and flight. Wing flaps, rud
and wheels respond as if in takeoff and landing modes as the plane makes an im
inary seven-minute flight *(the best place to view the spectacle is from the balc*
opposite the huge plane on the second floor).

Next to the Transportation Zone, a **chick hatchery** fascinates children as it qui
incubates eggs and houses the downy babies.

★**Navy: Technology at Sea** – This section in the far-flung east pavilion gives v
tors a chance to "tour" three different types of modern Navy vessels
reconstructing the aircraft elevator of the carrier USS *George Washington*,
bridge of the fast-attack submarine USS *Chicago* and the control center of
destroyer USS *Arleigh Burke*. For many, the highlight of the galleries is a ride
one of two authentic F-14 Tomcat **flight simulators**★, complete with visuals of a m
bombing run and radio chatter. Taking off, evasive maneuvering, banking a
other in-flight drills are so realistic that you are advised to hold on; landing on
aircraft carrier is a thrilling finale.

Whispering Gallery – Beyond the Communications exhibit, the classic Whisper
Gallery still astonishes visitors as it has for years by demonstrating the pecu
ability of sound waves to bounce between two widely spaced parabolic shells.

★★**Imaging: The Tools of Science** – This fascinating exhibit explores a more mod
phenomenon. "Imaging" refers to the high-tech science of gathering, process
and displaying data in visual forms, with the computer as its primary tool. It enat
us to picture the far reaches of space, the inner depths of the microworld,
body's interior, and climatic changes, even on other planets. Computers through
the exhibit invite visitors to manipulate images of their faces, investigate how N
and CT scans work, and create computer "art" by image enhancement and m
eling. Indeed, part of the wonder of this exhibit is the overlap it reveals betw

science and art, technology and creativity. A "Mystery Lab" at the end goes further in describing the practical forensic applications of this technology to age faces by computer, match fingerprints and enhance microscopic analyses. A small section on virtual reality gives visitors a taste of the virtual world.

Petroleum Planet – Since crude oil provides 97 percent of our transportation fuels in America, the importance of petroleum in daily life is a point that bears stressing. Interactive exhibits here do just that: help deliver crude oil from Saudi Arabia to Chicago; then navigate your way through the molecular Mirror Maze to the Speedway, where you can ride **racecar simulators**.

Balcony

The second-floor balcony encircles the entire perimeter of the building and houses a variety of exhibits pertaining largely to the basic sciences: chemistry, astronomy, geology, biology, physics, health and so on. Live demonstrations in the **Grainger Hall of Basic Science** animate fundamental physical theories with discussions and experiments in chemistry and physics.
Next to Grainger Hall, 40 human fetal specimens illustrate prenatal development from 25 days old to full term. Once controversial, the display is presented in a straightforward and scientific manner.
Also on the Balcony level, MSI Presents Lego Mindstorms® provides facilitated workshops where kids can build, design and program a robot or a Mars rover *(40min; $5 per computer station, $1 on Thu; reservations required: ☎ 773-684-1414)*.

★**Heart Balcony** – Exhibits on the heart, brain, sickle-cell anemia and AIDS—all part of this thematic zone—address not only basic issues of anatomy but timely health concerns as well. The museum's classic "walk-through" heart, a perennial favorite since 1952, has been incorporated into an updated exhibit on cardiac health called **Your Heart**. Computer exercises in concentration, memory, reasoning and other brain functions highlight **Learning and Learning Disabilities**, which explores the human mind in the context of how we learn. A brightly illustrated explanation of the origins and effects of different types of virus introduces **AIDS – The War Within**, the first major permanent museum exhibit on AIDS. Through easy-to-understand text, comic-book graphics and hands-on activities, the younger visitor learns the characteristics of the HIV virus and its prevention.

Reusable City – Hands-on environmental science displays educate visitors about some of the consequences of modern life. Water and air pollution, recycling and waste treatment are all topics for experimentation here. Try your hand at measuring ozone levels or taste-test drinking water.

Take Flight – The eastern portion of the balcony makes a dandy exhibit space for the 133ft cutaway Boeing 727 that visitors marveled at from below, enticing the visitor to wander up and down the aisle and learn about thrust, drag and lift as part of this exhibit. Donated by United Airlines, the aircraft was the seventeenth 727 ever built and remained in service between 1964 and 1991. During its journey to the museum, it became the largest plane ever to land at Meigs Field, Chicago's lakefront commuter airport. Floated south by barge to the museum, the huge craft stopped traffic as it was rolled across Lake Shore Drive. Along the balcony outside the craft, interactive experiments demonstrate how planes fly, and cutaway aircraft parts reveal the complexity of modern flight mechanics.

© Don Jiskra/Museum of Science and Industry

Take Flight Exhibit

211

Located in an industrial district on the Far South Side, this fascinating enclave was created by railroad-car magnate George Pullman in 1881 as an experimental company town. After years of neglect, the community was lovingly restored and today offers an architectural unity and unique history best sampled by a stroll down the 19C streets.

Historical Notes

George Pullman: Entrepreneur – George Mortimer Pullman (1831-97) was an inventor who embodied both the American dream and Chicago's "I Will" spirit. He made his first fortune in the 1850s when Chicago raised the street grade to construct sewers in the perennially muddy town. Downtown hotels and banks with elegant lobbies were faced with the prospect of rebuilding or losing a clientele who would not descend into luxury. Pullman figured out a way to elevate the buildings by placing hundreds of jackscrews around the foundation, and having workers turn them in unison. He bragged that he could raise a hotel "without disturbing a guest or cracking a cup." For his next venture, George Pullman developed luxurious train coaches—dining cars, club cars, rolling barbershops and his famous sleeping cars—to cater to the tastes of America's wealthy. At first railroads did not want the weighty, oversized cars that would require alterations to platforms and new tracks. However, when Abraham Lincoln was assassinated in 1865, Pullman offered his "Pioneer" sleeping car to transport executives on the slain president's funeral train back to Springfield, Illinois, and the railroads finally complied for the fallen national hero. Pullman incorporated the Pullman Palace Car Co. in 1867, with a starting capital of $1 million.

Pullman's Vision: Peace, Planning and Profits – The 1877 railroad strike shocked the nation and many expected open conflict between capital and labor. Wishing to isolate his workers from the strike- and strife-prone city, Pullman built a new factory town 13mi south of Chicago at Lake Calumet. By creating a clean, orderly environment far from the city's evils, Pullman hoped to live at peace with his employees. In 1880 he hired architect **Solon Spencer Beman** and landscaper **Nathan F. Barrett** to design not only the factories of the Pullman Palace Car Co., but also a comprehensive town plan. For the next 14 years Beman created rows and rows of red brick Queen Anne homes for the workers, along with a livery, churches, a hotel, shops and a library set in formal, French- and English-inspired landscapes. The result was a stunning, unified architectural vision, soon called the most perfect town in the world.

From the start, the community was a business for Pullman. The factory was to provide an eight-percent profit, the town, six. He collected rents from the two-thirds of his workers who lived in town, from the shopkeepers, and even from the church. In turn, Pullman provided conveniences like daily garbage pickup, paved alleys, water and sewer and fire protection. Sewage water was used to irrigate fields that produced vegetables for the town, and the huge Corliss engine that ran the factories provided steam heat to many of the homes. The only thing lacking in Pullman were taverns, since Pullman thought they would detract from his workers' productivity. Only visiting businessmen could be served alcohol at the Hotel Florence, which was off-limits to workers. One consequence of this policy was the construction by the Schlitz brewing company of a huge public saloon just outside Pullman's border.

"The Best Laid Schemes..." – Pullman's paternalism was tempered by his capitalism. Just as he retained ownership of all of his railroad cars, which he leased to the railroads, he maintained ownership of all the property in his community, setting rents and refusing to let anyone own individual houses in Pullman. The town grew to 12,000 persons, half of whom toiled in the factories, which produced not only Pullman cars at costs of up to $25,000, but railroad cars of every type.

Many visitors to the 1893 World's Columbian Exposition went to see the model town. Shortly after, the severe depression that struck the American economy that year would turn Pullman's dream into his nightmare. By 1894 Pullman was forced to fire workers and cut piecework wages to maintain the profits from his factories. To keep the town profitable, rents and food prices stayed high. Workers caught in the bind revolted, joining Eugene V. Debs' American Railway Union and striking in May 1894. The union asked its workers nationwide to stop handling Pullman cars, and the strike became national. Pullman refused to negotiate, assembling a group of railroad magnates who convinced President Grover Cleveland to send federal troops, since the strike was interfering with the US Mail. Bloody conflicts led to a victory for Pullman and loss for the strikers, but the "perfect town" was exposed as a failure.

Pullman died bitter in 1897, leaving the company to Robert Todd Lincoln. In 189 the company was ordered by the Illinois Supreme Court to sell its non-industrial property, and by 1909 the residential sections had been purchased by individuals and former renters. The community declined and its population dwindled, but the factor continued to turn out Pullman cars until 1981. In 1971 Pullman was listed on th National Register of Historic Places, and restoration efforts began under the leade ship of the Historic Pullman Foundation, which bought the Hotel Florence in 1975. In 1988 the State of Illinois drew up plans for a railroad museum for the site *(work is expected to start in 2001)*, purchasing the Clocktower Building and the Hotel Florence in 1991.

Visiting Pullman

Pullman is located about 13mi south of the Loop. To access Pullman by car, drive south on I-94 and exit at 111th St. westbound (Exit 66A). The Pullman Historic District is four blocks west of the expressway. To access Pullman by train, take the Metra Electric District Line from the Randolph Street Metra Station; exit at 111th St. *(fare & schedule information:* ☎ *312-836-7000)*.

Begin your visit at the **Historic Pullman Foundation Visitor Center** *(11141 S. Cottage Grove Ave.; open year-round daily 11am–2pm; closed major holidays: $3;* ♿ 🅿 ☎ *773-785-8901; www.pullmanil.org)*, which features a video presentation and exhibits, and stocks maps and brochures. Departing from the visitor center, **guided walking tours** *(1hr 30min)* are offered May through October on the first Sunday of each month at 12:30pm and 1:30pm *($4)*. A number of historic homes are open for viewing the second weekend in October *(11am–5pm)* for the Annual Pullman House Tour *($15)*. The Chicago Architecture Foundation also conducts tours of the district; for recorded information, call ☎ *312-922-8687*.

WALKING TOUR *Distance: .6mi*

A variety of Victorian homes make up the 16 blocks of the **South Pullman** residential district. The larger homes of managers face 111th Street, while smaller row houses and double houses of craftsmen and workers line the streets south to 115th Street. The homes, all designed by architect Solon S. Beman in the Queen Anne and Shingle styles, sport varied and picturesque rooflines despite their modest scale. Beman also platted and designed **North Pullman**, between 104th and 108th Streets, for workers of Allen Paper Wheel Works and Union Foundery. South Pullman became a historic city landmark in 1972, while North Pullman was only so-designated in 1993. An active community organization is restoring many of the five blocks of original North Pullman houses, which are similar in design, but often simpler in detailing. In 1999 the Chicago City Council renamed the area—including the original residential units and the factories in the center of town—the Pullman District. The most picturesque stretch is along Cottage Grove Avenue at 107th Street where the houses are staggered along the angling thoroughfare.

Begin at the Hotel Florence.

★★**Hotel Florence** – *11111 S. Forrestville Ave. Museum open year-round Mon–Fri 11am–2pm, Sat 10am–2pm, Sun 10am–3pm. Closed major holidays. $2.* ✗ 🅿 ☎ *773-785-8181.* This grandiose structure (1881) exhibits a picturesque roofline with dormers above red brick walls, a wide Eastlake-style verandah and a Joliet limestone foundation. Wooden trim is painted in the color scheme seen throughout Pullman, which combines maroon and two shades of green to set off the red brick and gray roofs. The interior contains a lobby with several small displays, the hotel bar and a restaurant ornamented with wood and stained glass and original furnishings. The second floor includes several restored hotel rooms and numerous items from Pullman's demolished home on Prairie Avenue. The hotel functioned until 1975, when it was purchased by the Historic Pullman Foundation. Locals frequent the

© Robert Holmes

Hotel Florence

Hotel Florence Restaurant *(open for lunch weekdays)* for its all-you-can-eat buffet Sunday brunch, which features lunch entrées, soups, and casseroles served in 1890's-style ambience *(10am–3pm; ☐ ☎ 773-785-8900)*.

Walk south through Arcade Park.

The pleasant **Arcade Park**, restored in 1977, is embellished with 19C gaslight-style lanterns and three formal planting beds. A series of double houses built for factory foremen flank the park to the east on St. Lawrence Avenue. Most of these structures feature a central shared porch and a roofline punctuated by three dormers, although the compositions are varied and subsequent alterations have created very individual homes.

To the south on 112th Street stands the **Livery/Stables Building★**, now an automotive-repair facility. Like the other structures, the livery has a picturesque roofline studded with dormers as well as two carved horses' heads between the central arches. Across 112th Street the gray, modern **Historic Pullman Foundation Visitor Center** occupies the former site of the Arcade Building, a massive structure that contained the library, post office, theater and shops until it was demolished in the 1920s.

Walk east on 112th St. to St. Lawrence Ave.

At the southeast corner of 112th Street and St. Lawrence Avenue is the **Greenstone Church★** (Pullman United Methodist Church), a handsome structure dominated by a rich roofline of dormers and monitors and a square corner tower. The Romanesque-style walls are faced with unusual green stone, and trimmed with black stone. The church was intended to service any denomination and was available for rent. Pullman wanted every element of his community to turn a profit, including religious edifices! During the 1894 strike, Rev. William H. Carwardine preached a "social gospel" against Pullman's policies here, and his book *The Pullman Strike* gained public support for the strikers.

Designed for skilled craftsmen, the houses to the south on St. Lawrence Avenue included marble fireplaces and plaster walls.

Continue east on 112th St. to Champlain Ave.

Today in the course of being restored, **Market Hall** was originally three stories high. The first floor housed a market, which sold the commodities of life to Pullman workers, while the second floor contained an assembly hall and gymnasium; the third floor consisted of meeting rooms. The building is flanked on all four corners by the curved **Colonnade Apartments and Town Houses★**, creating a unique and attractive streetscape. Both the hall and apartments were built in 1892 for the Columbian Exposition.

Continue east on 112th St. to Langley Ave.

The block houses north of 112th Street on the east side of Langley Street were the meanest in Pullman, designed for unskilled labor. Similar blocks are found in North Pullman.

Return to Champlain Ave. and walk north to 111th St.

This block is lined with workers' homes—simple two-story brick row houses. Many have been restored with new porches and trim work painted in the Pullman colors. The homes are small, but the backyards and alleys are ample, rare amenities in the 1880s. The larger structures at the north end of the block were reserved for company managers and officers. At 111th Street look north to the **Pullman Firehouse**, recognizable by its distinctive Tuscan tower, originally used for drying fire hoses.

Walk west on 111th St.

The homes on 111th Street, created for company executives, were the finest in Pullman. The home of Pullman Company doctor John McLean, at no. 623, has been exquisitely restored. The chief superintendent's residence at no. 605 now houses a restaurant.

Walk north on Cottage Grove Ave.

A stroll north along Cottage Grove Avenue affords a view of the remains of the **Clocktower Building and Erection Shops**, which were burned by an arsonist's fire in 1998. The blaze rekindled the State of Illinois' decade-old plan to restore the building as a museum of transportation and industry. Various other factory buildings surround the landmark, which once faced an artificial lake to the west.

OAK PARK★★★

Population 54,217
Map pp 218-219

A prosperous integrated suburb bordering Chicago on the west, **Oak Park** is known worldwide as the birthplace of Prairie-school architecture and the modern American house. Attracting hordes of architecture buffs as well as lay folk, the town boasts the highest concentration of houses designed by American icon of architecture **Frank Lloyd Wright**. True to his vision of creating a style of architecture that could embody America's frontier spirit, Wright designed hundreds of unique houses distinguished by horizontal lines, ribbons of stained-glass windows and low, projecting profiles. The adjacent town of **River Forest** encompasses additional Prairie designs, including six by Wright.

Historical Notes

Frank Lloyd Wright: "Truth Against the World" – Born in Richland Center, Wisconsin in 1867, Frank Lloyd Wright credited the educational Froebel blocks, given to him by his mother and his musician father, as his earliest influences toward the design of form and space. After briefly attending the University of Wisconsin, Wright came to Chicago in 1887 and was hired as a draftsman by the firm of Adler & Sullivan. He worked on the Auditorium Building, becoming "a good pencil in the Master's hand" to Louis Sullivan, the only architect whose influence he ever acknowledged. In 1889 he married Catherine Tobin and moved to Oak Park, where he built a home and fathered six children.

© Balthazar Korab

Frank Lloyd Wright at Taliesin East (1958)

The restless Wright began designing on his own and left the employ of Adler & Sullivan in 1893 at the age of 25, developing his distinctive Prairie style of architecture over the next decade. In 1909 Wright left his wife and six children for the wife of an Oak Park client, effectively ending his practice in the socially conservative community. His architecture became more expressionistic in the 1910s and 20s, and in 1931 he established Taliesin in his home state of Wisconsin to train architects. Following construction of the stunning 1936 Fallingwater House in western Pennsylvania, Wright opened his Taliesin West studio in Arizona and remained in the limelight, refining his iconoclastic image until his death in 1959 at age 91.

His own home and studio, now restored to their 1909 appearance, trace the evolution of Wright's horizontal, organic architecture, introduced to the world in the 1911 Wasmuth folio printed in Berlin. Wright apprentices William Drummond, Marion Mahony, Walter Burley Griffin, Barry Byrne and John Van Bergen became prominent in their own right, and contemporaries George W. Maher, Robert C. Spencer and E.E. Roberts also designed many Prairie-style buildings in Oak Park and throughout the region.

Oak Park: A Suburb Evolves – Oak Park was settled in the years after the fire in 1871 by a prosperous Puritan population that kept the tiny suburb free of immigrants, alcohol and other harbingers of moral decay. After supporting the annexation of neigh-

215

boring Austin by the City of Chicago in 1899, Oak Park preserved its independence by seceding from the township of Cicero and becoming an independent village in 1902. The population grew rapidly, from 5,000 in 1890 to almost 20,000 by 1910. Novelist **Ernest Hemingway** was born on Oak Park Avenue in 1899. Like Wright, his progressive ideas led him to abandon Oak Park for a world of adventure in 1918, later deriding the conservative suburb for its "wide lawns and narrow minds." Author Edgar Rice Burroughs also dwelled here until called to Hollywood to supervise the filming of the *Tarzan* movies starring Chicago native Johnny Weissmuller.

Linked to the city by two rapid-transit lines and commuter rail, Oak Park became a suburb of choice for progressive suburbanites in this century, swelling its population to 50,000 by mid-century. As racial change swept across Austin in the 1960s and 70s, Oak Park resolved to become an integrated, middle-class community, setting up a housing center to mix arriving African Americans into its increasingly diverse population, while buttressing its border against the city. In 1973 the Frank Lloyd Wright and Prairie School of Architecture Historic District was listed on the National Register of Historic Places, marking the beginning of restoration efforts in the community. Today Oak Park is known as an economically stable, socially progressive, well-educated community that easily accommodates lifestyles and ideas more radical than those of residents Wright and Hemingway three generations ago.

Visiting Oak Park

Oak Park lies 10mi west of Chicago's Loop along the Eisenhower Expressway (I-290) between Austin Blvd. and Harlem Ave. To access Oak Park by car, drive west on I-290 and take the Harlem Ave. Exit. Turn right onto Harlem and proceed north to Oak Park. To access Oak Park by public transportation, take the ▨▨ Green or Blue line, or take the Metra West commuter rail line from the Metra station at W. Madison and Canal Sts. Exit all train lines at Oak Park Ave. or Harlem Ave. stops *(for schedules and fares; ☎ 312-836-7000)*.

Begin your visit at the **Oak Park Visitor Center** *(158 N. Forest Ave.; open year-round daily 10am–5pm; closed Jan 1, Thanksgiving Day & Dec 25; 1hr audio tour available, $6; ⚒ ᓬ 🅿 🚾 708-848-1500; www.visitoakpark.com)*, which offers maps and brochures and sells tickets to various Oak Park attractions.

An audio cassette and map *($9)* for **self-guided tours** of the historic district are available from the Ginkgo Tree Bookshop in the **Frank Lloyd Wright Home and Studio**. Guided district walking tours begin at the Home and Studio on weekends *(year-round Mon–Fri 11am, 1pm & 3pm. Weekend tours available from 1pm–4pm; $8; ☎ 708-848-1976)*. Ten privately owned homes and architecturally significant buildings are opened to the public the 3rd Saturday in May for the "Wright Plus" tour *(prices vary)*. Advance tickets required *(tickets go on sale Mar 1)*. For additional information and tickets, contact **Ginkgo Tree Bookshop** *(951 Chicago Ave.; open year-round daily 10am–5pm; closed major holidays; ᓬ ☎ 708-848-1600)*.

For shopping and dining, visit Lake St., Chicago Ave. and Oak Park Ave. where you'll find a cluster of specialty shops and restaurants.

Oak Park is best experienced by strolling the pleasant, tree-lined streets. While feasting your eyes on the architectural marvels, keep in mind that most of the homes are not open to the public, and respect owners' privacy.

SIGHTS

The following descriptions cover Oak Park's highlights.

★★ **Frank Lloyd Wright Home and Studio** – *951 W. Chicago Ave. Visit by guided tour (45min) only, year-round Mon–Fri 11am, 1pm & 3pm; weekends 11am–3:30pm. Closed Jan 1, Thanksgiving Day & Dec 25. $8. ☎ 708-848-1976. www.wrightplus.org.* Opened to the public in 1974, this National Historic Landmark helped usher in Oak Park's era as an essential architectural pilgrimage. Wright first built the house in 1889, and continued to remodel and add to it over time; his alterations offer visitors the opportunity to view his architectural growth. The house has been restored to its 1909 appearance, when Wright last lived there and the studio was fully operational.

"The prairie has a beauty of its own.
A building on the prairie should recognize the features of its quiet level and accentuate them harmoniously. It should be quiet, broad, inclusive, a welcome associate of trees and flowers, not a nervous, fussy interloper, and should be 'married' to the ground. Hence, broad, sheltering eaves over determined masses, gentle roofs, spreading base and outreaching walls."

Frank Lloyd Wright

The tour begins with the 1889 Forest Avenue house that resembles a Shingle-style Victorian but for its horizontal bands of windows and low, earth-hugging profile. The **living room** is centered on the rectilinear hearth and inglenook that would characterize the later Prairie houses. The 1895 **dining room** reveals the emerging Prairie style in elegant, if uncomfortable, high-backed chairs framing the table beneath a false skylight. The tour continues to the modified second floor, where Wright's first office became a bedroom for his growing family. Wall murals in the master bedroom evoke Native-American themes also seen in the 1895 **children's playroom★**, a marvelous barrel-vaulted space with balconies that distort perspective, banded windows and sphere-in-square lanterns. Returning to the main floor, visitors pass a tree that grows through the house (Wright endeavored to keep natural elements as part of his designs). The two-story **studio★** addition of 1898 affords a glimpse into the busy, creative world where Prairie architects apprenticed to the master. The oc-

© Balthazar Korab

Frank Lloyd Wright Home and Studio, Living Room

tagonal library and low office entrance include intricate leaded-glass patterns that mimic the environment and intersecting volumes that defy and define interior space. A forest of columns and sculpture by Richard Bock ornament the Chicago Avenue entrance. The basement contains archives, while the Ginkgo Tree Bookshop occupies the former garage.

Farther west on Chicago Avenue stand the **Robert P. Parker** (**A**), **Thomas H. Gale** (**B**) and **Walter H. Gale** (**C**) Houses *(nos. 1019, 1027 and 1031)*, "bootleg" homes Wright designed in violation of his exclusive contract with Adler & Sullivan. These 1892-93 Queen Anne structures betray the emerging sensibilities of the 25-year-old Wright with their horizontal clapboards and banded windows.

★**Nathan G. Moore House** – *333 N. Forest Ave. Visit by guided tour (45min) only. For hours, contact Oak Park Visitor Center (☎ 708-524-7800).* With its steep roofline, Sullivanesque balustrade fence and Tudor Revival style, the 1895 Moore House presents a dramatic contrast to Wright's later horizontal compositions. The house was a remodeling of an earlier structure that all but disappeared under the busy hand of Wright. The architect rebuilt the home after a 1922 fire, providing Oak Park visitors a rare glimpse of his 1920s experimentation with Japanese themes in encrusted ornament.

★**Arthur Heurtley House** – *318 N. Forest Ave.* Wright's admired 1902 design here prefigures many of the elements of his 1909 Robie House, including a raised living space curtained by ornate stained glass, a wide roof that hovers above a band of windows, and horizontally textured brick walls. The front door is hidden by a wall but revealed by a rounded arch, suggesting a serene and organic fortress.

Wright moved and remodeled the 1883 Stick-style **Hills DeCaro House★** *(313 N. Forest Ave.)* in 1900, adding horizontal shingling and flattening the roof.

★**Laura Gale House** – *6 Elizabeth Ct.* Anticipating Europe's International style of the 1920s, the broad cantilevered planes of this 1909 home also prefigure Wright's 1936 work, Fallingwater. The porches both anchor and expand the living spaces, "breaking the box" of architecture and shifting it into the landscape.

The **Joseph D. Everett House** (**D**) *(228 N. Forest Ave.)*, an 1888 Queen Anne Victorian, represents the dominant residential style in the years that Frank Lloyd Wright wreaked his revolution on the serene side streets of Oak Park.

★**Frank W. Thomas House** – *210 N. Forest Ave.* Considered the first true Prairie-style house by Wright, this 1901 commission abandons all elements and ornaments of Victorian design. The entrance arch below the main floor leads not to a door but to a staircase proceeding to the hidden entry. Bands of art-glass windows are squeezed and sheltered between flattened roofs and high stucco walls. Immediately south, Victorian row houses from 1892 illustrate the architectural shift Wright led at the turn of the century.

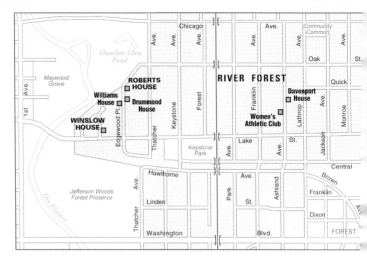

★★Unity Temple – *875 W. Lake St. Open Memorial Day–Labor Day Mon–Fri 10am–5pm, weekends 1pm–4pm. Rest of the year daily 1pm–4pm. $4 (self-guided audio-cassette tour). Guided tours (45min) available weekends only 1pm, 2pm & 3pm ($6). Closed Jan 1, Thanksgiving Day & Dec 25. ☎ 708-383-8873. www.unitytemple.org.* In 1905 Frank Lloyd Wright took a small site and a limited budget and created one of his great works of architecture. Called "my little jewel" by Wright, Unity Temple is an endlessly intriguing succession of form and space inside and out. The small budget ($45,000) dictated the use of unadorned reinforced concrete for the interlocking rectangular forms of the worship space and social hall. The two are joined with a low lobby shielded from busy Lake Street by a "pathway of discovery" leading from Kenilworth Avenue onto a raised entrance behind a high wall. Entered from behind the lectern, the worship space seems at once massive and intimate. Framed by rectilinear balconies, three levels allow 400 persons to sit no more than 45ft from the pulpit. Bathed by a grid of square skylights and clerestory windows, the room is framed with wood trim in a deceptively simple series of borders and inset rectangles and hung with sphere-in-square chandeliers. The clamor outside is forgotten behind high concrete walls as the eye travels along forms that simultaneously embrace and overreach the room itself, suggesting the spiritual quest at the heart of Unitarian-Universalism. The smaller social hall is filled with familiar Prairie forms and centers on a hearth, as in Wright's houses, reinforcing the human scale and purpose of this space.

Additional Sights

East of Forest Avenue, Kenilworth Avenue offers a wealth of large-scale Victorian mansions and early modern houses. On the southwest corner of Oak Park Avenue and Lake Street, **Scoville Square** (1908, E.E. Roberts) exhibits the influence of the Prairie school on commercial architecture with its broad rooflines. Euclid Avenue near the Oak Park and River Forest High School hosts an array of expansive mansions, including early works by Wright and Maher, and the **Edward W. McCready House** at no. 231 (1907, Spencer & Powers), with its stately entrance and elegant integration into the landscape.

Ernest Hemingway Birthplace – *339 N. Oak Park Ave. Open year-round Thu, Fr & Sun 1pm–5pm, Sat 10am–5pm. $6. Guided tours available. ☎ 708-848-2222 www.hemingway.org.* This restored Victorian home (1890, Wesley A. Arnold) recreates the comfortable family upbringing of celebrated author Ernest Hemingway (1899-1961), who won the Nobel Prize for literature in 1954. A visit here provides a glimpse of Oak Park's social order in the early 20C, and the impact that the community had on Hemingway's early development.

Two blocks south, at 200 North Oak Park Avenue, the **Hemingway Museum** *(same hours, phone & Web site as Hemingway Birthplace; $6)* offers a core exhibit that focuses on the first 20 years of Hemingway's life. Additional special exhibits treat periods of the author's adult years, such as Hemingway in Hollywood and Hemingway at war.

★"Pleasant Home" (Farson-Mills House) – *217 S. Home Ave. Visit by guided tou (1hr) only, Mar–Nov Thu–Sun 12:30pm–3:30pm. Rest of the year Thu–Su 12:30pm–2:30pm. Closed major holidays. $5 (free Thu). ▯ ☎ 708-383-265* George Washington Maher (1864-1926) is unique among Prairie school architect both for his symmetrical, straightforward facades and his motif-rhythm theory design, where ornamental elements and local flora are repeated throughout th

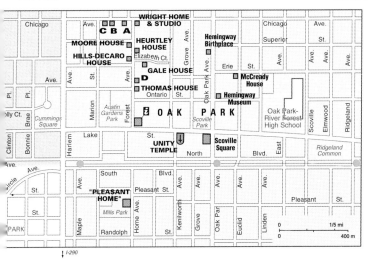

composition. Owned by the Park District of Oak Park since 1939, Pleasant Home is set in Mills Park, originally the mansion's grounds. This 1897 house was the first in Maher's modern (or Prairie) style, with its broad facade, hipped roof and use of four repeated motifs—the honeysuckle, Roman tray or shield, lion's head and segmented arch—in exterior decoration, art glass and light fixtures, interior furnishings and trim. The main hall features exquisitely detailed quartersawn oak trim studded with lights. Adjacent sunny parlors are being restored to reflect their original Arts and Crafts design, and the dining room contains the table and chairs intended for the space by Maher. Tours also include upstairs bedrooms and the second-floor collections of the Oak Park and River Forest Historical Society.

★RIVER FOREST

The more exclusive town of River Forest encompasses several notable Prairie school designs. Frank Lloyd Wright's 1893 **William Winslow House**★ *(515 Auvergne Pl.)* was his first significant independent commission. Centered on a square, Sullivanesque arch, the flat and symmetrical facade begins to reach for prairie-like horizontality in its Roman brick, low-pitched roof and shaded second story. On nearby Edgewood Place, an elm tree grows through the parlor of Wright's 1908 split-level **Isabel Roberts House**★ *(no. 603)*. The home was restored by Wright in 1955. Next door at no. 559, the **William Drummond House**, designed by its owner in 1910, exemplifies the work of Wright's student with its broad porch and flat roof, while the **Chauncey Williams House** at no. 530 (1895, Frank Lloyd Wright) is a rare high-roofed Wright design with Japanese influence. Ashland Avenue features Wright's 1901 **Arthur Davenport House** at no. 559, and the elegantly scaled **Women's Athletic Club** at no. 526 (1911, Drummond and Guenzel).

BROOKFIELD ZOO★★

Map p 10 and plan p 220

Covering 216 acres in west suburban Brookfield, this expansive zoo in a garden is home to more than 2,800 animals inhabiting carefully re-created rain forests, seascapes, savannahs and deserts both indoors and out. For its human denizens, 15mi of footpaths wind through the lovely grounds, and shady stretches of lawn invite picnicking. Formal flower beds complement the patchwork of animal habitats. Nearly two million people each year enjoy this animal haven, leaving with a heightened respect for our fragile environment.

Historical Notes – Brookfield Zoo's meticulous attention to habitat continues a long tradition of cageless homes for its animals. The idea behind Brookfield was to create a zoo big enough to accommodate natural outdoor habitats, thereby eliminating the use of small, spartan enclosures, and emulating conditions in the wild to provide more realistic study and breeding opportunities. Such was the trend in European zoos, and the Bronx Zoo in New York had incorporated naturalistic settings into its plan when it debuted in 1899. Built on land donated to the Forest Preserve District of Cook County by Edith Rockefeller McCormick in 1919, Brookfield, modeled largely after the Hagenbeck Zoo in Hamburg, Germany, would finally open in 1934 after years of controversy over taxes and public funding. The "barless" Bear Grottos, Goat Mountain and Monkey Island were among the first habitats completed, along with the Small Mammal House, the Reptile House and the Pachyderm House. In the last several decades, the trend toward cageless habitats has moved indoors with the construction of Tropic World: A Primate's Journey (among the world's largest zoo exhibits), The Fragile Kingdom, The Swamp and The Living Coast. Scheduled to open in summer 2001, the Hamill Family Play Zoo (located in the former small mammal house) will teach children about nature through a range of hands-on activities.

Visiting Brookfield Zoo

8400 W. 31st St. Open Memorial Day–Labor Day daily 9:30am–6pm. Rest of the year daily 10am–5pm. $7 (free Oct–Mar Tue & Thu). & (&) ($4) ☎ 708-485-0263. www.brookfieldzoo.org. Check at entrances or information kiosks located throughout the zoo for schedule of special shows and demonstrations.

The zoo is located 14mi southwest of the Loop in Brookfield. To access the zoo by car from the Loop, drive west on I-290 to the 1st Ave. Exit, then continue south on 1st Ave. to 31st St. Follow signs to the zoo. To access the zoo by train, take the Burlington Northern Metra train line from Union Station in the Loop. Get off at the zoo stop at Hollywood Station and walk north four blocks (fare & schedule information: ☎ 312-836-7000).

Discovery Center Theater offers visitors a variety of multimedia presentations to orient them to the zoo. Here you'll also find the Elephant's Trunk gift shop. Plan to visit Tropic World and Seven Seas Panoramas early in the day to avoid long lines.

Departing just west of the gates, the Motor Safari tour offers a narrated overview of the zoo. The tram can also be used to shuttle to the various areas of interest since passengers can disembark and reboard at any of four tram stops throughout the day (operates daily early spring–late fall, weather permitting; round-trip 45min; commentary; $2.50; &). During the winter months, you can ride the Snowball Express free of charge. Fast-food restaurants offering varied cuisine are located primarily in the eastern and southwestern sections of the zoo. A full-service, sit-down restaurant, Bocaditos, is located in the South American Marketplace next to The Living Coast. Restrooms can be found throughout the zoo. Public telephones are available at the Discovery Center and at both zoo entrances.

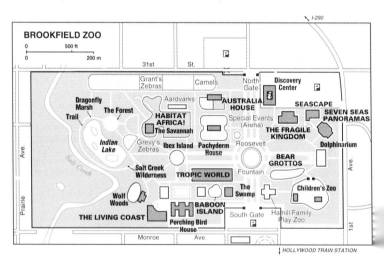

THE GROUNDS

The park fans out from Roosevelt Fountain, the formally landscaped heart of the grounds approached from four directions by grassy esplanades and pathways. Favorite sights around the zoo include Wolf Woods, home to a pack of gray wolves and the Bear Grottos★, where polar, brown, sloth and spectacled bears cavort. The Art Deco Pachyderm House and outdoor enclosures are home to black rhinos, Nile hippopotamuses and African elephants. In the Perching Bird House, iridescent avian gems reside behind "jewel-box" window enclosures.

★The Fragile Kingdom – To the northeast of the fountain, a large three-part exhibit explores the complex webs of life and survival in an African desert and an Asian rain forest. In these naturalistic habitats species commingle as they would in the wild, and the experience envelops the visitor as each setting extends to the public areas of the space. Linger a moment to spot and identify each creature: a flash of orange gives the rain forest's Prevost's squirrels away, but the camouflage of the elegant clouded leopard makes finding him more of a challenge. The Fragile Desert tells a story of survival in a seemingly inhospitable climate and how such animal as meerkats make a home there. Tiny windows reveal a subterranean world of burrowing creatures, including the fascinating naked mole-rats, hairless mammals that live in colonies like bees and feed on underground plant parts. Outside, the big cats are displayed as part of The Fragile Kingdom in the context of their increasingly difficult struggle to survive as hunters in their vanishing ecosystems.

★★**Seven Seas Panoramas** – ||||| Likely the most popular attraction at the zoo, Seven Seas consists of two parts. The **Seascape**★ features a series of outdoor pools designed to resemble a Pacific Northwest shoreline environment stocked with pinnipeds—seals and sea lions. An underwater viewing area beneath the pool allows visitors to enjoy the animals at their most graceful. Next door, the **Dolphin Show**★ *(several 20min performances daily; $2.50; &)* has been a perpetual favorite since its inception in 1961 as the first inland dolphin exhibit. Spectators generally jam the 2,000-seat **Dolphinarium** at several showtimes each day to view the antics of Atlantic bottle-nosed dolphins. The zoo uses the performance to reinforce its conservation message, and trainers are careful to explain the significance of dolphin behaviors in the wild. Natural dolphin feeding strategies, for instance, include smashing prey with its heavy tail, known to scientists as "fish-whacking." To demonstrate, trainers cue dolphins and audience to volley beach balls back and forth, the animals' powerful tails often catapulting the balls high into the stands.

Dolphin Show

Children's Zoo – Taking up most of the quadrant southeast of the fountain, this busy place provides ample opportunities for kids to interact with barnyard and other gentle animals *(open Memorial Day–Labor Day daily 10am–6pm; rest of the year daily 10am–5pm; $1, free Nov–Feb; &)*. The beguiling Nubian and pygmy goats are particularly popular, along with the llamas and reindeer. Demonstrations of "Animals in Action," including cow and goat milking, take place daily in summer, weather permitting.

★★**Tropic World: A Primate's Journey** – ||||| Opened in the 1980s, this ground-breaking exhibit southwest of the fountain comprises three indoor rain-forest habitats: Asia, Africa and South America. One of the first exhibits to group compatible species together as they might live in nature, Tropic World offers visitors a dramatic treetop perspective on life in these tropical realms. Realistic trees, foliage, waterfalls, rockwork and pools combine in a

■ **Famous Zoo Residents**

The Brookfield Zoo's animal collection started with the gift of 143 mammals, 123 birds and 4 reptiles from a private zoo in Holland, Michigan. In the ensuing years, Brookfield has had its share of famous inhabitants, including the first giant pandas in an American zoo, Su-lin (arrived in 1937), Mei-mei (1938) and Mei-lan (1939). Museka, the first okapi in America, arrived in 1955. Temperamental Asian bull elephant Ziggy (named for his original owner Florenz Ziegfield) lived to a ripe old age of 55, and the popular walrus Olga died in 1988 at 27, the oldest walrus in captivity. The zoos' resident heroine is an ape named Binti Jua who rescued a three-year-old boy who fell into her enclosure and knocked himself unconscious in 1996.

breathtaking and cavernous environment bustling with activity. The exhibit guides visitors through all three regions explaining the daily lives of primates and what choices they must make to survive. Most intriguing of all are the animals themselves, from the tiny Brazilian golden lion tamarin to the lordly western lowland gorillas that reside on their own island in Tropic World-Africa.

Nearby, **The Swamp: Wonders of our Wetlands** (in the former Primate House) offers insight into a North American cypress swamp populated by alligators, snakes and a variety of birds, as well as an Illinois wetland alive with otters and alligator snapping turtles. **Baboon Island★** (the zoo's original Monkey Island, refurbished) houses a large colony of rambunctious Guinea baboons whose interactions are fascinating to watch.

The greatest expanse of zoo lies to the north and west of Tropic World. **Ibex Island**, a prominent landmark due west of the fountain, is the artificial mountain home of a herd of surefooted ibex. In **Australia House★** audio stations guide visitors through a nocturnal "walk-about" past wombats and into a space alive with free-flying fruit bats. Kookaburras, echidnas, kangaroos, cassowaries and ostriches can be found outdoors.

★**Habitat Africa!** – The first phase of an ambitious undertaking that is transforming 30 acres of the zoo's northwest section into various African immersion exhibits, **The Savannah** covers five acres of exhibits highlighting the Dark Continent's diverse wildlife. Giraffes, wild dogs and other inhabitants of the African savannah populate the dusty plain, while a variety of hoofed animals slake their thirst at the **water hole**. A reconstructed **kopje** (KAH-pee), a grassland oasis surrounded by granite outcroppings, shelters a complex ecosystem that includes the delicate klipspringer, a tiny rock-climbing antelope, and the rock hyrax, a small mammal that judges the width of its rockbound hideaways with its whiskers.

Phase two, **The Forest**, replicates the pristine Ituri rain forest in central Africa's Democratic Republic of Congo. Enter this leafy world, created by combining 545 trees and 775 shrubs with fabricated elements, and discover the diversity of animal life in the rain forest, from the emperor scorpion to the hoofed okapi. Along the path, signs introduce the human residents of the Ituri: the Mbuti people who call the forest home, the Bila villagers who farm the edges of the forest, and the researchers and reserve rangers who study and work there. These groups "narrate" the journey via trailside signage, presenting contrasting views of lifeways and resources. The deepest part of the rain forest, where only one percent of light filters through to the floor, is re-created indoors with a dark understory of vines, ferns and trees. Here you'll find crocodiles, pythons, African giant rats, and the blue duiker, a tiny antelope.

★**The Living Coast** – Here visitors can explore—without getting wet—the "underwater" world of the west coast of South America, from the Open Ocean to the Near Shore Waters to the Rocky Shores. In Open Ocean, a ceiling-high tank swirls with seaweed, sea turtles and a host of fish, while in Rocky Shores, waves crashing overhead elicit cries of surprise. Along the way you'll see jellyfish, sea turtles, Inca terns and even vampire bats, while displays relate the surprising connections that exist between the animals, plants and coastal environment. A domed indoor habitat features the endangered Humboldt penguin.

At the western edge of the zoo lies man-made **Indian Lake**, surrounded by **Salt Creek Wilderness**, which teems with local plant, bird and animal life. A cedar-chip **trail** (.25mi) circles the far side of the lake past the **Dragonfly Marsh** and provides a restful break from the zoo crowds. Guideposts along the way identify resident wildlife.

MORTON ARBORETUM★

Map p 16

Sprawling over 1,700 acres, this outdoor museum is both a serious scientific laboratory of woody plants from around the world and a very pleasant place to spend the day. Visitors who wander by car and on foot among 35,000 individual plants and 3,300 species may not realize the contributions to horticulture, botany and ecology that this arboreal microcosm makes possible. Open year-round, the arboretum attracts professional landscapers and gardeners, horticultural hobbyists, bird-watchers and inexhaustible hikers.

Historical Notes – Joy Morton, founder of the arboretum in 1922, came by his love of trees naturally. His father, J. Sterling Morton, had been secretary of Agriculture under Grover Cleveland and is well remembered as the creator of Arbor Day. Using his fortune, made at the helm of the Morton Salt Co., which he founded, Joy established the arboretum on 400 acres at Thornhill (his Du Page County estate) and proceeded to carry out the family motto to "Plant Trees." From the beginning, Morton intended the arboretum to be a place to preserve and study trees suitable for growing in Illinois' temperate climate—a veritable "museum of woody plants."

Today the arboretum's far-flung collection is divided into four general categories: botanical groups (plants in the same genus or family, such as the *Quercus*, or oaks), landscape groups (plants with a similar use, such as the ground-cover garden), geographic groups (plants from the same region, such as the Japanese collection) and special habitat groups (plants that live in "amended" soil or in special sites, such as those in the sand beds). The grounds also support native landscapes: oak groves, wetlands and prairie. Particularly strong among the arboretum's collections are its Rosaceae (rose family), its elms and its sugar maples (especially beautiful in the fall).

Visiting Morton Arboretum

Open Apr-Oct daily 7am-7pm. Rest of the year daily 7am-5pm. ✗ ♿ ☐($7/car, Wed $3/car) ☎ 630-719-2465. www.mortonarb.org.
The arboretum is located on Rte. 53, 25mi west of the city, just north of I-88 and west of I-355. To access the arboretum by car from the Loop, take I-290 West and then continue west on the I-88 tollway. At Rte. 53, turn north toward the arboretum. Begin at the **Visitor Center** on the east side to gather information about the grounds, pick up trail maps and find out what is in bloom. Several gardens can be reached on foot from here, including the ground covers, roses and dwarf shrubs. Open-air **tram tours** depart from the visitor center (Apr-Oct daily 10:45am, noon, 1:15pm & 2:30pm, weather permitting; round-trip 45min; $3; ♿). Other specialized tours are available; contact the visitor center (☎ 630-719-2465) for details. Visitors can also drive the 11mi one-way route in their car (a driving map is provided at the entry gate). Along the way, 26 parking areas make it possible to stop and hike any of the 10 major trails or explore the ancillary tracks and paths. In all, 25mi of trails wind through the grounds and visitors have virtually unlimited access to the woods, glades and meadows (a compass is recommended on the lesser paths as there is little signage). Light snacks are available at the Coffee Shop (daily 9am-5pm) and a seasonally changing lunch menu is offered at Ginkgo Restaurant (daily 11am-3pm), both located in the visitor center. Public restrooms and telephones can be found in the visitor center and across from the Thornhill Education Center.

THE GARDENS

In the elegant **hedge garden★**, formal rows of woody plants extend into a stately pinetum, or plantation of pine trees. The four columns at its east end represent Joy Morton and his three brothers, Carl, Paul and Mark. It's an easy stroll from here around Meadow Lake, one of several man-made lakes on the grounds, along the first loop of the **Illinois Trees Trail★**. Interpretive labels identify local trees along this paved path. For more hiking, follow the second and third loops past the azaleas and rhododendrons and deeper into the forest to view wildflowers, meadows and marshes.

To see the rest of the arboretum, take the hour-long narrated open **tram tour★**, an excellent nonstop excursion that follows the main route from east to west and affords a complete overview of the grounds.

A particularly interesting walk winds through the **geographic collections★** of specimens from Asia, the Balkans, Appalachia and the eastern US wetlands.

Located on the west side, the **Thornhill Education Center** is the site of the original Morton estate. An exhibit in the Founder's Room, the only remaining wing of the home, provides a brief history of the arboretum and the family. Outside, in the lovely **fragrance garden★**, the aromas of peonies, mock oranges and mint combine enticingly. The nearby daffodil glade, planted with 130,000 bulbs, makes an incredible springtime sight.

On the far perimeter of the west side, at parking lot 25, a narrow trail makes a circuit through a reconstructed 100-acre **prairie★**, which blooms beautifully during the summer. The prairies of Illinois have been largely eliminated since the settlement of the area, and restorations such as this one are important keys to understanding the native ecology of the Midwest. Over 90 varieties of grasses and plants blanket the prairie.

The arboretum is a haven for at least 20 varieties of mammals, including raccoons, red foxes and coyotes. Birds abound as well, and 70 nesting boxes provide homes for eastern bluebirds.

ILLINOIS & MICHIGAN CANAL NATIONAL HERITAGE CORRIDOR★

Maps p 225 and pp 226-227

The Illinois & Michigan (I&M) Canal, running 96mi from Bridgeport to LaSalle/Peru, first linked the Great Lakes to the Mississippi and helped Chicago build its reputation as an industrial powerhouse. Today a popular recreational area hosting over five million visitors yearly, the National Heritage Corridor encompasses historic canal towns offering a glimpse into bygone days, as well as native prairies and state parks laced with miles of pleasant hiking and biking trails.

Historical Notes

Between 15,000 and 10,000 years ago, meltwaters from retreating glaciers carved a wide valley southwest of Chicago to the Mississippi River. As the glacial lake drained, a low, 12ft-high ridge rose slowly between the Des Plaines and Chicago rivers, separating the watershed of the Mississippi from the Great Lakes. Native Americans traveled by canoe through this corridor, and guided the first Europeans, explorer Louis Jolliet and missionary Jacques Marquette, to the Chicago Portage between the two rivers in 1673. As the French continued to explore Illinois and establish a lucrative fur trade, they realized that a canal through this low divide would open the continent to commerce.

After the area became part of the US in 1782, a canal was proposed and by the 1820s, a federal commission was established to create the channel connecting Lake Michigan to the Illinois River. Along with the Erie Canal, the I&M Canal would provide an inland link from New York to New Orleans. The towns of Chicago and Ottawa were platted in 1830, and canal construction began at Bridgeport on July 4, 1836. Despite a three-year hiatus caused by Illinois' unstable financial condition, the canal was completed in 1848. Chicago's population boomed from 4,000 to over 20,000 during construction, and other canal towns blossomed as well. As the narrow, 60ft-wide channel brought grains and livestock from Illinois' rich prairie soils to eastern markets, Chicago more than quadrupled its population to over 112,000 by 1860. Stone quarrying, steel production, and coal, zinc and sand mining thrived throughout the corridor in the 19C. Horses towed passenger boats and mules pulled boats laden with lumber, stone and grains. Although railroads made their appearance in the corridor by 1854, the canal continued to carry freight, reaching its apogee in 1882 when steam-powered boats had replaced the mule teams. Unlike most canals, the I&M paid off its debt by 1871, and was deepened that year from 6ft to 8ft in an attempt to reverse the flow of the Chicago River. The effort was not entirely successful, and after cholera and typhoid epidemics decimated the city in the 1880s, Chicago created a Metropolitan Sanitary District to dig a much larger drainage canal from Chicago to Lockport; completed in 1900, it permanently reversed the Chicago River. By 1914 the northern section of the I&M Canal was replaced as a shipping channel by the new Sanitary & Ship Canal. In 1933 the Illinois River was made navigable, and the obsolete I&M began to be developed for recreational use. The section of the canal in Chicago was filled in for construction of the Stevenson Expressway (I-55) in the 1950s. In 1963 the I&M Canal was designated a National Historic Landmark, and nine years later, the southern section became a state park. Efforts to develop the canal's recreational and historic potential culminated in the designation by Congress of the entire canal route (120mi) as a National Heritage Corridor in 1984. Today numerous historic buildings have been preserved and new trails and wayside exhibits promote the region's historic, recreational and economic resources.

NORTHERN SECTION DRIVING TOUR

Chicago to Joliet *Distance: about 90mi round-trip*

The highly industrialized northern section of the canal borders Chicago and includes several evocative historic sites as well as recreational and natural areas. Note that some sections of the drive are highly commercialized or wind through ordinary suburban landscapes, offering few vistas of the canal. However, quaint canal towns and various museums make this a worthwhile day trip from Chicago. Follow the map and the directions carefully, as this stretch is sometimes difficult to navigate.

Leave Chicago on I-55 (Stevenson Expwy.) and exit at LaGrange Rd./Rte. 45 (Exit 279A); bear right and follow the signs to Rte. 171/Archer Ave. South.

Built in 1836 as a construction route for the canal, Archer Avenue leads through the suburb of Willow Springs, where a 9mi-loop bicycle trail follows the canal towpath, and into the 14,000-acre Palos Forest Preserves. After about 5mi, to the left before Route 83, stands the historic **St. James at Sag Bridge★** (founded in 1833), the oldest church and cemetery complex in Cook County. The simple local limestone church building (c.1850) sits on a hill surrounded by graves dating back to 1846, containing the remains of hundreds of canal workers, including a large number of Irish immigrants.

Practical Information

Access – Northern section driving tour: follow itinerary directions in driving tour text. Southern section: drive south on I-55 for 46mi to Rte. 6 West toward Channahon. For other sights in southern section, drive south on I-55 and then west on I-80; exit at Rte. 47 for Morris, Rte. 23 for Ottawa, Rte. 178 for Utica and Starved Rock State Park, and Rte. 351 for LaSalle.

Visitor Information – The I&M Canal is best visited on summer weekends when most activities occur. The route can be difficult to follow as signs bearing the canal logo *(below)* are sometimes hard to locate. The following agencies provide maps and information about accommodations and recreation: **Illinois & Michigan Canal National Heritage Corridor Commission**, 15701 S. Independence Blvd., Lockport IL 60441, ☎ 815-740-2047 *(contact for location and hours of visitor centers along the canal)*; **Heritage Corridor Visitors Bureau**, 81 N. Chicago St., Joliet IL 60432 ☎ 815-727-2323 or 800-926-2262 (US & Canada only); the **Forest Preserve District of Cook County**, 536 N. Harlem Ave., River Forest IL 60305 ☎ 773-261-8400.

Tours – National Heritage Corridor cruises of the northernmost section of the I&M Canal are conducted September weekends *(depart from Mercury Cruise Line dock at the southwest corner of Michigan Avenue Bridge at 9am Sept 10, Sept 30 & Oct 1; round-trip 7hrs; $69; commentary; reservations required; Mercury ☎ 312-332-1366).*

Recreation – **Hiking:** I&M Canal State Trail (61mi) from Joliet to Peru; other trails found in state parks and forest preserves in the corridor. **Cross-country skiing** permitted on most hiking trails. **Canoe trails:** Des Plaines River from Lyons to Romeoville *(20mi)*; I&M Canal from Channahon to Morris *(15mi)*.

Dining and Accommodations – Hotels and restaurants can be found in the major commercial areas of Joliet, Morris, Ottawa and LaSalle. **Campsites** are available at Starved Rock, Illini and Channahon state parks and at designated sites along the I&M Canal State Trail.

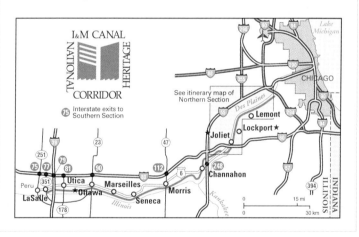

Continue on Rte. 171 as it turns left at Rte. 83.

The road crosses the Calumet Sag Channel, built in 1911 to link the Sanitary & Ship Canal with Chicago's southern port at Lake Calumet.

Keep right to follow Rte. 171; turn right after about 3mi at McCarthy Rd., which becomes Stephen St., and drive into Lemont.

Lemont – Known in the 19C for its dolomite-limestone quarries, Lemont is a well-preserved historic canal town set on a bluff in the Des Plaines River Valley. The **Lemont Area Historical Society Museum** *(306 Lemont St.)*, located in an 1861 limestone church, offers exhibits and research facilities; pick up a self-guided brochure to the downtown area here *(open May–Oct Tue, Thu, Fri 10am–2pm, weekends 1pm–4pm; rest of the year Thu–Fri 10am–2pm, weekends 1pm–4pm; closed major holidays; $1 contribution requested;* 🅿 ☎ *630-257-2972; www.township.com/lemont).* The downtown shopping area *(Main and Stephen Sts.)* is dominated by 19C Italianate buildings constructed of Lemont stone, including the 1870 Norton Building *(101 Stephen St.)*, today home to the Strand Antique Emporium, and the highly ornate 1870s Friedley Building *(311 Canal St.)*. A 4mi canal trail begins at General Fry Landing, located on Stephen Street west of the canal.

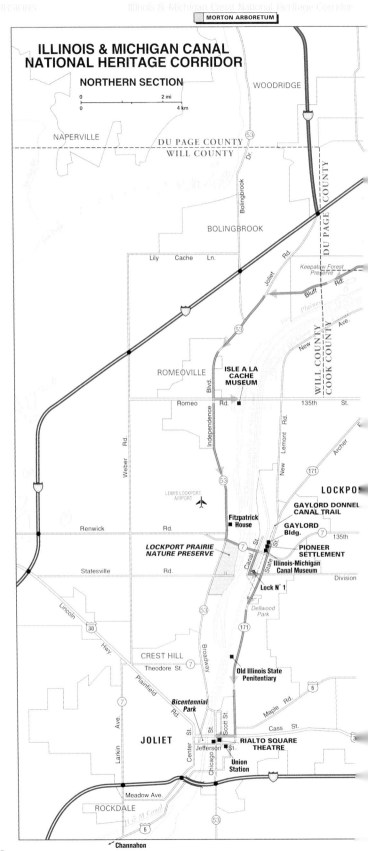

MORTON ARBORETUM

ILLINOIS & MICHIGAN CANAL NATIONAL HERITAGE CORRIDOR

NORTHERN SECTION

WOODRIDGE

0   2 mi
0   4 km

NAPERVILLE

DU PAGE COUNTY
WILL COUNTY

53

Bolingbrook Dr.

BOLINGBROOK

Lily   Cache   Ln.

Joliet   Rd.

Keepataw Forest Preserve

Bluff   Rd.

WILL COUNTY
COOK COUNTY

New   Ave.

53

ROMEOVILLE

Blvd.

ISLE A LA CACHE MUSEUM

Romeo   Rd.

135th   St.

New   Lemont   Rd.

Independence

Weber   Rd.

171

Archer

LEWIS LOCKPORT AIRPORT

53

LOCKPORT

GAYLORD DONNEL CANAL TRAIL

Fitzpatrick House

GAYLORD Bldg.

7   135th

Renwick   Rd.

Canal   St.

State   St.

PIONEER SETTLEMENT

LOCKPORT PRAIRIE NATURE PRESERVE

7

Illinois-Michigan Canal Museum

Statesville   Rd.

Lock N° 1

Division

Lincoln   Hwy.

30

53

Dellwood Park

171

Broadway

CREST HILL

Theodore   St.

7

Old Illinois State Penitentiary

6

Plainfield   Rd.

Maple   Rd.

Bicentennial Park

Cass   St.

Larkin   Ave.

Scott St.

JOLIET

Center   St.

Jefferson   St.

Chicago   St.

RIALTO SQUARE THEATRE

Union Station

Meadow   Ave.

ROCKDALE

I & M Canal

6

53

Channahon

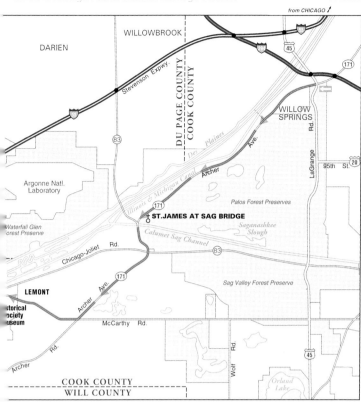

From downtown, backtrack on Stephen St. to Illinois St. and turn right. Continue to State St. and turn right, following State St. over the bridge west of town. Turn left at Bluff Rd. on the other side of the valley and continue for 3mi. At Joliet Rd. (Rte. 53), turn left and continue south 3mi to Romeo Rd. (135th St.). Turn left and drive .5mi.

★**Isle a la Cache Museum** – *501 E. Romeo Rd. Open year-round Tue–Sat 10am–4pm, Sun noon–4pm. Closed major holidays. Guided tours (15min) available.* 🅿 ☏ *815-727-8700.* This small island in the Des Plaines River was named by the French *coureurs de bois* who used the 80-acre haven to hide their trade goods. The museum presents historical exhibits highlighting daily life during the French-Indian fur-trade era, including a reconstructed wigwam. Occasionally, interpreters in Native American and 18C French costume demonstrate how to build a fire, portage a canoe and fire a musket. The modern building imitates a typical French Colonial structure with its steeply pitched roof overhanging a pavilion.

Return to Rte. 53 (Independence Blvd.) and continue south 2.5mi.

Just before the intersection with Route 7, on the left, stands the **Fitzpatrick House**, headquarters of the Illinois & Michigan Canal National Heritage Corridor Commission. The restored 1850s limestone farmhouse once anchored a 1,000-acre farm.

Continue south to Rte. 7 and turn left.

Immediately south of Route 7, on the right, extends the 269-acre **Lockport Prairie Nature Preserve**★, designated in 1983 as the largest presettlement prairie in northern Illinois *(access from Division St., .5mi south of Rte. 7 off Rte. 53; open Apr–Oct daily 8am–8pm; rest of the year daily 8am–5pm; closed Jan 1 & Dec 25; ☏ 815-727-8700; www.fpdwc.org).* An easy .5mi trail winds through native prairie grass and a profusion of wildflowers.

The Route 7 bridge crosses over the meandering Des Plaines River and then the Sanitary & Ship Canal, flanked by large grain elevators, before entering Lockport.

Turn right on Canal St. before the I&M Canal and continue .5mi to view Lock no. 1. Then turn left at Division St. just past the lock, and left again on State St. (Rte. 171) to enter downtown Lockport. Turn left on 8th St. one block after the intersection with Rte. 7 and park in the lot for the Gaylord Building.

★**Lockport** – Founded in 1836 as the canal headquarters, this picturesque canal town features a lovely downtown listed on the National Register of Historic Places. A short drive along the canal leads to **Lock no. 1**, a featured sight on the 2.5mi **Gaylord Donnelley Canal Trail**★ that follows the canal through Lockport and includes several wayside exhibits. This lock was the first of 15 locks used to raise and lower the boats plying the canal.

The **Gaylord Building**★ *(200 W. 8th St.)* was restored in the 1980s to its 1860s appearance. In 1996 the Gaylord became the first industrial building acquired as a historic property by the National Trust for Historic Preservation. The two-story western section of the local limestone building, completed in 1838 as a warehouse for canal construction, now contains the Public Landing restaurant. The three-story 1859 Italianate addition served as the store and offices of the grain companies who occupied the building from 1848 to 1890. Today the structure houses the **I&M Canal Visitor Center** on the first two levels, featuring exhibits, videos and educational programs relating to the history of the building, the canal and the Heritage Corridor *(open year-round Tue–Sat 10am–6pm, Sun noon–6pm; closed major holidays; hours vary seasonally, call ahead;* ⚒ & ⓟ ☎ *815-838-4830).* On the upper levels, the Illinois State Museum-Lockport Gallery offers rotating art exhibits and special programs *(open year round Tue–Sat 10am–5pm, Sun noon–5pm; closed major holidays and weekends between exhibits;* & ⓟ ☎ *815-838-7400).*

Extending south from the Gaylord Building, **Pioneer Settlement**★ comprises a collection of 19C buildings including a schoolhouse, blacksmith shop, jail and log cabins *(open mid-Apr–Oct 1 daily 1pm–4:30pm; closed major holidays;* & ⓟ ☎ *815-838-5080).* South of the parking lot on State Street stands the **Illinois-Michigan Canal Museum** *(803 S. State St.),* located in the original 1837 headquarters of the I&M Canal Commission. Costumed docents conduct tours of this former canal headquarters building, today crammed with artifacts documenting the canal era *(visit by 1hr guided tour only, year-round daily 1pm–4:30pm; closed major holidays, Thanksgiving week & Dec 15–Jan 2;* & ⓟ ☎ *815-838-5080).*

Continue south on State St. (Rte. 171) into Joliet. Turn right on Cass St. (Rte. 6).

★**Joliet** – The entrance to Joliet is marked by the **Old Illinois State Penitentiary** (1857, William W. Boyington) resembling the architect's Chicago Water Tower with its castlelike limestone walls and towers.

Cass Street leads into downtown Joliet and toward the riverboat casinos that boosted its economy in the early 1990s. Historic highlights include the restored **Union Station** *(Scott and Jefferson Sts.)* from 1907, and **Rialto Square Theatre**★ *(Chicago and Van Buren Sts.),* erected in 1926 by Rapp & Rapp. An opulent mirror-lined lobby leads into the rotunda dominated by an enormous, hand-cut crystal chandelier, claimed to be the largest in the US *(performances Sept–May; 1hr guided tours available year-round Tue 12:45pm; hours vary, call to confirm; closed major holidays; $3;* ☎ *815-726-7171).* Also of interest is **Bicentennial Park** *(Cass and Bluff Sts.)* with its waterside walk, mosaic mural and boulders commemorating important events in a city defined in the 19C by limestone quarrying and the steel industry *(open year-round Mon–Thu 8am–4:30pm, Fri 8am–noon, weekends for scheduled events only; closed mid-Dec–Jan 1;* & ⓟ ☎ *815-740-2216).*

Return to Chicago via Rte. 30 and I-55 (about 40mi).

SOUTHERN SECTION – Channahon to LaSalle/Peru

The following sights are not part of a driving tour. The visitor may choose to spend an entire day at one of the state parks, hike or bike along the 61mi canal trail, or rent a canoe and paddle down the canal. Access to each sight has been given from I-80. If you wish to drive through the various towns, follow Rte. 6 West into Ottawa, then continue on Dee Bennett Rd. to Utica, returning to Rte. 6 for LaSalle.

Though industrialized, the southern section of the Heritage Corridor boasts numerous recreational opportunities in the wide Illinois River Valley. Fishing aficionados will find a wealth of choice spots, while hiking and biking enthusiasts can follow the canal for miles along the rambling trails.

Channahon – *From I-55 (Exit 248), follow Rte. 6 for 2mi through the town and turn left at Canal St. onto I&M Canal State Trail.* The scenic 61mi **I&M Canal State Trail**★ (from Rockdale to LaSalle) provides a historic route for hiking, bicycling, canoeing and snowmobiling. Offering access to the trail, a lovely park at Channahon includes **Lock nos. 6 and 7**, a weir where the Du Page River crosses the canal, and an original 1840s **Locktender's House**.

Morris – *From I-80 (Exit 112), follow Rte. 47.* Downtown Morris retains the feel of a canal town and county seat. Just outside town the **Aux Sable Aqueduct**, near the Locktender's House and Lock no. 8, carries the canal over a creek. **Gebhard Woods State Park**★ *(401 Ottawa St.)* includes a visitor center and the Nettle Creek

© Balthazar Korab

I & M Canal at Channahon

Aqueduct. Picnic tables scattered under oak and maple trees make this a pleasant lunchtime spot *(visitor center open year-round daily 10am–4pm;* △ ᯓ ▯ ☏ *815-942-9669; www.imcanal.org).*

Farther west along Route 6 lie the old canal towns of Seneca and Marseilles, as well as Lock nos. 9 and 10. In **Seneca**, note the 65ft-tall, 70,000-bushel capacity **grain elevator** erected in 1861; a rare survivor from the canal's heyday, it towers over the canal, today nothing more than an overgrown ditch. **Marseilles** comprises a quaint downtown of pubs and antique shops.

★**Ottawa** *– From I-80 (Exit 90), follow Rte. 23.* Here the visitor will find a wealth of history, including Washington Park, where Abraham Lincoln and Stephen A. Douglas held the first of their famous 1858 debates, an event reenacted each August. The park is surrounded by historic buildings, most notably the large Italianate **Reddick Mansion**★ from 1856 *(Lafayette and Columbus Sts.; open year-round Mon–Fri 9am–5pm, Sat 10am–4pm, Sun 10am–2pm; closed major holidays;* ᯓ ▯ ☏ *815-433-9836; www.visit-ottowa-il.com).* The canal itself is dry in Ottawa, but the 100ft **Fox River Aqueduct**, which carried the canal over the intersecting stream, still stands at the eastern edge of the community, while the famous Ottawa silica sand quarries lie to the west.

Several historic sites are located on Dee Bennett Road *(access off Rte. 23)* along the Illinois River between Ottawa and Utica. At **Buffalo Rock State Park**★ take the River Bluff Trail down to two overlooks affording fine **vistas**★ of the Illinois River *(open year-round daily 8am–dusk; water turned off Nov–Mar;* ᯓ ▯ ☏ *815-433-2224).* At the western end of the parking lot, a wooden platform provides views of the **Effigy Tumuli**, giant earth sculptures in the form of indigenous aquatic animals completed as part of a strip-mine reclamation by artist Michael Heizer in 1985 *(trail access from platform).*

Farther west is the modern **Illinois Waterway Visitor Center**★ erected by the US Army Corps of Engineers *(open Memorial Day–Labor Day daily 9am–8pm; rest of the year daily 9am–5pm; closed Jan 1, Thanksgiving Day & Dec 25;* ᯓ ▯ ☏ *815-667-4054).* Exhibits describe the workings of the modern waterway connection between the Great Lakes and the Mississippi River that superseded the I&M Canal in 1933. From the observation deck, visitors can watch the lock in operation as barges enter the lock chamber and are slowly raised or lowered. Near Utica, the four-story sandstone **Sulphur Springs Hotel** (1852) marks the halfway point on the old stagecoach trail between Chicago and Peoria. West of the hotel is the Grand Village of the Illinois, an archaeological site where 10,000 Illinois Indians and members of related tribes lived in the late 17C.

Utica *– From I-80 (Exit 81), follow Rte. 178.* The **LaSalle County Historical Society Museum** *(Rte. 178 and Canal St.),* located in an 1838 canal warehouse, features an eclectic collection of artifacts related to the county's history, including furnishings, clothing, tools and even a carriage used by Abraham Lincoln in 1858 *(open Apr–mid-Dec Wed–Fri 10am–4pm, weekends & holidays noon–4pm; mid-Jan–Mar Fri–Sun noon–4pm; closed major holidays & Dec 15–Jan 15; $1;* ▯ ☏ *815-667-4861).*

The canal can be canoed from Utica to LaSalle, and bicycles can be rented here to visit Split Rock, a dramatic limestone outcrop through which the canal was carved. Utica is also the gateway to the popular **Starved Rock State Park★**, 2,600 acres of forested bluffs. Some 13mi of trails lead down canyons to lovely waterfalls and pools along the Illinois River *(open year-round daily 5am–10pm;* △ ✕ 🅿 ☎ *815-667-4726; http://.dnr.state.il.us/)*. The rustic **lodge** was built by the Civilian Conservation Corps in the 1930s. Step inside to view the massive fireplace dominating the Great Room.

LaSalle – *From I-80 (Exit 77), follow Rte. 351.* The twin towns of LaSalle and Peru mark the end of the canal and the Heritage Corridor. Located in downtown LaSalle, **Lock no. 14★** is the only restored lock on the canal. The 15-lock system allowed barges to conquer the 160ft difference in water level between Chicago and the Illinois River.

Adjacent Peru contains the remnants of a historic waterfront district along **Water Street**.

Return to Chicago via Rte. 351 and I-80 (about 100mi).

NORTH SHORE★★

Map p 231

Each with its own personality, Chicago's northern suburbs collectively conjure up a vision of elegant living called the North Shore. The lovely—and unusual—geography of ravines, bluffs, beaches and woodlands, and the area's architecture and history combine to make a drive up the shore a pleasant one-day excursion.

All of the North Shore communities described here were established in the mid- to late 19C. Prosperous city folk, drawn by the beauty of the lakeshore and tired of life in an increasingly crowded, industrial Chicago, moved north with the help of the railroad (operating here by 1855) and the development of Sheridan Road. The Chicago Fire in 1871 and the Haymarket Riot in 1886 hastened the exodus; the sylvan glades to the north seemed far removed from such urban cataclysms. As a result, an array of building styles crafted largely by prominent architects spread from Evanston to Lake Forest. Today Sheridan Road twists, turns and dips up the lakeshore, revealing grand vistas of homes and landscape. Visitors will have ample opportunities to stop and admire architecture and nature on foot, shop and dine or pick up picnic supplies for lunch in a lakefront park.

Practical Information

Access – The excursion to the North Shore is 62mi round-trip; from Chicago drive north on Lake Shore Dr., which turns into Sheridan Rd. and continue through Rogers Park toward Evanston. To return to Chicago, take Rte. 41 to I-94. The ▦ Purple line reaches Evanston; the Metra North line *(schedules & fares:* ☎ *312-836-7000)* accesses each suburb's downtown and is particularly convenient for visiting Ravinia Park and Market Square in Lake Forest. Note that parking may be difficult along this itinerary. Trains leave Chicago from North Western Metra Station at W. Madison and Canal Sts.

Public Parks and Beaches – **Evanston** beaches are open for swimming from mid-Jun–Labor Day; lifeguards on duty daily 10:30am–7:30pm; $6 daily fee payable at beach entrances *(mid-Jun–Labor Day only)*. Gillson Park in **Wilmette** is open for swimming Memorial Day–Labor Day 9am–8pm; lifeguard services provided; $5 nonresident fee required to enter park. Public parks in Kenilworth are open to nonresidents year-round at no charge; a $5 nonresident fee is charged at Kenilworth Beach payable at entrance; lifeguards are on duty from mid-Jun–Labor Day daily 9am–6pm. **Winnetka** beaches are open mid-Jun–Labor Day; lifeguards on duty daily 9am–7pm; $8 daily fee, plus $5 parking fee payable at beach entrances *(mid-Jun–Labor Day only)*. Beaches in **Glencoe** are open Jun–Labor Day; lifeguards on duty daily 10am–8pm; $6 daily fee for nonresidents.

Shopping and Dining – **Evanston**'s main shopping and dining areas cluster along Main, Dempster, Davis and Central Sts. Many art galleries are located on Sherman Ave. **Highland Park** also boasts a small gallery district on Central Ave.; specialty shops and restaurants can be found along St. John's Ave. In **Wilmette** several boutiques, restaurants and gourmet-food shops crowd the Plaza del Lago mall on Sheridan Rd. **Lake Forest** draws avid shoppers to its Market Square neighborhood.

★EVANSTON

A cosmopolitan community, Evanston makes a good segue from city to suburbs. First settled in the 1830s, Evanston blossomed in the 1850s around a new Methodist university later to be known as Northwestern. Four bursts of growth characterized the town's development, and many of its homes date from the 1870s, 1890s, 1920s (marked by a flurry of apartment building) and 1950s.

At the city line, Sheridan Road *(which briefly turns into Burnham Pl. and then Forest Ave.)* enters the **Evanston Lakeshore Historic District★**, listed on the National Register since 1980. You can best explore this compact district on foot, beginning at the Dawes House *(225 Greenwood St.)*.

The **Charles Gates Dawes House★** serves as the home of the Evanston Historical Society *(visit by 1hr guided tour only, year-round Thu–Sun 1pm–5pm; closed major holidays; $5; ⅋ ☎ 847-475-3410; www.evanstonhistorical.org).* One of the few area

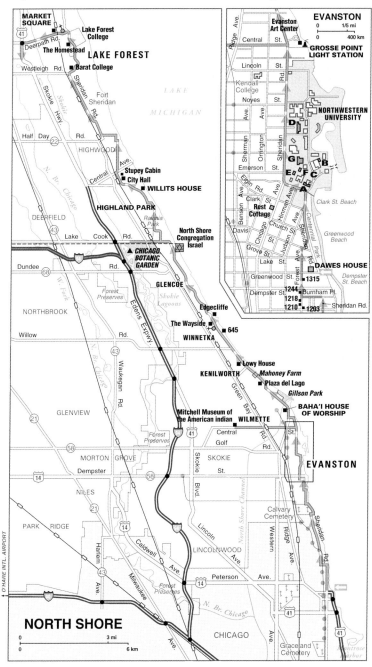

houses open to the public, it offers a rare glimpse into opulent 19C North Shore life. Perhaps the finest example of the Châteauesque style in the region, the mansion was designed in 1894 by Henry Edwards-Ficken for Northwestern University treasurer Robert Sheppard. The house has been beautifully restored to the residency of Charles Gates Dawes, who purchased it in 1909. Dawes won the Nobel Prize for his part in developing an economic recovery plan for Europe following World War I. He also served as vice president under Calvin Coolidge, and composed popular music in his spare time. The home comprises 28 rooms and 14 fireplaces; among the restored and furnished rooms on display are the elegantly wood-paneled library and second-floor nursery.

Walk south on Forest Ave.

Houses in the surrounding blocks span years of development and many styles, from the post-Chicago Fire cottages planned by Luther Greenleaf in the 1870s—**1218** and **1244 Forest Avenue**—to the imposing Tudor structures of Ernest Mayo dating from the 1910s, as seen at **nos. 1210** and **1203 Forest Avenue**, and the Prairie school work of Tallmadge and Watson. Note the lovely windows at **1315 Forest Avenue**, built in 1907. Now subdivided, the block bounded by Burnham Place, Forest Avenue, Dempster Street and Lake Michigan was once the estate of renowned city planner and architect **Daniel Burnham**, who moved there in 1887. The circuitous course of Sheridan Road (actually Burnham Place to Forest Avenue) undoubtedly reflects the influence of Burnham and his neighbors.

Drive north on Forest Ave., which merges with Sheridan Rd. To tour Northwestern University, park along Sheridan Rd. at Centennial Park just south of campus.

★**Northwestern University** – *The academic campus extends east of Sheridan Rd. to Lake Michigan, between Lincoln St. and Clark St. ☎ 847-491-3741. www.northwestern.edu. Parking permits are required for all university lots; visitor permits are available at the Parking Office (1819 Hinman Ave.; open 8am–4pm; ☎ 847-491-3319).* This prestigious Big Ten university originated as the dream of a group of devout Methodists in 1850, who selected a swampy parcel of land along Lake Michigan about 14mi from downtown Chicago as the place to plant their college. By 1855, with one building (since demolished) and 10 students, the school already formed the nucleus of a growing town. Responsible for the platting of Evanston (named for Dr. John Evans, a founder of Northwestern), the university fathers also set forth the temperate moral tone that would come to influence the sweep of the North Shore. The university's charter established the notorious "4mi limit" that prohibited the sale of alcohol within that radius of the campus.

Architecturally, Northwestern never developed along a master plan and seems today a random collection of buildings that bridge two centuries. Past **Fisk Hall** (**A**) (1899, Daniel Burnham & Co.), which fronts Sheridan Road and houses the renowned Medill School of Journalism, lies the Arts Circle, a cluster of buildings devoted to the fine and performing arts. The **Mary and Leigh Block Museum of Art** (**B**) *(1967 South Campus Dr.; open Sept–May Tue–Thu noon–5pm, Fri–Sun noon–8pm; rest of the year Tue–Sat noon–5pm; ⅙ ▯ ☎ 847-491-4000; www.nwu.edu/museum)* reopened to the public in late 2000, following completion of an expansion that tripled its size to 6,000sq ft of exhibit space. The new space allows the museum to display its permanent collection of some 5,000 works on paper. An **outdoor sculpture garden**★ (**C**) surrounding the museum includes works by Jean Arp, Jacques Lipchitz, Joan Miró and Henry Moore. For an extended walk providing fine views, take the path around the man-made lagoon behind the Arts Circle. The tower of **Garrett-Evangelical Theological Seminary** (**D**) (not affiliated with the university) rises above the monochromatic assembly of lecture halls, laboratories and offices that form the core of the campus and date mostly to the early 1970s. At the heart of the old campus west of the Arts Circle stands its most venerable building, the Gothic-style **University Hall** (**E**) (1869, Gordon P. Randall), surrounded by lush greenery. **Annie May Swift Hall** (**F**) (1895, Charles Robert Ayars) contrast with its warm red decorative brickwork and Arts and Crafts styling. The classically collegiate **Deering Library** (**G**) (1932, James Gamble Rogers) was augmented in 197 with three connecting pavilions (Skidmore, Owings & Merrill).

From the corner of campus at Sheridan Road and Chicago Avenue, it is a shor walk to **Rest Cottage** *(1730 Chicago Ave.)*, the home of Frances E. Willard, well known educator, suffragist and national president of the Women's Christia Temperance Union (WCTU) from 1879 until her death in 1898. Run as a museum by the WCTU, the home is furnished with period pieces and Willard's persona belongings. It was built in 1865, a lovely example of residential Gothic style *(vis by appointment only; contribution requested; ☎ 847-864-1397).*

Drive north on Sheridan Rd. Turn left on Central St. and continue to Central Park Av

Mitchell Museum of the American Indian – *2600 Central Park Ave. Open yea round Tue–Sat 10am–5pm (Thu til 8pm), Sun noon–4pm. Closed major holida & last two weeks of Aug. $5. ⅙ ▯ ☎ 847-475-1030. www.mitchellmuseum.or* Founded in 1977, the museum presents the history, culture and arts of Nativ

Americans via a collection of 10,000 objects dating from the Paleo-Indian period to the present day. Permanent exhibits *(1st floor)* explore the native cultures of the Woodlands, Plains, Southwest, Northwest Coast and Arctic regions. Five "touching tables" 🎨 give visitors the opportunity to handle pottery, baskets, clothing and stone tools made by American Indians. The second-floor gallery is devoted to temporary exhibits of historic and contemporary Indian arts.

Return to Sheridan Rd.

★**Evanston Art Center** – *2603 Sheridan Rd. Open year-round Mon–Thu 10am–4pm & 7pm–10pm, Fri & Sat 10am–4pm, Sun 2pm–5pm. Closed major holidays & the 4th Thu evening of the month. $3.* ♿ 🅿 ☎ *847-475-5300. www.evanstonart-center.org.* Beautifully situated at the edge of the lake, the art center occupies a one-time private home built in 1926 by Richard Powers and presents changing exhibits of contemporary Midwestern artists. Outside, the naturalistic landscaping of Jens Jensen makes a lovely buffer between house and beach. Jensen, who designed several Chicago parks, was a leading proponent of Prairie school principles as they applied to landscape architecture. He advocated a return to natural prairie where possible and used native plants extensively. His influence pervades the parks of the North Shore. The beach has been restored as a small **dune ecosystem** to convey a sense of the primordial Lake Michigan shoreline.

Built in 1873, the adjacent **Grosse Point Light Station**★ *(2601 Sheridan Rd.; visit by 45min guided tour only, Jun–Sept weekends 2pm–5pm; $5;* 🅿 ☎ *847-328-6961)* comprises a 90ft tower, two 1880 structures used to house steam-powered fog sirens (removed in 1922) and a lightkeeper's cottage. On summer weekends, visitors can climb 141 stairs to the top of the tower for a wonderful view. The lighthouse is a stunning reminder of the time when thousands of ships plied the hazardous waters of Lake Michigan. The collision of the paddle wheeler *Lady Elgin* with a lumber schooner off Wilmette's shores in 1860, resulting in the loss of nearly 300 lives, provided considerable impetus for a landmark at this location. The lighthouse structure was restored in 1980 and still serves as a beacon to mariners.

Continue north on Sheridan Rd. to Wilmette.

WILMETTE

Early developers envisioned Wilmette (so named for its first settler, fur trader Antoine Ouilmette) as a true railroad suburb and successfully lobbied for a train stop there by 1871. One year later Wilmette's population swelled to 300 and the village became incorporated. In contrast to booming Evanston, however, Wilmette remained a sleepy rural community until well into the 1880s when suburban amenities—sewers, library, schools, telephone service—became available. The question of consolidation with Evanston hindered Wilmette's independence until voters finally rejected the possibility in 1897.

★**Baha'i House of Worship** – *100 Linden Ave. Open May–end Sept daily 10am–10pm. Rest of the year daily 10am–5pm. Guided tours (1hr) available.* ♿ 🅿 ☎ *847-733-3469. www.us.bahai.org.* The lacy, opalescent dome of the Baha'i temple startles motorists on Sheridan Road passing from Evanston into Wilmette. The mammoth, nine-sided structure, rising 191ft to its pinnacle and set about with beautifully landscaped gardens, cuts an exotic profile against the low

© David R. Frazier

Baha'i House of Worship

suburban skyline. This is the North American seat of the Baha'i faith, which maintains six other equally monumental houses of worship around the world. Its presence in the Chicago area dates to the religion's introduction here at the World's Columbian Exposition in 1893. Baha'is, who follow the teachings of the 19C Persian prophet Baha'u'llah, believe in the "oneness" of religion and of humankind, and hopefully anticipate complete equality among people and the evolution of a global civilization. They draw inspiration from all of the world's great faiths and consider Buddha, Christ, Mohammed and the other major prophets to have been messengers from a single God.

Although the origins of the Baha'i faith are Persian, and the temple itself bears a distinctly Eastern look, in fact its design elements are eclectic and intended to represent unity in their blend. A close inspection of the intricate interlocking patterns that inscribe most surfaces of the building reveals the influence of the organic ornamentation of Louis Sullivan. Icons of the world's great religions decorate the outside columns. Other aspects of the temple carry symbolic significance for the Baha'i, such as the circular plan and the nine entryways, each surmounted by an inscription.

The temple is the work of French-Canadian architect Louis Bourgeois, who began its planning in 1909. Construction did not start until 1920, however, and proceeded slowly until completion in 1953, beset by funding and technical problems. The elaborate lacework on the dome posed the biggest challenge; crafted of quartz and white cement, the panels were shipped by rail from Earley Studio in Rosslyn, Virginia and hung on the temple's steel framework.

The interior space, infused with natural light, soars elegantly to the apex of the dome where the invocation "O Thou the Glory of the Most Glorious" appears in Arabic calligraphy. The auditorium seats 1,191. An exhibit with a distinctly missionary tone in the visitor center on the lower level explains the faith through the sayings of Baha'u'llah and other Baha'i writings.

Continue north on Sheridan Rd.

Just around the bend from the temple is the 59-acre lakefront **Gillson Park**, a nice spot for a picnic lunch. Farther along, **Plaza del Lago** shopping center offers several restaurants as well as Convito Italiano (☏ *847-251-3654*), a trendy food shop and bistro, where you can sit down to lunch or purchase fixings for a gourmet picnic. Built in 1928, the stores and apartments along the north side of the plaza comprised one of the nation's first shopping centers. Located in a no-man's-land outside Wilmette proper, the complex included a speakeasy that was popular among Chicago's Prohibition-era drinking crowd. When the notorious roadhouse caught fire in 1932, adjacent villages refused to send fire fighters and cut off the water supply, ensuring its destruction. Wilmette annexed the area in 1942, and the shopping center filled with hot-dog and ice-cream stands befitting its lakefront location. In 1968, after high-rise apartment buildings blocked the beach, Plaza del Lago opened in its present form. Its bell tower is original to the 1920s.

Continue a short distance north on Sheridan Rd. to Kenilworth.

KENILWORTH

Incorporated in 1896, the town of Kenilworth, named after Sir Walter Scott romantic novel, is the youngest North Shore community. Inspired by the English countryside, businessman Joseph Sears envisioned a genteel village that would attract a certain caliber of residents. In 1889 he purchased the land and developed the amenities that would entice property buyers, platting the village with such care as to insure that its houses would enjoy so many hours of daily sunlight. He spared nothing on public works and even laid the first stretch of macadam road on the North Shore.

Contemporary of Frank Lloyd Wright, renowned Midwestern architect **George W. Maher** designed more than 40 buildings in the community, his work chronicling the transition in architectural styles from late Victorian to Prairie. Today Kenilworth retains an air of exclusivity.

Just north of the southern gates of Kenilworth lies **Mahoney Farm**, which straddles Sheridan Road. This land was deeded to Kenilworth for use as a park, and in 1933 the village asked Jens Jensen to design a sanctuary for birds and flowers there. In addition to native plantings, Jensen included seven **"council rings"**—stone seating areas meant for quiet contemplation that grace many of his landscapes. The park was restored and added to the National Register in 1985. *To visit the sanctuary, park at Plaza del Lago (north of Gillson Park on Sheridan Rd.) and walk north.*

East of the intersection of Sheridan Road and Kenilworth Avenue, note the two adjacent houses closest to the lake. Both built in the early 1890s, they typify the elegance that characterized the village's early homes.

Continue north on Sheridan Rd. to Winnetka.

WINNETKA

Although it grew slowly, Winnetka (from an Indian word meaning "beautiful land") developed a political and cultural milieu apart from its neighbors, largely due to the influence of Henry Demarest Lloyd, who made his home there in 1878. Lloyd, essayist and social reformer with a strong belief in direct democracy, viewed family and community as the linchpins of society and eschewed the power of corporations and monopolies. As a leading citizen of Winnetka, he succeeded in applying his theories of government on a practical level, striving to involve the people in municipal decision making. Around Lloyd grew something of a cultural and political salon; he often entertained the likes of social worker Jane Addams and railroad union founder Eugene Debs.

At 140 Sheridan Road, the **Felix Lowy House** (1925, Mayo & Mayo) is a fine example of the Tudor style popular in the 1920s. The lakefront home at **no. 645** was built in 1902, and the grounds and lovely cemetery at **Christ Church** *(784 Sheridan Rd.)* date to 1876. At no. 830 stands Henry Lloyd's home, **The Wayside**, some parts of which date to the 1850s. It was listed on the National Register in 1966. At no. 915 the twin gatehouses of **Edgecliffe**, designed in 1930 by Samuel Marx for businessman Max Epstein, signal the elegant formality of the mansion beyond.

Continue north on Sheridan Rd. to Glencoe.

GLENCOE

After a poorly planned scheme to develop Glencoe fell apart in the 1870s, the village lagged behind its growing neighbors. Its lovely ravines and woods continued to attract excursionists and picnickers and the village gradually blossomed. Poet Archibald MacLeish was born here in 1892.

At 1185 Sheridan Road stands **North Shore Congregation Israel**. The curvilinear, organic lines of the temple to the north (1963, Minoru Yamasaki) contrast sharply with the geometric post-Modern cylinder of the smaller sanctuary created by Hammond, Beeby & Babka in 1983.

Continue north on Sheridan Rd. until it turns westward as Lake Cook Rd. (a half mile farther on, Sheridan Rd. continues north). Follow Lake Cook Rd. straight ahead 1mi to the Chicago Botanic Garden.

★★**Chicago Botanic Garden** – *1000 Lake Cook Rd. Open year-round daily 8am–dusk. Closed Dec 25.* ✗ ᴋ ⬛*($7/car).* ☎ *847-835-5440. www.chicago-botanic.org.* This 385-acre preserve makes a lovely stop any time of year. With 23 garden areas, over a million individual plants of 7,000 different varieties and a plethora of bird life, the site attracts half a million people annually. Established in 1965 under the auspices of the venerable Chicago Horticultural Society, the garden considers itself a "Noah's Ark for plants" devoted to collection, education, research, plant testing and conservation. Begin at the **Gateway Center** for a film orientation. The **tram tour**, which provides a general overview of the grounds, is a good way to see the far-flung 11-acre **prairie** *(tram tours depart from Gateway Center Apr–Oct daily 10am–3pm every hour, Jul–Aug 10am–4:30pm every 15min; round-trip 45min; commentary; $4;* ᴋ*).*

© Don Smetzer/Tony Stone Images

Japanese Garden, Chicago Botanic Garden

Changing exhibits in the **Education Center** explore botanical topics, while greenhouses feature exotics, succulents and topiary. The heart of the garden occupies the largest of nine islands in the 60-acre man-made lagoon. Each garden setting rivals the next. In the formal **Rose Garden★**, 5,000 plants include 100 varieties of fragrant blossoms. The **English Walled Garden★** encompasses a charming collection of six "rooms" representing various English gardening styles. The tactile and fragrant plantings of the **Sensory Garden** encourage visitors to use every sense to enjoy them. Across the lagoon note the **carillon**, whose 48 bells chime on the hour and play evening concerts in the summer. The **Regenstein Fruit and Vegetable Garden** demonstrates the variety of ways local gardeners can succeed in small balcony planters or extensive backyard plots. The **Japanese Garden★**, *Sansho-En* ("The Garden of Three Islands"), offers a peaceful and contemplative refuge. A bridge connects two of the islands; the third is to be observed from afar. In Japanese style, shape and form create serene spaces, a concept that works beautifully in the quiet "dry garden" of sand, rocks and carefully placed vegetation.

Return to Sheridan Rd. and continue north to Highland Park. Follow the signs carefully as the route takes some unexpected turns.

HIGHLAND PARK

One of the larger North Shore communities, Highland Park was incorporated in 1869 and grew through several annexations, including that of Ravinia in 1899. The Highland Park Building Co. shaped its early development, selling lots and building houses from pattern books. The natural beauty of the ravines and the extensive hardwood forests of the area attracted year-round and summer residents alike, and made the perfect setting for the work of Jens Jensen (who lived in Ravinia) and other naturalistic landscape architects.

Highlighting this town is 36-acre **Ravinia Park**, home to the world-renowned **Ravinia Music Festival**. Originally intended as an amusement park to attract riders on the adjacent interurban railroad, the grounds were converted in 1911 to a venue for opera and symphony performances. Wildly successful over the years, Ravinia has hosted Arthur Rubinstein, George Gershwin, Ella Fitzgerald, Placido Domingo and hundreds of other internationally acclaimed performers. The summer home of the Chicago Symphony Orchestra since 1936, Ravinia today also offers everything from jazz, popular and chamber music to folk, dance and children's programs. The complex includes restaurants, covered seating in the pavilion, and two indoor theaters. Most fun, however, is to enjoy performances with a picnic dinner on the expansive lawn.

At 1445 Sheridan Road stands Frank Lloyd Wright's masterpiece, the **Ward W. Willits House★**, familiar to students of architecture as an archetype of the Prairie school. This 1902 commission—six years before Wright's Robie House—gave the architect his first full-blown opportunity to apply his theories of "organic simplicity." The house exhibits beautifully the hallmarks of Prairie school design: strong horizontal lines, a symbiosis with its natural surroundings and the influence of Japanese domestic architecture. Beyond the Willits House, circuitous Sheridan Road passes through Highland Park's business district as St. John's Avenue. Note the stately **City Hall** *(1707 St. John's Ave.)*, built in 1930, and the adjacent **Stupey Cabin**, which dates from 1847, the oldest building in town. Moved to this site in 1969, it has been restored and furnished to reflect the year 1850.

Continue north on Sheridan Rd. Follow signs as the itinerary makes a short detour on Central Ave. and then Oak St. before returning to Sheridan Rd.

Fort Sheridan was established in 1887 following the Haymarket Riot and deactivated in 1993, a victim of cuts in defense spending. The military base is unusual in that most of it was designed by the private architectural firm of Holabird Roche. In the distance rises the fort's 167ft stone water tower (1890). Today the base has been largely converted into a new residential community featuring both historic and contemporary homes.

Continue north on Sheridan Rd. through Highwood to Lake Forest.

★LAKE FOREST

Lake Forest has long cultivated a reputation as Chicago's most elite suburb, though its creation was inspired by a group of Presbyterians who chose that locale to build a college in the 1850s. They hired a St. Louis landscape architect named Hotchkiss to lay out the town in 1857, and he designed picturesque streets to curve along the natural contours of the ravines and hills and wind through the forest with calculated leisure. The spacious lots offered privacy for the most gracious homes. Lake Forest's high society grew more so as wealthy summer visitors took up residence year-round, bringing with them the entertainments and trappings of Chicago's aristocracy. F. Scott Fitzgerald later equated Lake Forest with Newport and South Hampton, and that sense lingers today.

As Sheridan Road passes into Lake Forest, note **Barat College**, founded in 1858. The middle campus of **Lake Forest College**, established by Presbyterians as Lind University in 1857, occupies the intersection of Sheridan and College Roads. Its buildings date to several eras. Immediately on the right, the handsome **Reid Memorial Library** (1899, Frost & Granger) blends Gothic, Norman and English-abbey elements into a suitably collegiate whole. Farther ahead, one of the earlier buildings, **Young Hall** (1878), comprises three stories of yellow brick topped with a mansard roof. Hidden in the trees to the east, stout **Hotchkiss Hall** (once the gymnasium) is worthy of note for its solid Romanesque lines and massive redstone construction. It was designed by Henry Ives Cobb in 1890.

On a small rise immediately across from the campus sits **The Homestead** *(570 N. Sheridan Rd.)* built in 1860 for Devillo R. Holt, a Chicago lumberman and a founder of Lake Forest. The house's exterior remains unaltered today and features lovely Italianate details. Its construction is of brick sheathed in clapboard.

Continue north on Sheridan Rd. to Deerpath Rd.

The massive Shingle-style **First Presbyterian Church** (1887, Charles Frost) at the corner of Sheridan and Deerpath Roads is a testament to the Presbyterians who founded Lake Forest. Unusual on the North Shore, this Shingle church exudes the summer-resort ambience that once characterized the town. Across the street, on the north campus of Lake Forest College, note the **Durand Art Institute** (1891), another of Henry Ives Cobb's Richardsonian Romanesque edifices. A frieze above the main entryway spells out the building's name in elaborate foliate ornament.

Turn left on Deerpath Rd.

Just west of the train tracks at 700 North Western Avenue, **Market Square★** has defined the character of downtown Lake Forest since 1916. Designed by Howard Van Doren Shaw to resemble an English town market, the square includes elements derived from several European traditions. Among America's earliest planned suburban shopping centers, Market Square today houses boutiques and restaurants but has otherwise changed 'little over the years.

To return to Chicago, drive west on Deerpath Rd. to Rte. 41 South, which merges with the Edens Expwy. (I-94). Head south on I-94 toward Chicago.

© Willard Clay/Tony Stone Images

Prairie Flowers

INDIANA DUNES NATIONAL LAKESHORE★

Map p 11

A sliver of pristine land lining the southern edge of Lake Michigan, the Indiana Dunes National Lakeshore encompasses 14,000 acres of windswept beaches, dunes, marshes and forests containing a great diversity of species. Over the years, much of the area around the dunes was industrialized, and today parklands are interrupted by steel and power plants. Yet this industrialization has not thwarted the mass of urban dwellers who crowd the trails and beaches in their ubiquitous search for unspoiled land.

Historical Notes

Glaciers that carved the Great Lakes sculpted the first chapter in the history of the dunes some 15,000 years ago. As the glaciers retreated to the north, they left moraines—ridges formed from glacial till—south of present-day Lake Michigan. Glacial meltwaters created further ridges as the shoreline shrank to the north by stages. As the Ice Age drew to a close about 11,000 years ago, various ecosystems developed between the various ridges. Ice Age plants such as bearberry and jack pine persisted, while cacti and other southern plants began to thrive in the warmer climate.

Prevailing northwesterly winds and lake waves continue to create new sand dunes at the lakeshore, while older dunes beyond the shoreline gradually evolve from sparse grasslands and marshes into dense forests. When University of Chicago ecologist **Henry Chandler Cowles** (1869-1939) began to study the dunes in the 1890s, he was fascinated not only by the evidence of glacial action, but also by the fact that the plant forms on each ridge continue to change over time. Cowles discovered that plants alter their environment, providing fertile ground for new species that will crowd out the originals. Marram grasses become established on sand dunes, gradually collecting water and humus until a pine or cottonwood forest takes root, eventually to be succeeded by oak-hickory and then beech-maple forests.

The effort to preserve the Indiana Dunes began in 1911 when landscape architect Jens Jensen and other Chicago conservationists formed the Prairie Club, leading train excursions to the then-unbroken 25mi stretch of dunes between Gary and Michigan City, Indiana. In 1913 Dr. Cowles led 10 European botanists on a trip to the dunes, which they determined to be one of the four most important natural sites in America, along with Yellowstone, Yosemite and the Grand Canyon. Chicago-based efforts to preserve the dunes met great resistance in rural Indiana, but a small state park was established in 1923, comprising 2,000 acres by 1927.

As industry grew again after World War II, Bethlehem Steel bought large tracts of the Central Dunes for a steel plant, harbor and sand mine. A new effort to save the dunes as a national park was led by Illinois senator Paul Douglas. Legislation was passed in 1966 to preserve a 6,400-acre area split in two by the Bethlehem complex, designated the Indiana Dunes National Lakeshore. Park expansion continued into the 1980s even as lakefront industry mushroomed. Today the national lakeshore, which includes **Indiana Dunes State Park**, encompasses more than 1,400 plant species—from arctic wildflowers to prickly pear cacti—within its confines. Indeed, vistas unfolding along the numerous trails take in swirling dunes, lowland marshes and dense forests in the space of a few hundred yards.

Practical Information

Access – By **car**: drive south on I-94/I-90 (Dan Ryan Expwy.) to Chicago Skyway tollroad (I-90). Past Gary, Indiana, exit at US-20/US-12 (Dunes Hwy.) and continue eastbound. Stay on US-12, forking left as US-20 forks right. All Dunes sights can be accessed from US-12. From Chicago Loop to West Beach entrance is 37mi; to Buell Visitor Center, 49mi; to Mt. Baldy, 54mi. By **train**: the South Shore Railroad *(schedules & fares: ☎ 219-926-5744)* departs daily year-round from the Randolph Street Metra station; get off at Dune Park and walk north.

Visitor Information – Encompassing two park sections separated by an industrialized area, this popular venue measures about 20mi in length and is accessible in all seasons. Contact the following agencies for maps and additional information about camping and recreation: **Indiana Dunes National Lakeshore**, 1100 N. Mineral Springs Rd., Porter IN 46304, ☎ 219-926-7561, www.nps.gov/indu; **Indiana Dunes State Park**, 1600 N. County Road 25 East, Chesterton IN 46304, ☎ 219-926-1952, www.ai.org/dnr/statepar/parks/indunes/indunes.htm.

Camping and Recreation – **Campsites** are available mid-Mar–mid-Nov at Dunewood Campground *($10)*, and year-round at Indiana Dunes State Park *($7-$11)*. Pleasant **hiking trails** crisscross the area. Most trails have a detailed trail map and brochure placed in boxes at trailhead. Trail maps are also available at visitor centers. The Calumet **bike trail** (9mi) begins at Mt. Baldy and ends near the park headquarters. **Cross-country skiing** is allowed on most park trails. **Swimming** is recommended only at West and Kemil beaches, and in the state park *(West Beach manned by lifeguards 9am–6pm daily Memorial Day–Labor Day; no lifeguard services at other national lakeshore beaches)*.

Water Safety – Swimmers may find **rip currents**, sometimes mistakenly called **undertow** (strong, narrow lakeward flows), all along the shore during periods of high wind and waves. If caught in a rip current, swim parallel to the shoreline until out of the current. Strong winter currents coupled with continual freezing temperatures create **shelf ice** along the shore. Deceptively thin in places, this ice is unstable and dangerous.

Amenities – A **bathhouse** containing rest rooms, interpretive displays and a first-aid station is located at **West Beach** *(open Memorial Day–Labor Day 9am–9pm)*. Comfort stations in the state park are open Apr–Oct. You'll find snack bars at West Beach and Lake Street Beach *(open Memorial Day–Labor Day)*. Motels, restaurants and service stations are located in nearby towns.

VISIT

★**West Beach Area** – *Turn left on County Line Rd. shortly after entering the park. Open mid-May–Sept 9am–9pm. Rest of the year 8am–dusk. Closed Jan 1, Thanksgiving Day & Dec 25. $4/car, mid-May–Sept. ⅹ(May–Sept) ♿ ⊞. Pets prohibited. Trails through sand dunes can be more strenuous due to the sandy soil and rapid elevation changes.* Known primarily for its popular **West Beach**, this large section of the park also includes Long Lake and 3.5mi of hiking trails. Behind the visitor center, "blowout" dunes that have eroded to a great degree slowly evolve as water collects in the center and forms interdunal ponds, stabilizing the dune and allowing it to mutate into the next ecosystem—a cottonwood or conifer stand, to be succeeded by oak savanna and oak-hickory forest.

A walk along the **Dune Succession Trail**★ offers a look at the park's surprising biological diversity, constantly changing between seasons and over the years. The 1mi boardwalk trail runs from the beach near the bathhouse to the parking lot near the visitor center and provides one of the best views of rapid ecosystem change. Beginning with sand dunes and marram grasses located on the waterfront, the trail leads past a blowout dune and then abruptly comes upon a conifer forest thick with evergreens and vines. At another interdunal pond, the conifer forest ends just as suddenly and is succeeded by oaks and hardwoods. The short trail offers several excellent **viewpoints**★.

Inland Marsh – *Access to the right off US-12, about 1.5mi past West Beach.* The 4mi trail *(1.5hrs)* follows the Tolleston Beach ridge, formed 10,000 years ago by melting glacial waters. Sand dunes form the basis of the soil, supporting cottonwood, wildflowers and prickly pear cacti around a large marsh. New plants appear around each bend, delicately layered from ground to sky, springing from sand ridge and wetland marsh.

★**Bailly-Chellberg Visitor Center and Trail** – *Drive 6mi east of Inland Marsh, passing through a heavily industrialized area before re-entering the park. Turn right on Mineral Springs Rd. and continue about 1mi. Open Memorial Day–Labor Day daily 10am–4:30pm. Rest of the year weekends only 10am–4:30pm. ♿ ⊞ ☏ 219-926-7561, ext. 225.* This stop provides a historic counterpoint to the natural wonders of the dunes. A 2mi trail burrowing through a lush forest of basswood, beech and sugar maple leads to an 1820s farm consisting of several log structures and the two-and-a-half-story **Bailly Homestead** *(open Memorial Day–Oct Sun 1pm–4pm)*, illustrating early European settlement of the region. The trail follows an old Indian path before reaching a French-Canadian cemetery noteworthy for the elaborate raised stone structures, and then loops back to a preserved 1880s Swedish farm and outbuildings.

Indiana Dunes State Park – *From Bailly-Chellberg Visitor Center, go east on US-12 and turn left on Rte. 49. Open daily year-round 7am–11pm. $2/vehicle for Indiana residents; $3/vehicle for others. ⚠ ♿ ⊞ ☏ 219-926-1952, www.state.in.us/dnr/park lake/parks/indianadunes. html.* With 3mi of beachfront and 16.5mi of hiking trails, the state park offers myriad recreational opportunities. Amenities here include a bathhouse/pavilion, picnic areas and a nature center. Try your skill at scaling Mt. Tom, the park's tallest dune *(192ft; height varies due to shifting sands)*.

Dorothy Buell Memorial Visitor Center – *Access to the right off US-12, about 4.5mi east of Mineral Springs Rd. Open Memorial Day–Labor Day daily 8am–6pm. Rest of the year daily 8am–5pm. Closed Jan 1, Thanksgiving Day, &*

Indiana Dunes National Lakeshore

239

Dec 25. ♿ 🅿 ☏ *219-926-7561, ext. 218.* Named for the woman who founded the Save the Dunes Council in 1952, the visitor center presents a 10min audio-visual introduction to the park, its glacial formation and its continuing evolution by the forces of the wind and lake. A boulder in front of the center commemorates the work of Jens Jensen, Stephen Mather and Henry Cowles in preserving the dunes. Informative exhibits explain the ecosystems, plant and animal life, including examinations of specific native and "foreign" species. Regular guided nature walks are listed in the activity schedule, and a bookshop sells useful field guides.

Kemil Beach Area *– From the Buell Visitor Center, cross US-12 and continue on Kemil Rd. to Kemil Beach. The parking area for the beach is on the right, .25mi before the beach. Access the 1mi Dune Ridge Trail from the parking area.* In summer, the long stretch of sandy beach welcomes visitors as well as nearby home-owners in Beverly Shores. The 4mi drive to **Central Beach**, another popular swimming area, affords spectacular **views**★ of the vast blue expanse of Lake Michigan. *No life-guard service is available on either of these beaches.*

★**Mount Baldy** *– To the left off US-12, about 6mi east of Kemil Beach. Mt. Baldy is located 54mi east of Chicago.* One of the largest *(123ft)* dunes in the park is constantly shifting by a process called saltation, in which the lake winds whip the sand inland across the surface of the dune to the forests behind. Mt. Baldy is moving inland at a rate of 4-5ft a year, killing the trees behind its crest. The walk up and around the dune to the beach is short *(.5mi)* and very steep *(use caution).* A great bowl of sand leads down to the beach from the summit, which provides a grand **panorama** of the lake and the dunes, unfortunately disrupted by the massive cooling tower of a power plant to the east.

■ Fun for kids

Sights in this guide that are specifically geared toward children are indicated by the [KIDS] symbol. A selection of such sights described in THE GREEN GUIDE Chicago are listed below with their address and the entry under which they appear in the guide.

Sears Tower Skydeck – Entrance on Jackson Blvd. between Wacker Dr. & Franklin St., The Loop.

Nike Town Chicago – 669 N. Michigan Ave., Magnificent Mile.

The Hancock Observatory – 875 N. Michigan Ave., Magnificent Mile.

American Girl Place – 111 E. Chicago Ave., Magnificent Mile.

Navy Pier★★ – E. Grand Ave. at Lake Michigan, Magnificent Mile.

Chicago Children's Museum★ – Navy Pier, Magnificent Mile.

ESPN Zone – 43 E. Ohio St., River North.

Disney Quest★ – 55 E. Ohio St., River North.

Thorne Miniature Rooms★★ – 111 S. Michigan Ave., Art Institute of Chicago

Field Museum of Natural History★★★ – 1400 S. Lake Shore Dr., Museum Campus.

John G. Shedd Aquarium★★★ – 1200 S. Lake Shore Dr., Museum Campus.

Adler Planetarium★★ – 1300 S. Lake Shore Dr., Museum Campus.

Lincoln Park Zoo★★ – 2200 N. Cannon Dr., Lincoln Park.

Farm in the Zoo★ – 1901 N. Stockton Dr., Lincoln Park.

Peggy Notebaert Nature Museum★ – 2340 N. Cannon Dr., Lincoln Park.

Museum of Science and Industry★★★ – 57th St. at S. Lake Shore Dr., Hyde Park/Kenwood.

Brookfield Zoo★★ – 8400 W. 31st St., Excursions.

Steve Leonard/Tony Stone Images

Chicago's "L" Train

© Mark Segal/Tony Stone Images

Practical
Information

Calendar of Events

Listed below is a selection of Chicago's most popular annual events; some dates may vary each year. For more information about events in Chicago, consult local newspapers or contact the Chicago Office of Tourism (☎ 312-744-2400) or the Mayor's Office of Special Events (☎ 312-744-3370).

St. Patrick's Day Parade

Date	Event/Location	
Spring and Summer		
Mar 14	**St. Patrick's Day Parade**	312-744-337
	Dearborn St. from Wacker Dr. to Van Buren St.	
early Apr–mid May	**Chicago Park District Spring Flower Show**	
	Garfield Park Conservatory	312-746-510
	Lincoln Park Conservatory	312-742-773
1st weekend in May	**Annual Mayor Daley's Kids & Kites Fest**	312-744-331
	Museum of Science and Industry	
2nd weekend in May	**Art Chicago Navy Pier Festival Hall**	312-587-330
1st weekend in Jun	**57th St. Art Fair**	773-493-324
	E. 57th St. at Kenwood Ave.	
	Printer's Row Book Fair S. *Dearborn St.*	312-987-989
	Chicago Blues Festival	312-744-331
	Petrillo Music Shell	
	Chicago Gospel Festival	312-744-331
	Petrillo Music Shell	
	Park West Antiques Fair	773-477-510
	W. Fullerton Pkwy. & N. Orleans St.	
2nd weekend in Jun	**Old Town Art Fair**	312-337-193
	W. Menomenee & N. Orleans St.	
	Wells Street Art Festival	312-951-610
	1520 N. Wells St.	
mid-Jun	**"Celebrate on State" Festival**	312-782-916
	State St., between Wacker Dr. & Van Buren St.	
mid-Jun–late Aug	**Grant Park Music Festival**	312-742-763
	Petrillo Music Shell	
mid-Jun–Labor Day	**Ravinia Music Festival** *Highland Park*	847-266-500
late Jun–Jul 9	**Taste of Chicago** *Grant Park*	312-744-331
1st weekend in Jul	**Chicago Country Music Festival**	312-744-331
	Petrillo Music Shell	

Jul 3	**Independence Day Concert & Fireworks** *Petrillo Music Shell*	312-294-2420
3rd weekend in Jul	**Magnificent Mile Art Festival** *N. Michigan Ave., near Equitable Bldg.*	954-472-3755
mid-late Jul	**Chicago to Mackinac Island Yacht Race** *starts at Monroe Harbor*	312-861-7777
late Jul	**Venetian Night** *Lake Shore Dr. & Congress Pkwy.*	312-744-3315
early Aug	**Northalsted Market Days** *N. Halsted St. between W. Belmont Ave. & Addison St.*	773-868-3010
2nd Sat in Aug	**Bud Billiken Parade & Picnic** *39th St. & Martin Luther King, Jr. Dr. to 51st St. (Washington Park)*	312-225-2400
2nd weekend in Aug	**Gold Coast Art Fair** *Ontario to Huron Sts. & LaSalle to Wells Sts.*	312-787-2677
late Aug	**Chicago Air & Water Show** *North Avenue Beach*	312-744-3315
3rd weekend in Aug	**New East Side Artworks**, *E. Lake St. east of S. Michigan Ave.*	773-404-0763
last weekend in Aug	**Viva Chicago Latin Music Festival** *Petrillo Music Shell*	312-744-3315
Labor Day weekend	**Chicago Jazz Festival** *Petrillo Music Shell*	312-744-3315
	African Festival of the Arts *Washington Park*	773-955-7742

Fall and Winter

2nd weekend in Sept	**Around the Coyote** *N. Damen & Milwaukee Aves. (Wicker Park)*	773-227-5522
mid-September	**Annual Celtic Fest Chicago** *Petrillo Music Shell*	312-744-3315
3rd weekend in Sept	**Celtic Fest Chicago** *Petrillo Music Shell*	312-744-3315
Oct 1	**Annual Mayor Daley's Kids & Kites Fest** *Montrose Park*	312-744-3315
2nd Sun in Oct	**Chicago Marathon**	773-779-3250
early–late Oct	**Chicago International Film Festival** *Various theaters*	312-644-3400
Nov 1	**Day of the Dead Celebration** *Mexican Fine Arts Center Museum*	312-738-1503
mid-Nov	**Magnificent Mile Festival of Lights**	312-642-3570
Day after Thanksgiving Day	**City of Chicago Tree-Lighting Ceremony** *Daley Center Plaza*	312-744-3370
1st Sun in Dec	**Caroling to the Animals** *Lincoln Park Zoo*	312-742-2283
early Dec	**Chicago Park District Christmas Flower Show** *Garfield Park Conservatory* *Lincoln Park Conservatory*	312-746-5100 312-742-7736
mid-Dec	**Kwanza Festival** *Location varies*	312-744-2400
Dec 31	**New Year's Eve Celebration** *Navy Pier*	312-595-7437
late Jan–Feb	**Chinese New Year Parade** *Wentworth Ave. from Cermak Rd. to 24th St.*	312-225-6198
early–mid-Feb	**WinterBreak Chicago** *Various locations*	312-744-3315
mid-Feb	**Chicago Auto Show** *McCormick Place*	630-495-2282

Over the years Chicago has managed to capture and preserve the essence of myriad ethnic groups in its quaint and diverse neighborhoods. Other areas have developed distinct characteristics as artists' meccas or shopping havens. Together the districts combine to form a colorful "city of neighborhoods."

Downtown

Center of the city, the **Loop** offers a lesson in American urban architecture—bar none. Lined with department stores, **State Street** is the city's original shopping thoroughfare. Since the 1960s, it has been eclipsed by the **Magnificent Mile**, a boulevard of glitzy shops of international renown. Trendy and upscale **River North** has garnered a reputation for its art-gallery district and charming bistros and boutiques; the neighborhood has also become a favorite of tourists who flock to its celebrity-owned restaurants. In the South Loop, recently rehabilitated **Printer's Row** caters to a young crowd with its coffee shops and bookstores.

North Side

The affluent **Gold Coast**, most of it preserved as a landmark historic district, provides a restful retreat from bustling Michigan Avenue. One of the city's oldest neighborhoods, **Old Town** includes an offbeat assortment of comedy clubs, shops and

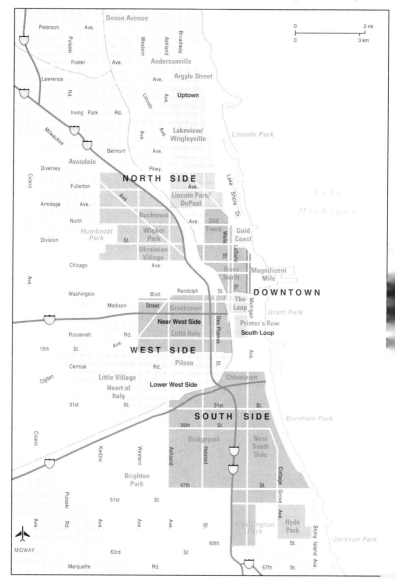

estaurants. Just west of Lincoln Park, gentrified **Lincoln Park/DePaul** encompasses the
ulk of the city's theaters and jazz and blues clubs, as well as a wide range of eateries.
onsidered the artistic area of Chicago, **Wicker Park** and **Bucktown**, both found along
lilwaukee Avenue, present quaint coffeehouses, alternative performance venues and
nique bookshops to a motley crew of yuppies and Hispanic immigrants. Just south
f Milwaukee Avenue, **Ukrainian Village** forms the core of a small but lively Ukrainian
ommunity, distinguished by unique ethnic shops and cozy eateries. A large number
f Chicagoans of Polish origin reside north of Logan Square in **Avondale**. Located in the
lorth Clark Street area, the Swedish community of **Andersonville** offers Scandinavian
rafts and foods. Center of the city's gay population, **Lakeview/Wrigleyville** is a diverse
rea boasting funky nightclubs, vintage-clothing stores and inexpensive restaurants.
rgyle Street, just north of Uptown, is home to a large community of recent Asian immi-
rants, who have set up Vietnamese and Korean shops and restaurants along the
olorful thoroughfare. Farther north lies **Devon Avenue**, lined with a variety of ethnic
estaurants reflecting the different waves of settlement in the area: Pakistani, Indian,
ewish and Thai.

West Side

ocated in the Near West Side, **Little Italy** offers a choice concentration of Italian restau-
ants and markets; just north, the delicious aromas of Greek fare pervade the streets
f **Greektown**. Heart of the Hispanic community, **Little Village** and **Pilsen** in the Lower West
ide feature stores selling imported goods as well as a variety of Mexican restaurants.
lso in the Lower West Side is **Heart of Italy**, one of Chicago's original Italian neigh-
orhoods, where restaurants serve traditional Italian meals. Along Western Avenue
nd 47th Street, the **Brighton Park** neighborhood is home to Lithuanian immigrants.

South Side

he predominantly African-American **Near South Side** features renowned blues and jazz
lubs and some of the city's oldest religious edifices. Nearby, **Chinatown** boasts
umerous restaurants and markets offering authentic oriental goods. **Bridgeport** is
amous for its Irish mayors, including Richard J. Daley (who served six terms, 1955-
'6), who have for years presided over Chicago politics. A liberal and eclectic area
urrounding the University of Chicago campus, **Hyde Park** is best known for its well-
tocked bookshops and student hangouts.

Neighborhood Festivals

Date	Event/Location	☎
st weekend in May	**Cinco De Mayo** *Douglas Park* *19th & Sacramento Sts.*	773-762-6565
2nd weekend in Jun	**Old Town & Wells St. Art Fairs** *1800 North Ave., Lincoln Park West*	312-337-1938
mid-Jun	**Taste of the Heart of Italy** *2400 S. Oakley Ave.*	773-625-0506
ast Sat in Jun	**Prairie Historical Festival** *3100 S. Calumet St.*	312-225-2257
st Sat in Jul	**Kwanza Summer Festival,** *Abbot Park, 95th & State Sts.*	773-264-1298
2nd weekend in Jul	**Rock Around the Block** *Lincoln Ave. from Belmont Ave. to School St.*	773-665-4682
	Brighton Park Festival *4700-4900 S. Western Ave.*	773-847-0664
ate Jul	**Chinatown Summerfair** *S. Wentworth Ave. at Cermak Rd.*	312-225-6198
1st weekend in Aug	**North Halsted Market Days** *Halsted St. from Belmont Ave. to Addison St.*	773-868-3010
ast weekend in Aug	**Bucktown Arts Fest** *2300 N. Oakley Blvd.*	312-409-8305
2nd weekend in Sept	**Ukrainian Fest** *Smith Park, 2500 W. Grand Ave.*	773-252-1228

Planning the Trip

Visitors can contact the following agencies before their trip to obtain maps and information on points of interest, accommodations and seasonal events, and complimentary copy of the *Chicago Official Visitors Guide*, published quarterly by the Chicago Convention and Tourism Bureau. For additional information about Chicago access the Chicago Office of Tourism's Web site or www.metromix.com.

Chicago Office of Tourism – Chicago Cultural Center, 78 E. Washington St. Michigan Ave., 4th Floor, Chicago IL 60602, ☎ 312-744-2400 or 800-487-244 *(North America only)*; www.ci.chi.il.us/tourism.

Chicago Convention and Tourism Bureau – McCormick Place Complex, 2301 S. Lake Shore Dr., Chicago IL 60616, ☎ 312-567-8500.

CHICAGO'S SEASONS

Chicago's temperatures can drop as low as -20°F during the winter and soar up to 100°F in the summer months. The city averages 33in of rain and 40in of snow each year. Lake Michigan has a noticeable effect on the city's weather: temperatures near the lake are markedly cooler in summer and warmer in winter. Most tourists visit Chicago between Memorial Day and Labor Day.

Spring – A brief and generally unpredictable season, spring begins in late March and lasts through the end of May. Daytime highs usually reach the 50s (10-15°C) and nighttime lows rarely dip below 35°F (2°C). Snow remains a possibility well into April

Summer – From Memorial Day to Labor Day, Chicagoans flock to parks and beaches to take their fill of sun. Daytime temperatures are hot, averaging in the 80s (26-31°C). The relative humidity can be uncomfortably high, and a haze often settles over the city. In the evenings temperatures are normally in the 60s (15-20°C); bring a light jacket or sweater if you're strolling along the lakefront.

Autumn – Lasting from mid-September through October, autumn may be the most pleasant time to visit Chicago. Crisp, clear days with temperatures in the 50s and 60 (10-20°C) give way to cool nights, usually dropping into the 40s (4-8°C). Hints of the impending winter may appear with an occasional frost and freeze warning.

Winter – This is Chicago's longest season and is a part of the city's culture. It can extend from mid-October through April. Brutal winds sweep through tunnels created

Weathering Chicago's Winter

Temperature Chart			
Month	avegerage high	avegerage low	precipitation
Jan	29°F (–2°C)	14°F (–10°C)	1.6in (4.1cm)
Apr	59°F (15°C)	39°F (4°C)	3.7in (9.5cm)
Jul	83°F (28°C)	63°F (17°C)	3.6in (9.3cm)
Oct	64°F 18°C	43°F 6°C	2.3in 5.8cm

by the towering buildings, and windchills are known to fall to a dangerous 60° below zero (-51°C). Daytime temperatures average between 20-40°F (-7°C to 4°C); nights drop to 15-20°F (-9°C to -7°C). **Lake-effect snow** occurs throughout the season. These small storm systems often reach several miles inland and bring with them large amounts of snow (12-24in/30-60cm) in short periods. Protective clothing (coats, boots, gloves, hats) is essential when venturing outside. Note that the abundantly used road salt will leave a white residue on shoes and boots.

Getting There

PLANES

O'Hare International Airport – ☎ 773-686-2200. www.ohare.com. *14mi northwest of the Loop via I-90 West.* Most international flights arrive and depart from O'Hare, the nation's second-busiest airport (after Atlanta's Hartsfield International). **Airport information booths** *(open daily 6am–10pm)* are located on the lower level of the domestic terminals (no. 1-3), as well as the upper and lower levels of the international terminal (no. 5); there is no terminal 4. Departing passengers should allow themselves the maximum amount of time recommended by their airline. Travelers must present valid photo identification at the ticket counter when checking in. **Restaurants** with table service are located in terminal 1, concourses B and C; in terminal 2, concourse F; in the rotunda of terminal 3 and in concourse K; and in terminal 5, on the upper and lower levels of concourse M. Smoking is prohibited in the airport, except in designated areas. A **medical clinic** is located in terminal 2. **Foreign Currency Exchange** is located on the lower level of terminal 5 at Arrivals Door A.

An **Airport Transit System** provides free transportation between the terminals and long-term parking lots. **Trains, buses and hotel shuttles** depart from the level below baggage-claim. For buses and hotel shuttles, follow the red signs for the bus/shuttle center located across from the airport Hilton hotel.

Taxis – The "starter" taxi system is in effect at O'Hare Airport. Passengers are obligated to wait in line and allow a starter to hail the next available cab. Taxi service to the Loop takes approximately 50min in rush hour *($30-$35)*. All cab companies offering airport service participate in the **Shared-Ride** discount program, wherein individual riders willing to share a cab to downtown pay a flat rate of $15. Inform the Starter or driver if you wish to participate; maximum of four passengers (discounted rate applies even if there are no additional riders). The program is designed for individual riders; groups pay regular posted fares.

Shuttles – **Airport Express** offers transport between O'Hare, downtown hotels and North Shore suburbs year-round. Shuttles run between the airport and downtown hotels daily 6am–11:30pm *(transit time: 45-60min; $17.50 one-way/$31 round-trip; ☎ 312-454-7800 or 800-654-7871; www.airportexpress.com).*

Rental Cars – Rental-car service counters are located on the lower level of terminals 1, 2 & 3. Most major rental-car agencies have shuttle buses offering transportation to their lots. Conduct all rental-car business in the terminal before boarding a shuttle.

Trains – **CTA Blue Line** trains operate between O'Hare and downtown daily 24hrs/day *(transit time 40-45min; $1.50; ☎ 312-836-7000; www.transitchicago.com).* Trains depart every 5-15min *(daily midnight–11:45pm)* from the O'Hare station, located in terminal 2 under the Hilton Hotel.

Chicago Midway Airport – ☎ 773-767-0500. www.ci.chi.il.us/aviation/Midway. *10mi southwest of the Loop via Rte. 50 South/Cicero Ave.* Many travelers find this smaller airport easier to navigate. Flights are limited to domestic carriers. **Airport information booths** *(open daily 10am–6pm)* offering airline and transport information are located between concourses A and B. Midway is undergoing construction of a new terminal building, scheduled to open in 2001.

Taxis and Shuttles – Taxis are located outside the front of the terminal building *(service to downtown 30min; $20-$23)*. Operators participate in the **Shared-Ride** discount program *($10)*. **Airport Express** offers transport between Midway and downtown hotels. Shuttles are located across from the Southwest Airlines ticket counter and depart daily 6am–11:30pm every 15min *(transit time: 30-45min; $12.50 one-way, $23 round-trip; ☎ 312-454-7800 or 800-654-7871; www.airportexpress.com).*

Rental Cars – Rental-car-agency shuttle buses depart near taxi stands. Conduct all rental-car business in the terminal before boarding a shuttle.

Trains – **CTA Orange Line** trains operate between Midway and downtown *(Mon–Sat 6am–11:20pm, Sun & holidays 7:30am–11:20pm; transit time 20-30min; $1.50; ☎ 312-836-7000; www.transitchicago.com);* Trains depart every 6-10min from the Midway station, located across Cicero Avenue (a covered walkway can be found on level 2 of concourse A).

The **Amtrak** rail network offers a relaxing alternative for the traveler with time to spare. Advance reservations are recommended to ensure reduced fares and availability of desired accommodations. Passengers can choose from first-class, coach, sleeping accommodations and glass-domed cars that allow a panoramic view. First-class fares are comparable to air travel; coach is more economical. Major long-distance routes to Chicago are: *Lake Shore Limited* from Boston and New York along the Great Lakes *(21hrs)*; *Capitol Limited* from Washington, DC *(18hrs)*; *City of New Orleans* from New Orleans *(19hrs)*; *Texas Eagle* from Houston and San Antonio *(30hrs)*; *Southwest Chief* from Los Angeles along the Santa Fe Trail *(39hrs)*; *California Zephyr* from San Francisco *(42hrs)*; *Empire Builder* from Seattle *(43hrs)*; *International* from Toronto *(12hrs)*. Travelers from Canada should ask their local travel agents about Amtrak/VIARail connections. **All-Aboard America Fare** allows travel within up to four regions. The **North America Rail Pass** offers travel via both Amtrak and VIARail Canada for up to 30 days. Chicago's **Amtrak station** is located at Union Station, 225 S. Canal St. Schedule and route information: ☎ 800-872-7245 (outside North America, contact your local travel agent) or access the Web site www.amtrak.com.

© Robert Holmes

Bridges Connect the Loop *(left)* to River North and the Magnificent Mile

Greyhound offers access to Chicago at a leisurely pace. Overall, fares are lower than other forms of public transportation. **Ameripass** allows unlimited travel for 7, 14 or 21 days (some travelers may find long-distance bus travel uncomfortable due to the lack of sleeping accommodations). Advance reservations are suggested. The main Greyhound station in Chicago is located at 630 W. Harrison St. Schedule and route information: ☎ 312-408-5980 or 800-231-2222 (US only); www.greyhound.com.

Travelers driving to Chicago will find it easily accessible by major interstate highways. The Dan Ryan Expressway *(I-90/I-94)*, the Chicago Skyway *(toll road)* and I-57 serve the South Side while the Stevenson Expressway (I-55) offers access to the Southwest Side. The Eisenhower Expressway (I-290), called Congress Parkway within downtown Chicago, provides the quickest route to reach the western suburbs. The Kennedy (I-90) and Edens (I-94) expressways service the Northwest and North Sides respectively. Lake Shore Drive (Route 41) follows the lakefront through the city.

International Visitors

BEFORE YOU GO

Visitors from outside the US can obtain information from local tourism agencies *(listed in the* Planning Your Trip *section)* or from the US embassy or consulate in their country of residence.

Foreign Consulates – In Chicago, international visitors can contact the consulate of their country of residence.

Country	Address	☎
Brazil	401 N. Michigan Ave., Suite 3050	312-464-0244
Canada	180 N. Stetson Ave., Suite 2400	312-616-1860
France	737 N. Michigan Ave., Suite 2020	312-787-5359
Germany	676 N. Michigan Ave., 32nd Floor	312-580-1199
India	150 N. Michigan Ave., Suite 1100	312-781-6273
Indonesia	72 E. Randolph St.	312-345-9300
Japan	737 N. Michigan Ave., Suite 1100	312-280-0400
Mexico	300 N. Michigan Ave., 2nd Floor	312-855-1380
Switzerland	737 N. Michigan Ave., Suite 2301	312-915-0061
United Kingdom	400 N. Michigan Ave., 13th Floor	312-346-1810

Entry Requirements – Citizens of countries participating in the Visa Waiver Pilot Program (VWPP) are not required to obtain a visa to enter the US for visits of less than 90 days. For more information, contact the US consulate in your country of residence. Citizens of nonparticipating countries must have a visitor's visa. Upon entry, nonresident foreign visitors must present a valid passport and round-trip transportation ticket. Canadian citizens are not required to present a passport or visa to enter the US, although identification and proof of citizenship may be requested (a passport or Canadian birth certificate and photo identification are usually acceptable). Naturalized Canadian citizens should carry their citizenship papers. Inoculations are generally not required but check with the US embassy or consulate before departing.

Health Insurance – The US does not have a national health program. Before departing, visitors from abroad should check their health-care insurance to determine if doctor's visits, medication and hospitalization in the US are covered. Prescription drugs should be properly identified, and accompanied by a copy of the prescription.

US Customs – All articles brought into the US must be declared at the time of entry. **Exempt** from customs regulations are: personal effects; one liter (33.8 fl oz) of alcoholic beverages (providing visitor is at least 21 years old); up to 200 cigarettes and 100 cigars; and gifts (to persons in the US) that do not exceed $100 in value. **Prohibited items** include plant material; firearms and ammunition (if not intended for legitimate sporting purposes); and meat or poultry products. For other prohibited items, exemptions and information, contact the US embassy or consulate before departing, or check with the US Customs Service, Chicago District Office, 610 S. Canal St., Chicago IL 60607 *(open Mon–Fri 8:30am–5pm; ☎ 312-353-6100).*

FAST FACTS

Credit Cards and Traveler's Checks – *(For additional information about money, see the* Basic Information *section.)* Rental-car agencies and many hotels require credit cards. Most banks will cash brand-name traveler's checks and give cash advances on major credit cards (American Express, Visa, MasterCard/Eurocard) with proper identification.

1 penny= 1 cent
1 dollar bill= 100 cents
10 dollar bill
dime= 10 cents
5 dollar bill
nickel=5 cents
quarter=25 cents
20 dollar bill

Currency Exchange – Many banks located in the Loop offer foreign currency exchange, including **American National Bank & Trust** *(33 N. LaSalle St.; ☎ 312-661-5000)* and **Northern Trust Bank** *(50 S. LaSalle St.; ☎ 312-630-6000)*. Banks charge a small fee for this service. Private companies generally charge higher fees: **Thomas Cook**, 111 W. Washington St., ☎ 312-828-1126; and **World Money Exchange**, 203 N. LaSalle St., Suite M11, ☎ 312-641-2151. **O'Hare International Airport Currency Exchange** offices *(☎ 773-686-7965)* are located on the lower level of the international terminal (no. 5), at Arrivals Door A.

Driving in the US – Visitors bearing valid driver's licenses issued by their country of residence are not required to obtain an International Driver's License to drive in the US. Drivers must carry vehicle registration and/or rental contract, and proof of automobile insurance at all times. Rental cars in the US are usually equipped with automatic transmission, and rental rates tend to be less expensive than overseas. Gasoline is sold by the gallon (1 gallon=3.8 liters) and is cheaper than in other countries. Most self-service gas stations do not offer car repair, although many sell standard maintenance items. Road regulations in the US require that vehicles be driven on the right side of the road. Distances are posted in miles (1 mile=1.6 kilometers).

Electricity – Voltage in the US is 120 volts AC, 60 Hz. Foreign-made appliances may need AC adapters (available at specialty travel and electronics stores) and North American flat-blade plugs.

Emergencies – In all major US cities you can telephone the police, ambulance or fire service by dialing **911**. Another way to report an emergency is to dial **0** for the operator. *(See the Basic Information section for other important telephone numbers.)*

Mail – *See* Basic Information.

Taxes and Tips – *(See also* Basic Information.*)* Prices displayed or quoted in the US do not generally include **sales tax** (8.75% in Chicago). Sales tax is added at the time of purchase and is not reimbursable as in other countries (it can sometimes be avoided if purchased items are shipped to another country by the seller).
In the US it is customary to give a **tip** (a small gift of money) for services received from waiters/waitresses, porters, hotel maids and taxi drivers.

Telephone/Telegram – *(For important telephone numbers, see the* Basic Information *section.)* For **emergencies** (police, fire, ambulance), dial **911**. Instructions for using **public telephones** are listed on or near the telephone. Some public telephones accept credit cards, and all will accept long-distance calling cards. For **long-distance calls** in the US and Canada, dial 1 + area code (3 digits) + number (7 digits). To place a **local call**, dial the 7-digit number without 1 or the area code (unless the local calling area includes several area codes). The cost for a local call from a pay phone is generally 35¢ (any combination of nickels, dimes and quarters is accepted). To find a local number (within your area code), dial **411** for **information**. For **long-distance information**, dial 1 + area code + 555-1212. For further information or operator assistance, dial **0** for the local operator or **00** for the long-distance operator.
To place an **international call**, dial **011** + country code + area code + number. A list of country and city codes can be found in the beginning of local phone directories. To place a collect call (person receiving the call pays charges), dial **0** + area code + number and tell the operator you are calling collect. If it is an international call, ask for the overseas operator.
Most telephone numbers in this guide that start with **800** or **888** are toll-free (no charge) in the US and may not be accessible outside of North America. Dial **1** before dialing an 800 or 888 number. The charge for numbers preceded by **900** can range from 50¢ to $15 per minute. Most hotels add a surcharge for local and long-distance calls.
You can send a **telegram** or money, or have money telegraphed to you, via the Western Union system *(☎ 800-325-6000; www.westernunion.com)*.

Basic Information

Business Hours – Most businesses operate Monday to Saturday 9am–6pm. Banks are usually open Monday to Friday 9am–5:30pm although some may have later hours. Shopping centers operate Monday to Saturday 10am–7pm or 9pm, Sunday noon–6pm and offer extended hours between Thanksgiving Day and Christmas Day.

Fax Services – Many hotels, as well as businesses that offer copying or mailing services, will send or receive faxes for a per-page fee.

Liquor Law – The legal age for purchase and consumption of alcoholic beverages is 21. Proof of age is normally required. Most bars and taverns are open until 2am and some have extended weekend hours until 4am or 5am. Almost all package-goods stores sell beer, wine and liquor.

Mail – Chicago's main post office *(433 W. Harrison St. at Canal St.; ☎ 312-983-6000)* is open Monday to Friday 7am–9pm and Saturday 8am–5pm. The post office at the Federal Center *(540 N. Dearborn St.; ☎ 312-644-7528)* in the Loop is open Monday to Friday 7:30am–5pm and Saturday 7:30am–1pm. For information and hours for other branches, contact the **Postal Customer Service Center** *(☎ 312-654-3895; same hours as main post office).*

First-class rates within the US: letter 33¢ (1oz), postcard 20¢. Overseas: letter 60¢ (1/2oz), postcard 50¢. Letters can be mailed from most hotels. Stamps and packing material may be purchased at post offices, grocery stores and businesses offering postal and express shipping services located throughout the city *(see the Yellow Pages phone directory under "Mailing Services").*

Major Holidays – Most banks and government offices in the Chicago area are closed on the following legal holidays *(many retail stores and restaurants remain open on days indicated by an asterisk*):*

New Year's Day	January 1
Martin Luther King, Jr.'s Birthday*	3rd Monday in January
Presidents' Day*	3rd Monday in February
Pulaski Day*	1st Monday in March
Memorial Day*	Last Monday in May or May 30
Independence Day*	July 4
Labor Day*	1st Monday in September
Columbus Day*	2nd Monday in October
Veterans Day*	November 11
Thanksgiving Day	4th Thursday in November
Christmas Day	December 25

Money – Most banks are members of the network of Automated Teller Machines (ATMs), allowing visitors from around the world to withdraw cash using bank cards and major credit cards. ATMs can usually be found in banks, airports, grocery stores and shopping malls. Networks (Cirrus, Honor, Plus) serviced by the ATM are indicated on the machine. To inquire about ATM service, locations and transaction fees, contact your local bank, call Cirrus *(☎ 800-424-7787)* or Plus *(☎ 800-843-7587)*. **Traveler's checks** are accepted, with photo identification, in banks, most stores, restaurants and hotels. **American Express Company Travel Service** offices are located at: 625 N. Michigan Ave., ☎ 312-435-2570; 122 S. Michigan Ave., ☎ 312-435-2595; and at 2338 N. Clark St., ☎ 773-477-4000. To report a lost or stolen **credit card**, call: American Express, ☎ 800-528-4800; Diners Club, ☎ 800-234-6377; MasterCard, ☎ 800-307-7309 or the issuing bank; Visa, ☎ 800-336-8472.

■ **Safety Tips**

Chicago is a relatively safe city. Visitors should remember these common-sense tips to ensure a safe and enjoyable visit:

- Avoid carrying large sums of money, and don't let strangers see how much money you are carrying.
- Keep a firm hold on purses and knapsacks, carry your wallet in your front pocket and avoid wearing expensive jewelry.
- Stay awake when riding public transportation, and keep packages close by. CTA buses and trains are equipped with devices that enable riders to notify personnel of emergencies.
- Always park your car in a well-lit area. Close windows, lock doors and place valuables in the trunk. Exercise caution when visiting areas in the South and West Sides of Chicago.

Newspapers and Magazines – Chicago's two main daily newspapers, the *Chicago Tribune* and the *Chicago Sun-Times*, are distributed in the morning. The arts and entertainment sections appear in the *Tribune* on Friday and Sunday, and in the *Sun-Times* on Friday. The *Chicago Defender*, another popular newspaper, caters to the African-American population. Weekly alternative publications available at bookstores and restaurants around town include *New City* and the *Chicago Reader*.

Senior Citizens – Most attractions, hotels and restaurants offer discounts to visitors age 62 and older (proof of age may be required). The **American Association of Retired Persons** (AARP) offers additional discounts to its members *(601 E St. N.W., Washington DC 20049;* ☎ *202-434-2277; www.aarp.com).*

Taxes and Tips – In Chicago, the sales tax is 8.75 %. Tax on food items in grocery stores is 2 %; magazine and newspapers are exempt. The tax rate for rental cars is 18 %. The hotel occupancy tax within the city of Chicago is 14.9 %; tax percentages vary in outlying suburbs. Since hotel and rental-car rates do not reflect the taxes, travelers should be aware of these added charges.

In restaurants it is customary to tip the server 15-20 % of the bill. At hotels, porters should be given $1 per suitcase and hotel maids $1 per day of occupancy. Taxi drivers are usually tipped 15 % of the fare.

Telephone – A local call from a pay phone generally costs 35¢—or more, depending on the telephone number being called (any combination of nickels, dimes or quarters is accepted). *(For more information, see the* International Visitors *section.)*

Area Codes

Chicago (Downtown)	312	Western suburbs	630
Chicago (other areas)	773	Southern suburbs	708
Northern suburbs	847	Outer suburbs	815

Important Numbers

Emergency/Police/Ambulance/Fire *(24hrs)*	**911**
Police *(non-emergency, 24hrs)*	312-746-6000
Special Events	311
Medical Society Referrals *(Mon–Fri 8:30am–4:30pm)*	312-670-2550
Dental Association Referrals *(Mon–Fri 9am–5pm)*	312-836-7300
24-hour pharmacy Walgreens	800-925-4733
(over 30 locations in Greater Chicago area, call for closest store)	
Time	312-976-1616
Weather	312-976-1212

Television and Radio – In Chicago, many network television programs run an hour earlier than in other US time zones.

MAJOR TV NETWORKS

ABC	Channel 7	FOX	Channel 32
CBS	Channel 2	WGN	Channel 9
NBC	Channel 5	PBS	Channel 11

MAJOR RADIO STATIONS

AM		FM		FM	
670	News/talk	88.1	Jazz, R&B	98.7	Classical
720	News/talk	91.5	NPR	99.5	Country
780	News	93.1	Rock	101.1	Alternative Rock
820	Sports	95.5	Contemporary Jazz	103.5	Oldies
1160	Sports	97.1	Classical/Jazz	104.3	Oldies

Time Zone – Chicago is located in the Central Standard Time (CST) zone, which is one hour behind Eastern Standard Time (EST) and six hours behind Greenwich Mean Time (GMT). Daylight Saving Time is observed from the first Sunday in April (clocks are advanced one hour) to the last Sunday in October.

Travelers with Disabilities – *Throughout this guide wheelchair access is indicated in admission information accompanying the sight description by the* ♿ *symbol.* Most public buildings, attractions, churches, hotels and restaurants provide wheelchair access. On all **CTA** transportation a designated seating area is available, as are reduced fares, for persons with disabilities. Over half the CTA and **Pace** lines are wheelchair accessible, and **Metra** is adding lift-equipped cars to all lines. Disabled travelers using

Amtrak and **Greyhound** bus lines should contact these companies prior to their trip to make special arrangements and receive useful brochures. For information about travel for individuals or groups, contact the **Society for the Advancement of Travel for the Handicapped** *(347 Fifth Ave., Suite 610, New York NY 10016; ☎ 212-447-7284).*

Getting Around

LAY OF THE LAND

Bordered on the east by Lake Michigan, Chicago is divided into North, West and South sides by the Y-shape of the Chicago River. The Loop, bounded by the lake, the Main Channel and the South Branch of the river, forms the heart of the metropolis. Chicago's most fashionable neighborhoods lie on the North Side of the city. The South Side is home to the city's large African-American population, while the West Side attracts immigrants to its myriad ethnic neighborhoods.

How to Find an Address – Chicago's street system makes it easy to locate any address based on its north and south coordinates. The intersection of State and Madison Streets is the zero-mile point. Running north to south, State Street serves as the east/west baseline, while Madison Street, running east to west, functions as the north/south baseline. Every address north of Madison is preceded by "North," every address east or west of State is designated "East" or "West," and so forth. In addition, address numbers originate from this point, usually in increments of 100 for each block (400=.5mi).

PUBLIC TRANSPORTATION

The **Chicago Transit Authority** (CTA) runs an extensive network of rapid-transit trains (elevated and underground) and buses that serve the city and numerous adjacent suburbs. Other suburbs are served by the **Pace** bus line *(Pace buses run every 30-60min; CTA transit cards and transfers may be used)* and **Metra** commuter trains. *For information on wheelchair accessibility,* see Basic Information. *For route and fare information for all systems in the Metro Chicago area,* call ☎ *836-7000 (daily 5am–1am; no area code is needed for this telephone number if you are calling from the 312, 773, 630, 847 or 815 area codes).*

■ Free Trolley System

Summer 2000 saw the addition of a **free trolley** that runs the length of Michigan Avenue from Water Tower Park *(Rush and Pearson Sts.)* to the Museum Campus *(daily 10am–7pm; Thu til 8pm)* and provides connecting service to the Navy Pier trolley at Illinois Street *(lower level).* The Navy Pier trolley runs from State Street to the Pier *(Sun–Thu10am–11pm, Fri & Sat 10am–1am).* Trolleys run every 15-20min and maps are available at the Water Works visitor center *(Pearson St. at Michigan Ave.).* For more information, call ☎ *312-744-3565 or access www.cityofchicago-.org/transportation.*

Chicago Transit Authority

In this guide, rapid-transit and bus stops are indicated with the ▣▣ *symbol.* System maps and the publication, *Downtown Transit Sightseeing Guide,* are available *(free)* at both airports, all train stations, downtown hotels and visitor information centers throughout the city. Detailed system timetables are available from the CTA customer service office at 181 W. Madison St. (at Wells St.), Chicago IL 60602 *(open Mon–Fri 8:30am–5pm; ☎ 312-836-7000; www.transitchicago.com).*

Rapid Transit System – *See map on inside back cover.* Originally, all routes for the city's rapid-transit and railway trains ran on ground-level tracks. However, the advent of the automobile caused the city to pass an ordinance that required the tracks to be elevated. Today CTA operates elevated and underground trains; the nickname "L" (short for elevated) designates lines circling the Loop. Train-station entrances are indicated by blue "Rapid Transit" signs. Access stairwells to the above-ground (elevated, or "L," lines) and below-ground trains may look somewhat foreboding, but stations and waiting areas are generally clean and well lit. Many trains are accessible to riders with disabilities, and some stations are equipped with elevators. Trains run every 3-12min during weekday rush hours, 6-20min at most other times, and every 30min overnight. The seven different lines are referred to by color (note that route names indicate destination or end points). Transfers are not needed for changes within the rapid-transit system.

CTA Lines		Service Hours
■ RED	(Howard-Dan Ryan)	24hrs daily
■ BLUE	(O'Hare-Congress-Douglas)	24hrs daily (O'Hare & Congress); Mon–Fri 4am–1am (Douglas)
■ PURPLE	(Evanston)	Mon–Fri 5am–1am (Linden & Howard); Sat 6am–2am; Sun 7am–2am; peak period service only between Howard & the Loop
■ GREEN	(Lake-Englewood/Jackson Park)	Mon–Fri 4am–1am; Sat 6am–1am; Sun 7am–1am
■ ORANGE	(Midway)	Mon–Sat 5am–11:20pm; Sun & holidays 7:30am–11:20pm
■ BROWN	(Ravenswood)	Mon–Fri 5am–10pm, Sat 5am–8pm; additional late evening, Sun & holiday hours (Kimball & Belmont)
YELLOW	(Skokie Swift)	Mon–Fri 5:15am–10pm

Times given are approximate; call the Rapid Transit Authority
(☎ 312-836-7000; www.transitchicago.com) for specific information.

Buses – CTA buses generally operate daily 6am–midnight; some routes run 24hrs/day. During the weekday rush hour, most buses run about every 5-15min, and about every 8-20min at other times. Stops (clearly marked by blue and white signs) are customarily made at posted locations only, one to two blocks apart, and may be verified with the driver. Oversized street signs are helpful in identifying upcoming stops. Many routes are accessible to riders with disabilities.

Fares – All CTA fares are $1.50 one-way *(exact fare required for buses; $1 bills accepted)*. Discounted fares are available for senior citizens and persons with disabilities; children under 12 can ride free when accompanied by an adult. CTA transit cards automatically deduct fares and transfers and can be used on trains and buses for any amount between $1.50 and $91. Transit cards are available at CTA train stations, banks, currency-exchange offices, and Jewel and Dominick's grocery stores. Transfers cost 30¢. A 25¢ surcharge is added from downtown on certain express bus routes. Visitor Passes, allowing unlimited travel on buses and trains, are available for 1 day*($5)*, 2 days *($9)*, 3 days *($12)* and 5 days *($18)*. You can purchase passes at both airports, at Union Station and at visitor centers, or online at www.transit chicago.com.

Commuter Trains – *See map on inside back cover.* Pullman Historic District, Oak Park, Brookfield Zoo and other outlying sights can be reached by commuter train. In downtown Chicago, Metra operates commuter trains from four downtown terminals: LaSalle Street Station, Randolph Street Station, Union Station (Amtrak) and North Western Station (Ogilvie Transportation Center). In all, 12 lines service some 220 suburban stations including O'Hare International Airport and outlying cities in Illinois and neighboring states. During rush hour, trains run frequently; at other times, departures are every one to three hours. Fares range from $1.75 to $6.60, depending upon distance traveled. Metra's $5 weekend pass offers unlimited rides on all Metra lines. Children under 12 ride free with Family Fares. *For schedules & fare information, call* ☎ *312-836-7000 or access www.transitchicago.com.*

Chicago taxis are metered. All Chicago cab companies share the same rate schedule: $1.60 for the first mile, $1.40 for each additional mile within Chicago; $2.10 for each additional mile outside Chicago; and 50¢ for each additional passenger. There are no extra fees for baggage handling or assistance for passengers with physical disabilities. Cabs are easily hailed in the downtown area. Taxi stands are located at most hotels and major attractions (in other areas, telephone for service). To report lost property, call ☎ 312-744-2900; be sure to give taxi identification number. The main cab companies in Chicago are: **Checker Taxi Co.** *(☎ 312-243-2537)* and **Yellow Cab Co.** *(☎ 312-829-4222; www.yellowcabchicago.com)*.

DRIVING IN CHICAGO

For information about Chicago road conditions, call the Illinois Department of Transportation Information Line: ☎ 847-705-4650.

Given the efficiency of the public transportation system, and the ease with which many sights can be reached on foot, a car is not necessary to visit downtown Chicago. However, a car is recommended for visiting other areas. Keep in mind that roads are often congested, street parking can be difficult to find and public parking lots are expensive. **Rush hour**, the peak transit time for business commuters, is weekdays between 7:30am–9:30am and 4pm–6pm. Expect roadways to be clogged and traveling to be slow during these times.

Road Regulations – The maximum **speed limit** on major expressways is 55mph (90km/h). Speed limits within the city range from 25mph (40km/h) in residential areas to 35mph (56km/h) on major streets. Use of **seat belts** is mandatory for passengers in the front seat of the car, and for children age 4-6 years in the back seat. Child-safety seats are required for children under 4 years (seats are available from most rental-car agencies). Illinois law requires motorists to bring vehicles to a full stop when warning signals on a **school bus** are flashing. Drivers must always yield the **right of way to pedestrians**. Unless otherwise posted, drivers may turn right on a red traffic light after coming to a complete stop.

Parking – Metered street parking is available on most downtown and arterial streets; note that vehicles will be towed if left overnight. Many streets are designated Snow Routes (indicated by red, white and blue signs); parking is not allowed on either side of these streets overnight during winter or when there are two or more inches of snow on the ground. No parking is allowed on many streets during rush hour and during specific street-cleaning days; note signs. Major parking facilities are indicated on maps in this guide with the ◲ symbol. Parking in some residential areas is by permit only (restricted to area residents). Parking spaces identified by the ♿ symbol are reserved for people with disabilities; anyone parking in these spaces without proper identification is subject to a heavy fine.

Rental Cars – Most major car-rental companies have offices downtown and at both O'Hare and Midway airports. Rental cars are available for persons at least 25 years old, but some rental-car agencies will rent to drivers under 25 for a daily surcharge. The agency has the right to check the renter's driving record for violations before approving the rental. A major credit card and valid driver's license are required for rental (some agencies also require proof of insurance). The average daily rate for a compact car, when renting for 5-7 days, ranges from $30-$65. Note that rental cars are taxed at the rate of 18%.

Rental Company	☎ Reservation	Rental Company	☎ Reservation
Alamo	800-327-9633	Hertz	800-654-3131
Avis	800-831-2847	National	800-227-7368
Budget	800-527-0700	Thrifty	800-331-2277
Enterprise	800-325-8007		

(Toll-free numbers may not be accessible outside North America.)

Accommodations

The Chicago area offers a wide range of accommodations from elegant downtown hotels *($200-$350 and up)* located in the Loop and around North Michigan Avenue to more moderately priced motels *($90-$150)* found throughout the city. Rates tend to be lower in suburban areas (including O'Hare Airport) and on weekends. Amenities can include television, restaurant, swimming pool and smoking/nonsmoking rooms. The more expensive hotels also offer room-service dining and valet service. Most downtown hotels charge a fee for parking. Some hotels located near Lake Shore Drive may be within walking distance of a public beach; inquire when making reservation. *All rates quoted are average prices per day for a double room.*

Hotels/Motels – The *Metro Chicago Hotel Guide* and *Hotel/Motel Illinois Directory* are available *(free)* from the tourism offices. Below is a list of major hotel chains with locations in Chicago. *For information about specific hotels in the city, see the* Address Book *section in the front of this guide.*

Hotel ☎	Hotel ☎
Best Western 800-528-1234	Hyatt 800-233-1234
Comfort Inn...........800-228-5150	Marriott 800-228-9290
Days Inn...............800-325-2525	Omni 800-843-6664
Four Seasons 800-332-3442	Radisson....................800-333-3333
Hampton Inn 800-426-7866	Ramada Inn................800-272-6232
Hilton 800-445-8667	Westin Hotels 800-228-3000
Holiday Inn 800-465-4329	Wyndham 800-996-3426

Reservation Services ☎

Accommodations Express ....800-444-7666 (US only)
Accommodations Express ....800-444-7666 (US only)
Hotel Reservations Network 800-964-6835
Hot Rooms 800-468-3500
	or 773-468-7666
Illinois Reservation Service...800-491-1800
Quikbook ....800-789-9887 (US only)
RMC Travel Centre...212-754-6560
	or 800-782-2674 (US only)

Bed and Breakfast Inns – Most of the B&Bs in Chicago are located downtown and in the Gold Coast, Old Town and Lincoln Park areas. Many B&Bs are privately owned historic homes *($95-$295)*. Continental breakfast is customarily included. Private baths are not always available. Smoking indoors is usually not allowed. **Bed and Breakfast Chicago** *(P.O. Box 14088, Chicago, IL 60614; ☎ 773-248-0005 or 800-375-7084; www.bnbchicago.com)* offers reservation service for most of the area B&Bs. Furnished **apartment rentals** *($155-$350)* are available through Bed and Breakfast Chicago for periods ranging from three nights to a year.

Hostels – A no-frills, economical alternative to pricey hotels, **hostels** average $18-$45/day. Amenities include community living room, showers, laundry facilities, full-service kitchen and dining room, dormitory-style and private rooms *(guests must bring their own towels)*. The Chicago International Hostel is located at 6318 North Winthrop Ave., Chicago, IL 60660, ☎ 773-262-1011.
Hostelling International *(www.hiayh.org)* operates the following facilities *(fees quoted are for HI members)*. **Chicago Summer Hostel** at Columbia College provides room rentals from June to early September *(731 S. Plymouth Ct., at Polk St. between Dearborn & State Sts. in the South Loop; dorm rooms $22-24, private rooms with baths $25-$27; reservations recommended; P.O. Box 0452, Chicago, IL 60690; ☎ 773-327-5350 summer, or ☎ 312-360-0300 off season)*. The new state-of-the-art facility at **Hostelling International-Chicago** *(24 E. Congress Pkwy. at Wabash St., P.O. Box 0452, Chicago, IL 60690; $18-$20; reservations recommended; ☎ 312-360-0300)* features 24hr access, self-service kitchen, dining room, on-site cafe, laundry, parking and Internet access.

ndex

A

B

C